W9-ASO-095

Products Liability and the Reasonably Safe Product

KF
1296
.P77

Products Liability and the Reasonably Safe Product:

A Guide for Management, Design, and Marketing

Alvin S. Weinstein
Carnegie-Mellon University

Aaron D. Twerski
Hofstra Law School

Henry R. Piehler
Carnegie-Mellon University

William A. Donaher
Duquesne Law School

Tennessee Tech. Library
Cookeville, Tenn.

A WILEY-INTERSCIENCE PUBLICATION

JOHN WILEY & SONS, New York • Chichester • Brisbane • Toronto

283272

Copyright © 1978 by John Wiley & Sons, Inc.

All rights reserved. Published simultaneously in Canada.

Reproduction or translation of any part of this work
beyond that permitted by Sections 107 or 108 of the
1976 United States Copyright Act without the permission
of the copyright owner is unlawful. Requests for
permission or further information should be addressed to
the Permissions Department, John Wiley & Sons, Inc.

Library of Congress Cataloging in Publication Data:

Main entry under title:

Products liability and the reasonably safe
    product.
    "A Wiley-Interscience publication."
    Includes indexes.
    1. Products liability—United States.
I. Weinstein, Alvin S., 1928–

KF1296.P77   346'.73'038   78-8749
ISBN 0-471-03904-7

Printed in the United States of America

10 9 8 7 6 5 4 3 2 1

To my parents
Samuel J. and Miriam Weinstein
and to MARSH

A.S.W.

To Kreindel
Who suffered through what the kids call "another crazy book"

A.D.T.

To my wife
Margaret Forbes Piehler
and sons
Michael and Christopher

H.R.P.

To my parents
John C. Donaher and Margaret McDonald Donaher

W.A.D.

Preface

This book testifies to the proposition that lawyers and engineers can really understand each other if they will only make the effort. In fact, once the dialogue is undertaken, professionals in both disciplines will find they share common problem-solving techniques. We—two lawyers and two engineers—have been associated over a period of six years, analyzing the role of technology and its interface with the law. We are in a position to announce to our respective professions that it is really worthwhile to take the time to get to know each other well. The quality of the work engineers and lawyers do is certain to reflect the shared sense of professionalism.

The initial impetus for our association was provided by the two engineers, both professors at Carnegie-Mellon University, who sensed from their involvement as consultants in products liability litigation that practicing engineers would benefit from, perhaps even require, formal training in the legal and technical aspects of this process. To implement such a legal/technical course in products liability, the engineers established contact with the Duquesne University School of Law and later with the Hofstra University School of Law, and this led to the association among the authors. As a result, a highlight of a course developed and taught at Carnegie-Mellon was the inclusion of in-depth case studies that the students analyzed and documented in experts' reports and later presented in a moot court at Duquesne Law School. Our involvement in these case studies revealed substantial unresolved problems involving the interaction of law and technology in both the framework and practice of products liability litigation, and these questions led to the research component of our association.

Very early in our work it became apparent to us as both lawyers and engineers that, rather than being fundamentally opposed in our thinking, we shared common perspectives in solving problems. Recognition of this was a fundamental step in pursuing a joint research effort funded by the National

Science Foundation.* Transcripts of litigated cases were the basic data used in this joint study, which sought to examine whether the practice of products litigation was based on established legal principles and to evaluate whether the litigation process was consistent with technological reality as well. From these dual evaluations of the products liability process at the trial level, we perceived substantial legal and technical deficiencies. Enunciation of these deficiencies led to proposals for substantive and procedural modifications of the existing products liability law. In addition, the technical community responded with proposals for standardizing the role of the technical expert. In an effort to implement these modifications we presented an extensive series of publications and lectures, based on our observations and conclusions, to both the legal and technical communities.

The responses and concerns voiced at these presentations, especially from the technical community, prompted the preparation of this book. Our purpose is not only to summarize the insights from our research and experience but also to provide guidance and direction for decision-making. In this way the same approaches used retrospectively by the courts in litigation can be used prospectively by engineers and managers in the design and manufacture of products.

We express our appreciation to Kay O. Curry, Esq., Denise Lepicier, Esq., and Margaret Forbes Piehler for their critical comments and editorial assistance in the preparation of this manuscript. To E. Jean Stiles we express our gratitude and thanks for her patience, talent, and good humor while typing its many iterations.

Permission to quote from the following is gratefully acknowledged:

1.   The American Law Institute for permission to reprint § 402A and § 402B with the comments of the Restatement of the Law, Second, Torts, copyright 1965 by the American Law Institute. Reprinted with the permission of The American Law Institute.

2.   Cornell Law Review for permission to quote from Twerski, Weinstein, Donaher, and Piehler, "The Use and Abuse of Warnings in Products Liability—Design Defect Litigation Comes of Age," 61 Cornell Law Review 495 (1976), copyrighted by Cornell Law Review, 1976.

3.   Duquesne Law Review for permission to quote from Weinstein, Twerski, Piehler, and Donaher, "Product Liability: An Interaction of Law and Technology," 12 Duquesne Law Review 425 (1974), copyrighted by Duquesne Law Review 1974; and from Mitchell, "Products Liability, Workmen's Compensation and the Industrial Accident," 14 Duquesne Law Review 349 (1976), copyrighted by Duquesne Law Review 1976.

4.   Hofstra Law Review for permission to quote from Twerski, "From Codling, to Bolm to Velez: Triptych of Confusion," 2 Hofstra Law Review 489 (1974), copyrighted by Hofstra Law Review 1974.

*Grant No. GI-34857, Product Liability: A Study of the Interaction of Law and Technology.

5. Indiana Law Review for permission to quote from Twerski, "The Use and Abuse of Comparative Negligence in Products Liability," 10 *Indiana Law Review* 797 (1977), copyrighted by Indiana Law Review 1977.

6. Iowa Law Review for permission to quote from Twerski, "Old Wine in a New Flask—Restructuring Assumption of Risk in the Products Liability Era," 60 *Iowa Law Review* 1 (1974), copyrighted by Iowa Law Review 1974.

7. Marquette Law Review for permission to quote from Twerski, "From Defect to Cause to Comparative Fault, Rethinking Some Product Liability Concepts," 60 *Marquette Law Review* 297 (1977), copyrighted by Marquette Law Review 1977.

8. *Science* and the American Association for the Advancement of Science for permission to rely throughout Chapter Six of this book on material contained in Piehler, Twerski, Weinstein, and Donaher, "Product Liability and the Technical Expert," *Science,* Vol. 186, No. 4169, 20 December 1974, pp. 1089–1093, copyright 1974 by the American Association for the Advancement of Science.

9. Texas Law Review for permission to quote from Donaher, Piehler, Twerski, and Weinstein, "The Technological Expert in Products Liability Litigation," 52 *Texas Law Review* 1303 (1974), copyrighted by Texas Law Review 1974.

Alvin S. Weinstein
Aaron D. Twerski
Henry R. Piehler
William A. Donaher

Pittsburgh, Pennsylvania
Hempstead, New York
July 1978

Contents

Products Liability and the Reasonably Safe Product:

CHAPTER 1

Products Liability—
A Page of History
and the Basic Theory

1.1 A CONFRONTATION WITH PRODUCTS LIABILITY

This book confronts the reader with difficult issues. Those engaged in designing, manufacturing, marketing, and selling products are seriously concerned about their legal responsibilities when an injury occurs from the use of a product. Some of the concern is well founded and some stems from a lack of understanding.

We believe that it is now time to deal with these difficult questions in a manner comprehensible to those who bear the day-to-day burdens of decision-making in the business enterprise. These problems are not the private preserve of lawyers. The following sampler of questions highlights some of the issues we address in this and the following chapters.

- Will you be held liable even though your product was manufactured to the most exacting quality control procedures available? (See pp. 5, 8, and 137.)
- Does the law require that the manufacturer guarantee or insure that the product will not cause injury? (See pp. 5, 8, 17, and 137.)
- Does making a product or part exactly according to your buyer's specifications protect you? (See pp. 25–27, and 138.)
- Must you incorporate safety features as part of the basic product, or can you sell them as optional equipment? (see pp. 26 and 138.)

1

- Will making safety changes in an updated product haunt you in a lawsuit involving an older model without the new features? (See p. 139.)
- If a product is considered safe at the time of sale, are you absolved from liability if later technological advances can make that product safer? (See pp. 55 and 139.)
- Should a manufacturer be required to undertake the safety retrofit of old products? Who should bear the cost? (See p. 139.)
- Can a product become too old for a products liability suit? (See pp. 37–40 and 81–82.)
- If you warn about dangers that could have been designed out of a product, could you still be in trouble? (See pp. 40–42, 60–62, and 138.)
- Suppose the machine you sold is used negligently by an employer. Can an injured employee sue you and win? (See pp. 82–84, 104–109, and 137.)
- Manufacturers and sellers are often confronted with unimagined uses and users of their products. How far should manufacturers go in anticipating how their products will be used and by whom? (See pp. 12–16, 18, 23–25, 27, 51–53, 87–91, 91–94, 137, and 140.)
- If a product is substantially modified by the user and then causes injury, how much responsibility will the product manufacturer have to assume? (See pp. 53–55.)
- Can distributors, wholesalers, and retailers (even lessors) be responsible for product defects that they could not have detected? (See pp. 10, and 95–99.)
- Are commercial sellers of used products held to the same standards as the manufacturer or seller of new products? (See pp. 101–103.)
- If a product danger is open and obvious to the user, does a manufacturer need to be concerned about liability? (See pp. 45–47, 56–57, 88–91, and 140.)
- Are warnings the cheapest way to make a product safe? (See pp. 62–65.)
- Can a seller rely on a contract with his buyer that absolves the seller of all liability? (See pp. 11, 15–16, and 69–74.)
- What is the responsibility of a manufacturer or seller if the product defect played an insignificant role in causing the injury? (See pp. 19–21, and 23.)
- If a user decides to take his chances with a bad product, can the manufacturer still be liable? (See pp. 86, and 90–92.)
- If a product malfunctions and causes injury because it needed repair, could the manufacturer still have a liability problem? (See pp. 82–84.)
- Can a safe product be made unsafe by Madison Avenue? (See pp. 11–12, and 138.)
- Is making your product as safe as your competitor's good enough? (See p. 7.)

- Can a product complying with governmental standards ever be legally unsafe? (See pp. 7, 57–59, and 139.)

1.2   OVERVIEW

In June 1970 the National Commission on Products Safety issued its final report. Included were some hair-raising statistics. Each year, 20 million Americans are injured in the home in incidents connected with consumer products. Of those injured 110,000 are permanently disabled and 30,000 are killed. These statistics *do not* include injuries and deaths associated with foods, drugs, cosmetics, motor vehicles, firearms, cigarettes, radiological hazards, and certain flammable fabrics [1]. Incidents connected with industrial products account for an additional 7 million injuries per year [2].

Personal injuries are the primary source of the burgeoning number of products liability cases entering our courts. In 1969 approximately 300,000 such cases were filed, a threefold increase over 1968. The number of products liability suits will inevitably continue to rise, spurred primarily by the public's increased awareness of the potential defects in consumer products and industrial machinery. Recent estimates place the number of product lawsuits at nearly 1 million for the year 1976.

The public's heightened sensitivity to product-related problems has, of course, elicited concern from the manufacturing community. Increased exposure to litigation, large judgments, and insurance difficulties, and pervasive federal regulatory activities, were among the issues raised by industry before the Commerce Department's Interagency Task Force on Product Liability in 1976.

All of this has resulted from society's questioning of the efficacy of product design and manufacture viewed from the dimension of safety. The courts have posed searching and ofttimes discomforting questions about the design process. Human frailties in behavior can no longer be ignored or considered aberrant in the marketing of products.

As a consequence corporate decision-making in the design, fabrication, and marketing of products, whether they are for industrial, commercial, or consumer use, is increasingly constrained by concern for products liability. The questions raised by the law are difficult, sometimes enigmatic, and frequently disconcerting. The law is confronting technology with responsibilities that have never been so direct and searching.

The purpose of this book is to explore the interface between law and technology so that business enterprise—through its management, design, production, and marketing staffs—may come to understand the demands of

the law with regard to product safety. Much of the products liability literature directed to technology has focused on the role of the engineer as an
expert witness [3]. While this is an important function, it brings technology
into contact with the law at a stage when there is little else to do except
reflect with hindsight.

There is, however, a more hopeful and helpful role for product planners,
designers, and producers who understand just what the law demands of
them. To be sure, part of this endeavor will be to avoid liability by meeting
the standards imposed by law. But more importantly, we shall demonstrate
that the ultimate objective of the law is to outline the boundaries for socially
acceptable products. This concept of "societal acceptability" may seem
unpalatable to those accustomed to dealing with more precise and quantitative measures of performance. We shall, however, find that the art forms of
the law and of the design engineer speak to similar if not identical problems,
whose solutions are derived from similar methodologies.

It is decidedly not the purpose of this book to add to the storehouse of
facts, figures, and equations that are part of the library of the design process.
The purpose is, instead, to sensitize the industrial community to the balancing process by which the legal system integrates human behavior and product behavior in determining whether or not the product is societally acceptable. The goal is clear. By acquiring a fundamental understanding of the
legal process, the product planners, designers, and producers will develop a
mind set in which legal factors become an integral part of their thought
processes. Safety and legal standards will cease to be a nuisance to contend
with after the fact of design and will become healthy and welcome additions
to the design process from its very inception.

One word of caution is in order. This book is not written to perpetuate the
state of misinformation that is so prevalent today. We believe that those
responsible for management and design decisions must appreciate the response of the legal system to their work product. An in-depth understanding
of the structure of a lawsuit is a requisite for understanding the implications
of those decisions. It is in the legal theater that their decisions, correct and
incorrect, will be tested. We thus make no apologies for the sophistication of
this volume. It is a timely antidote to the fables, myths, and untruths that are
part of the lore of the business or engineering community.

1.3   PRODUCTS LIABILITY—A DEFINITION

Products liability is the legal term used to describe an action in which an
injured party (plaintiff) seeks to recover damages for personal injury or loss
of property from a seller (defendant) when it is alleged that the injuries
resulted from a defective product. The term has also been used when a

consumer or business enterprise has suffered commercial loss owing to the breakdown or inadequate performance of a product [4]. However, the products liability explosion of the past decade has arisen primarily from personal injury cases in which a product is implicated in the injury.

In most instances an action based on products liability requires the establishment of a defect in the product. Product defects arise from two sources. The first and most basic is the production or manufacturing defect. This is a defect arising from an error occurring during the manufacture of the product. The classic example of a production defect is the soda pop bottle that explodes as a result either of an imperfection in the glass structure of the bottle or of inadvertent overcarbonization. In other words a production defect arises when a product does not meet the manufacturer's own standards for that product. This would presume that products that meet the manufacturer's standards are not defective, at least from the viewpoint of production errors. In contrast, when a product that meets the manufacturer's own standards does cause injury, it may be alleged by the plaintiff that the design or the manufacturer's standards were inferior and should be judged defective. This would be termed a design defect.

1.4 EXPLORING THEORIES OF LIABILITY

An injury occurs and a product is implicated as a possible cause of the injury. Where does one begin in assessing whether the law will assess liability on either the manufacturer or seller of the product? The mere occurrence of an injury in which a product played a role is *not, ipso facto*, grounds for imposing liability. The manufacturer or seller is not an insurer [5]. He does not normally guarantee that no ill will befall the user of his product. Products liability is *not* absolute liability. It must be established that the manufacturer violated a legal responsibility to the user or consumer. These responsibilities are expressed in the principles of law against which either the conduct of the defendant or the quality of the product must be tested.

The following three basic legal principles can be used in most states as the framework within which the plaintiff can bring an action in products liability:

1. Negligence, which tests the *conduct of the defendant*.
2. Strict liability and implied warranty, which test the *quality of the product*.
3. Express warranty and misrepresentation, which test the *performance of products against the explicit representations* made on their behalf by the manufacturer and sellers.

1.4.1 Negligence

Negligence has been defined as "conduct which involves an unreasonably great risk of causing damage" [6]. Alternatively, it has been described as conduct "which falls below the standard established by law for the protection of others against unreasonably great risk of harm" [7]. To make out a cause of action in negligence, it is not necessary for the plaintiff to establish that the defendant either intended harm or acted recklessly in bringing about the harm. The test requires that the conduct of the defendant be measured against a norm. The norm that has been established by the courts is the "reasonable person" test.

All human activity involves an element of risk. The defendant's conduct is deemed negligent only when it falls below what a "reasonable" person would have done under similar circumstances. It could be argued that such a standard would be too vague for courts to use in everyday litigation, but in fact it provides a flexible tool for judging behavior. For example, a soda pop bottle that exploded owing to a flaw in the glass may be defective. It does not necessarily follow that the defendant manufacturer of the bottle was negligent. If the manufacturer took "reasonable care" as demonstrated by the level of his quality control techniques, his conduct was not unreasonable, even though the product that came off the assembly line was *in fact* defective and caused injury to the plaintiff.

The flexibility that is the hallmark of the negligence standard is achieved by permitting the interplay of three factors. In every negligence action the court must consider (a) the probability of the harm's occurring; (b) the gravity of the harm, if it should occur; and (c) the burden of precaution to protect against the harm, that is, what the manufacturer might have done to minimize or eliminate the harm. The more remote and improbable that the defendant's conduct will result in harm, the less reason he has to protect against it. If, however, the harm can result in serious injury, the actor must consider the serious implications of even improbable or unlikely harm. Finally, the two aforementioned factors must be weighed against the "burden of precaution," that is, the cost of preventing harm. Thus, in the exploding soda pop bottle case, on the assumption that more exacting inspection techniques existed at the time of manufacture, it still must be determined whether the cost of instituting such procedures would have been justified. The difference in the cost of the alternative procedures must be weighed against the increased probability of discovering flawed bottles through the more sophisticated inspection techniques, as well as against the seriousness of the injuries that can occur from exploding soda pop bottles. Thus the negligence principle admits the existence of real risks associated with product use. The question that must be answered in each case is whether the risk is justified.

In assessing the manufacturer's conduct, the negligence test focuses on the technology and information available to him at the *time of manufacture* of the product. Note, however, that a plaintiff can allege a cause of action based on what a reasonable manufacturer *should have known* about products manufactured at the time the defective product was produced. Thus the reasonable manufacturer is expected to maintain an awareness of industry-wide standards and improving technology. At the same time even an entire industry may be found negligent for the continuation of unacceptable standards of manufacture [8]. Thus negligence may be imposed for the failure of an industry to adopt or undertake technological improvements. An example of the operation of this principle is found in *Marsh v. Babcock and Wilcox* [9]. The plaintiff, who had suffered injury as a result of an exploding boiler, successfully established negligence on the part of the boiler manufacturing industry in their continued use of a hydrostatic test to establish boiler integrity. The court found that it was reasonable for a jury to determine that a more sophisticated test that had recently been developed by a professor of metallurgy at the University of Wisconsin was a feasible alternative to the hydrostatic test and had a higher probability of discovering flaws in the metal.

Since the determination of negligence arises on a case-by-case basis, initiated by a plaintiff who seeks recovery for harm done to him by a defective product, it is possible that the same conduct may be judged both negligent and nonnegligent in two different legal proceedings. Although this is somewhat unsettling, there is a core concept of "reasonableness" that governs negligence cases. The issue is not left to the vagaries of the jury. If a judge reaches the conclusion that the core concept of "reasonableness" has been met, based on precedents set in similar decisions, he will direct a verdict for the defendant manufacturer (i.e., he will not let the jury decide the case). Thus a manufacturer may take guidance from the general flow of product cases about whether his future conduct will be judged substandard. Based on the results of litigated cases, a sense can be developed about the considerations that determine an acceptable level of risk.

Evidence that a manufacturer has met self-imposed standards, voluntary consensus standards, or even statutory standards is significant in a negligence action. But such evidence alone does not establish that a manufacturer is nonnegligent. These standards are often used as a floor, not as a ceiling, for establishing the "acceptable" conduct. A 1971 Pennsylvania case illustrates this principle [10]. A helicopter manufacturer had met FAA standards for the time available to the pilot for engaging the autorotation control after engine failure. This manufacturer could not raise as an absolute defense to liability the fact that he had conformed to governmental standards. The court held that a jury could well find that a reasonable manufacturer would design the controls to allow the pilot more time after the engine failure to activate the autorotation control than is required by FAA standards. The lesson is clear: regardless of existing standards, either industrial or governmental, the final responsibility for reasonable behavior rests with the manufacturer.

1.4.2   Strict Liability and Implied Warranty

1.4.2.1   *Strict Liability*

In 1964 the concept of strict liability emerged as an alternate avenue for establishing an action in products liability. The clearest expression of the strict liability concept is found in the Restatement (Second) of Torts, Section 402A (1965).* It reads:

(1) One who sells any product in a *defective condition unreasonably dangerous* to the user or consumer or to his property is subject to liability for physical harm thereby caused to the ultimate user or consumer, or to his property if
    (a) the seller is engaged in the business of selling such a product, and
    (b) it is expected to and does reach the user or consumer without substantial change in the condition in which it is sold.

(2) The rule stated in Subsection (1) applies although
    (a) the seller has exercised all possible care in the preparation and sale of his product, and
    (b) the user or consumer has not bought the product from or entered into any contractual relation with the seller.

The differences between the negligence and strict liability theories are significant and far-reaching. Fundamentally, in deciding whether a product is or is not unreasonably dangerous, the focus in strict liability is on the *product* and not on the *conduct* of the manufacturer. The shift from negligence to strict liability requires, if nothing else, that the inquiry be focused on the product and its use and away from what the manufacturer should or should not have done or perceived.

Recall that, in regard to the exploding soda pop bottle, it was established that under the negligence theory a manufacturer could claim that his quality control techniques met the standard of reasonableness and that he should not be found liable for a flawed bottle that exploded. Under the theory of strict liability it is *no defense* that the manufacturer acted reasonably. If the product is in fact unreasonably dangerous and it caused the plaintiff's injury, the manufacturer can be held liable. Liability will attach, even though "the

---

*See Appendix B for the comments contained within the Restatement.

seller has exercised *all possible care* in the preparation and sale of his product," and it will be of no avail to the defendant in a production defect case to argue that better quality control procedures are prohibitively expensive.

If plaintiff's claim is, however, that the defendant's product is defective because of a *design* feature, it is essential, as in the theory of negligence, to weigh the burden of precaution to protect against the harm together with the probability and gravity of the harm. In testing a design defect, then, these basic considerations, balancing the probable risks inherent in the use of the product against its utility, remain common to both the negligence and strict liability causes of action.

Use of this balancing process is crucial. Take, for example, the recent Texas case [11] in which the plaintiff, who was attending a party, walked from the living room toward the patio. Unbeknown to her, a clear glass door separated the living room and the patio. The glass was cleanly polished and the plaintiff mistook the glass for open space. The result was a plaintiff with a bruised face. In prior years plaintiff would have gone home and applied a steak to her black eye. But the year was 1971, and so plaintiff sued the glass company for manufacturing an "unreasonably dangerous" door. The court rejected the plaintiff's claim. In doing so it decided that the value of clear glass doors, which give home dwellers the "outdoors" feeling, exceeded the danger level of the occasional situation in which someone mistakes the door for open space. To reach this conclusion, the court was deciding whether it ought to establish a standard for glass doors that would lessen the risk of injury. By implying that the existing criteria for the manufacture and installation of glass doors were adequate and that no design alterations or warnings were necessary, the court was stating that the product was reasonably safe and not defective.

The need for an external standard is obvious because the design of a product cannot be measured against the manufacturer's own internal standard. By definition in a design defect case the manufacturer has met his own internal standard. The difference between negligence and strict liability in a design defect case is thus a subtle one. The key to understanding the difference is again the distinction between defendant conduct and product performance. Negligence questions the reasonablness of the manufacturer's conduct at the time that the product left his hands. Strict liability focuses on the reasonableness of the product in the environment of its use. We leave to later discussion a full exploration of the subtleties that distinguish negligence and strict liability in confronting the design problem.

Another major distinction between negligence and strict liability theory arises from the potential liability of defendants in the distributive chain. Under strict liability, any seller who has sold the product in a defective condition will be held liable to the plaintiff for his injury. Thus potential liability exists for the retailer, the wholesaler, and the distributor, as well as the manufacturer. In addition the manufacturer of a component part of the final product is also potentially liable. The only *caveat* is that the product that caused injury must have left the hands of the particular defendant containing the "defective" condition complained of. Thus, if the plaintiff is able to establish that a component part of a product left the hands of the component-part manufacturer in a defective condition and was later assembled into the final product, the component-part manufacturer can be held liable, as well as the assembler of the final product. The distributor, the wholesaler, and the retailer, will be held liable, even though there is no duty upon them to inspect the product and even when there is no way in which they could have learned of the defective condition. It should be clear that under the negligence theory many of the members of the distributive chain would not be at fault, since there would be no practical way for them to inspect and discover the defect. They would thus have been acting "reasonably" in failing to inspect. Since strict liability focuses, not on the conduct of any party, but rather on the condition of the product in its use environment, liability may attach to any member of the distributive chain regardless of the reasonableness of his conduct.

1.4.2.2 Implied Warranty of Merchantability

A parallel guarantee of product quality, similar to that of strict liability, is given to the user or consumer by the Uniform Commercial Code, Section 2-314.* The code has been adopted in every state except Louisiana. Section 2-314 provides as follows:

(1) Unless excluded or modified, a warranty that the goods shall be merchantable is implied in a contract for their sale if a seller is a merchant with respect to goods of that kind. . . .

(2) Goods to be merchantable must be at least such as. . . .
    c. are fit for the ordinary purposes for which such goods are used. . . .

Although the interpretation of this section of the Uniform Commercial Code by the courts is somewhat unclear, there is general agreement that Section 2-314, which defines an implied warranty of merchantability, provides the same consumer protection as the Restatement requirement that a product be reasonably safe. There may be understandable confusion when it appears that there are two alternate theories of law that accomplish almost the same purpose. Without delving into subtle legal complexities, suffice it to say that, in proceeding under the Uniform Commercial Code (a statute designed primarily for commercial entrepreneurs and not directed specifi-

*See Appendix B.

cally to consumers), special care must be taken to comply with all the requirements set forth by the complex provisions of the Uniform Commercial Code. Thus, for example, failure of an injured party to give notice of the defect in the product to a manufacturer within a reasonable time after his injury may preclude his ability to bring suit [12]. In addition the common practice of manufacturers to disclaim the implied warranty of merchantability must be given special consideration. When the plaintiff proceeds under the Uniform Commercial Code, he may be faced with an argument that the disclaimer prevents his recovery [13]. Courts have differed sharply on whether a disclaimer of the implied warranty of merchantability should be effective in a case where the plaintiff has suffered personal injury. Further, the validity of a disclaimer between parties of unequal bargaining power has been seriously questioned [14]. There is a real ambiguity in the Code on this subject. There is, however, no question that strict liability admits of no disclaimers of any kind [15].

1.4.3 Express Warranty and Misrepresentation—Implied Warranty of Fitness

The previous discussion has focused on legal theories requiring that plaintiff establish some form of product defect. There is, however, an alternate theory for recovery that does not require the establishment of a defect; that is, it is not necessary to establish that the product is unreasonably dangerous. Where a seller expressly warrants or represents that a product has certain characteristics or will perform in a certain manner and the product fails to meet the seller's own warranty or representations, then, if the buyer can prove that his injury resulted from the failure of the product to meet the warranty, liability is established. The Uniform Commercial Code provides in Section 2-313:

Section 2-313. Express Warranties by Affirmation, Promise, Description, Sample

(1) Express warranties by the seller are created as follows:
  (a) Any affirmation of fact or promise made by the seller to the buyer which related to the goods and becomes part of the basis of the bargain creates an express warranty that the goods shall conform to the affirmation or promise.
  (b) Any description of the goods which is made part of the basis of the bargain creates an express warranty that the goods shall conform to the description.
  (c) Any sample or model which is made part of the basis of the bargain creates an express warranty that the whole of the goods shall conform to the sample or model.
(2) It is not necessary to the creation of an express warranty that the seller use formal words such as "warrant" or "guarantee" or that he have a specific intention to

make a warranty, but an affirmation merely of the value of the goods or a statement purporting to be merely the seller's opinion or commendation of the goods does not create a warranty.

There is often a question about whether a certain statement is a warranty or a representation, or whether it is merely "puffing." Thus, at what point a representation of the qualities of a used car becomes a warranty rather than puffing depends on the type and age of the car and the nature and strength of the representations. The statement that a car is in "A-1 shape" may not mean a great deal if the car is seven years old with 100,000 miles on the odometer. A somewhat stronger representation (e.g., "Factory New") applied to a demonstrator model may qualify as a warranty. No hard and fast rules exist about where to draw the line. It is all a question of good common sense.

The caution to manufacturers not to oversell the product is important. If a manufacturer markets beyond the capability of the product to perform, liability may result. This will be true even though the manufacturer honestly believes in the truth of the representations and is reasonable in his belief. An excellent example of courts' holding a manufacturer to his own rhetoric is *Crocker v. Winthrop Laboratories* [16]. Defendants had developed Talwin® —a fairly strong painkiller that they advertised to the medical profession as nonaddictive. The plaintiff, who had been injured in an industrial accident, took Talwin regularly, as prescribed by his physician, to relieve the pain and became addicted to it. Sometime thereafter the plaintiff died as a result of taking a large enough dose so that it was toxic. In finding for the plaintiff, the court did not declare Talwin to be an "unreasonably dangerous" drug. Instead it held the defendant to its promise that Talwin was "nonaddictive." It was irrelevant that the defendant drug company believed the truth of its own assertion at the time of marketing the product. Thus an express warranty is a form of absolute liability.

There is yet another representation theory. The Uniform Commercial Code Section 2-315 expresses it as follows:

Where the seller at the time of contracting has reason to know any particular purpose for which the goods are required and that the buyer is relying on the seller's skill or judgment to select or furnish suitable goods, there is unless excluded or modified under the next section an implied warranty that the goods shall be fit for such purpose.

Thus, for example, a seller of shoes who knows that a purchaser is relying on his judgment to choose a good pair of mountain climbing shoes for him will be held liable if the shoes are not fit for the stated task. Note that the seller will be held liable, even though the shoes are not defective and even though he has not expressly warranted to the buyer that they will perform well in mountain climbing. The seller is thus held liable if he "has reason to know" of the particular purpose for which the goods are to be used.

1.5   THE DEATH OF PRIVITY IN NEGLIGENCE LAW—MACPHERSON V. BUICK MOTOR CAR COMPANY

No discussion of products liability law can proceed without an examination of the privity doctrine. Very simply, in the early development of the law concerning manufacturer's liability the law provided that a manufacturer who was at fault in producing a dangerous product could not be held liable if injury occurred to anyone except his immediate buyer. This rule requiring "privity of contract," that is, a direct relationship between buyer and seller, provided almost absolute immunity to manufacturers since users rarely contracted directly with the manufacturer. Intermediaries such as wholesalers and retailers provided the necessary insulation to accomplish manufacturer's immunity from liability. In 1916 in the landmark case of *MacPherson v. Buick Motor Company* [17] the court held that an action in negligence could be maintained against a *remote* manufacturer of an automobile with a defectively made wheel that broke, causing injury to the plaintiff. The court said that if "the nature of a thing is such that it is reasonably certain to place life and limb in peril when negligently made, it is then a thing of danger." The impact of *MacPherson* was thus to remove the special immunity of manufacturers that existed because of the lack of a contractual relationship and to hold them liable for a cause of action in negligence brought by the ultimate user.

1.6   THE DEATH OF PRIVITY IN WARRANTY—HENNINGSEN V. BLOOMFIELD MOTORS

The same disability that faced buyers in the pre-MacPherson era when they brought suit on a negligence theory faced buyers until recently when they sought to base their claim on a theory of implied warranty of merchantability. The problem with regard to the warranty theory was a more difficult one to hurdle. Negligence law is based on a theory of tort* law, that is, that a defendant owed the plaintiff a duty not to wrongfully harm him through his negligent manufacture of a dangerous product. A warranty theory appeared to be more in the nature of a contract right. In general, only the parties to a contract could enforce rights arising out of the contract. However, times

*A tort can be defined as a civil wrong.

were changing and the courts were forced to reframe legal doctrine to the realities of modern marketing.

In 1960 *Henningsen v. Bloomfield Motors* [18] crashed upon the legal scene with a bang equivalent to the impact of the ill-fated car with the brick wall that caused the accident in this case. The plaintiff, Mrs. Henningsen, was driving a brand-new 1955 Plymouth (10 days old, 488 odometer miles) when she heard a loud noise "from the bottom of the hood." It "felt as if something cracked." The steering wheel spun in her hands and the car veered sharply to the right and crashed into a highway sign and a brick wall. Mrs. Henningsen was injured and brought an action against Chrysler Corporation, the manufacturer of the car.

In a brilliant and far-reaching opinion, the court laid to rest the doctrine that an injured plaintiff could sue only his immediate seller for a breach of an implied warranty of merchantability. The court concluded that:

Under modern conditions the ordinary layman, on responding to the importuning of colorful advertising, has neither the opportunity nor the capacity to inspect or to determine the fitness of an automobile for use; he must rely on the manufacturer who has control of its construction, and to some degree on the dealer who, to the limited extent called for by the manufacturer's instructions, inspects and services it before delivery. In such a marketing milieu his remedies and those of persons who properly claim through him should not depend "upon the intricacies of the law of sales. The obligation of the manufacturer should not be based alone on privity of contract. It should rest, as was once said, upon 'the demands of social justice'." *Mazetti v. Armour & Co.* (1913). "If privity of contract is required," then, under the circumstances of modern merchandising, "privity of contract exists in the consciousness and understanding of all right-thinking persons."

Accordingly, we hold that under modern marketing conditions, when a manufacturer puts a new automobile in the stream of trade and promotes its purchase by the public, an implied warranty that it is reasonably suitable for use as such accompanies it into the hands of the ultimate purchaser. Absence of agency between the manufacturer and the dealer who makes the ultimate sale is immaterial.

It is important to recognize what *Henningsen* accomplished. *Henningsen* stands for the proposition that a manufacturer can be sued by remote users for selling a defective product, without regard to whether the manufacturer was at fault. This is strict liability—plain and simple. It was not to be very long before courts would abandon the theory of implied warranty, which was based in contract, and recognize that what was really at work was a strict liability tort theory that inured to the benefit of personal-injury plaintiffs. Indeed, the theory of strict liability in tort has now become the predominant approach to products liability law. However, some courts that have clearly switched to the tort theory for personal injury and property damage claims still retain the "privity" doctrine when the claim is not for personal injury and property loss [19]. In such "commercial loss" claims, some courts believe it wise to retain the limitation that the plaintiff must be in direct privity with the defendant in order to enforce contract rights.

1.7 STRICT LIABILITY AS A TORT DOCTRINE—GREENMAN V. YUBA POWER PRODUCTS, INC.

The fulfillment of the New Jersey court's prophetic opinion in *Henningsen* was accomplished three years later in the landmark case of *Greenman v. Yuba Power Products, Inc.* [20]. In that case the California court was faced with a plaintiff who brought a products liability action against both the retailer and the manufacturer of a Shopsmith combination power tool. The plaintiff had seen the Shopsmith demonstrated by the retailer and studied a brochure prepared by the manufacturer. He decided he wanted a Shopsmith for his home workshop, and his wife bought him one for Christmas in 1955. In 1957 he bought the necessary attachments to use the Shopsmith as a lathe for turning a large piece of wood he wished to make into a chalice. After he had worked on the piece of wood several times without difficulty, it suddenly flew out of the machine and struck him on the forehead, inflicting serious injuries. About 10½ months later, he gave the retailer and the manufacturer written notice of their breach of warranties and filed a complaint against them alleging such breaches and alleging negligence.

The court was faced with a dilemma. If the only strict liability theory it had at its disposal was the implied warranty of merchantability, then the court was faced with the problem that the buyer had given the seller tardy notice of the breach of warranty. Under the California Commercial Code timely notice was necessary for a cause of action based in contract. Rather than give a tortured reading of the language of its commercial code, the California court said that it was time to recognize a theory of strict liability based, not in contract, tied to the intricacies of the law of sales, but rather one based in the law of torts. If it was no longer necessary to prove a privity relationship between buyer and seller, it was only because the problem was no longer contractual. Thus, reasoned the court, why not recognize the obvious and remove all the impediments of contract law to permit an action based on strict liability in tort? The court argued as follows:

The purpose of such liability is to insure that the costs of injuries resulting from defective products are borne by the manufacturers that put such products on the market rather than by the injured persons who are powerless to protect themselves. Sales warranties serve this purpose fitfully at best. Under these circumstances, it should not be controlling whether plaintiff selected the machine because of the statements in the brochure, or because of the machine's own appearance of excellence that belied the defect lurking beneath the surface, or because he merely assumed that it would safely do the jobs it was built to do. It should not be controlling whether the details of the sales from manufacturer to retailer and from retailer to plaintiff's wife were such that one or more of the implied warranties of the sales act arose. "The remedies of injured consumers ought not to be made to depend upon the intricacies of the law of sales." To establish the manufacturer's liability it was sufficient that plaintiff proved that he was injured while using the Shopsmith in a way it was intended to be used as a result of a defect in design and manufacture of which plaintiff was not aware that made the Shopsmith unsafe for its intended use.

Thus, with one fell swoop the California court abolished many of the stumbling blocks to a plaintiff intent on bringing an action against a remote manufacturer. No longer would a plaintiff have to be concerned with whether he had given notice of the breach of warranty to the manufacturer [21]. No longer would the plaintiff be barred from recovery because the contract statute of limitations, running from the time of sale, had expired [22]. His cause of action was in tort, and the tort statute of limitations begins to run at the time of injury [23]. No longer would a plaintiff be barred because a contract disclaimer precluded his recovery [24]. The cause of action was in tort, and the seller could not disclaim the legal liabilities imposed on him by the law of torts with a contract disclaimer [25]. And the dreaded enemy known as privity was dead forever in a tort action.

To conclude, then, the basic legal principles of negligence, strict liability/implied warranty, and express warranty/misrepresentation in their present states of evolution provide sometimes parallel and sometimes overlapping paths for a plaintiff to chart a course of liability to a manufacturer or seller. What is important to recognize, however, is that the law is the framework for measuring the responsibilities and duties of the parties. While the case-by-case application of the principles may sometimes go awry, those principles stand as the sole tests for measuring the interactions between society and technology.

CHAPTER 2

A Tort Action—
Defining the Basics

2.1 AN OVERVIEW OF PLAINTIFF'S CASE

To make out a case in products liability, regardless of the theory of the liability, the plaintiff must establish the following:

1. The product was defective.
2. The defect existed at the time the product left the defendant's hands.
3. The defect caused the harm.
4. This harm is appropriately assignable to the identified defect.

Where the plaintiff's theory is that of negligence, he must establish, in addition to these elements, that the defendant's conduct was unreasonable.

With some reflection it will be seen that, if the plaintiff fails to establish any of these elements, his cause will fail.

2.1.1 Product Defect

Although we leave to a later discussion the intricacies of the defect question, it is obvious that the plaintiff must in some way establish that the product is substandard. If a product meets all the requisite demands that society sets forth and the plaintiff is injured nonetheless, then we can hardly blame the manufacturer. Thus, a knife can realistically be termed a dangerous product. It will cut meat but also has the inherent danger of cutting human flesh. Yet no court will permit the manufacturer of a knife to be sued because a housewife is cut while preparing vegetables. The product may be considered dangerous but not defective.

2.1.2   Defect in the Hands of the Manufacturer

Products often lead tortured lives. Products that meet even the most demanding specifications can be used and abused so that at the time of injury they are clearly defective. But such defects cannot be automatically assigned to the manufacturer. It must be determined when the defect was introduced into the product. Unless it is established that the defect existed when the product was in the hands of the manufacturer, liability will not attach. Often structural weaknesses or design problems do not manifest themselves until the product is put to a certain use. The mere fact that a defect did not become evident until later does not, of course, mean that the defect was not present when the product left the hands of the manufacturer. In each case a careful factual examination must be conducted to determine whether the defect was attributable to the defendant manufacturer or seller or whether it was present in the product when it left the defendant's hands.

2.1.3   The Defect Caused the Harm

The mere presence of a defect in a product at the time of injury is not enough. A defect may exist in a product but have had little or no bearing on the incident that caused the injury. The defect may have been dormant, and the operating cause of the accident may have been human failure totally unrelated to the product. This is often very difficult to ferret out. Sometimes after the violent event of a product accident, the product appears defective. Thus, in a recent case [1] in which motor mounts were found broken after a car accident, the question arose as to which came first, the chicken or the egg? Did the motor mounts break prior to the accident and thus cause the driver to lose control, or did the collision impact cause the motor mounts to break? It is often impossible to determine whether the defect played a causal role or became apparent only as a result of the traumatic event. It is here that experts often clash in their assessment of what occurred.

2.1.4   Is the Harm Assignable to the Defect?

Even when it is clear that the defect played a role in the injury event, it is often necessary to determine whether that role was significant in assessing the defendant's liability. Even defective products can be abused and misused beyond reason. Thus, for example, if a manufacturer sold a kitchen blender with a gross structural weakness in the glass, and the plaintiff dropped metal objects in the blender, causing the glass to shatter and injure him, it may well be argued that, defect or not, it is not fair to impose liability on a manufacturer for an injury resulting from such use. The harm is not fairly assignable to the defect as a matter of elemental justice. This is the issue of "proximate cause," which is examined in greater depth at a later point.

It may be argued that the blender example really illustrates misuse of the product. Yet the law must find some way of determining whether liability should attach to a defective product when, in addition to the defect that may have played some role in the injury-causing event, misuse occurred as well. Here the courts must judge whether the injury that occurred is properly assignable to the defect. Thus misuse in this context is labeled by the courts as the proximate-cause issue.

2.2 PLAINTIFF'S CONDUCT

2.2.1 Action Based on Negligence—Contributory Fault

In any action in products liability the plaintiff will not emerge victorious merely by establishing the defectiveness of the product and its causal relationship to his injury. In each case the plaintiff's behavior can come under scrutiny. It is generally the legal responsibility of the defendant, who seeks to exculpate himself from liability, to prove that the plaintiff has been at fault in his use of the product. It is here that it becomes crucial to distinguish between the cause of action based on negligence and that based on either implied warranty or strict liability. In some states, when the action is negligence based, a defendant can totally defeat the plaintiff's claim by proving that the plaintiff has been "contributorily negligent." This means that, in evaluating the plaintiff's behavior, if the defendant can establish that the plaintiff failed to act as a reasonable person would under the same or similar circumstances and that plaintiff's conduct contributed to his injury, the plaintiff will be denied recovery. Thus the plaintiff's conduct is judged relative to a community standard for behavior just as the defendant's is [2]. If the plaintiff has failed to discover an obvious defect in the product, or misused the product, or abused the product, in a manner that society would deem unreasonable and if his conduct has contributed to his own injury, recovery will be denied, despite whatever negligence may be assigned to the manufacturer.

2.2.2   Action Based on Strict Liability—Assumption of Risk

In an action based on strict liability, however, the defendant cannot defeat a plaintiff's claim by proving that the plaintiff failed to discover a defect or unknowingly misused the product. Instead, the defendant must prove that plaintiff *voluntarily and unreasonably encountered a known risk* [3]. It is not enough to prove that a reasonable person would have discovered the risk. The defendant must establish that the plaintiff, himself, saw the risk and unreasonably encountered it. Note the subjective element of this test. The plaintiff's claim will not be defeated simply because he failed to meet the general community standard of reasonableness in his actions. The courts are willing to go far in the interpretation of the subjective element of this test.

In a recent case a steelworker had for 15 years been using his ungloved hand to steady a rapidly moving sheet of steel entering a slitting machine [4]. On the day of the accident his hand was caught by a slight burr protruding from the steel sheet. His hand was pulled into the slitting blades and severely injured. The defendant argued with some justification that the plaintiff must have appreciated the danger of keeping his ungloved hand so close to the cutting knives of the machine. The court found, however, that the plaintiff did not know of the presence of the burr on the sheet of steel and thus did not assume a known risk. This conclusion was reached even though plaintiff had 15 years of experience with the machine and should have appreciated the general danger of working so close to the unguarded cutters of the machine. The plaintiff may well have been contributorily negligent with use of a community standard to measure his behavior, but that is not sufficient in an action for strict liability. The defendant must prove that the plaintiff himself appreciated the specific risk in the moments before his injury and voluntarily (and unreasonably) decided to take the risk.

2.2.3   Action Based on Express Warranty—Assumption of Risk

The test of the plaintiff's conduct in an action in express warranty is the same as in strict liability. Did the injured party voluntarily and unreasonably encounter a known risk? It is not based on a community standard of whether a reasonable person would have discovered that the product did not have the warranted quality [5]. It must be proved by the defendant that the injured plaintiff actually knew that the product did not contain the warranted quality and then voluntarily and unreasonably faced this risk. In addition serious product abuse, beyond the scope of reasonable product use (or, again, the issue of proximate cause), is also a defense, as it is in strict liability.

2.2.4   The Comparative-Fault Doctrine

This principle involves an evaluation of the plaintiff's fault in comparison to that of the defendant [6]. Thus, for example, a defendant may be considered 80 percent at fault and the plaintiff 20 percent at fault. Various formulas are used to determine the effect of such a finding on the amount of a plaintiff's recovery. It is clear however that, when the plaintiff proceeds on a theory of negligence, a jurisdiction that follows a *comparative negligence* rule will reduce his recovery in proportion to his fault in the accident. The strict liability case presents a more complex problem. It may seem somewhat anomalous to speak of contributory fault, when under theories of strict liability, express or implied warranty, it is not necessary to prove the defendant's fault at all [7]. Nevertheless, some courts have attempted the impossible when faced with a plaintiff who is somewhat at "fault." The courts apparently compare his conduct with the gravity of the defect in the product and seek to work out a percentage allocation for the damages. Assumption of the risk is treated in many states as a variant of plaintiff's fault.

2.3   THE DUTY QUESTION—SOME GENERAL CONSIDERATIONS

The duty concept in the law of torts is a threshold issue that must be surmounted before a court will entertain a cause of action. If a court determines, for whatever policy reason, that the defendant has no duty to the plaintiff, then, even if the defendant's conduct or product is unreasonable and harms the plaintiff, no liability will attach [8].

Perhaps this concept can best be explained by an example using a common nonproducts liability situation. An elderly man has a heart attack in the middle of the street in broad daylight. He asks a passerby to summon an ambulance for him. The passerby refuses and the elderly gentleman dies. If the deceased's next of kin sought to bring a wrongful death action against the passerby for his failure to call for help, the defendant would prevail. The law imposes no duty upon a person to rescue another with whom he has no established relationship [9]. Note that the courts are not saying that the defendant has acted reasonably under the circumstances. That is simply not so in this instance. Instead the law has, for policy reasons that transcend the facts in the case before it, sought to define certain relationships (or nonrelationships) and grant certain ones immunity from liability. In the developing field of products liability, courts are still attempting to define the basic legal obligations (duties) that they ought to impose.

2.3.1   Privity: A No-Duty Concept

The question of privity was discussed earlier in Sections 1.4 and 1.5. Within the present context it appears that the privity rule, which required that a plaintiff and defendant be in a direct contractual relationship as a prerequisite to a products liability action, was actually a no-duty rule. The courts were not saying that, without privity, a product was reasonably safe. They simply refused to acknowledge a responsibility from the manufacturer to the buyer unless there existed a direct contractual relationship.

The privity problem illustrates how courts proceed in the process of developing the law. The courts' treatment of the duty issue expresses the social mores and economic realities of the day. When mores and social realities change, the courts are empowered (when there is no legislation to the contrary) to change their conclusions about the legal obligations. Thus, in the late nineteenth and early twentieth centuries, when courts sought to protect the emerging industrial economy, it was quite natural for them to conclude that the insulation afforded by privity should be granted to the manufacturers. When the economic facts of life changed and it became clear that consumers were the disadvantaged class needing protection, the privity rule was abandoned.

A recent example of this principle lay in the expansion of strict liability law in favor of bystanders. Originally the rule had been granted to favor users and consumers of products [10]. But what of the bystander plaintiff who happened to be struck by an automobile whose steering was defective and went out of control? The New York court in *Codling v. Paglia* [11] expanded duty to include bystanders. Their language in support of doing so was most eloquent:

> Today as never before the product in the hands of the consumer is often a most sophisticated and even mysterious article. Not only does it usually emerge as a sealed unit with an alluring exterior rather than as a visible assembly of component parts, but its functional validity and usefulness often depend on the application of electronic, chemical or hydraulic principles far beyond the ken of the average consumer. Advances in the technologies of materials, of processes, of operational means have put it almost entirely out of the reach of the consumer to comprehend why or how the article operates, and thus even farther out of his reach to detect when there may be a defect or a danger present in its design or manufacture. In today's world it is often only the manufacturer who can fairly be said to know and to understand when an article is suitably designed and safely made for its intended purpose. Once floated on the market, many articles in a very real practical sense defy detection of defect, except possibly in the hands of an expert after laborious and perhaps even destructive disassembly. By way of direct illustration, how many automobile purchasers or users have any idea how a power steering mechanism operates or is intended to operate, with its "circulating worm and piston assembly and its cross shaft splined to

the Pitman arm"? Further, as has been noted, in all this the bystander, the nonuser, is even worse off than the user—to the point of total exclusion from any opportunity either to choose manufacturers or retailers or to detect defects. We are accordingly persuaded that from the standpoint of justice as regards the operating aspect of today's products, responsibility should be laid on the manufacturer, subject to the limitations we set forth.

2.3.2 Second-Collision Liability

Recently courts have been asked to create legal obligations that have not previously existed. Plaintiffs who have suffered injury in automobile collisions have instituted actions against manufacturers for enhanced injuries arising from either a production defect or a design defect that did not actually *cause* the initial accident.

A plaintiff who was injured when her car collided with another claimed that her injuries were enhanced when, in the ensuing impact, her face was seriously scarred by a three-pronged emblem on the steering wheel [12]. It is obvious that the three-pronged emblem did not cause the accident (first collision) but merely enhanced or increased the plaintiff's injuries suffered in the accident when the second collision occurred with the emblem. These are the so-called "crashworthiness" or "second-collision" issues. To date, such claims have received a mixed reception by the courts. Two landmark cases have come down squarely on either side of the issue [13]. In any event, plaintiff can recover from the defendant manufacturer only for those damages arising from the enhancement of his injuries. He cannot recover for the damages caused by the initial impact itself. The resolution of this question requires addressing difficult matters of proof involving complex expert testimony, not the least of which is the extent to which the injuries were increased by the defect.

The second-collision cases demonstrate the duty principle in operation. Those courts that impose liability believe that we have reached the point in the development of safety considerations where it is fair to impose responsibility on manufacturers to design with collisions in mind. Furthermore, they believe that expert testimony can be of sufficient clarity to aid the court in determining how much more seriously the plaintiff was injured as a result of the second collision. The courts that deny liability believe that the duty question presented by the second-collision issue should not be decided by courts but rather by administrative agencies and legislatures. They further believe that the expert testimony cannot provide a clear picture of how much a plaintiff's injury was enhanced by the second collision. They view this evidence to be ephemeral and somewhat suspect. The conclusion these courts have reached is that there is no duty to manufacture a crashworthy car

[14]. It is thus clear that "duty" or "no duty" is the indicator the courts use to signal to the world that they have concluded that the law has or has not reached the point where it is fair to assess liability.

2.3.3 Duty to the Sophisticated User

The duty problem must be addressed in defining the relationship between a manufacturer and a class of sophisticated users. In this instance the question is whether the manufacturer owes a full duty of due care to a group of people whose level of sophistication in the use of the product is very high. *West v. Broderick and Bascom Rope Company* [15] exemplifies the problem. In this case a manufacturer of steel cable was sued when a cable broke while lifting a weight well beyond its tensile strength (breaking point). From long experience Broderick and Bascom knew the ultimate breaking point of the cable it manufactured. To avoid the possibility of injury to personnel or damage to the cable itself, the manufacturer rated cable for use at one-fifth its tensile strength. It is accepted practice in the industry that steel cable should not be used beyond its rated capacity. The evidence indicated that the cable was rated for 2.7 tons but was actually being used to haul a weight of 15–20 tons. As a result of this overload the cable literally exploded, causing serious permanent injuries to the plaintiff, an ironworker, who was standing in the vicinity.

The negligence alleged was that the defendant failed to attach a permanent tag to the cable to indicate that its rated capacity was 2.7 tons. The defendant did distribute literature about the rated capacity of various size cables and apparently also tagged them. Although the opinion is somewhat unclear on this point, it appears that the tag was somehow knocked off in service.

The warning problem in such a case raises serious duty questions. The court assumed that ironworkers who work with cables are well aware that using a cable beyond its rated capacity is extremely dangerous. One witness testified that only a fool would use a cable beyond its rated capacity, let alone use one at five times its rated capacity. One must then question how the cable, *without* a tag indicating its rated capacity, is an unreasonably dangerous product.

The Iowa court agreed with a jury finding that the defendant had a duty to warn by placing a nonremovable or permanent tag on the cable. The court reasoned that the cost of such a warning was minimal compared to the possible danger in using the wrong cable. Unlike other kinds of warnings that bear a substantial societal cost (see Section 5.2), the tag in this case would be convenient and would have no adverse effect on the believability of warnings in general. As we note later on, warning about dangers that are remote may have negative effects on the credibility of danger warnings. But mere convenience should not be viewed as equivalent to unreasonable danger. If the steel cable did not represent itself as capable of carrying any particular load and was to be used by a sophisticated user, what grounds are there for imposing liability?

The answer the court gives is both simple and simplistic: it would be nice to have the tag and cheap to put it on. Even admitting that this conclusion is valid, it has little to recommend it as a standard for determining when to impose a duty to warn. It is the court that must make a threshold decision on whether in any case the danger level and the nature of product use are such that society ought to consider the imposition of safety features. It is especially important in warning cases that the courts face the duty question before they commence with their analysis of any other issues. The reason is simple. The inexpensive nature of convenience-type warnings can easily lure a court to conclude that a warning should be imposed. Yet somewhere the judicial process must focus attention on factors other than minimal cost and convenience and address the question of whether the law is prepared to impose legal liability when the danger level of a product is minimal in the hands of a sophisticated user. The duty question permits a court to take into account a broad range of policy factors that lie well beyond risk-utility balancing. Thus factors such as the normal use patterns of the workers, their relative sophistication, the demands of the work environment, the spectrum of use and users of the product, the ultimate impact of the warning, and the safety record of the industry should be addressed at this initial stage of the legal analysis.

2.3.4 Shifting Duty—Primary Suppliers and Managerial Decision-making

Another area that must be watched carefully in developing product law is the potential liability of primary suppliers of materials. The problem is difficult. Clearly the manufacturers of basic materials who sell on an open market cannot be held liable if improper use is made of the material they supply. On the other hand the sellers of the basic material, who are in close contact with the manufacturers using this material in specific ways or in specific products and who consult with these manufacturers about their needs for appropriate material, may well be open to a products liability suit if the material chosen is not appropriate to the product. Although it is less clear, it may be that a material supplier who was not consulted about a specific need but who knows how his basic materials are being used may also have ultimate responsibility for the inappropriate use of that material. Thus steel suppliers who sell to surgical implant manufacturers may be required to insist on the use of certain kinds of metals to minimize the possibility of fatigue failure of these metals when the implants are inserted in patients [16].

The same problems arise with regard to complex machinery requiring the attachment of safety features before it can be put to proper employee use. Often the manufacturers will offer the safety equipment as an optional feature. Depending on the nature of the machinery and how it is to be used, the courts have imposed primary liability on the machine manufacturer for failure to attach the required safety features as part of the basic machine. Although some may view this as an improper interference with managerial decision-making, recent cases have suggested that the manufacturer, who has full knowledge of the foreseeable use of his machinery as well as of its attendant hazards, bears significant responsibility for building safety into the machine and not offering it as an optional feature [17].

On the other hand, if a machine has many uses, as a press does, and if the press manufacturer has no reason to know of a special guarding or safety requirement for a specific end use of the press, it may be inappropriate to hold the press manufacturer liable for failure to supply a special safety device unique to that use. It may be more appropriate for this duty to be assumed either by the actual seller of the equipment or by the purchaser, both of whom may be aware of the specific use intended.

It would seem inappropriate to burden the manufacturer with supplying safety equipment for every conceivable use as part of the machine. Indeed, to incorporate all such safety equipment in each machine may make the machine inoperable for certain appropriate uses. Yet the machine manufacturer can well recognize that certain of his potential purchasers are unsophisticated in recognizing the need for or existence of safety equipment. Thus it may very well be the duty of the machine manufacturer to insist that some type of guarding or safety equipment be part of every sale, although he may place the duty of appropriate selection on the distributor or buyer, who may be in a better position to make an intelligent choice consistent with his needs.

The courts have yet to fully explore the subtle duty questions raised here. To the extent that materials suppliers, manufacturers, distributors, and sellers can anticipate and formulate duty policies through contractual arrangements, the courts may be better able to understand the issues and adopt similar principles of duty.

Each of these questions helps to set the legal parameters for the relationships between primary suppliers and those who buy from them. Where is it that the law seeks to impose responsibility for safety? Each situation will call for an understanding of the economic realities of the industry, the sophistication of the purchaser, the ability of the seller to impose safety on the buyer, as well as of other issues. The court will then decide, taking all of these factors into account, whether it is fair to impose a duty on the primary supplier or whether it is best to impose responsibility for safety further down the distributive chain.

2.4 DUTY IN PERSPECTIVE

The interplay of the concepts of duty, proximate cause, and contributory fault may appear to introduce needless complexity into the determination of liability. More often than not, the pragmatic view of the manufacturer and design engineer is that any product use outside the boundaries of the intended use (perhaps prescribed by the instructions with the product) should deny any right of the plaintiff to recover.

The courts have refused to adopt such an approach. The issues are not simple but subtle and complex and differ in each situation. Whereas the plaintiff may fail to recover for injuries when metal objects caused the blender with a defective container to shatter, the courts may rule in favor of the same plaintiff if, instead, the defective container shattered when ice cubes were inserted, despite the fact that the instructions may have cautioned against such use.

The courts, with their myriad of concepts, are saying that manufacturers must recognize and respond to a range of human frailties in designing and marketing products. The legal system is seeking to define, in a very qualitative way, the boundaries of responsibilities for each of the actors in the chain from the manufacturer to the bystander.

This concept of responsibility underlies the entire question of duty. Should the manufacturer make the safety guard an integral part of the machine, or should it be available only as an option? Should the primary material's supplier insist on knowing the use to which an item will be put by a remote fabricator to prevent an inappropriate use of a material? To what extent should a component-part manufacturer rely solely on the specifications of the assembler of the entire product to ensure that the component part will function properly relative to all the other elements that comprise the product?

These are some of the questions being raised by the courts in searching for resolution of the duty issue, as well as of the issues of proximate cause and contributory fault. Our premise, both express and implied, is that these are the questions and the issues that ought to be raised and answered *before* the product leaves the designer's hands.

CHAPTER 3

Product Defects—
What Are They?

3.1 INTRODUCTION

Prior discussion has intentionally taken for granted the notion of defect in setting forth both the theories of liability and the issues involved in prescribing liability. The central focus in any products liability action is the existence of a defect in the product.

Abstractly, a defect is that state, quality, or condition of a product that makes it substandard. Having said that, one is really no closer to understanding the legal framework, but it does point toward the two steps involved in considering defect: identifying what it is about the product that gives rise to the problem (i.e., state, quality, or condition) and then attempting to demonstrate that, as a result of this, the product did not meet some established criterion (i.e., it was substandard).

3.2 THE FLAWS OF NATURE: PRODUCTION AND DESIGN

At this point it is necessary to introduce new terminology concerning defect. One goal of the plaintiff's case is to have the jury conclude that the product in question was defective because the product state, quality, or condition was substandard. An irregularity in the state, quality, or condition of a product is termed a "flaw." If that flaw is judged substandard within the context of litigation, then the flaw may be said to have emerged as a defect.

Whether it is among the expected fraction of products that does not meet prescribed manufacturing standards or results from the inadvertent act of an employee, the production flaw is what arises when a given product of an entire line fails to meet the standards met by the majority of these products. A production flaw can be a weld with little or no penetration, the wrong bolt fastening two pieces, the inclusion (or foreign particles) in the metal part, the failure to grind the appropriate fillet radius, the wrong label on a container, the missing vent hole in a cap, and so on. Inevitably, despite the existence of sophisticated quality control procedures, products flawed during the manufacturing process will find their way to the market place.

Products can be flawed even if they are made precisely according to manufacturing standards. As the California court said in *Cronin v. J. B. E. Olson Corporation*, "a defect may emerge from the mind of a designer as well as from the hand of the workman" [1]. The design flaw is what exists in all products of that make or of that kind.

The absence of a guard on a machine or device is the prototype of the design flaw. Among other possible design flaws are the intentional selection of a certain material, the size of a given part, the location of a feature, or the absence of a warning.

The distinction between production errors and design flaws is not always as clear as the examples suggest. While at the two extremes of the frequency at which flaws occur the distinction between design and production flaw has meaning, it must be recognized that there exists a gray area in which the distinction becomes blurred. For example, assume that a leaf spring of a truck is flawed by gouge marks on the surface of some of its leaves or plates. If a very small fraction of the leaf springs produced by a given manufacturer contained these gouge marks, the flaw could be described as a production error. If, however, a significant fraction of these springs, as produced, contained the gouge marks, then one might consider the problem to be generic and inherent in the choice of a production process, and hence it should be considered a design flaw. The point at which the shift was made from the former perspective to the latter is of little consequence, as long as the context in which the flawed product is viewed in litigation is the same regardless of whether the origin of the flaw is production or design.

The crucial question, then, is whether as a result of the flaw, the product's performance is substandard and, if so, does that performance make the product defective?

3.3 PRODUCTION DEFECTS—NEGLIGENCE AND STRICT LIABILITY

In establishing the concept of defect in a negligence case, as distinguished from a case based on strict liability, one must constantly keep in mind the basic dichotomy between the two theories. Negligence focuses on the conduct of the defendant and asks whether the defendant has acted reasonably. Strict liability focuses on the product and seeks to determine whether the product is defective, irrespective of *how* or *why* it got to be defective.

The doctrine of strict tort liability for products was first recognized in the context of production defect cases. The typical case was, not surprisingly, that of the exploding soda pop bottle. An injured plaintiff who sought to sue the glass manufacturer or bottler for negligence was faced with the defense that the defendant had acted reasonably in its manufacturing process. The quality control system of the defendant became the battleground for the lawsuit. If the defendant had in fact acted reasonably, the fact that a defective bottle had slipped through quality control would be insufficient grounds for imposing liability.

Thus, while it might be easily established that the product was defective, that is, that it was flawed in production and its substandard performance resulted in injury, the defendant might not be negligent. That is, despite the defective product that caused the harm, the manufacturer had still acted reasonably in marketing it.

In still other cases the defendant manufacturer could introduce into evidence the details of its quality control program that was persuasively reasonable. However, the extent to which that program was adhered to, or deviated from, although critical to the plaintiff's case, may well be beyond the resources of the plaintiff to prove. In response to these difficulties the courts developed evidentiary rules to assist the plaintiff in proving his case. The most significant of these rules is the doctrine of *res ipsa loquitur*—literally, "the thing speaks for itself" [2]. This meant that courts were permitted to allow cases to go to a jury for determination in the absence of hard evidence of negligence when there was a commonsense inference that negligence was the most logical explanation of the defect in the product.

To be sure, the doctrine of *res ipsa loquitur* was of immeasurable assistance to plaintiffs, for it permitted an inference of negligence even in the absence of proof of the specific negligence of the defendant. Yet, strange as it may seem, the effective use of the *res ipsa* doctrine was probably the tipping point for strict liability. In those instances in which plaintiffs were prevailing on the basis of *res ipsa*, even when confronted with a strong defendant showing of nonnegligence, strict liability was in fact the doctrine being applied. In *Escola v. Coca Cola Bottling Company*, Justice Traynor expressed that view in 1945 in a dissenting opinion. He said:

An injured person, however, is not ordinarily in a position to refute such evidence [of negligence] or identify the cause of the defect, for he can hardly be familiar with the manufacturing process as the manufacturer himself is. In leaving it to the jury to decide whether the inference has been dispelled, regardless of the evidence against it, the negligence rule approaches the rule of strict liability. It is needlessly circuitous to make negligence the basis of recovery and impose what is in reality liability without negligence [3].

When the defendant did prevail, the fact that the plaintiff was unable to successfully counter the defendant was attributed to the defendant's control of the evidence (i.e., the manufacturing process). Thus, win or lose, there was a strong feeling that negligence should not be the governing theory. It was thus the *production* defect case that spurred the development of strict products liability.

In a production defect case it is not difficult to identify the defect in the product. Generally, one needs only to compare the defective product with a "good" product from the defendant's assembly line. The standard of reference is internal—it is the manufacturer's own quality standard. If the defendant's product fails to measure up to that standard, it can, with relative assurance, be identified as defective. If the defect caused the plaintiff's harm, a *prima facie* case has been established. Thus it rarely makes a difference in a production defect case whether the standard given to the jury for deciding whether a defect exists is that the product is "defective" or "unreasonably dangerous" or "defective and unreasonably dangerous to the user or consumer." The decision process remains the same. The internal manufacturing standard is the bench mark for assessing the presence of defect.

Although this statement is a good working definition of a defect, it is not theoretically sound. The test for defect is in reality the same for both production and design defect cases. The practical effect of administering the test may result in a finding that in a production defect case the product is unreasonably dangerous in most cases. For example, the manufacturer's alternative in a production defect case may be for the manufacturer not to market the flawed product that comes off the assembly line. Contrast this with the manufacturer's alternative in a design defect case in which the effect of identifying the flaw as a defect may be to cause an alteration in an entire product line. It is crucial to note that in a production defect case the defendant may not know which of the products of the assembly line is flawed and thus may not be negligent. But if strict liability focuses on whether the product is defective, then the question of defendant's ability to know is irrelevant. Thus a product with a manufacturing flaw can be termed defective, since the defendant, if he had the knowledge, would have decided against marketing the flawed product. Herein lies the crucial difference between negligence and strict liability. The product may be defective, yet the defendant may have used the very best quality control and thus may not be negligent. The doctrine of *res ipsa loquitur*, which permits an inference of negligence in many production defect cases, even in the face of strong quality control evidence to the contrary, most probably bastardized the negligence standard. This doctrine thus became a way station for the courts, who were in fact marching to the ultimate conclusion that strict liability should be the governing doctrine.

3.4 DESIGN DEFECTS—NEGLIGENCE AND STRICT LIABILITY

In sharp contrast to the production defect case the design defect case does not provide a built-in internal standard for establishing defect. The product by definition meets the manufacturer's own internal standard. In attempting to define an external standard for establishing defect in design, it is clear that a balancing process must help determine the standard. And that standard must essentially be one of reasonableness (see Section 4.4).

When the test is the conduct of the defendant, the reasonableness standard is fully understandable. When, however, it is the product itself that must be considered to establish defect (as it must be in strict liability), then the standard of "unreasonable danger" requires some explanation.

Products are not capable of reasoning—only persons are. When we speak of the "unreasonably dangerous" product, we begin with the premise that all products present risks to the consuming public. Some risks, when balanced against the important functions the product performs and the cost of providing for greater safety, are deemed "reasonable." This means that a reasonable person who had actual knowledge of the product's potential for harm would conclude that it was proper to market it in that condition.

How does this differ from negligence? Strict liability theory, unlike negligence, is not concerned with the conduct of the defendant that brought about the unreasonably dangerous condition. Thus, for example, assume that a defendant manufacturer has acted reasonably in designing a product and has adequately tested it before it is marketed. After the product is in actual use in the marketplace, however, it is discovered that the testing and design process failed to account for certain dangers, and even though it was reasonable *not* to anticipate those dangers, the design is in fact substandard. It will *not* be a defense in this case that the defendant *acted* reasonably. If we can proclaim that the product is *in fact* not reasonably safe—that a reasonable person who had knowledge of the danger would have decided against marketing without the design alteration or additional warning—then the product is unreasonably dangerous.

3.5 THE BALANCING PROCESS—MCCORMACK V. HANKSCRAFT COMPANY

To illustrate how the standard of "reasonableness" is determined after an evaluation of the trade-offs of product risk versus the utility of the product, consider the case of *McCormack v. Hankscraft Company* [4].

A major manufacturer of steam vaporizers placed an inexpensive model on the market. One of its features was a lift-off cap to which was attached the heating element that produced the steam (Figure 3-1). The container with the lift-off cap was placed on a kitchen stool in a child's bedroom. In the middle of the night the child awoke and walked through the darkened room, tripping over the electrical cord attached to the vaporizer, causing the vaporizer to tip over on its side. The scalding water flowing from the overturned vaporizer severely burned the child. An action brought against the manufac-

Figure 3-1. Three-piece vaporizer for home use. (Artist's sketch; not actual unit.)

turer on behalf of the child claimed that the design of the vaporizer was defective.

Using the balancing process for reasonableness, it is possible to identify the factors necessary for determining whether or not the design of the vaporizer was unreasonably dangerous. The utility of a vaporizer is generally unquestioned. It is entirely foreseeable, however, that steam vaporizers will be used in close proximity to children, and often in darkened bedrooms. Placing the vaporizer on a stool or chair so that the steam is directed toward the child in bed is also a common and expected practice. Thus there is a good chance that a vaporizer will be inadvertently tipped by a child or an adult. Given this chance, one must consider the implications of heated water's flowing out of the tipped container.

Since the water in the container was hot enough to cause third-degree burns, one is compelled to ask whether it is possible to eliminate the danger without seriously impairing the usefulness of the product or making it unduly expensive. It seems reasonable to examine possible alternatives to the design of this inexpensive vaporizer. Plaintiff, through the use of expert testimony, established that a screw-on cap, in place of the lift-off cap, was both feasible and relatively inexpensive. Defendant countered that the screw-on cap raised other design problems, since there would be a possible buildup of pressure within the vaporizer in addition to the increased cost of adding this feature. Plaintiff's experts countered with testimony that a small vent hole in the cap would serve to relieve the pressure buildup. While small dribbles of water might flow from the vent hole of a tipped vaporizer with a screw-on cap, there would be a significant lessening of the danger of extensive burns arising from such small amounts of water. In other words the risk of injury, while not completely eliminated, would be substantially reduced. In considering the acceptability of the manufacturer's design, the court also took into account the fact that there was no real way for the user, in this case the mother, to know with clarity that the water in the container was scalding hot, and she thus could not realistically assess the danger that could arise from a tipped vaporizer.

Note that the danger of the vaporizer was assessed in the context of its use environment. Unlike negligence, where the emphasis is on the conduct of the manufacturer, strict liability assesses the issue of unreasonable product danger from the vantage point of the environment of its use by a consumer. It is thus clear that the conclusion of whether a given design is, or is not, unreasonably dangerous is an expression, through the litigation process, of society's willingness to accept or reject that design. When the cost of an alternative to make the product safer outweighs the probable danger, then the product will be declared "reasonably safe" as is. When the risk of the product exceeds its inherent utility, the product will be declared "unreasonably dangerous."

3.6   THE BALANCING PROCESS—PERFORMANCE STANDARDS

This risk-utility theory finds its principal application in questions of design defect. As noted earlier in Section 3.3, in a production defect situation the plaintiff establishes that an identified production flaw precipitated the product failure and that this failure caused the injury. Risk-utility theory has no relevance in these situations, since the flawed product has not met the manufacturer's *own* production standards. In instances where the alleged production flaws have promoted product failure after substantial use, however, the question of defect must be framed relative to expected *performance* standards of the product rather than to the *production* standards used by the manufacturer. The focus in addressing *expected standards of performance* is the reasonable expectation of the consumer, which necessarily will reflect questions of societal significance. When risk-utility theory emerges in this manner in an alleged production defect case, in reality, a design defect question is being approached from a different point of view.

   To illustrate, a one-year-old tractor trailer truck that had traveled 90,000 miles collided with an automobile. Following a slight impact between the truck's right front end and the car's left rear end, the truck swerved off the right side of the road, struck an embankment and overturned. The plaintiff truck driver reported that the right front end of the truck "dropped down" prior to its impact, with the car. Examination of the truck following the accident revealed that the right front leaf spring was completely broken just behind the front shackle connection (Figure 3-2). "Gouge marks" were discovered across the surface of the main leaf spring in the vicinity of the fracture surface. Additionally, the microstructure of the steel on the fracture faces near the leaf surface appeared to be significantly different from the microstructure of the remaining material in the leaf. The plaintiff contended that these two conditions were manufacturing flaws. He alleged that the "gouge marks" resulted from using a worn mandrel in fabricating the front eye of the spring and that the aberrant microstructure near the surface resulted from improper quenching of the leaf spring during the heat treating operation. The plaintiff claimed that either or both of these flaws would contribute to *premature* spring failure that would cause the truck to go out of control. Thus he insisted that the spring was defective and unreasonably dangerous.

   To contrast the concept of *production defect* with *performance standards* we must ask the question, can the fracture of a truck spring after 90,000 miles of use in one year be classified as *premature* failure? Admittedly, there were flaws in the leaf spring, but all products are flawed at some level. The real question is whether or not these flaws have risen to the level of defect. To answer this question affirmatively, one must first conclude that failure at 90,000 miles is premature. If, on the other hand, 90,000 miles is considered

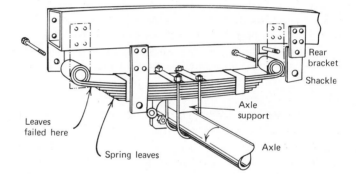

Figure 3-2. Right-front truck spring showing detail of mounting and point of failure.

a reasonable lifetime for the majority of leaf springs with or without the gouge marks or heat treating flaws, then one must ask whether such implied performance standards (i.e., a spring that lasts only 90,000 miles with no indication of when it should be examined or replaced) meet minimal levels of societal acceptability.*

*The jury in this case concluded that the spring broke prior to the truck's impact with the embankment, as a result of its flawed condition, and that they believed the leaf spring to have been defective.

3.7   USEFUL PRODUCT LIFE

There is another way of looking at the question of performance standards. To the extent that a product is being used beyond its capacities or beyond its reasonably expected life, the issue may be a function of inadequate communication between the manufacturer and the consumer. Thus, if a product fails "prematurely," it may be because the consumer has expectations that the product will last longer. It might then appear that unrealistic expectations of product performance are more a function of failure to warn or inadequate communication and less that of improper design [5]. This is certainly a reasonable way of looking at the problem. As we demonstrate in a later chapter, however, the interplay between warning and design is a rather intricate matter. Manufacturers often exaggerate their ability to communicate with consumers. Often, the only realistic way to deal with a performance problem is to design the problem out of the product. Thus, for example, if the leaf spring in the cited case was subject to "early" failure because of expected road loads, apart from any flaws, when compared with the longer life of other similarly loaded truck components, it might be found that warnings would be insufficient to convince consumers to replace the leaf spring. Thus we would come full circle by recognizing that we are facing a problem of faulty design again, inferred from a lack of reasonable performance of the part.

The problem of product performance need not necessarily result from inadequate communication. The product itself may be the purveyor of false impressions about its performance abilities. Consider, for example, an aluminum ladder that does not rust and that keeps its appearance well for many years; however, through constant use, rivets that fasten the rungs to the siderails may become loosened and fail, causing the user to fall and injure himself. In such a case the product itself gives no warning that it is about to fail. The very opposite is true. It deceptively communicates a good state of product health. Having chosen a metal that does not appear to age, the manufacturer may have to employ other design choices increasing product life that will match the metal's appearance. The standards of performance may have to meet real life expectations determined by product use. Alternatively, the manufacturer may attempt to limit product life by a sharply worded warning. Whether such an approach to performance standards is acceptable depends on the availability and cost of alternative designs, which would eliminate the hazards. In any event the manufacturer must be sensitive to what his product communicates to consumers. If the product overrepresents itself (implying an unrealistic performance standard), then the manufacturer may have to limit consumer expectations by warnings. Even that may sometimes be insufficient to eliminate the hazard. It is, however, at this point that the manufacturer may defend his product design as a reasonable compromise in light of the inherent limitations in both warning and design.

3.8   STATUTES OF LIMITATION—FIXED LIMITATIONS ON PRODUCT LIABILITY

Statutes of limitation are legislative enactments that limit the period within which a plaintiff is permitted to bring a lawsuit. Products liability has been a fertile field for statute of limitations problems because these statutes are directed to various causes of actions. The law provides certain time periods for contract actions and other time periods for tort actions. Furthermore, the statutes of limitation begin to run upon the occurrence of different events. The contract statute usually begins to run upon sale or tender of delivery of the product, whereas the tort statute usually runs from the date of injury. Since products liability actions have their origin in both contract (warranty) and tort law, there has been much confusion about which statute of limitations should govern.

The impact of different statutes of limitation on a products liability case was graphically demonstrated in *Victorson v. Bock Laundry Machine Co.* [6]. In *Victorson* the defective product was a laundry extractor. This machine is used in laundromats immediately following the washing but before drying. Using centrifugal force through drum rotation at high speed, the extractor draws out much of the moisture from the clothes and thus permits the wash to dry more quickly in the clothes dryer. Plaintiffs were injured in three separate incidents when the extractor top disengaged prematurely while the machine was still running. The three cases were consolidated for the appeal. In each instance the plaintiff believed that the machine had come to a stop and had placed his hand in the machine with devastating results. The statute of limitations problem arose from the fact that the injuries had taken place 21, 10, and 8 years respectively from the time of the sale of the machine.

The plaintiffs brought their action on three basic theories: (a) negligence, (b) strict tort liability, and (c) implied warranty of merchantability. If the plaintiff had been satisfied to proceed under the negligence theory, in which he would have been required to prove fault on the part of the manufacturer, he would have been subject to the regular tort statute of limitations. The tort statute of limitations in New York is three years, which begins to run from the date of injury. It would thus be irrelevant that the product was sold from 8 to 21 years before the accident happened.

The plaintiffs in this instance sought, however, to bring a strict liability action. In previous New York decisions the court held that strict liability was in truth the implied warranty of merchantability. The Uniform Commercial Code that prescribes the time limit for warranty actions under Section 2-725 sets forth four years from the time of sale as the statute of limitations. The court was thus faced with the decision of whether strict liability could be a tort action or must be based in implied warranty. In *Victorson* the court overruled its previous position and held that strict liability could be based in tort so that a plaintiff could have the advantage of either the three years from time of injury rule or four years from the time of sale, whichever is longer. Plaintiffs will thus normally plead their case in both tort and warranty to take advantage of the longer statute of limitation. Generally, the tort statute is the more advantageous, since it begins to run from the time of injury. But it is possible for the injury to occur shortly after purchase. If the plaintiff should fail to bring his action until three years from the time of injury, some time may remain of the four-year period from the time of sale.

Some courts have taken what the authors believe to be a more sensible view of the entire question [7]. Instead of permitting a choice between the warranty and tort statute of limitations, they have said that a products liability action that results in personal injury or property damages is essentially tortious in nature. As such, the contract statute of limitations should not apply at all.

It must be recognized that the present law on statute of limitations is of little solace to manufacturers. Their major concern is that 10 or 15 years after a product has been marketed they may be the subject of a products liability action. The traditional tort statute of limitations gives no assurance of final repose to the defendant until several years *after the injury*. This results in what the legal profession has come to call the "long tail," which means that the manufacturer must wait an inordinate number of years before he can have any confidence that he will not be sued. Even then the possibility of suit remains, since it is always conceivable that even a very old product can be proved to have been defective at the time of sale. Several states have sought to resolve this problem by passing "final repose" statutes that bar any action for products liability after a certain number of years have passed from the time of sale [8]. The trade-offs between relief to the manufacturing community and fairness to consumers raise sensitive issues and have not yet been articulated clearly. Final repose statutes tend to favor manufacturers of long-use items in which the possibility of injury after many years is still very real. They provide little solace to defendants whose products tend not to be usable after their short life has passed. These defendants may still have to face the prospect of lawsuits resulting from injuries caused after the normal life of the product has run but that are still within the final repose statute of limitations. To be sure, there may be legitimate substantive defenses to such actions, but the defendant will not have the luxury of the statute of limitations as an unquestioned bar to the action. This points out the problem with an across-the-board statute of limitations. It is an inexact and indiscriminate tool that may accomplish either too much or too little. Ultimately the answer to statutes of limitations questions lies *not* in the legal response but with the manufacturer's response to the question of product life. Product life must become an important element of both design and marketing. In that arena it addresses not the lawsuit but the question of reasonable product use. As such, it becomes a finely honed tool in the hands of a sensitive manufacturer who can calibrate his product to the needs and the patterns of product usage by the consuming public.

3.9 WARNINGS AND INSTRUCTIONS

Closely allied to the issue of unreasonable danger, and often determinative of it, are the warnings and instructions that accompany a product. A product may meet the most exacting production and design requirements and still be judged defective if the warnings and/or instructions are inadequate, because the danger level of the product can be substantially reduced by carefully worded warnings and instructions on product use and the possible conse- quences of misuse. Since warnings are relatively inexpensive and require no major redesigning of the product, the natural tendency of manufacturers is to *warn* against rather than *redesign* against a foreseeable danger. On the other hand, manufacturers may be reluctant to warn about all the foreseeable dangers for fear that such warnings will negatively affect the product's mar- ketability.

It is difficult to generalize about the efficacy of warnings in reducing the manufacturer's exposure to liability. Depending on the nature of the prod- uct, the kind of harm involved, and the kind of consumer, a warning may or may not be sufficient to insulate the manufacturer from liability. By and large, effectively worded and prominently displayed warnings have been recognized by courts as an effective method of reducing the liability expo- sure of manufacturers. Manufacturers should not, however, view warnings as a substitute for intelligent design decisions. Manufacturers, in deciding whether to design out a hazard or warn against it, should undertake the same risk-utility balancing described for judging the adequacy of a given design. For example, in the vaporizer case discussed earlier, it may well be that a court would consider a sharply worded warning dealing with the scalding hot water in the container an effective deterrent to reduce the risk of inadver- tent tipping. On the other hand, the greater likelihood is that a court would find that the inexpensive alternative design of the screw-on cap that substan- tially reduced the possibility of serious injury was a far superior method of reducing the risk of injury. Given the frequent use of vaporizers near chil- dren, the proclivity of parents to be forgetful about where they place va- porizers, and the recognition that the most likely victims of these accidents, children, cannot appreciate the danger even if warned against it, it is understandable that a court would opt for the design change rather than the warning [9]. Thus a warning does not necessarily protect the manufacturer from liability.

It is crucial to distinguish between warnings and instructions. Instructions tell the consumer how to use the product effectively. Warnings inform the consumer of the dangers of improper use and tell how to guard against those dangers, if possible. Whether a given statement is a warning or an instruction is often hard to tell. One often shades imperceptibly into the other. The court in *Muncy v. Magnolia Chemical Company* [10] set forth its requisites for adequate warnings:

(1) it must be in such *form* that it could reasonably be expected to catch the attention of the reasonably prudent man in the circumstances of its use; the (2) *content* of the warning must be of such a nature as to be comprehensible to the average user and to convey a fair indication of the nature and extent of the danger to the mind of a reasonably prudent person . . . the question of whether or not a given warning is legally sufficient depends upon the language used and the impression that such language is calculated to make upon the mind of the average user of the product.

Implicit in the duty to warn is the duty to warn with a degree of *intensity* that would cause a reasonable man to exercise . . . the caution commensurate with the potential danger. . . . A clear cautionary statement setting forth the exact nature of dangers involved would be necessary to fully protect the seller. . . .[Emphasis added.]

While the court has accurately described the attention-getting process for an effective warning, another element is necessary when the warning function is to reduce the danger to the consumer. In these instances the third element of an adequate warning is to tell the consumer *how* to act to avoid the danger. *Tucson Industries v. Schwartz* [11] demonstrates that this problem must be addressed specifically.

The plaintiff suffered severe eye injuries when fumes from an adhesive, a generally recognized toxin, were circulated to the plaintiff's vicinity by an air conditioning system. The label on the adhesive container bore, among other warnings, the following statements:

DANGER, Extremely flammable, read the instructions, be sure to provide adequate ventilation and safety first.

The air conditioning system for the building was turned on in an attempt to remove the fumes from the room in which the adhesive was being used. The air conditioning system was merely cooling and recirculating air, without bringing in any fresh air. As a result the essentially undiluted fumes were continually recirculated throughout the building.

The question is whether it was possible to formulate a warning adequate to reduce the danger to an acceptable level within the environment of the adhesive's use. The phrase at issue is, "be sure to provide adequate ventilation." Because this kind of adhesive is widely distributed, the spectrum of users will range from the relatively untutored to those with highly specialized knowledge of ventilating system designs. The warnings must communicate the nature of the risk to be guarded against and, equally important, they must provide adequate instructions about how to minimize or eliminate the risk.

In this situation the first requirement was probably adequately met by the following message:

VAPORS HARMFUL. TOXIC. Keep out of reach of children. Avoid prolonged or repeated breathing or contact with skin.

But the instruction, "Provide adequate ventilation," falls short of communicating information essential to the consumer's understanding of the term "adequate ventilation." The warning, which was useless in protecting the bystander-plaintiff, contained language that would be inadequate even for the ordinary user's protection, simply because the phrase "adequate ventilation" is imprecise and ambiguous.

An adequate warning, in this case the *only* feasible alternative to withdrawing the product from the market, must describe what action the user must take either to obviate the hazard or reduce it to an acceptable level. An adequate warning might read as follows:

Fumes are dangerous. They *must* be exhausted directly to the *outside air.* Use as near as possible to open window or outside door. Fans or blowers can be used *only* if they exhaust to *outside air.* Exposure to fumes can cause blindness or other serious injury.

The techniques for effectively communicating to the user the appropriate actions for minimizing the risk of injury are not well understood. No guidelines exist for the design of adequate warnings, but they should be formulated with great care by someone who thoroughly understands the risks and how to reduce or eliminate them.

CHAPTER 4

Reasonable Safety or Unreasonable Danger— In Search of a Standard

4.1 THE DEFECT PROBLEM—A TERM IN SEARCH OF DEFINITION

The concept of "defect" in product liability law has been the cause of enormous confusion. Everyone agrees that for a product to be a likely subject for a products suit it must have a defect, but there is considerable disagreement about just what attributes of a product will, when added together, constitute a defect. Earlier a defect was defined as that state, quality, or condition of a product that makes it substandard. It was acknowledged that giving content to the definition would be difficult. Part of the reason for the elusiveness of the "defect" concept is the failure to clearly differentiate between: (a) "production" or "manufacturing" defect and "design" defect cases and (b) representational theories and "unreasonable risk" theories, as the basis for product liability law. The confusion resulting from the failure to indicate which theory is being advocated in a given case added to some holdover semantic problems from earlier products liability law has precluded the formulation of a workable definition of defect.

The "reasonableness" of the product has generally served as the operative test for the determination of "defect." This approach, which requires the balancing and trade-offs of risks versus benefits or utility, lies at the heart of the defect concept. But courts have also used other processes to determine "defect." A survey of products liability decisions will illustrate how the courts have explained the process by which they determined that a defect does or does not exist in a product.

4.2 THE DEFECT TEST

Several courts have maintained that no intrinsic difference exists between a strict liability case based on defective design and one based on defective manufacture. If defect is an acceptable term for one, it is acceptable for the other. The judicial statement of this view is clearly expressed in *Cronin v. J. B. E. Olson Corporation* [1].

We can see no difficulty in applying the Greenman [strict liability] formulation to the full range of products liability situations, including those involving "design defects." A defect may emerge from the mind of a designer as well as from the hand of the workman.

The most obvious problem we perceive in creating any such distinction is that thereafter it would be advantageous to characterize a defect in one rather than the other category. It is difficult to prove that a product ultimately caused injury because a widget was poorly welded—a defect in manufacture—rather than because it was made of inexpensive metal difficult to weld, chosen by a designer concerned with economy—a defect in design. The proof problem would, of course, be magnified when the article in question was either old or unique, with no easily available basis for comparison. We wish to avoid providing such a battleground for clever counsel. Furthermore, we find no reason why a different standard, and one harder to meet, should apply to defects which plague entire product lines. *We recognize that it is more damaging to a manufacturer to have an entire line condemned, so to speak, for a defect in design, than a single product for a defect in manufacture.* But the potential economic loss to a manufacturer should not be reflected in a different standard of proof for an injured consumer.* [Emphasis added.]

The court also concluded that a product is not required to be "unreasonably dangerous" to be "defective." In a footnote the court acknowledged that "defect" lacked a clear meaning in design defect cases but expressed faith that there has emerged an acceptable definition of the defect concept, despite the omission of the phrase "unreasonably dangerous."

---

*The court here explicitly notes that if a product is defectively designed, the economic consequences to a particular defendant will not save him from liability. Economic realities are, however, an integral part of the jury's decision-making in determining whether or not the product is unreasonably dangerous. For example, the cost of alternative designs must be addressed during trial and be part of the risk-utility balancing. However, once the determination has been made that a design is defective, it will be of no consequence to a defendant to argue that such a determination will spell financial ruin for him.

In a recent case the California Supreme Court decided to give substance to the defect concept. In *Barker v. Lull Engineering Company, Inc.* the court held that a product would be found defective in design (a) if the product failed to perform as safely as an ordinary consumer would expect when used in an intended or reasonably foreseeable manner *or* (b) if the benefits of the challenged design are outweighed by the risk of danger inherent in such a design. The court held that a consumer expectation test provides a base minimum below which no product can fall. There are products which meet consumer expectations but which are nevertheless "unreasonably dangerous." The test for unreasonable danger will require the balancing of risk versus utility to determine whether an acceptable level of safety has been met. The California court also held that once plaintiff alleged a design defect and was able to prove that the alleged defect caused his or her injury, the burden then shifted to the defendant manufacturer to prove that his product was *not* unreasonably dangerous. It is certain that this new California case shifting the burden onto the defendant will be critically received by the business community. It does indeed appear to place an unusually heavy burden on those responsible for product design.

4.3 THE CONSUMER EXPECTATION TEST

A more meaningful standard is found in the Restatement (Second) of Torts, which predicates liability upon a finding that a product is "in a defective condition unreasonably dangerous to the user or consumer." The comments to the Restatement seem to emphasize that the consumer expectation test is the essence of strict tort liability. A product is considered defective when "it is . . . in a condition not contemplated by the ultimate consumer, which will be unreasonably dangerous to him." And a product is to be found unreasonably dangerous when it is "dangerous to an extent beyond that which would be contemplated by the ordinary consumer who purchases the product, with the ordinary knowledge common to the community as to its characteristics."

The virtue of the consumer expectation test is that it focuses on the product as a functioning entity in the hands of the consumer and eliminates negligence considerations (which focus on the conduct of the defendant) from a design defect case.

The Restatement standard is, however, a mixed blessing. Although it forces an examination of the actual environment of product use, it suffers from the fact that this examination is undertaken from the viewpoint of the ordinary consumer. The test suggests that if the ordinary consumer "contemplates" the danger, then the product is not unreasonably dangerous. The difficulty with this test is that it suggests that a manufacturer has fulfilled all his duties to the consumer if the product's dangers are open and obvious. In many instances manufacturers have been absolved from liability when an obvious danger caused serious injury, even though that injury could have been averted by a design modification that would not have added significantly to the cost of the product or impaired its usefulness.

Professors Harper and James [2] recognized this problem long before strict liability emerged. They stated:

[T]he bottom does not logically drop out of a negligence [products liability] case against the maker when it is shown that the purchaser knew of the dangerous condition. Thus if the product is a carrot-topping machine with exposed moving parts, or an electric clothes wringer dangerous to the limbs of the operator, and if it would be feasible for the maker of the product to install a guard or safety release, it should be a question for the jury whether reasonable care demanded such a precaution, though its absence is obvious. Surely reasonable men might find here a great danger, even to one who knew the condition; and since it was so readily avoidable they might find the maker negligent.

In *Vincer v. Esther Williams All-Aluminum Swimming Pool Company* [3], the Wisconsin court illustrated that plaintiffs have good reason to fear a test that establishes liability solely on the basis of consumer expectations. In that case the plaintiff, a two-year-old child, suffered injury when he fell into a swimming pool in the backyard of his grandfather's home. The complaint alleged that a retractable ladder to the above-ground pool had been left in the down position, that the pool was unsupervised, and that the plaintiff climbed the ladder, fell into the water, and remained there for an extended period of time, resulting in severe brain damage. The plaintiff contended that the swimming pool was defectively designed because the defendant had failed to take the *reasonable and low-cost* precaution of building the swimming pool so that the fencing extended across the deck at the top of the ladder opening, with a self-closing, self-latching gate on the deck of the swimming pool. This suggested design alternative would have prevented access to the swimming pool area by children of the plaintiff's tender age, even when the ladder from the deck to the ground was in the down position.

The Wisconsin court dismissed the plaintiff's complaint, holding that, as a matter of law, the swimming pool was not defectively designed. Its reason for so holding was that the Restatement's consumer expectation test demanded such a result. The court said:

[T]he test in Wisconsin of whether a product contains an unreasonably dangerous defect depends upon the reasonable expectations of the ordinary consumer concerning the characteristics of this type of product. If the average consumer would reasonably anticipate the dangerous condition of the product and fully appreciate the attendant risk of injury, it would not be unreasonably dangerous and defective. This is an objective test and is not dependent upon the knowledge of the particular injured consumer.

Based upon the principles discussed above, we conclude that the swimming pool described in plaintiff's complaint does not contain an unreasonably dangerous defect.

By using the consumer expectation test, the Wisconsin court short-circuited the analytical process. The court removed from both the court's and jury's consideration an examination of the safety of the design of the swimming pool. If it could have been demonstrated that for a very slight additional cost it would be possible to virtually eliminate the danger of accidental drownings, such a design modification should be given serious consideration through the medium of a design defect case.

4.4   THE UNREASONABLE-DANGER TEST

Much of the discussion in Chapter 3 alluded to the unreasonable-danger test for defect. The suggestion in Section 4.3 that the safety of the swimming pool might have been enhanced by a design change at very little cost may be valid, but how can it be judged that the absence of such a feature is unreasonable, making the manufacturer liable?

The criteria against which the defective and unreasonably dangerous nature of any product is tested are broad. A leading scholar in the area of products liability, Dean Wade, has provided a list of seven explicit indicia for this purpose [4]:

(1) The usefulness and desirability of the product.
(2) The availability of other and safer products to meet the same needs.
(3) The likelihood of injury and its probable seriousness.
(4) The obviousness of the danger.
(5) Common knowledge and normal public expectation of the danger (particularly for established products).
(6) The avoidability of injury by care in use of the product (including the effect of instructions or warnings).
(7) The ability to eliminate the danger without seriously impairing the usefulness of the product or making it unduly expensive.

While certain of these indicia may be quantifiable and others require subjective evaluation, the final decision on whether a product is defective and unreasonably dangerous is an amalgam of all seven indicia. The determination of defect and unreasonable danger is, in one sense, subjective, because each product must be viewed in the particular context of its function and use. The use of the same product in two different environments, domestic and industrial, for example, may lead to different conclusions regarding defectiveness and unreasonable danger. Thus it is critical that the product be understood thoroughly within its use environment before the appropriate focus is established for application of the Wade indicia.

Let us attempt such an analysis within the context of a litigated case.

The product that was the subject of litigation was a printer-slotter machine (see Figure 4-1). The basic functions of the machine are to print advertising and labeling material on corrugated cardboard and to cut and score the cardboard for later assembly as cartons. Printing dies are stapled on large rotating wooden rolls. The ink is transferred from the upper portion of the machine to these rolls by a series of smaller rolls. Because this machine is equipped to print in two colors, there are two sets of ink-transfer and die-mounting rolls. The machine was designed to open to a width of 30 inches to give workers access to the dies so that they can be changed. Thus, when the machine opens, there is a clear passageway in the center of the machine.

The back (feed) end of the machine is equipped to feed the cardboard into the first set of rolls for printing. The cardboard then passes through the second set of printing rollers located on the front or exit end of the machine. When the cardboard emerges from the second set of rollers, it passes into the slotter section of the machine, which is integrally attached to the front set of

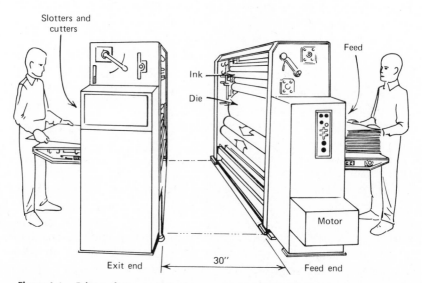

Figure 4-1. **Printer-slotter machine in open position revealing 30-inch passageway.**

printing rolls. Adjustable knives are located in this section to score and cut the cardboard.

The principal driving motor is located at the back end of the machine and transfers power to both sets of printing rolls and the knives and scores, using gears. When the machine is opened, only the front end rolls, knives, and scores are mechanically disconnected from the driving motor and are inoperative, even though the primary motor may be energized. Even though the machine is open, the back or feed end of the machine can still function from the primary motor. The passageway created by the opening of the machine is thus bordered by the inoperative front rolls on one side and by the rotating back rolls on the other, if the primary motor is on. An automatic washing attachment was subsequently added to this machine. In order for washing to take place, the rolls to be washed must be rotated by the primary motor. If both rear feed and front exit ends are to be washed, the machine must be run in the closed position. The back (feed) end can be washed alone when the machine is separated, since the back feed-end rolls can still be driven by the primary motor.

The injury to the plaintiff occurred when he entered the open passageway of the printer-slotter. Since the machine separation only prevented power transfer to the front end, there was still power available to the rolls on the back (feed) end, and they were rotating, presumably washing the rear set of rolls, at the time of injury to the plaintiff.

Plaintiff walked through the open passageway of the machine to get to an auxiliary piece of equipment, a staple gun, which was located at the far end of the passageway. His motive for doing so was not altogether clear, but he apparently hoped to save time by getting the staple gun so that he could begin the next step in the operation and thus reduce the amount of nonworking time (or downtime) of the machine and thereby increase his earnings. Plaintiff was carrying a rag at the time, and somehow the rag was drawn into the moving back rollers. His hand followed the rag and his arm followed his hand into the machine. The end result was that the plaintiff's arm was amputated.

The design defect claimed by the plaintiff was that the machine was not equipped with a breakaway switch shutting down the primary motor and automatically cutting off power to both front and rear rolls when the machine was opened up. With such a switch the power to the back rolls would have been shut off and those rolls would not have rotated when the passageway was open. The plaintiff's expert testified to the feasibility of a breakaway switch—a switch similar to a refrigerator door switch that makes the interior light go on and off. Plaintiff's counsel focused on three factors—the breakaway switch, the open passageway, and the amputated arm. The trilogy was hammered home effectively and appeared to be the crux of the case as it was presented in court.

In applying the unreasonable-danger balancing test, it is important to recognize that the printer-slotter was designed and operated with several complex trade-offs in mind. Among these trade-offs must have been an assessment of the cost of having a machine setup where the operator in the passageway could change front roll dies while the back rolls were rotating in a wash cycle versus the increased cost of having a setup where the back rolls could not operate if the operator was changing front roll dies. If a simultaneous setting of dies and washing of back rolls was inadvisable from a safety standpoint, machine downtime would probably increase substantially. This consideration was directly related to the actual operation of the machine, for this machine's downtime affected the efficiency of the entire production process.

A comprehensive list of the competing factors that might come into play in the design of a printer-slotter would include the following:

1. The necessity for the machine to open for the purpose of changing dies on one or both sets of rollers (front and feed ends).

2. The necessity of having the feed end of the machine operative when machine sections are separated.

3. The effect of subsequent design modification as a result of the installation of automatic washers for the cleaning of rolls.

4. The functional advantage of simultaneously setting scorers and knives on the inactive front end while permitting operation of the automatic washers and rollers on the feed end.

5. An understanding of the time sequence in setting up, cleaning, and operating the machine within the pay incentive scheme of the plant.

6. The operational feasibility, cost, and effectiveness of various kinds of breakaway switches.

7. The necessity of cleaning both sets of rolls subsequent to single color printing.

8. A precise description of the location and direction of rotation of all rotating rolls.

9. The location of all controls and auxiliary power sources with a clear understanding of their functional purposes.

10. The perception of the open machine as an access route to auxiliary equipment.

11. The necessity of two auxiliary power sources, one for die changing and color registration and the other for opening the machine.

When one considers these competing trade-offs within the context of the Wade indicia, it becomes clear that the test of unreasonable danger is complex and intimately dependent on the factual situation. Perhaps the machine was unreasonably dangerous or perhaps the trade-offs were sound for the device as designed, but the issue cannot be determined without a comprehensive understanding of the product and its overall environment of use [5].

To be sure, the battles will be fought by experts, each attempting to demonstrate the validity of his own judgment and the deficiencies of that of his opponent. For the jury to be able to understand the issues involved in deciding on product defectiveness, each side must clearly address the indicia of unreasonable danger and reveal the reasoning process that leads to the conclusion of whether or not the product contains an unreasonably dangerous defect.

Thus the unreasonable-danger test is really asking a question of societal acceptability: is the product, as marketed, a reasonable balance of risk and utility, or should it be sold in an altered, less dangerous form?

4.5   RECONCILING THE DEFECT TESTS

Any attempt at total reconciliation of the varying tests just set forth may appear to be sophistry. Perhaps the courts are all saying the same thing. If so, why have they chosen such differing ways to say it? A total exploration of this problem is beyond the scope of this work. Nevertheless, it would seem that "reasonableness" is the operating rule for the defect concept.

The California "defect" test [6] does not hold up when one asks, "How does one test for defect?" The "consumer expectation" test must ultimately ask not only what the consumer expected but also what he had a *right to expect*. To answer that question, one must turn to the question of societal acceptability and thus return to "reasonableness" as the operative concept. To be sure, in some cases where the consumer's expectations are clearly disappointed, there will be no need to test the societal acceptability of the product. Liability will follow almost automatically. But in cases of any complexity where the issue is close—the test will be that of unreasonable danger determined by a sensitive balancing process. All the tests seem ultimately to lead back to the process of balancing risk and utility.

4.6   DESIGNING FOR FORESEEABLE MISUSE

The problem of product misuse can become a factor in a product liability action at several junctures. First, it may be argued that the injury was totally a function of the consumer's misuse of the product and that the product is reasonably safe. Thus, for example, if a geologist's hammer, intended for chipping away at small rocks, is used to pound a spike into a concrete wall, shatters, and the chips penetrate the plaintiff's eye, it may be that the hammer is not defective at all. It may be a perfectly good geologist's hammer that has been subjected to a use so inappropriate that it failed. Second, it may be argued that, even if the product is *defective*, the plaintiff's use of the product was so beyond the norm that liability should not attach.

Ritter v. The Narragansett Electric Company [7] illustrates this type of case. The defendant, American Motors, manufactured a small 30-inch gas range. The plaintiff, a four-year-old girl, was injured when she opened the oven door and used it as a step stool to look into a pot on top of the stove. The stove tipped forward, seriously injuring the plaintiff. The plaintiff's expert testimony concluded that the stove was in fact defectively designed, since the stove door could not hold a weight of 30 pounds without tipping.

Under the circumstances of this case the issue is *not* whether the stove was designed improperly. If the stove had tipped because a housewife used the open door as a shelf for a heavy roasting pan, the issue would properly be the design of the unit, since it could be argued that one of the intended uses of the door was as a shelf for checking food during preparation. Here, however, the issue was whether the use of the open door as a step stool was so unforeseeable that it is not correct to assign liability to the manufacturer for the harm caused to the child. The court held that it was proper for liability to attach to the manufacturer in a case such as this.

This thought was echoed by the Texas Court of Civil Appeals in *Magic Chef v. Sibley* [8] in an analogous case where a five-year-old child was burned as she stood on a chair and leaned over the top of the stove, inadvertently turning on one of the burners. They said:

> It has been held by our Supreme Court that foreseeability is significant in product liability cases when the product is what it is intended and known to be, but injury is suffered because the product is misused. . . .[Citations omitted.] A product is not "misused" merely because the manufacturer intended that it be used in a different manner; the manufacturer must show that the use which caused the injury was not *reasonably foreseeable*. [Emphasis added.]

The question of misuse obviously centers around the plaintiff's behavior in the use of the product and on whether this behavior is so aberrant as to bar his recovery.

Note that the clear trend of cases is that the defendant will have to design for foreseeable misuse of the product. This is highlighted by a decision of the Pennsylvania Supreme Court in *Berkebile v. Brantly Helicopter Corporation* [9], described in a different context in Section 1.3.1. In that case the plaintiff took off in a helicopter with a nearly empty gasoline tank. Shortly after takeoff the helicopter crashed while still in climbing flight. The charge of defect was that the helicopter system of autorotation required that the pilot be able to throw the helicopter into autorotation within one second. It was the plaintiff's contention that this was too short a time period and that this was the cause of the crash. The defendant responded with the contention that the plaintiff had put the product to an "abnormal use" (taking the helicopter up with an almost empty gasoline tank). The court responded that:

The autorotation system is a safety device existing for the sole purpose of preventing a crash in the event of engine failure *for any reason*. The reason the engine failed is irrelevant. Even defendant's argument that decedent was flying without gas, would be no "abnormal use." The autorotation system only comes into use in the event of engine failure for whatever the reason may be.

It is thus clear that the manufacturer may have to allow for and design against various kinds of plaintiff behavior. In the *Berkebile* case the design that would have prevented the accident (a longer period of time to activate autorotation) may have been necessary to protect the pilot even in accidents *not* attributable to abnormal use. The manufacturer's responsibility may, however, go farther, and he may be required to design against dangers that can occur only when the product is being used abnormally. As long as the abnormal use is within the range of foreseeability, liability may properly attach.

Further elucidation of this principle will be found in Section 5.1 in the discussion of the safety guarding of industrial machinery. These cases all arise from similar fact patterns. A machine is manufactured without a given safety device. As a result of working at the machine plaintiff either inadvertently or intentionally engages the dangerous aspect of the machine (e.g., the point of operation) and loses an arm or leg. It is uniformly argued by the defendant that the machine was put to an abnormal use. The argument usually fails. The use, though not intended by the manufacturer, is hardly abnormal and generally results from predictable, hence reasonably foreseeable, human behavior.

4.7 THE SUBSTANTIAL-CHANGE QUESTION

Few topics engender more vehement reaction by manufacturers and designers than that of their liability when their product has been subjected to substantial change after it has left their hands. There is much misunderstanding about this problem.

The Restatement (Second) of Torts, Section 402A, comment g, sets the basic ground rules for handling the problem.

The rule (of strict liability) . . . applies only where the product is, at the time it leaves the seller's hands, in a condition not contemplated by the ultimate consumer, which will be unreasonably dangerous to him. The seller is not liable when he delivers the product in a safe condition, and subsequent mishandling or other causes make it harmful by the time it is consumed. The burden of proof that the product was in a defective condition at the time it left the hands of the particular seller is upon the injured plaintiff; and unless evidence can be produced which will support the conclusion that it was then defective, the burden is not sustained.

It is axiomatic that the question of substantial change can be addressed only by focusing on the causal elements of the injury. That is, if the alterations in the product bear no relationship to the defect claimed to have caused the injury, they are not substantial changes in the sense that they were significant in causing the injury.

For example, the facts that a conveyor was moved from its original above-ground location to below ground and that its angle of inclination was altered cannot be viewed as substantial change when the alleged defect is the absence of a scraper bar that necessitated a workman's reaching into an in-running nip point to clean the rotating drum.

A substantial change in a product, then, is one that created a risk that did not exist before the change was made. What, however, of the product that was defective when it left the hands of the manufacturer and was then subjected to a substantial change that *increased* an already present risk? This problem was addressed in *Finnegan v. Havir Manufacturing Company* [10].

A punch press when sold by Havir was equipped only with a mechanical foot treadle for press operation and did not contain any guard at the point of operation, the closure point of the press. Sometime later, the machine owner replaced the mechanical foot treadle with an electrical foot switch on a long cord.

The defendant claimed that this change "reduced the 'safety aspect' of the machine in that it increased the chances of accidentally kicking the switch and activating the press" and thus was the cause of the accident.

The court, in addressing the issue of substantial change, concluded:

Although the defendant's expert testified that the substituted pedal increased the likelihood of accidentally activating the press and that that change was the cause of the accident, he conceded that had the machine been equipped with an effective point of operation safety device the accident would not have occurred. The jury could infer that because of a lack of a safety device the accident would have occurred notwithstanding the change to an electrical foot pedal. Thus, it could conclude that the substitution had little or nothing to do with the happening of the accident.

4.8 THE SCIENTIFICALLY UNKNOWABLE HAZARD

Strict liability focuses on the product in the actual environment of its use, and the plaintiff is not required to prove that the defendant's conduct was negligent to establish a cause of action. A serious question has, however, arisen about whether it is proper to hold a manufacturer liable when, at the time he manufactured his product, there was no technological knowledge available that would have permitted him to discover the hazard and take action to minimize its effects. This problem can arise in both production and design defect cases. The problem is difficult to resolve. If manufacturers are to be held responsible for hazards that are not within the realm of technical knowledge or for production design defects that are beyond the current capability of technology to eliminate, they can legitimately claim that they are being faced, not with *strict* liability, but with a form of *absolute* liability. The countervailing argument is that if at the time of trial the product is declared "unreasonably dangerous" it is because the defect has been identified, and after balancing the risk-utility factors, the court has concluded that the defect is unreasonably dangerous. Placing the burden on the plaintiff to prove what information or capabilities could have been developed by the defendant if he had possessed adequate technology or if he had been involved in appropriate research is to force the plaintiff to prove one of the most difficult factual questions imaginable [11]. The courts adopting this view have implied that it is sufficient if, at the time of the trial, the product is "unreasonably dangerous." There is as yet no clear resolution to this question. The few cases that have appeared on this matter have split sharply [12].

The Interagency Task Force Report on Product Liability, published under the direction of the United States Department of Commerce, reaches the conclusion that, with isolated exceptions, courts have been unwilling to hold manufacturers liable when they establish that the hazard causing the injury was scientifically unknowable at the time of manufacture. Sometimes courts express this by saying that a manufacturer is required only to meet the "state of the art." In Section 4.10 we examine another use of the term *state of the art*. In this second meaning courts uniformly hold that a manufacturer cannot base an absolute defense on its conformance with industry standards. As the Interagency Task Force Report properly notes, this is a far different issue, since the question is not technological feasibility, but rather whether an industry can dictate its own standards to the consuming public.

4.9   THE OPEN-DANGER PROBLEM

It was indicated earlier that courts often established broad no-duty rules that immunized manufacturers from liability in certain instances. One such rule that had a dominant influence in the formative stages of products liability law was the patent-danger rule. The rule that a manufacturer was not responsible for dangers in a product that were open and obvious had its origin in the landmark case of *Campo v. Scofield* [13]. In that case the plaintiff was feeding onions into an "onion topping" machine when his hands became caught in its revolving steel rollers and were badly injured. The plaintiff alleged that the onion topping machine was negligently designed because it lacked safety guards to prevent the user's hands from being caught in the machine. The court held that no liability would attach:

The cases establish that the manufacturer of a machine or any other article, dangerous because of the way in which it functions, and patently so, owes to those who use it a duty merely to make it free from latent defects and concealed dangers. Accordingly, if a remote user sues a manufacturer of an article for injuries suffered, he must allege and prove the existence of a latent defect or a danger not known to the plaintiff or other users.

After a long and disappointing relationship with the patent-danger rule, the New York Court of Appeals rejected the doctrine in *Micallef v. Miehle Company* [14]. The plaintiff was employed as an operator on a huge photo-offset printing press. One day while working on the press the plaintiff discovered a foreign object on the plate of the unit. Such a substance, known in the printing trade as a "hickie," causes a blemish or imperfection on the printed page. To correct this situation the plaintiff informed his superior that he intended to "chase the hickie." The process of "chasing hickies" consists of very lightly applying a piece of plastic about eight inches wide to the printing plate, which is wrapped around a circular plate cylinder that spins at high speed. The revolving action of the plate against the plastic removes the "hickie." While the plaintiff was engaged in this maneuver the plastic was drawn into the nip point and plaintiff's hand was caught between the plate cylinder and an ink roller. The photo-offset machine had no safety guards to prevent such an occurrence, and the plaintiff was unable to stop the machine quickly because the shut-off button was distant from his position at the machine.

The plaintiff, Micallef, was fully aware of the danger of getting his hand caught in the press while "chasing hickies." It was, however, the custom of the industry to "chase hickies on the run," because once the machine was stopped, it required at least three hours to resume printing. An expert witness testified that good engineering practice would dictate that a safety guard be placed near the rollers, since the danger of human contact at the point of operation was well known. The court realized that, even though this design modification was both reasonable and feasible, the *Campo* patent-danger rule demanded that recovery be denied. In rejecting its long-held position that the obviousness of the danger is to be the only criterion for judging the safety of a product, the court stated that it would henceforth judge a product for reasonableness, based on the totality of the product. The obviousness of the danger would be only *one factor* to evaluate in the overall judgment of whether or not the product is reasonable. Clearly this seems to be the preferable rule. Nonetheless, a number of courts still adhere to the patent-danger rule as the sole test for safe design.

4.10   THE ROLE OF VOLUNTARY AND GOVERNMENTAL STANDARDS

A major question that will require resolution in the developing law of products liability is what credence will be given to governmental or voluntary safety standards in establishing the appropriate risk-utility level for judging whether or not a product is unreasonably dangerous. Traditionally the courts have taken the position that all standards, even governmental standards, provide, at best, lower limits for product acceptability. This means that if a product falls below the statutory or regulatory standard of safety it will be deemed unreasonably dangerous (negligence *per se* or unreasonably dangerous *per se*). This is because it would be inappropriate for the judiciary to set a standard of product safety below that established by the legislature or an authorized standard-setting body. Although voluntary or consensus standards are less binding as a matter of law, and a court need not feel bound by such a standard, in practice, if a manufacturer falls below a consensus industry standard, the product will generally be deemed unreasonably dangerous.

A more difficult problem is that raised by manufacturers who seek the protection of the law when they have complied with either governmental or industry-wide standards.

Berkebile v. Brantly Helicopter Corporation [15], mentioned earlier in Sections 1.3.1 and 4.6, indicates the reluctance that courts have in withdrawing a case from jury consideration merely because the defendant has complied with a governmental standard. In that case a pilot was killed when he was unable to throw his helicopter into autorotation within the allotted design time of one second. The plaintiff contended that one second was inadequate. The defendant argued that it had met with FAA regulations, which had approved one second as an adequate reaction time. On appeal, the court commented on the approach taken by the trial court in approving the FAA standard.

In telling the jury that one second was adequate time to go into autorotation, and thus removing the question of whether such fact presented a dangerous condition, the court relied on the following FAA regulation: "In taking corrective action, the time delay for all flight conditions shall be based on the normal pilot reaction time, except that for the cruise condition the time delay shall not be less than one second." 14 C.F.R. § 6.121, as in effect 1959–1962. The court en banc concluded that the regulation should be the standard in judging whether the helicopter was defective and unreasonably dangerous. The court further concluded that the manufacturer should be able to rely on the federal regulatory standard and that if the jury could fix other standards the regulation would become meaningless.

The Federal Aviation Agency's standards are far from meaningless. Considering the pre-eminence of the federal government in the field of air safety and the importance and standing of the FAA we would incline to the view that failure of the manufacturer to comply with the regulations would be negligence *per se*. Our view is strengthened by the fact that the FAA is empowered to lay down minimum standards and violation of such standards, if the proximate cause of the injury, should submit the violator to liability.

In this case, however, we are not faced with a violation of the regulations, we are faced with compliance. Compliance with a law or administrative regulation relieves the actor of negligence *per se*, but it does not establish as a matter of law that due care was exercised. . . . "The care to be exercised in a particular case must always be proportionate to the seriousness of the consequences which are reasonably to be anticipated as a result of the conduct in question." *Maize*, supra at 56–57, 41 A.2d at 853. Compliance with the statute or regulation is admissible as evidence of the actor's exercise of due care, but such compliance "does not prevent a finding of negligence where a reasonable man would take additional precautions." Restatement (Second) of Torts § 288C (1965).

Courts do feel free, in appropriate instances, to send cases to the jury to determine whether or not governmental standards are adequate. This power lies within the discretion of the courts. It is they who determine whether governmental or voluntary standards provide an appropriate ceiling for the societally acceptable product. If past history is a guide, much will depend on the reputation of the agency setting governmental standards. Traditionally, those agencies that have maintained a high standard of professionalism in setting performance standards for products have been treated with deference by the courts. Note that the Consumer Products Safety Act specifically provides that standards set by the agency do not preclude the bringing of a private, common law action against a manufacturer whose product has met an agency's standards. Thus it may well be that much future litigation will revolve around the efficacy of promulgated governmental standards. In this way private litigation may act as a check on whether or not the risk-utility levels as implied in the governmental standards are appropriate or adequate.

It is apparent, however, that a federal agency such as the Consumer Products Safety Commission will be unable, through its own resources, to develop safety standards for the bulk of products requiring such standards. It is inevitable that such agencies will turn to private standards-setting constituencies such as the American Society for Testing and Materials (ASTM) and the American National Standards Institute (ANSI) for assistance in either writing or providing standards. Recognizing this need, groups such as ASTM, are reexamining their standards development process to be certain that it conforms to the legal guidelines. The weight which courts accord to voluntary standards will depend, as in the case of governmental standards, on the reputation and thoroughness of the standard-setting process.

CHAPTER 5

Warnings
and Disclaimers

5.1 THE DESIGN WARNING INTERPLAY

In an earlier chapter the role of warnings in products liability litigation was discussed. Having established the basic framework for the products action, it is appropriate to examine the interplay between the design defect case and the failure-to-warn case. A common pitfall is to view these two elements of a products case as disparate and unconnected. In reality a sensitive interplay exists between these two aspects of a product—the soft or communicating part and the hard or design aspect [1].

A recent Oregon case, *Phillips v. Kimwood Machine Company* [2], illustrates the problems that can arise when courts are not sensitive to this interrelationship. The plaintiff in this case was injured while feeding fiberboard sheets into a six-headed sanding machine. Three of the heads sanded the top of the fiberboard sheet and three sanded the bottom. The top half of the machine could be adjusted manually to accommodate fiberboard sheets of varying thicknesses. The adjustment was made to accommodate a production run calling for sheets of a different thickness. The bottom half of the machine had powered rollers that moved the fiberboard being sanded through the machine. Pinch rolls on the top half of the machine were pressed down on the fiberboard by springs to keep the sanding heads from forcefully ejecting the fiberboard from the machine.

On the day of the accident the plaintiff was feeding sheets of fiberboard into the sander. Because of the faulty operation of a press (unrelated to the sander), the plaintiff received a large group of sheets of increased thickness. To accommodate these new sheets, the sanding machine was reset. During the sanding of the thicker sheets a thinner sheet of fiberboard that had become mixed with the lot was inserted into the machine. The pressure exerted by the pinch rolls in the top half of the machine as reset was insufficient to counteract the force that the sanding belts exerted on the thin sheet of fiberboard. As a result the machine ejected the piece of fiberboard, which hit the plaintiff in the abdomen, causing serious injuries.

The case proceeded on both design defect and failure-to-warn grounds, following a familiar pattern. The court first discussed the inadequacies of the design and found that a jury could conclude that, for a relatively small cost, a line of metal teeth that would press lightly against the sheet could have been installed into the machine. In case of attempted ejection the teeth would bite into the sheet and thus stop its backward motion. The court then found that, in any event, the manufacturer had failed to warn properly of the danger of the machine's ejecting a sheet of fiberboard that was not of uniform thickness with the rest of the stack. Since the court was faced with a manufacturer who had failed to warn of the dangers, it had no reason to decide what would happen if the manufacturer had fulfilled his duty to warn.

The *Phillips* case is, however, an excellent vehicle for considering the efficacy of a warning, if it had been given. It seems clear that in evaluating the adequacy or appropriateness of a warning regarding this sanding machine the following questions must be asked:

1. How frequently does a thinner sheet of the material become intermixed with those of usual thickness?
2. Was the operator's location at the time of the injury the usual one for feeding sheets into the sanding machine?
3. How much thinner than normal must a sheet be to be forcefully expelled by the machine?
4. Would a sheet thin enough to be expelled be readily detectable, visually, by the operator in the course of his normal job of feeding sheets into the sanding machine?

If, for example, the normal operator position coincides with the ejection point of a thin sheet and if such a thin sheet cannot be easily detected by the operator during the feeding operation, then a warning, even prominently positioned on the face of the machine, may not serve to minimize the risk. Alternatively, if the operator is paid by piecework and if the only way to detect a thin sheet is to measure each one before feeding it into the machine, the employee is faced with what may be regarded as an unreasonable choice: either ignore the warning and not measure each sheet (to preserve a high production rate and hence a reasonable income) or obey the warning and accept a reduced income. In fact, even with an effective warning or instructions on the machine, the plant environment created by its management may not make a choice possible if high rates of production are expected.

It may be argued that appellate courts have gone through the trouble of deciding cases on both design and warning grounds because they have intuitively concluded that the warning issue cannot be decided in a vacuum. A warning may or may not be sufficient, depending on the probability of reducing the risk and the feasibility of the design alternatives that would eliminate the risk or substantially diminish it. Courts sensitive to the very real limitations that affect warnings have indicated their concern that in some instances even the best of warnings may not shield the manufacturer from liability. The vehicle for this instruction to manufacturers has been the design issue.

The message to the manufacturing community is clear. The ultimate design of a product must take into account design alternatives together with warnings in deciding how best to reduce the risk of injury. The ultimate decision of whether to design out a hazard or warn against it must consider human behavior within the environment of product use. The fact that a line of print is inexpensive cannot be the sole determining factor in the decision process.

5.2   HOW EXPENSIVE ARE WARNINGS—WHAT ARE THEIR SOCIAL COSTS?

The trial of a products liability case under a failure to warn theory may appear to be the simplest approach. Indeed, this is something of a trend in products liability law. It can be simply stated—when in doubt warn. The reason for the trend is clear. Warnings are an apparently inexpensive mode of dealing with risks that cannot be designed out of a product without adding substantially to its cost or otherwise affecting its utility.

In deciding whether to declare a product unreasonably dangerous because it lacked a warning against a hazard, courts are faced with a unique problem. The test for unreasonable danger requires balancing the probability and gravity of harm, if care is not exercised, against the cost of taking appropriate precautions. Where the issue is failure to warn, and the probability of harm is quite remote, the question whether or not to warn against it arises. The attitude of the court on this point in *Moran v. Fabergé, Inc.* [3] is not atypical:

[W]e observe that in cases such as this the cost of giving an adequate warning is usually so minimal, amounting only to the expense of adding some more printing to a label, that this balancing process *will almost always weigh in favor of an obligation to warn of latent dangers*, if the manufacturer is otherwise required to do so. [Emphasis added.]

The unexamined premise that warnings are not costly in risk-utility balancing is highly questionable. Warnings, to be effective, must be selective. They must call the consumer's attention to a real and significant danger. One must warn discriminately if one expects the consumer to heed the warning. The story of the boy who cried wolf is an analogy worth contemplating in considering warning against a marginal risk. The possibility that multiple warnings decrease the effectiveness of all warnings should be considered when a court decides whether a warning should be required or a design change mandated in a products liability case. Those who argue for warning as *the* judicial solution to latent-defect cases appear to believe that one can warn against all significant risks. The truth is that this is not feasible. The warning process, to have impact, must select carefully the items that are to become part of the consumer's mental apparatus while using the product. Making the consumer account mentally for trivia or guard against risks that are unlikely to occur imposes a very real societal cost. Even when the risks are significant, one must consider whether the consumer will perceive them as significant. If the only way to ensure that the consumer will consider them significant is to oversell the warning by increasing its intensity, one may again face the problem that all warnings will come into disrepute as overly alarming. This does not mean that warnings do not have a major role to play in the area of product safety. It does mean, however, that there is a real question about which dangers must be warned against and which dangers should be designed out of products. Furthermore, for every danger that is designed out it may become possible to warn against others that still remain as potentially dangerous.

Moran v. Fabergé, Inc. strikingly illustrates the problem. The plaintiff, Nancy Moran, a 17-year-old, went to visit her girlfriend, Randy, on a warm summer night. The two girls, apparently bored that evening, focused their attention on a lit candle on a shelf behind the couch in the gameroom. The girls began to discuss whether or not the candle was scented. After agreeing that it was not scented, Randy exclaimed: "Well, let's make it scented!" Randy impulsively grabbed a "drip bottle" of Fabergé's Tigress Cologne that Randy's mother kept in the basement for use as a laundry deodorant and began to pour its contents onto the lower portion of the candle somewhat below the flame. Instantaneously, a fire burst out and burned Nancy's neck and breasts as she stood nearby watching, not fully aware of what her friend was doing. Evidence was introduced that cologne has a high percentage of alcohol, is dangerously combustible, and has a flash point of 73°F. On the other hand Tigress Cologne had a 27-year accident-free history.

The major question dividing the court was whether the foreseeability of misuse of the product was high enough to require a warning of flammability. The majority found that the general fire hazard was sufficiently foreseeable that the issue of whether a warning would be required should be decided by a jury. The dissent stated that, given the safety history of the product in the context of its normal use, the hazard was too remote to require a warning.

The quotation cited earlier, from the majority opinion in the *Moran* case, indicated that the court approached a failure-to-warn case with the bias that warnings are inexpensive—costing only a few extra words on a label. Neither the majority nor the dissent raises the question of whether a manufacturer is required to warn of other equally remote risks (e.g., not to ingest, keep away from children). If so, one could expect that a cologne bottle might be required to have a laundry list of warnings on the label—all to be equally disregarded .by consumers. The court approached the warning question in isolation, rather than within the context of the general problem of warnings. More important, however, is the failure of the court to take into account the societal cost of warning of a risk as remote as the one before it. The words "Danger-Flammable" are intended to alert a consumer to a real risk that can arise from reasonable use of the product. If the "Danger—Flammable" label is overused, one can only expect that consumers will become jaded about its message. If even remote risks are to be forced to the consumer's attention, the danger signal is diluted. If the bottle had not been equipped with a "drip-cap" that ensured that cologne would not come out of the bottle in large quantities, then perhaps the risk would have been more substantial. But the consumer knows that cologne comes out in drops. To tell him that flammability is a problem will bring into disrepute the danger signal that must service more serious situations.

In short, when calculating the burden of precaution that is part of the risk-utility calculus, one must focus on costs other than the cost of label printing. The efficacy of warning is a societal cost of substantial importance. Thus the courts cannot rely on warnings alone to ensure product safety. The range of risks is so broad, and the type of consumer response so varied, that the courts cannot avoid asking "what is a reasonably safe product?" or "how much product safety is enough?" The answers will sometimes lie with an adequate warning, sometimes with redesign of the product, but very often with a blend of warning and design to provide an adequate safety level.

5.3 WARNINGS THAT DO NOT REDUCE THE INHERENT RISK

In the past several years a new breed of failure-to-warn cases has emerged. In these cases the warning, even if given, could not reduce the incidence of injury by making the consumer more careful in his use of the product. Courts have proceeded on a failure-to-warn rationale and have concluded that without a warning the product is unreasonably dangerous.

5.3.1   The Warning That Can Only State That the Product Should Never Be Used

An instance in which a court found that liability should be imposed because of a failure to warn, but in which any conceivable warning could have no functional utility, appears in *Nissen Trampoline Company v. Terre Haute National Bank* [4]. The product there was known as an "Aqua Diver," a circular trampoline with a metal frame 36 inches in diameter and a canvas bed 16 inches in diameter. The bed was attached to the frame by an open network of elastic cables. Two feet above this trampoline was a platform for jumping onto the 16-inch bed, as a springboard into the water. A 13-year-old boy jumped from the platform, aiming for the trampoline bed, and landed with one foot on the bed and the other becoming entangled in the support cables. The injuries sustained by the boy later required amputation of a leg. The court concluded that, solely on the basis of the manufacturer's failure to warn that a user's foot could become entangled in the supporting cables, the product was defective.

Such a warning, in and of itself, can serve no useful purpose. Specifically, it cannot give the user, at the moment of jumping from the platform, any way to adjust his fall if he senses that he may land incorrectly. If a warning could make this product reasonably safe, it would have to instruct a user in how he might jump so as always to land with *both* feet in a patch of canvas only 16 inches in diameter. No such warning can be written or adequately communicated. Indeed the only warning that, *if heeded*, would be of any utility would state *"Don't Use This Product!"* Obviously no such warning will be given and no court would suggest that its absence constitutes a product defect.*

The only intelligent resolution of the hazard problem in the trampoline case is a redesign of the Aqua Diver so that the bed would be substantially larger and/or the supporting cables would be covered in some way to prevent a foot from passing between them. To address the question in the context of a missing warning is to mislead the manufacturer and ultimately to maintain a high hazard level for the consumer.

---

*Indeed, Justice Hunter of the Indiana Supreme Court, in his dissenting opinion in this case, expressed many of these same reservations. 358 N.E. 2d 974 at 980.

5.3.2 The Warning That Only Alerts the User to an Unascertainable Risk—Informed Consent

In *Davis v. Wyeth Laboratories, Inc.* [5] the plaintiff, a 39-year-old male, responded in March, 1963 to a mass polio immunization campaign in which residents of eastern Idaho and western Montana were being inoculated with Sabin Type III vaccine. Within 30 days after taking the vaccine the plaintiff contracted polio, ultimately resulting in paralysis from the waist down. Plaintiff sued Wyeth Laboratories, the manufacturer of the vaccine, on theories of negligence, breach of warranty, and strict liability. The plaintiff relied on the fact that, in September 1962, almost simultaneous reports were issued by the Surgeon General and a national association of health officers suggesting that there was a small but definite risk of contracting polio from the use of the vaccine. The risk was remote—in the range of less than one case for every 1 million doses. On the other hand the risk of contracting polio without taking the vaccine, for persons over the age of 20, was calculated by the Surgeon General to be somewhat less than one in a million as well. It was therefore the recommendation of the Surgeon General that Type III oral vaccine be administered primarily to preschool and school-age children and that it be used for adults "only with the full recognition of its very small risk."

The Ninth Circuit analyzed the case under the failure-to-warn rubric. Judge Merrill recognized that in this case he was faced with a rather special type of warning problem:

> There are many cases, however, particularly in the area of new drugs, where the risk, although known to exist, cannot be . . . narrowly limited and where knowledge does not yet explain the reason for the risk or specify those to whom it applies. It thus applies in some degree to all, or at least a significant portion, of those who take the drug. This is our case; there seems to be no certain method of isolating those adults who may be affected adversely by taking Type III Sabin vaccine.
>
> In such cases, then, the drug is fit and its danger is reasonable only if the balance is struck in favor of its use. Where the risk is otherwise known to the consumer, no problem is presented, since choice is available. Where not known, however, the drug can properly be marketed only in such fashion as to permit the striking of the balance; that is, by full disclosure of the existence and extent of the risk involved.

The court concluded:

> As comment k [to section 402A] recognizes, human experimentation is essential with new drugs if essential knowledge ever is to be gained. No person, however, should be obliged to submit himself to such experimentation. *If he is to submit it must be by his voluntary and informed choice or a choice made on his behalf by his physician.* [Emphasis added.]

As a result of this analysis the court found that the failure to warn in this case "rendered the drug unfit in the sense that it was thereby rendered unreasonably dangerous."

The court may be correct that the consumer is entitled to know the dangers inherent in the drug; nevertheless, the court is decidedly incorrect in reasoning that the failure to warn makes the drug unreasonably dangerous. The desired information, even if given to the consumer, would not make the drug safer nor lessen the risk of harm. The warning does not alter the inherent probability of harm, since the consumer has about the same probability of contracting polio whether he takes the vaccine or not. There are no precautions that the doctor or consumer can undertake either in the administration or the monitoring of the drug that would reduce the incidence of risk. There is no method by which a user can determine a priori whether or not he is one of those susceptible to the polio threat inherent in the drug. The warning in this case does not reduce the theoretical risk level but does serve the legitimate purpose of communicating sufficient information so that the consumer can intelligently choose whether or not to ingest the drug.

The determination of whether or not sufficient information has been communicated to the plaintiff so that he can intelligently judge whether or not he wishes to expose himself to the drug has little to do with the inherent safety of the vaccine. The issue rests on the choice-making mechanism of the consumer. It is clear that the defendant need not inform the plaintiff of all risks. The most liberal test of informed consent adopted by the courts requires only that the plaintiff be given the information that a reasonable person in the plaintiff's position would like to have before making a decision of such moment. The advantage, however, of focusing on the issue of choice rather than on the unreasonably dangerous nature of the product is substantial. By determining whether the plaintiff's consent must be obtained before exposing him to the risk, it becomes possible to distinguish rationally those cases in which courts believe that the information would have no impact on the plaintiff's decision. Two products may have the same risk potential, but because of the diverse nature of product benefits, consumers may desire to have the risk-potential information in one case and yet may not be particularly concerned with the matter in the other. This is generally a jury issue. Note here that the product's danger itself is but one element of the overall question of consumer choice. Whether the plaintiff has the information that a reasonable person would want before submitting himself to potential harm (reasonable or unreasonable) depends on factors far more complex than the risk of harm that may be incurred in using the product.

It becomes important at this point to differentiate Davis from the standard failure-to-warn case where the purpose of the warning is to reduce the risk potential of the product. When dealing with risks of varying seriousness and frequency in failure-to-warn cases, it has become fashionable to cite Davis as authority that even remote risks should be warned against. But it does not appear that *Davis* stands for the proposition that one must warn against remote risks where the purpose of the warning is to alert the consumer to risks that will reduce the incidence of harm. In the failure-to-warn case, where the warning tells the consumer how to act in relation to the product so as to minimize the chance of harm, the consumer is asked to make the warning part of his mental apparatus when using the product. It is something about which he must remain ever vigilant. As pointed out earlier, there are limits to the number of risks for which one can hope to hold the consumer accountable. The overuse of warnings invites consumer disregard and ultimate contempt for the warning process. This is not true of the warning that merely informs the consumer that he has a "take-it-or-leave-it" option because of a remote risk in the product. In this latter kind of warning situation, as in *Davis*, the consumer need not carry the baggage of the warning with him. He needs only to make the choice at the outset about whether he wishes to use the product. It is thus not unreasonable to ask the manufacturer to list even remote risks for a product that is generally reasonably safe.

If this leads to a somewhat paradoxical situation wherein the manufacturer of a product that embodies a remote risk that cannot be avoided no matter how much caution is exercised is required to warn of its presence, whereas the manufacturer of a product that embodies a remote risk that can be avoided by caution need not warn of it, so be it. The paradox arises out of the different goals to be accomplished by sharing information with consumers.

It may well be that, even with regard to the kind of warning that must be affixed to the product, significant differences can result, depending on the function of the warning. Cautionary labels designed to impress on the consumer the dangers attendant to the use of a product may require attention-getting words designed to place the consumer on guard and keep him on guard. The information-type warning whose purpose is merely to present the consumer with a one-time "take-it-or-leave-it" choice might not have to be quite as alarming and attention riveting. Analysis cannot proceed in failure-to-warn cases unless a careful evaluation is undertaken of the nature and function of the proposed warning and its relationship to possible design modifications.

5.4 DOES STRICT LIABILITY APPLY TO WARNING CASES?

The assumption here has been that failure-to-warn cases can proceed under both negligence and strict liability theories. That assumption may be somewhat questionable, since some courts have taken the position that a failure-to-warn case can go forward only under a negligence theory [6].

The reason for the difficulty is understandable. It does seem somewhat awkward to hold a manufacturer liable for failing to warn about a danger that he had no reason to foresee. Strict liability would demand a finding that, if the warning should have been there, the product is unreasonably dangerous irrespective of whether the defendant was acting reasonably in his failure to discover the danger. On the other hand, as has been discussed in Section 5.1, it is difficult to draw a meaningful distinction between failure-to-warn and design defect cases in general. If strict liability should apply in one case, it should apply in the other.

It should be recognized that the area of disagreement is narrow, since in a failure-to-warn case the defendant would not only have to plead ignorance of the danger but also would have to justify that ignorance. With the exception of drug cases a defendant can rarely exculpate himself from recovery on the grounds that he neither knew nor had reason to know of the dangers inherent in the use of the product.

5.5 THE ROLE OF DISCLAIMER IN AVOIDING LIABILITY

It must be remembered throughout that much of products liability law developed from the implied warranty of merchantability (see Section 1.3.2.2). Much of warranty law was responsive to the needs of merchants and businessmen and did not focus on the ordinary consumer. Since warranty essentially arose out of a contractual setting, there developed the notion of disclaimer; that is, the seller could disclaim, by contract, his liability that would normally arise out of the sale. This is reflected in Section 2-316 (2) of the Uniform Commercial Code. It reads:

(2) Subject to subsection (3), to exclude or modify the implied warranty of merchantability or any part of it the language must mention merchantability and in case of a writing must be conspicuous, and to exclude or modify any implied warranty of fitness the exclusion must be by a writing and conspicuous. Language to exclude all implied warranties of fitness is sufficient if it states, for example, that "There are no warranties which extend beyond the description on the face hereof."

(3) Notwithstanding subsection (2)

    a. unless the circumstances indicate otherwise, all implied warranties are excluded by expressions like "as is," "with all faults" or other language which in common understanding calls the buyer's attention to the exclusion of warranties and makes plain that there is no implied warranty; and

    b. when the buyer before entering into the contract has examined the goods or the sample or model as fully as he desired or has refused to examine the goods there is no implied warranty with regard to defects which an examination ought in the circumstances to have revealed to him; and

    c. an implied warranty can also be excluded or modified by course of dealing or course of performance or usage of trade.

The question that came to plague the courts was whether or not strict liability in tort could be disclaimed. The implied warranty of merchantability could be disclaimed under the statute just set forth, subject to certain exceptions. One of the possible exceptions, depending on statutory interpretation, was personal injury damages. Section 2-719 (3) of the Uniform Commercial Code could lead one to the conclusion that personal injury damages could be disclaimed. Since, however, strict liability in tort was no longer based on a contract theory, could disclaimer have any validity?

The position of the Restatement (Second) of Torts, Section 402A, comment m, was unequivocal on the matter. Disclaimers were not to be honored:

> m. "*Warranty.*" The liability stated in this Section does not rest upon negligence. It is strict liability. . . . The basis of liability is purely one of tort.
>
> A number of courts, seeking a theoretical basis for the liability, have resorted to a "warranty," either running with the goods sold, by analogy to convenants running with the land, or made directly to the consumer without contract. In some instances this theory has proved to be an unfortunate one. Although warranty was in its origin a matter of tort liability, and it is generally agreed that a tort action will still lie for its breach, it has become so identified in practice with a contract of sale between the plaintiff and the defendant that the warranty theory has become something of an obstacle to the recognition of the strict liability where there is no such contract. There is nothing in this Section which would prevent any court from treating the rule stated as a matter of "warranty" to the user or consumer. But if this is done, it should be recognized and understood that the "warranty" is a very different kind of warranty from those usually found in the sale of goods, and that it is not subject to the various contract rules which have grown up to surround such sales.
>
> The rule stated in this Section does not require any reliance on the part of the consumer upon the reputation, skill, or judgment of the seller who is to be held liable, nor any representation or undertaking on the part of that seller. The seller is strictly liable although, as is frequently the case, the consumer does not even know who he is at the time of consumption. The rule stated in this Section is not governed by the provisions of the Uniform Sales Act, or those of the Uniform Commercial Code, as to warranties; and it is not affected by limitations on the scope and content of warranties, or by limitation to "buyer" and "seller" in those statutes. Nor is the consumer required to give notice to the seller of his injury within a reasonable time after it occurs, as is provided by the Uniform Act. The consumer's cause of action does not depend upon the validity of his contract with the person from whom he acquires the product, and it is not affected by any disclaimer or other agreement, whether it be between the seller and his immediate buyer, or attached to and accompanying the product into the consumer's hands. In short, "warranty" must be given a new and different meaning if it is used in connection with this Section. It is much simpler to regard the liability here stated as merely one of strict liability in tort.

The judicial response to this question has been less than clear. An excellent example of the confusion that reigns in this area is provided by the New York Court of Appeals in *Velez v. Craine and Clark Lumber Corporation* [7].

The *Velez* facts are simple. The job superintendent for a contractor ordered a quantity of lumber from the defendant lumber company. The superintendent claimed that he specified that the lumber was to be scaffold planking. Defendant's vice-president, who took the order, contended that the order was for rough spruce planking and that he had not been given any indication of how the planking was to be used. The planking was delivered and later used for scaffolding. The plaintiffs, a carpenter and a laborer, stepped out on the plank platform at the same time. A few seconds later a plank cracked, causing the plaintiffs to fall some 25 to 30 feet to the foundation below. The uncontroverted testimony was that the plank that broke was rotted on one side, with a split all the way across the rotted area.

Plaintiffs brought the action against the defendant lumber company on both negligence and breach of warranty grounds. The trial court dismissed the negligence cause of action, and the plaintiffs ultimately won a verdict on warranty grounds alone. As to the breach of warranty charge, the plaintiff was faced with a disclaimer problem. The invoice for the lumber that was received in evidence bore the following legend in large capital letters:

NO CLAIMS ALLOWED UNLESS *MADE IMMEDIATELY AFTER DELIVERY*

Immediately below this legend appeared the following:

NOTE—The purchaser shall be deemed to have accepted these goods as is, the seller having made no representations or warranties whatsoever with respect to their quality, fitness for use, or any other regard thereto.

The word "NOTE" was printed in the largest type used in the body of the invoice, but the text of the disclaimer is printed in the smallest type used on the invoice.

The plaintiffs contended that the disclaimer should be disregarded because it did not meet the *Uniform Commercial Code* requirements that it be "conspicuous." Although the trial court sustained this contention, the Court of Appeals decided to bypass this issue and face the validity of a disclaimer as it would affect a nonbargaining third party. The court concluded that a disclaimer would not be effective. It reasoned as follows:

Subdivision (2) or Section 2-316 of the Uniform Commercial Code in pertinent part provides: "to exclude or modify the implied warranty of merchantability of any part of it the language must mention merchantability and in case of a writing must be conspicuous, and to exclude or modify any implied warranty of fitness the exclusion must be by a writing and conspicuous. Language to exclude all implied warranties of fitness is sufficient if it states, for example, that 'there are no warranties which extend beyond the description on the face hereof.' " This provision is obviously addressed to the language and form to be used if any exclusion of warranties is to be effective. The section does not undertake, nor does any other section of the code undertake, to specify who shall and who shall not be found by an exclusion of warranties which meets the requirements of Section 2-316.

We are then thrown back on broad principles of contract law. Although strict products liability sounds in tort rather than in contract, we see no reason why in the absence of some consideration of public policy parties cannot by contract restrict or modify what would otherwise be a liability between them grounded in tort.

In this case, however, we find no basis for holding that these plaintiffs should be barred from recovery by reason of the imprint of the exclusion of warranties legend on the invoice in this case. Plaintiffs were complete strangers to the contract; there is no evidence that either of them ever saw the invoice in question or knew of its contents. No authorities or rationale are tendered to support the extension of the disclaimer to plaintiffs with reference to claims predicated on strict products liability. We agree with the position of the dissenters at the Appellate Division that these plaintiffs were not bound by the terms of the contract between their employer and defendant lumber company. We see no necessity to labor the point that, in the absence of special circumstances not present here, buyer and seller cannot contract to limit the seller's exposure under strict products liability to an innocent user or bystander.

The most important question is not, however, liability to third-party strangers, but rather the validity of the basic disclaimer. If the disclaimer is invalid, then there is no question of its applicability to a third party. As already noted, the court sees "no reason why in the absence of some consideration of public policy parties cannot by contract restrict or modify what would otherwise be a liability between them grounded in tort."

It would appear that the New York court has signaled that, except in very special circumstances, disclaimers between parties in privity will be recognized even in an action under strict liability.

Thus it cannot be stated with assurance that disclaimers are totally invalid. Clearly, in commercial transactions, their validity is unquestioned. In consumer cases much will depend on the particular facts of the case. If there is a lack of arms-length bargaining and if there are take-it-or-leave-it provisions in a sales contract, it is hard to believe that such disclaimers will be given much effect. The *Velez* case instructs us, if nothing else, to be cautious about the future of disclaimers between bargaining parties.

The effect on disclaimers of warranty liability of the Magnuson-Moss Warranty Act, 15 USCS §§ 2301–2312, which became effective July 4, 1975, is not yet clear, but it could have considerable impact. It applies only to consumer products, defined as "any tangible personal property which is distributed in commerce and which is normally used for personal, family or household purposes." It does not compel a manufacturer or retailer to give a warranty in connection with the sale of any consumer product; it merely regulates the form and effect of those warranties that manufacturers and retailers choose to offer. It does, however, prohibit a seller from disclaiming or modifying any implied warranty (whether of merchantability or fitness) whenever he either offers a written warranty or enters into a service contract with the consumer within 90 days of the sale. The express purpose of the Act was to stop the commercial practice of using the written warranty as a vehicle for disclaiming implied warranties. Thus it invalidates disclaimers of implied warranties only where the seller offers a written warranty of some kind, or enters into a service contract with the buyer, and leaves the seller free to disclaim or modify implied warranties whenever no written warranty or service contract is present. Similarly a seller is not prevented from excluding all implied warranties by means of an "as'is" sale. Moreover, even when a warranty is given, the Act specifically permits the seller to limit or exclude liability for consequential damages arising from a breach of an implied warranty, so long as the exclusion or limitation conspicuously appears on the face of the warranty. However, UCC § 2-719(3), which declares limitations of consequential damages for injury to the person as *prima facie* unconscionable, remains fully applicable.

Note that a disclaimer is not to be confused with a warning. A disclaimer is a contractual attempt to avoid or mitigate liability. It does not address itself to the dangers attendant to the use of the product. It merely seeks to exculpate the defendant for all harms that may arise out of the use of the product. It is a Draconian measure and should be enforced only in circumstances where it is clear that buyer and seller were totally free to negotiate the terms of the sale. Even then it could be argued that such disclaimers are against public policy, since they permit unreasonably dangerous products in the marketplace. When such a product disintegrates or explodes, one has no assurance that only the bargaining party will be injured.

Perhaps the most eloquent statement in the judicial literature on this problem was that by Justice Francis of the Supreme Court of New Jersey in *Henningson v. Bloomfield Motors* [8]. In holding that the disclaimer of liability by Chrysler Corporation was invalid for a personal injury claim arising from a violent collision caused by a defective steering mechanism, he stated:

The warranty before us is a standardized form designed for mass use. It is imposed upon the automobile consumer. He takes it or leaves it, and he must take it to buy an automobile. No bargaining is engaged in with respect to it. In fact, the dealer through whom it comes to the buyer is without authority to alter it; his function is ministerial—simply to deliver it. The form warranty is not only standard with Chrysler but, as mentioned above, it is the uniform warranty of the Automobile Manufacturers Association. Members of the Association are: General Motors, Inc., Ford, Chrysler, Studebaker-Packard, American Motors (Rambler), Willys Motors, Checker Motors Corp., and International Harvester Company. Automobile Facts and Figures (1958

Ed., Automobile Manufacturers Association) 69. Of these companies the "Big Three" (General Motors, Ford, and Chrysler) represented 93.5% of the passenger-car production for 1958 and the independents 6.5%. And for the same year the "Big Three" had 86.72% of the total passenger vehicle registrations.

The gross inequality of bargaining position occupied by the consumer in the automobile industry is thus apparent. There is no competition among the car makers in the area of the express warranty. Where can the buyer go to negotiate for better protection? Such control and limitation of his remedies are inimical to the public welfare and, at the very least, call for great care by the courts to avoid injustice through application of strict common-law principles of freedom of contract. Because there is no competition among the motor vehicle manufacturers with respect to the scope of protection guaranteed to the buyer, there is no incentive on their part to stimulate good will in that field of public relations. Thus, there is lacking a factor existing in more competitive fields, one which tends to guarantee the safe construction of the article sold. Since all competitors operate in the same way, the urge to be careful is not so pressing. . . .

The task of the judiciary is to administer the spirit as well as the letter of the law. On issues such as the present one, part of that burden is to protect the ordinary man against the loss of important rights through what, in effect, is the unilateral act of the manufacturer. The status of the automobile industry is unique. Manufacturers are few in number and strong in bargaining position. In the matter of warranties on the sale of their products, the Automobile Manufacturers Association has enabled them to present a united front. From the standpoint of the purchaser, there can be no arms length negotiating on the subject. Because his capacity for bargaining is so grossly unequal, the inexorable conclusion which follows is that he is not permitted to bargain at all. He must take or leave the automobile on the warranty terms dictated by the maker. He cannot turn to a competitor for better security.

Public policy is a term not easily defined. Its significance varies as the habits and needs of a people may vary. It is not static and the field of application is an ever-increasing one. A contract, or a particular provision therein, valid in one era may be wholly opposed to the public policy of another. . . .

Public policy at a given time finds expression in the Constitution, the statutory law and in judicial decisions. In the area of sale of goods, the legislative will has imposed an implied warranty of merchantability as a general incident of sale of an automobile by description. . . . The lawmakers did not authorize the automobile manufacturer to use its grossly disproportionate bargaining power to relieve itself from liability and to impose on the ordinary buyer, who in effect has no real freedom of choice, the grave danger of injury to himself and others that attends the sale of such a dangerous instrumentality as a defectively made automobile. In the framework of this case, illuminated as it is by the facts and the many decisions noted, we are of the opinion that Chrysler's attempted disclaimer of an implied warranty of merchantability and of the obligations arising therefrom is so inimical to the public good as to compel an adjudication of its invalidity.

CHAPTER 6

Causation—
In All Its Forms

6.1 IS THE FLAW RESPONSIBLE FOR THE PRODUCT FAILURE?
TECHNICAL CAUSATION

For a plaintiff to prevail in an action in products liability, it is not sufficient for him to establish that a defect existed in the product and that it was unreasonably dangerous. He must also establish causation, that is, that the harm principally resulted from the defect in the product. The standard legal formulation of causation is the "but for" test. It asks: "*But for* the presence of the defect, product failure, or malfunction, would the injury have occurred?" If plaintiff cannot establish with clarity that the defect was both necessary and sufficient to the occurrence of his injury, he will not prevail.

Causation is, however, a multifaceted problem. Note that, particularly in products litigation, a special aspect of causation often surfaces as a threshold issue even before the issue of defect can be resolved. We term this special aspect of the question "*technical causation.*" Technical causation is intimately tied to the establishment of a production defect. Given the existence of a deviation from the manufacturer's standards, that is, a flaw, the technical causation question is simply, "Did this flaw cause this failure or malfunction of the product?"

A fascinating recent case [1], arising from a seemingly commonplace automobile accident, reveals the need for a clear understanding of the concept of technical causation.

The plaintiff, a 28-year-old veteran who had just returned from Vietnam, was driving his new car (12 hours old) on a dark and winding road late at night. Suddenly the car left the road and tumbled down a deep ravine, seriously injuring the driver. This car was equipped with retractable head-light covers. The thrust of the plaintiff's case was that the headlight covers closed spontaneously while he was driving, causing loss of illumination. As a result the plaintiff did not see a curve and the car hurtled into the ravine.

The case was fought on the dual battlegrounds of design and production defect. The headlight closure system was the focus of both allegations. For this system to function, a solenoid-operated valve activates a vacuum-controlled linkage that opens and closes the headlight covers. Current enters the solenoid and opens the valve when the lights are turned on. The open valve exposes the diaphragm to engine vacuum and activates the linkage, which transmits the force necessary to open and keep open the headlight covers. When no current flows through the solenoid, either as a result of shutting off the lights or an electrical failure, the headlight covers return by a spring action to their closed position.

The plaintiff began his testimony by challenging the wisdom of the closure-system design. As the case developed, the attack on the system became three pronged. The first attack charged that a combined electrical-pneumatic-mechanical system was overly complex and inherently less reli-able than a completely mechanical system for raising and lowering the headlight covers. The second charged that a fail-safe system should have been used, whereby the headlight covers would open or remain open when an electrical failure in the headlight cover circuit occurred. Finally it was alleged that the poor design of the electrical connectors (tabs) to the solenoid could lead to premature failure if inadvertently bent or subjected to normal car vibrations.

The production defects alleged by the plaintiff provided a graphic display of technological altercation. An electrical continuity check performed on the crashed vehicle (after it had been in a salvage yard for some time and had been cannibalized for parts) revealed an open circuit in the solenoid valve wiring. One of the plaintiff's technical experts, from x-rays of the assembly, traced the open circuit to a completely cracked tab connecting the electrical lead to the solenoid. In addition the expert discovered an external chip on the epoxy resin encapsulating all but the tip of the electrical tab; he also discovered an internal void in the resin at its juncture with the solenoid.

The plaintiff's technical experts proceeded in their investigation by exam-ining the fracture surfaces of the tab after grinding and filing away the encapsulating epoxy resin to expose the failure, and twisting the tab seg-ments for ease of observation. They discovered what appeared to them as solidified resin on that fracture surface of the hot-lead tab. This led them to conclude that the tab was partially cracked prior to being molded in liquid epoxy resin and that it was in that condition when sold to the plaintiff.

The critical question that should have been addressed by the plaintiff was, however, when, in the time period from car manufacture to the accident, the complete fracture of the tab occurred. If both the lawyers and technical experts had considered this question first, the litigation would have been directed exclusively to the origin, characteristics, and consequences of this crack. All other evidence concerning design defect, accident description, and injury to the plaintiff would have become relevant only after the origin and characteristics of the complete tab fracture were clearly addressed.

The reason for this conclusion is simple. If the tab did not fracture completely *prior* to the accident, then the headlight covers were apparently up and the accident occurred for reasons other than loss of illumination. If this were true, then the plaintiff obviously could not advance his case on either a production- or a design-defect theory. It may well have been that this solenoid tab was truly flawed in that a substantial crack did exist prior to the car's leaving the road, but that would have been of no consequence if it had been determined technologically that the tab could still carry the required current through its reduced cross-sectional area. Although it might well have been possible to use simpler and safer lighting system designs, that fact would have been of no consequence if the lighting system in the automobile had been operating prior to impact despite the flaw, that is, the cracked tab. This is the technical causation issue. This point was not absent in the trial as litigated; however, the presentation of evidence was such that this most significant question of technical causation, pivotal to the litigation on any premise, was never clearly and coherently addressed in the lengthy trial. Irrelevancies dominated, and the treatment of this major technological issue was sporadic and shallow.

The original trial resulted in a verdict favoring the defense. The decision was overturned on appeal because the original trial judge had refused to instruct the jury that they could find the defendant liable on the basis of the design defects. In view of the pivotal position of the issue of technical causation in this case, however, the reversal is puzzling. If the jury did not answer affirmatively the question of technical causation as it related to the production-defect theory of the case (did the preexisting crack cause complete failure prior to the accident?), then any consideration of a design-defect theory is irrelevant. The case was subsequently settled out of court.

The concept of technical causation is also applicable to the design defect. The question is, did the design flaw cause the product malfunction? This concept may at times be more subtle than the technical causation question in a production defect situation. This point is well illustrated in *Garst v. General Motors Corporation* [2].

In *Garst* three workmen were struck at a dam construction site by a scraper (a heavy earth-moving machine), resulting in the death of one and injury to the others. At the trial it was undisputed that the operator of the scraper first became aware of the presence of the workmen when the scraper was less than 15 feet away from them and was moving at approximately 10 to 12 miles per hour. The claim against the scraper manufacturer was based on two independent counts of design flaw: (1) the braking system on the scraper was not enclosed so as to exclude mud or other foreign materials that might impair braking, and (2) the hydraulic system delivered reduced oil flow to the power steering system at low-engine speed, requiring a longer time for altering vehicle direction.

The plaintiff's expert offered extensive testimony on the types of material and designs available for shields to enclose the brake drums to maintain braking efficiency. This was followed by a similar listing of possible modifications to the power steering pump and drive train for increasing pump speed at low engine speeds for more rapid steering. The defendant's reply dwelt on the technological inadequacies of the suggested design changes. Literally days were spent in discussion of the design modifications.

Yet, ironically, specific consideration of the braking and steering design alternatives raised in this case may have been totally irrelevant. It can be shown with a reasonable degree of technical certainty that *none* of the design alternatives suggested by the plaintiff would have been likely to have prevented the scraper from hitting the workmen, given the 10–12-mile-per-hour speed and the less than 15-foot distance available for stopping. It therefore appears unreasonable to state that the scraper malfunctioned. If this threshold question (i.e., whether the design alternatives would have sufficiently altered the scraper's performance so as to have reduced the likelihood of the injury-producing event) had been addressed initially, its resolution would have been a determination of no liability. This is the question of technical causation in the context of design defect.

6.2   IS THE PRODUCT FAILURE RESPONSIBLE FOR THE INJURY?

Although the flaw may have been the technical cause for the product's failure, there remains the question of whether the product failure was the cause of the harm. It may very well be that a product is defective and that the defect caused the product to fail in a significant manner at the time of injury, but that does not necessarily mean that the product failure was responsible for the injury. Thus in the case described earlier dealing with the failure of the headlight covers, it still remains incumbent on the plaintiff to establish that the product failure was responsible for the driver's losing control of the car, even if it could be established that a production flaw caused loss of illumination. Evidence that another car forced the driver of the defective car off the road or that the plaintiff was inattentive would render moot the question of liability of the car manufacturer. The defect must be the established cause of the injury. That is, if the injury would have occurred without regard to the defect, the defect is not the "but for" cause of the injury.

The use of the "but for" test as a break point for causation is extremely significant. It places a substantial burden on the plaintiff to account for the true cause of the accident. It also places a heavy burden on expert witnesses in products liability cases, since they are often asked hypothetical questions about whether the injury would have occurred without a defect. This point is discussed further in Chapter 9 dealing with the technologist as an expert witness. Suffice it to say that causation testimony is generally phrased in all-or-nothing terminology. Either a defect was or was not the cause of the injury event. This may satisfy purists but is often highly unrealistic, since causation is primarily a matter of probabilities. In light of the fact that this probability inquiry is rather sharply focused toward the liability question, it would be strange indeed if courts would not calibrate the degree of certainty that they require, depending on the nature of the specific inquiry before the court. The more significant the defect and the more serious the results of such a defect, the more pliant and pliable courts tend to be with the "but for" test. Thus the test is more a general guideline than a straitjacket preventing the imposition of liability.

The role of causation and the way in which we believe it should impact the products litigation process are illustrated in Figure 6-1. It is evident that the causation issue can short-circuit a lawsuit at the very outset. It is thus an issue that deserves the attention of counsel and experts at the earliest stages of litigation.

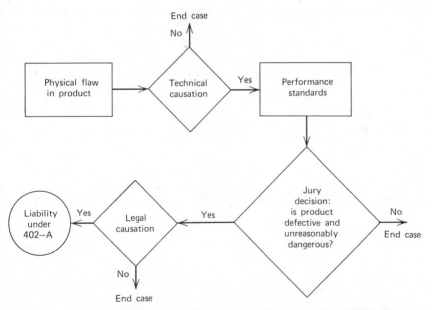

Figure 6-1.   Flow diagram highlighting technical and legal issues in products liability litigation.

6.3 IS THE DEFENDANT RESPONSIBLE FOR THE DEFECT?

In every products liability case based on a production defect, the plaintiff must establish not only that there was a defect in the product but also that the product was defective when it left the possession or control of the seller. It is not necessary under strict liability that the defendant-seller has brought the defect into being (e.g., a wholesaler or retailer); it is necessary only that the product was defective when it left his hands. This does not present a proof problem in many instances. When the plaintiff is able to establish the exact nature of the specific defect through expert testimony, or when the circumstantial evidence is such that an expert can conclude that a defect existed at the time of manufacture, this element of the case will not be difficult to establish. In many cases, however, this mode of proof is not possible. There are several reasons for this. First, products liability cases frequently arise from violent events. The evidence is often destroyed or damaged in the accident, and one has little more than the say-so of the plaintiff about how the accident occurred. Second, and more important, prior to the accident the product may have been through substantial use. Thus, even if at the time of injury there was a defect in the product, it may become very difficult to establish that the defect existed at the time of manufacture. In these instances the plaintiff must resort to some form of common sense inference. In a strict liability case the inference one must make is that, more probably than not, the accident would not have occurred in the absence of a *defect* and that the defect existed when the product left the hands of the manufacturer. For this inference to be a rational one, the courts have demanded that the plaintiff establish the "chain of control" with regard to the product, so that the plaintiff can negate other probable causes that could have introduced the defect in the product or that could themselves have caused the accident.

In *Jagmin v. Simonds Abrasive Company* [3] the court was faced with just such a problem. The plaintiff was injured when a grinding wheel on a portable grinder he was operating broke and struck him in the face. The grinding wheel, when new, was two inches thick and could be used until it was ground down to one-half inch in thickness. The plaintiff testified that he had put on a new wheel the night before the accident and had used it not more than three-quarters of an hour before quitting. He then used the new wheel for about half an hour the morning of the accident. He testified that the wheel was about one and one-half inches thick and had at least four or five hours of grinding time left on it. On these facts alone the *res ipsa*-type inference would have been fully warranted. There was, however, a real question of whether the grinding wheel in question had been used by someone on the night shift who might have misused it and thus have introduced a defect into the product. The problem was further complicated by the impossibility of establishing whether the wheel involved in the accident was the one that the experts examined or whether another wheel had been substituted instead.

The Wisconsin court resolved the problem by concluding that there was sufficient evidence for this case to go to the jury. It found that there was a legitimate fact question presented about whether the wheel had been used by the night shift and that this question was appropriately for the jury. It is hard to disagree with the court, which dealt carefully and sensitively with fact issues that it believed should not have been resolved by a directed verdict. It is, however, crucial that this problem be placed in a broader perspective.

In cases where defect cannot be definitively established by expert testimony, the proof problems appear in what, for want of better terminology, shall be referred to as the young, the middle-aged, and the old product. The cases at either extreme can be disposed of easily. The "young" product is best represented by the brand-new car in use for only several hundred miles. After plaintiff loses control of the car for unexplained reasons, the question of whether the car was defective arises. Since the car is so new, the plaintiff is able to account for almost every movement of the car. If plaintiff is able to negate the possibility of his own negligent conduct as a cause of the accident, the inference of defect is compelling. This was the scenario in some of the most celebrated products cases in the literature. *Henningson v. Bloomfield Motors* [4] and *Codling v. Paglia* [5] both involved new cars in which the steering mechanisms unexplainedly failed. Although the plaintiffs were not able to establish the defect with specificity, the inference of defect was so compelling that negating misuse was simply not a major problem. At the other end of the spectrum it is clear that when a product has been in use for a very long time, unless the plaintiff is able to isolate the defect and convincingly prove that it was in the product when it left the hands of the manufacturer, he is destined to lose his case. No court is prepared to hypothesize about the multitudinous causes that might have impaired the quality of an automobile that has been driven some 50,000 miles.

The problem arises, as the Wisconsin court correctly perceived, in the range of what is termed here the "middle-aged" product. The question is not only how long a product is supposed to last but also how much abuse a product is expected to take and how much abuse this particular product did take. The tendency of courts has been to treat this problem as an evidentiary one. Verdicts are either affirmed or reversed on the basis of whether the plaintiff has sufficiently negated the other possible causes of the defect. It is therefore necessary that the plaintiff trace his period of ownership and convince a court that nothing untoward or irresponsible was done to the product. One observes daily, in the exploding bottle cases, the charade wherein witnesses solemnly testify that they did nothing to the bottle that could have brought about the explosion. The evidence in this whole class of cases takes on a quality of fantasy, people testifying about their lifelong experience with a product with a wealth of detail that it is highly unlikely that they can accurately recall. Or the fortunes of a case are placed in the hands of third parties such as auto mechanics, who could have altered the product and introduced the defect into it. The question then becomes one of credibility, and as the number of intervening causes mount, the less credible the plaintiff's case becomes. The sheer waste of judicial effort in trying to discover the undiscoverable through the presentation of evidence is staggering.

The first step in resolving this problem is to recognize that marketing problems have been permitted to masquerade as basic liability questions. It is strange that the question of how long a product is supposed to last is viewed as within the purview of the jury in the standard products liability case. If a car, for example, becomes a dangerous instrument after six years, and a hair dryer is subject to serious failure after three years, manufacturers are well aware of those facts. Repair data and product life information are reasonably known by major industries and figure into the determination of production schedules and repair parts inventory. To be sure, these data are not sufficient to pinpoint product failure. But product deterioration information is available in the sense that the manufacturer knows when the troublesome period tends to set in. Yet for some reason this information is kept a deep, dark secret from the consuming public. It is only when plaintiffs bring a product claim that product life becomes a focal question. It does seem ludicrous to send the issue of how long a product should last to a jury when industry is better able to answer that question—and could affect consumer behavior by sharing it with the public.

The manufacturer's knowledge of product life could help resolve not only the question of how long a product should last but also that of what intervening causes could have contributed to the defect. To be sure, that problem cannot be totally eliminated, but if realistic guides on product life became part of the marketing scheme, there would be a ready method for resolving the alternate-cause question. Since products have a reasonable life expectancy and take normal abuse within that period, a *prima facie* case of product failure could be made out when the product fails within that period of time. The burden should then shift to the defendant to establish that the defect came into being through some abnormal cause, rather than as a consequence of normal consumer use. This would free the courts from speculating over the lists of things that could or might have happened within the normal life span of the product.

6.4 LIMITING THE RISK OR PROXIMATE CAUSE

In an earlier section (4.6) the question of foreseeable misuse of a product was addressed. It was established that, even if a product is determined to be defective, there must be some practical limit to the scope of manufacturer's liability attaching even to injuries caused by a defective product. Although courts have been willing to give the concept of foreseeable misuse a broad interpretation, the courts are unwilling to hold a manufacturer liable if they determine that the defect has been caused by outrageous misuse.

A recent Arizona case indicates that the limits can indeed be reached, and when that happens the manufacturer will be protected from liability by the courts. In *Roger v. Unimac Company* [6] the offending product was a washer-extractor used by automatic car washes for wringing water out of the wiping towels. The extractor operated at 175 rpm. To stop the machine, the lid of the extractor was raised. This action disconnected a microswitch in the motor circuit and simultaneously applied a mechanical brake activated by a rod attached to the rear of the lid. As the rod is pulled up, a cam arrangement forced two brake shoes up against the revolving disc fixed to the bottom of the extractor basket. At the time the Unimac 202 extractor was manufactured and shipped in 1967, this brake was capable of stopping the spinning extractor cylinder in approximately 10 seconds after the lid was raised.

The manager of the car wash was responsible for the maintenance and repair of the Unimac. He testified that when he began employment at the car wash in October 1969, he could adjust the brake according to the instruction manual supplied by Unimac so that the cylinder stopped within 10 seconds after the lid was raised. By November 1972, five and one-half years after delivery of the Unimac to the car wash, the brake mechanism of the appliance was in a state of great disrepair, and the brake itself was frequently inoperative. The manager testified that in his opinion the main reason for the excessive wear on the brake was its constant use, combined with the fact that the employees loaded the extractor basket unevenly, causing the unit to wobble and vibrate. According to the manager he was not authorized to order replacement parts from the Unimac company, because he was kept on a "tight budget." Those parts that he had replaced prior to the plaintiff's injury, the cams, the cam arm, and the brake linings, were fabricated by a local welder and installed by the manager himself.

When the brakes were not working, the car wash employees stopped the spinning extractor, after raising the lid, by taking a towel and pressing down on the rim or the hub of the basket with the towel. Earlier in the day on which the plaintiff was injured, the brake shoes of the Unimac fell off repeatedly and were replaced by the manager. The injury occurred when the plaintiff was pressing down on the hub of the spinning basket and a loose towel caught his arm and wrenched it into the mechanism.

An examination of the brake unit the next day revealed worn cams, a broken cam arm, a cracked brake shoe, and worn shock absorbers. The cam grooves on the top of the motor housing were worn so that the cams dropped through.

The case focused on the plaintiff's contention that the Unimac was unreasonably dangerous because (a) it did not have a lock to keep the lid from opening until the machine was at a complete stop, and (b) it did not have a warning on the extractor indicating the danger involved in reaching into the spinning cylinder. He argued that a warning was necessary because the machine was so designed that the operator had to lift the lid to apply the brake and was thus exposed to the spinning cylinder for at least 10 seconds or longer, depending on the condition of the brake.

The court, in addressing the claim that the failure to warn made the machine unreasonably dangerous, decided that, even if it should accept the plaintiff's argument, the injury could not be said to have been proximately caused by the failure to warn. Rather, the failure to repair the Unimac must be viewed as the cause of the injury. Relying on a similar case in Minnesota, the court cited that case for authority.

It is difficult to know where to draw the line on a manufacturer's liability in the sale of products. There must be a limit to such liability somewhere. We think this case lies outside the area where liability exists. The manufacturer here has done all anyone could reasonably expect it to do in making the chattel safe for the use for which it was intended. The responsibility for maintaining it in the safe condition in which it was sold rested with the user.

The message is clear. Even a defective condition that is operative at the time of injury (the failure to warn) may not be the grounds for imposing liability when the risk created by the defect is superseded by conduct that is much more significant. The risk as it eventually developed was more clearly a result of the outrageous behavior of the employer than it was of the defendant-manufacturer. When this conclusion can be reached with certainty, a court will direct a verdict for the defendant on the grounds that the defendant's conduct is not the proximate cause of the injury.

6.5 SUMMARY

It should be apparent that the word "cause" in the law of products liability covers a multitude of factors. It is first an inquiry into whether the flaw in a product was capable of causing the failure of the product. Second, it examines whether the product failure was the cause of the harm or whether some nonproduct phenomenon caused the harm. Third, it must deal with the practical limits that courts must place on a products liability action. There is a commonsense limitation in the law of torts stating that it is unfair to impose liability without regard to the kinds of risks that have subsequently developed and that have had considerable impact on the injury event. The use of the term "proximate" to modify the word "cause" adds little to an understanding of what the courts are actually doing. Asking the question of whether a causal element is closely or remotely related to the incident does not help in analyzing why the courts believe it appropriate to limit liability. It is only by focusing on the risks created by the original product defect that one can determine whether it is fair to assess liability on a defendant-manufacturer whose original conduct has now begun to fade into the background.

CHAPTER 7

The Role of the User

7.1 PLAINTIFF'S CONDUCT—AN OVERVIEW

After the occurrence of an injury the defendant often discovers that the injury was partially attributable to the way in which the plaintiff used the product. The desire to blame the foolish user is understandable, but the law will not necessarily bar the plaintiff from recovering because his conduct has been foolish or even foolhardy.

It is important to list the kinds of plaintiff conduct that can affect legal liability:

1. Plaintiff can fail to inspect a product to discover defects.
2. Plaintiff may discover the defect but forget about it subsequently and thus suffer injury.
3. Plaintiff may discover a defect, recognize that it presents a risk, but decide to use the product in spite of the risk.
4. Plaintiff may generally misuse or abuse the product in ways that are unrelated to any product defects.

In a normal negligence action, if the defendant is able to establish that the plaintiff has failed to act reasonably and that the plaintiff's conduct has a causal connection with his injury, that may be grounds for barring the plaintiff from recovery. Many states have today eliminated the contributory negligence of the plaintiff as a complete bar to recovery. Instead, the plaintiff's recovery can be reduced based on the percentage of his fault relative to that of the defendant. Thus the contributory fault of the plaintiff, as measured by comparing his behavior with that of the "reasonable" person, may either bar or substantially reduce the plaintiff's recovery.

A case based on a theory of strict products liability provides a significant advantage to the plaintiff. In order for the plaintiff's conduct to enter the picture, it must be of a very special nature. The Restatement (Second) of Torts, Section 402A, comment n provides:

Contributory negligence of the plaintiff is not a defense when such negligence consists merely in a failure to discover the defect in the product, or to guard against the possibility of its existence. On the other hand the form of contributory negligence which consists in voluntarily and unreasonably proceeding to encounter a known danger, and commonly passes under the name of assumption of risk, is a defense under this Section as in other cases of strict liability. If the user or consumer discovers the defect and is aware of the danger, and nevertheless proceeds unreasonably to make use of the product and is injured by it, he is barred from recovery.

The plaintiff's behavior as it can affect the issue of liability can assume various forms, each of which is examined here.

7.2 PLAINTIFF'S FAILURE TO INSPECT FOR DEFECT

The *Restatement* position, which has been widely adopted, specifically frees a plaintiff from a duty to inspect a product for defects. The reason for removing the burden from the consumer is clear; the thrust of strict liability law has been to place the duty of manufacturing a *reasonably safe product* on the manufacturer. The concern is no longer whether the manufacturer has acted reasonably in putting the product on the market. The shift from substandard manufacturer conduct to product defectiveness as the criterion for liability should mean, at the very least, that a *consumer has a right to expect a nondefective product* and is entitled to use the product under this premise. As long as negligence was the criterion for liability, a consumer had no absolute right to expect that a product would reach him in a nondefective condition. Manufacturers bore no responsibility for producing a defect-free product. If the defendant used reasonable care in the manufacturing process, he would not be held liable, even for injuries caused by his defective product. But once the criterion for manufacturer liability became product defectiveness, it made no sense to place on the consumer a duty to inspect before use. If he is entitled to a nondefective product, why should he be required to inspect it to assure himself that the product he is about to use is nondefective?

Nonetheless, there are courts that continue to apply the standard rules of contributory negligence. In *Velez v. Craine and Clark Lumber Corporation* [1], discussed earlier, the plaintiff was injured when he fell from a piece of unsound scaffolding lumber. The court had earlier stated in *Codling v. Paglia* [2] that to recover a plaintiff must establish:

1. That the product was being used for the purpose and manner normally intended.
2. That if the plaintiff was himself the user of the product, he would not, by the exercise of reasonable care, have both discovered the defect and perceived its danger.
3. That by the exercise of reasonable care the person injured would not otherwise have averted his injury.

Following the *Codling* principle, the appellate court in *Velez* returned the case to the trial court to learn whether reasonable persons in the plaintiff's position would have discovered the defect and appreciated its danger. Thus it is clear that the New York court has imposed a duty to discover the defect.

A further question is whether a court that is willing to impose the doctrine of comparative fault will be willing to consider the plaintiff's failure to discover the defect as a factor in assessing some percentage of the fault against the plaintiff. There is scant authority on the matter; however, the Alaska Supreme Court in *Butaud v. Suburban Marine and Sporting Goods, Inc.* [3] has indicated that it will be willing to take the full range of plaintiff's conduct into account in assessing liability. Several courts have applied comparative fault in products liability cases. It is not clear, however, that they will take into account, in apportioning fault, such plaintiff conduct as failure to discover defect [4].

7.3 THE PLAINTIFF WHO SEES AND THEN FORGETS THE RISK

Recent cases in the products liability field have highlighted the problem of the inadvertent or forgetful plaintiff who at an earlier stage of product use had become aware of the dangers that were ultimately to cause his injury. Consider, for example, *Bexiga v. Havir Manufacturing Corporation* [5]. Plaintiff, John Bexiga, Jr., 18 years of age, was employed by the Regina Corporation as a power punch press operator. The 10-ton punch press that he was operating, manufactured by Havir Corporation, was almost totally devoid of safety features. Plaintiff testified that the particular operation he was directed to do required him to place round metal discs, about three inches in diameter, one at a time by hand on top of the die. He would then depress a foot pedal activating the machine and causing a ram to descend about five inches and punch two holes in the disc. After this operation the ram would ascend and the equipment on the press would remove the metal disc and blow the trimmings away so that the die would be clean for the next cycle. The entire cycle just described would take about 10 seconds. The plaintiff related the events leading up to the accident as follows:

Well, I put the round piece of metal on the die and the metal didn't go right to the place. I was taking my hand off the machine and I noticed that a piece of metal wasn't in place so I went right back to correct it, but at the same time, my foot had gone to the pedal, so I tried to take my hand off and jerk my foot off too and it was too late. My hand had gotten cut on the punch, the ram.

Plaintiff's expert testified that the punch press amounted to a "booby trap" because there were no safety devices in its basic design. He described two different types of protective safety devices, both of which were known in the industry at the time of the manufacture and sale of the press. The trial court had dismissed the action at the close of the plaintiff's case, and the appellate division affirmed. The latter reasoned that, since it was the custom of the trade that purchasers, rather than manufacturers, provide safety devices on punch presses like the one in question, Havir could not be held liable. However, the New Jersey Supreme Court, in considering this same case, noted that "the only way to be certain that [safety devices] will be installed on all machines . . . is to place the duty on the manufacturer where it is feasible for him to do so," and remanded the case for trial, holding that a jury might well find the defendant negligent or the machine unreasonably dangerous.

Having resolved the duty issue in favor of the plaintiff, the court dealt with the defendant's contention that plaintiff must as a matter of law be held contributorily negligent:

We think this case presents a situation where the interests of justice dictate that contributory negligence be unavailable as a defense to either the negligence or strict liability claims.

The asserted negligence of plaintiff—placing his hand under the ram while at the same time depressing the foot pedal—was the very eventuality the safety devices were designed to guard against. *It would be anomolous to hold that defendant has a duty to install safety devices but a breach of that duty results in no liability for the very injury the duty was meant to protect against.*

The plaintiff, through inadvertence, placed his hand in a machine that was operational. He did not *voluntarily* choose to encounter the risk at the critical moment. Plaintiff simply was not assuming the risk at the moment of encounter.

7.4 VOLUNTARY AND UNREASONABLE ASSUMPTION OF A KNOWN RISK

Although courts have been reluctant to bar plaintiffs from recovery when their conduct is merely negligent, they have been willing to bar plaintiffs who have voluntarily and unreasonably decided to confront a known risk. "If the user or consumer discovers the defect and is aware of the danger and nevertheless proceeds unreasonably to make use of the product and is injured by it, he is barred from recovery" [6]. The requirements for this defense are that plaintiff: (a) voluntarily and (b) unreasonably confront a (c) known risk. All three elements must be proved to establish the defense. How voluntary is voluntary? How much reason must be missing before an act is unreasonable? How much knowledge of the risk is enough knowledge?

Vernon v. Lake Motors [7] is indicative of how far the courts can go in setting the boundary while examining the plaintiff's behavior. The Vernons had purchased a Mercury Marquis about 8½ months prior to the time in which the damage to their car occurred. On the day in question Mr. Vernon had driven the car and had noticed some smoke coming from the windshield wipers. The wipers also would not shut off. His local Ford agency refused to fix the car since Vernon had not purchased the car through that agency.

Mrs. Vernon decided to drive the car 40 miles to Salt Lake City that morning immediately following the "smoking event." Her reasons for doing so were several. First, she wanted to take the car to the agency from which she purchased the car for its 10,000-mile checkup. Second, she wanted to attend a dance recital in which her granddaughter was to perform. Being concerned about the smoking incident, Mrs. Vernon went out to the car, turned the motor on, and let it run to see if smoke was accumulating in the car. The wipers would not turn off, but since it was storming she needed them in any event. Her testimony was that she believed that the worst that could happen was that some fuses would blow out. About three-fourths of the way to Salt Lake City, a fire started under the instrument panel and the car was consumed by fire.

In deciding whether the plaintiff had voluntarily and unreasonably assumed a known risk, the court considered the fact that plaintiff might have had good reason to believe that nothing would be seriously wrong with a new car and remanded the issue for jury determination of whether plaintiff's conduct was a voluntary and unreasonable assumption of a known risk.

In deciding to leave this case for jury determination the court did not feel compelled to conclude that the smoking wiper incident was *ipso facto* knowledge of the risk that the car would be destroyed by fire. Nor did the court conclude that the grandmother's desire to see her granddaughter in a dance recital is clearly sufficient to make the act unreasonable as a matter of law.

Note that a jury could have concluded that plaintiff acted unreasonably (i.e., that her decision to drive the car with smoking windshield wipers was negligent), but that plaintiff did not have specific knowledge of the risk (i.e., the danger that the electrical problem would cause the car to burn up). Thus plaintiff might have been negligent but may not have assumed a known risk. In most jurisdictions, if this had been the finding of the court, the plaintiff would not be barred from recovery if the cause of action were based on strict liability.

Products are manufactured for use without particular knowledge of the myriad situations that may arise in which consumers will be put in what to them may be difficult choice situations, deciding whether to continue to use the product even though some serious risk of injury may surface. Whether the plaintiff acts voluntarily, reasonably, and with knowledge or not is a product of social pressures acting on the plaintiff at the moment of encounter. "Proceeding to voluntarily and unreasonably encounter a known risk" is a legal term without a standard of reference to give it meaning.* Yet, despite a lack of knowledge of a user's decision-making process in product use, the burden is clearly on the manufacturer to anticipate a wide range of human vagaries.

7.5 GENERAL CONTRIBUTORY NEGLIGENCE—UNRELATED TO THE PRODUCT

Consider the following hypothetical situation. Plaintiff was injured when an improperly beaded tire on his car blew out. At the time of the accident plaintiff was speeding 20 miles per hour (mph) over the limit, driving 55 mph in a 35-mph zone. The evidence is such that, if plaintiff had been driving at the appropriate speed limit, he would have been able to bring his car under control and could have avoided the impact that caused his injuries. Traveling at 55 mph is hardly an abusive use of a tire. But if plaintiff had been traveling at the speed limit, he would have been able to avoid the accident entirely. His contributory negligence is now clearly a substantial factor in the cause of his injury. Should contributory negligence be a defense? The Restatement position, Section 402A, comment n, would seem to say that it is not a defense, since he apparently did not voluntarily and unreasonably assume a known risk, that is, that his tire would blow out at 55 mph. This position appears to be clearly correct.

---

*In the context of this work we have not addressed the concept of "pure assumption of the risk." It is likely to be primarily of scholarly interest. For an extensive treatment of this subject, see reference 8.

The duty of producing a nondefective product has been placed on the manufacturer. The harm that has befallen the plaintiff is directly within the risk of the defect against which the manufacturer has a duty to guard. The defendant has a clear duty to manufacture tires that will not disintegrate at 55 mph, regardless of whether or not the plaintiff was negligent at the time of failure. By establishing the contributory negligence defense we are removing from the defendants' liability picture a whole range of foreseeable users to whom a clear duty is owed, that is, those people legally driving at 55 mph, whose tires should not blow out.

This argument notwithstanding, there are some courts that have recognized an across-the-board contributory-negligence defense to products liability [9]. Although they are in the minority, the groundswell toward comparative negligence may well lead us back to a general doctrine of contributory fault in which the plaintiff's behavior is taken into consideration in assessing the percentage of his contribution to the injuries. If this should happen, then the distinctions between failing to discover the defect, voluntary and unreasonable assumption of the risk, and general contributory fault may all become moot. This need not happen. Courts may still consider these distinctions in plaintiff's behavior in deciding whether or not to impose the doctrine of comparative fault. This is the open question for the next decade of products liability litigation.

7.6 COMPARATIVE FAULT

Under the rule of comparative fault or comparative negligence a plaintiff is not barred from recovery merely because the defendant establishes that the plaintiff acted unreasonably. Rather, the plaintiff's conduct is compared with that of the defendant and the plaintiff's recovery is then reduced by the percentage of his fault. Thus, for example, if defendant is deemed to be 70 percent at fault and plaintiff 30 percent at fault, the plaintiff will have his recovery reduced by 30 percent. So if the plaintiff suffered $100,000 worth of damages, he would recover only $70,000 [10]. Note that some jurisdictions deny plaintiff any recovery if the jury finds his percentage of fault exceeds 50 percent, while other courts still apportion the award beyond the 50-percent point.

Should the doctrine of comparative fault be applied to strict liability cases? Opposition to the comparative-fault doctrine in strict liability has been voiced by those who fail to see how one can compare the strict liability (a no-fault doctrine) of the defendant with the negligence (a fault doctrine) of the plaintiff.

This technical problem is capable of resolution. There are two mechanisms to accomplish the apportionment of fault.

7.6.1 Focus on Plaintiff's Conduct

If the purpose of comparative negligence is to reduce plaintiff's recovery by assessing the role that plaintiff's conduct played in causing the injury, then we are really not involved in a strict comparison of fault. Instead, what we are doing is viewing the injury event in totality and then asking ourselves whether or not it is fair to allow the plaintiff full compensation for an injury event to which he made an important contribution. To be sure, some comparison of fault is inevitable, but the percentage allocation is essentially accomplished by looking at plaintiff's conduct. The draft Uniform Comparative Fault Act [11] reflects this basic perspective. It provides:

(a) In an action based on fault, to recover damages for injury or death to person or harm to property, any contributory fault chargeable to the claimant diminishes proportionately the award of compensatory damages, but does not bar recovery . . . .

(b) "Fault" includes negligence, recklessness, breach of implied warranty, conduct subjecting the actor to strict tort liability, unreasonable assumption of risk, and failure to avoid or mitigate damage. The fault must have an adequate causal relationship to the damage suffered.

Note that the emphasis is not so much on the comparative aspects of the action but rather accomplishes the reduction by diminishing the award according to the plaintiff's contributory fault.

7.6.2 Equating Defect with Fault

The reasons for adopting strict liability stem from a desire to change risk distribution principles, to fulfill consumer expectations, and to free the plaintiff from the burden of proving fault when it is likely that fault is present but cannot be easily demonstrated. Given such a multiplicity of reasons for the adoption of strict liability, it is not untoward to suggest that the seriousness of defect be in some rough sense equated with a percentage of fault. Again the draft Uniform Comparative Fault Act suggests the following:

In determining the percentage of fault allocable to each party, the trier of fact shall consider, on a comparative basis, both the nature and quality of the conduct of the party and the extent to which and directness with which the conduct contributed to cause the damages claimed.

Having concluded that there is no technical impediment to applying the comparative-fault concept to strict liability cases, it is important that we consider whether there are philosophical objections to doing so. Here the arguments become much more substantial. In those cases where the defendant's duty is to protect the plaintiff from an inadvertent action (e.g., by installing a safety device) it would seem unwise to reduce the plaintiff's recovery by the percentage of his fault. The plaintiff's reaction to the product (and thus his contributory negligence) is not only foreseeable but also in a sense built into the product. If the defendant is duty bound to protect the plaintiff, that duty ought not to be diminished merely because the plaintiff has reacted in a predictable fashion to the product [12].

The question of comparative fault in strict products liability is very much up in the air. There are decisions on both sides of the question. But the widespread adoption of comparative fault is too new a phenomenon to be able to predict the reaction of the courts. This is one question that must await the verdict of the next several years.

CHAPTER 8

Who Is the Appropriate Defendant?

8.1 AN OVERVIEW

The thrust of strict tort liability was originally directed toward the manufacturer. It was at the point of design and manufacture where safety could best be enforced. But the marriage of implied warranty and strict tort liability into one common theory has accomplished a result that includes every seller in the distributive chain as a possible products liability defendant. Unlike negligence, where the tort is the negligent conduct of the defendant (whether he is retailer, wholesaler, or manufacturer), the tort in strict products liability is the *sale* of a *defective product*. Thus, if the defendant was the seller of the defective product and the product was the cause of the injury, the cause of action has been made out. We must, of course, establish that the defect existed when the product left the hands of the defendant (see Section 6.3). This is the thrust of strict tort liability and implied warranty (absent privity). The reasons for expanding the number of strict liability defendants to include every seller of a defective product up and down the distributive chain is set forth in Restatement of Torts (Second), Section 402A, comment c.

On whatever theory, the justification for the strict liability has been said to be that the seller, by marketing his product for use and consumption, has undertaken and assumed a special responsibility toward any member of the consuming public who may be injured by it; that the public has the right to and does expect, in the case of products which it needs and for which it is forced to rely upon the seller, that reputable sellers will stand behind their goods; that public policy demands that the burden of accidental injuries caused by products intended for consumption be placed upon those who market them, and be treated as a cost of production against which liability insurance can be obtained; and that the consumer of such products is entitled to the maximum of protection at the hands of someone, and the proper persons to afford it are those who market the products.

8.2   THE DISTRIBUTIVE CHAIN

The imposition of strict tort liability or warranty requires that the defendant be engaged in the business of selling. The occasional noncommercial sale is not covered under strict liability. In such an instance the plaintiff would be required to prove that the noncommercial seller failed to act reasonably (negligence). The clearest expression of this principle is set forth in Restatement (Second) of Torts, Section 402A, comment f:

> f. *Business of selling.* The rule stated in this Section applies to any person engaged in the business of selling products for use or consumption. It therefore applies to any manufacturer of such a product, to any wholesale or retail dealer or distributor, and to the operator of a restaurant. It is not necessary that the seller be engaged solely in the business of selling such products. Thus the rule applied to the owner of a motion picture theatre who sells popcorn or ice cream, either for consumption on the premises or in packages to be taken home.
>
> The rule does not, however, apply to the occasional seller of food or other such products who is not engaged in that activity as a part of his business. Thus it does not apply to the housewife who, on one occasion, sells to her neighbor a jar of jam or a pound of sugar. Nor does it apply to the owner of an automobile who, on one occasion, sells it to his neighbor, or even sells it to a dealer in used cars, and this even though he is fully aware that the dealer plans to resell it. The basis for the rule is the ancient one of the special responsibility for the safety of the public undertaken by one who enters into the business of supplying human beings with products which may endanger the safety of their persons and property, and the forced reliance upon that undertaking on the part of those who purchase such goods. This basis is lacking in the case of the ordinary individual who makes the isolated sale, and he is not liable to a third person, or even to his buyer, in the absence of his negligence. An analogy may be found in the provision of the Uniform Sales Act, § 15, which limits the implied warranty of merchantable quality to sellers who deal in such goods; and in the similar limitation of the Uniform Commercial Code, § 2-314, to a seller who is a merchant. This Section is also not intended to apply to sales of the stock of merchants out of the usual course of business, such as execution sales, bankruptcy sales, bulk sales, and the like.

The case law thus far supports the imposition of strict liability against the following members of the distributive chain*:

*For a discussion of the primary material's supplier as a defendant, see Section 2.3.4.

1. Producer of the raw material [1].
2. Maker of a component part [2].
3. Assembler or subassembler [3].
4. Packager of the final product [4].
5. Wholesaler, distributor, or middleman [5].
6. One who holds the product out to be his own [6].
7. Retailer [7].

In each instance the plaintiff must establish that the product was defective when it left the defendant's hands. With respect to a production defect this is easier said than done. For a product assembled from component parts supplied by a number of manufacturers, it may be fairly easy to establish that the assembled product was defective but to pinpoint the component part that contained the defect may be exceedingly difficult. The same problem exists with other members of the distributive chain. If the product could have been tampered with and the defect introduced after the defendant sold the product, he is not responsible for the after-acquired defect. Thus, adding defendants to the list of persons who may be sued for strict tort liability is not a guarantee of recovery even if the product was defective. It is not necessary that the defect manifest itself immediately. If the defect is a slumbering one that does not become evident until the product has been put to some use but it is still possible to identify that the defect was present in the product at the time of manufacture or sale, liability can attach [8]. Thus, for example, a metallurgical flaw may not manifest itself until the metal fails by fatigue. Nevertheless, expert evidence may clearly identify the failure as due to fatigue and pinpoint the structural deficiency of the metal from the date of the original processing. This would be sufficient to establish that the defect existed when the product left the hands of a defendant, conceivably the producer of the metal, in this instance.

8.3 OTHER DEFENDANTS

8.3.1 Commercial Lessors

The concepts of strict liability in tort or the implied warranty of merchantability had their origin in normal sales transactions. Modern marketing arrangements have, however, led the courts to apply the strict liability rule to sales-like transactions. One of the most important additions to the roster of strict liability defendants is the class of commercial lessors.

The leading case on this subject is *Cintrone v. Hertz Truck Leasing & Rental Service* [9]. In this case the New Jersey Supreme Court held that the lessor of a truck who had leased the truck to the plaintiff's employer could be held liable to the plaintiff-employee under a strict liability theory when he was injured owing to defective brakes on the truck. There was no evidence of negligence on the part of the lessor. Thus a commercial lessor who had acted reasonably in inspecting and caring for a leased vehicle would still be liable for defects arising during the leasing period under a strict liability theory (either strict tort or implied warranty of merchantability or fitness for a particular purpose). In support of its holding the court argued:

> The nature of the U-Drive-it enterprise is such that a heavy burden of responsibility for the safety of lessees and for members of the public must be imposed upon it. The courts have long accepted the fact that defective trucks and cars are dangerous instrumentalities on the highways. They present great potentiality for harm to other highway users as well as to their own drivers and passengers. Therefore the offering to the public of trucks and pleasure vehicles for hire necessarily carries with it a representation that they are fit for operation. This representation is of major significance because both new and used cars and trucks are rented. In fact, as we were advised at oral argument, the rental rates are the same whether a new or used vehicle is supplied. . . . To illustrate, if a traveler comes into an airport and needs a car for a short period and rents one from a U-drive-it agency when he is "put in the driver's seat" his reliance on the fitness of the car assigned to him for the rental period whether new or used usually is absolute. In such circumstances the relationship between the parties fairly calls for an implied warranty of fitness for use, at least equal to that assumed by a new car manufacturer. The content of such warranty must be that the car will not fail mechanically during the rental period.

The court was then faced with the question of how long the warranty would last. In other words, if a defect becomes manifest during the period of the lease, after considerable use by the lessee, should liability attach? The court resolved this question in the affirmative saying:

> Since the exposure of the user and the public to harm is great if the rented vehicle fails during ordinary use on a highway, the answer must be that it (the warranty) continues for the agreed rental period. . . . The operator of the rental business must be regarded as possessing expertise with respect to the service life and fitness of his vehicles for use. That expertise ought to put him in a better position than the bailee to detect or to anticipate flaw or defects or fatigue in his vehicles.

It thus appears that all the policy reasons for applying strict liability to manufacturers and sellers applied with equal force to commercial lessors. The Pennsylvania Supreme Court in *Francioni v. Gibsonia Truck Corp.* [10] reviewed the leading cases on the subject and concluded that strict liability against lessors was supported by the following considerations:

1. In some instances the lessor, like the seller, may be the only member of the marketing chain available to the injured plaintiff for redress.
2. As in the case of the seller, imposition of strict liability upon the lessor serves as an incentive to safety.
3. The lessor will be in a better position than the consumer to prevent the circulation of defective products.
4. The lessor can distribute the cost of compensating for injuries resulting from defects by charging for it in his business, i.e., by adjustment of the rental terms.

8.3.2 Real Estate Transactions

Products liability law is generally thought of as concerning itself with defective and dangerous movable property. In the past several years, however, strict liability has been applied to the sale of new homes by a builder-vendor. The leading authority is the now-famous *Schipper v. Levitt and Sons, Inc.* [11] case in New Jersey. In this instance the builder had installed a hot water system in which scalding hot water came from the tap. The manufacturer of the boiler, York-Shipley, had recommended that their water heater be installed only together with a mixing valve external to the boiler to avoid domestic use of excessively hot water, but the builder, Levitt, had deliberately not followed the recommendation. Plaintiff, a 16-month-old infant, turned on the hot water tap and was scalded.

In seeking to impose strict liability the court was faced with a well-established rule that the seller of real property implies no warranties whatsoever. In the absence of fraud or misrepresentation, the vendor is liable only for express warranties that he makes about the property. The court abandoned this approach and imposed strict liability against the developer. They argued:

When a vendee buys a development house from an advertised model, as in a Levitt or in a comparable project, he clearly relies on the skill of the developer and on its implied representation that the house will be erected in reasonably workman-like manner and will be reasonably fit for habitation. He has no architect or other professional advisor of his own, he has no real competency to inspect on his own, his actual examination is, in the nature of things, largely superficial, and his opportunity for obtaining meaningful protective changes in the conveyancing documents prepared by the builder vendor is negligible.

8.3.3 Sales-Service

To date the doctrine of strict liability has not yet reached the pure service-type case. Thus the plumber who does defective work is generally liable only for negligence. Similarly the architect who has failed to supervise the contractor properly can be sued only for negligence. He will not be liable for the defective result, absent negligence.

There are, however, hybrid cases that involve both a service and a product, and it becomes difficult to pigeonhole the case. Two cases—*Newmark v. Gimbel's, Inc.* [12] and *Magrine v. Krasnica* [13]—illustrate the scope of the problem. In *Newmark* the plaintiff was a customer of Gimbel's beauty parlor. One day the beautician suggested the use of a certain permanent wave solution. Following the use of the solution, the plaintiff suffered severe reddening of the scalp and loss of hair. The question before the court was whether the defendant should be liable on the basis of strict liability for the sale of the permanent wave solution. Gimbel's argued that it was involved in performing beautician services and could thus be liable only for negligence. According to the defendant it had not "sold" the permanent wave solution; it had only used it as part of its service.

In *Magrine* a patient of defendant-dentist was injured when a hypodermic needle being used, concededly with due care, to administer a local anesthetic, broke off in his gum or jaw. The break resulted from a latent defect in the needle. The plaintiff here, too, made the argument that the defendant-dentist should be strictly liable for the injuries caused by the defective needle. The defendant's position was that he was not involved in "selling" the needle but was merely using it for the performance of a service. He thus contended that he should be judged by a negligence standard. Since he acted reasonably, no liability should attach.

It should come as no surprise to the reader that the court imposed strict liability against Gimbel's for the use of the permanent wave solution but held the dentist to a negligence standard only and refused the imposition of strict liability. Articulating a rationale for the distinction is somewhat more difficult. The court offered the following explanation:

Defendants suggest that there is no doctrinal basis for distinguishing the services rendered by a beauty parlor operator from those rendered by a dentist or a doctor, and that consequently the liability of all three should be tested by the same principles. On the contrary there is a vast difference in the relationships. The beautician is engaged in a commercial enterprise; the dentist and doctor in a profession. The former caters publicly not to a need but to a form of aesthetic convenience or luxury, involving the rendition of non-professional services and the application of products for which a charge is made. The dentist or doctor does not and cannot advertise for patients; the demand for his services stems from a felt necessity of the patient. In response to such a call the doctor, and to a somewhat lesser degree the dentist, exercises his best judgment in diagnosing the patient's ailment or disability, prescribing and sometimes furnishing medicines or other methods of treatment which he believes, and in some measure hopes, will relieve or cure the condition. His performance is not mechanical or routine because each patient requires individual study and formulation of an informed judgment as to the physical or mental disability or condition presented, and the course of treatment needed. Neither medicine nor dentistry is an exact science; there is no implied warranty of cure or relief. There is no representation of infallibility and such professional men should not be held to such a degree of perfection. There is no guaranty that the diagnosis is correct. Such men are not producers or sellers of property in any reasonably acceptable sense of the term. In a primary sense they furnish services in the form of an opinion of the patient's condition based upon their experienced analysis of the objective and subjective complaints, and in the form of recommended and, at times, personally administered medicines and treatment. Compare, Gagne v. Bertran, 43 Cal. 2d 481, 275, P.2d 15 (1954). Practitioners of such callings, licensed by the State to practice after years of study and preparation, must be deemed to have a special and essential role in our society, that of studying our physical and mental ills and ways to alleviate or cure them, and that of applying their knowledge, empirical judgment and skill in an effort to diagnose and then to relieve or to cure the ailment of a particular patient. Thus their paramount function—the essence of their function—ought to be regarded as the furnishing of opinions and services. Their unique status and the rendition of these *sui generis* services bear such a necessary and intimate relationship to public health and welfare that their obligation ought to be grounded and expressed in a duty to exercise reasonable competence and care toward their patients. In our judgment, the nature of the services, the utility of and the need for them, involving as they do, the health and even survival of many people, are so important to the general welfare as to outweigh in the policy scale any need for the imposition on dentists and doctors of the rules of strict liability in tort.

It thus appears that whether a sales-service combination is treated as a "sale" and subject to strict liability or as a "service" subject only to negligence law depends on a whole host of policy factors that look toward whether society believes it is fair to impose the higher standard of strict liability on the defendant. As we move across the spectrum and approach the pure-service defendant, where no product is involved, liability is limited to the negligence doctrine.

8.3.4 Sellers of Used Products

The question of whether strict liability applies to the sale of used products is most difficult. To the extent that products liability law responds to the disappointed expectations of the consumer, it is clear that reasonable consumers would have adjusted their expectations vis-à-vis used products. Consumers simply don't expect product performance of a used product to match that of a new one. On the other hand the concept of unreasonable danger responds to the question of the defectiveness of the product at the time of sale. It may very well be that a used product is defective and unreasonably dangerous at the time of sale. In an earlier discussion we focused on the role of disclaimers with regard to the sale of new products. It was there indicated that many courts have refused to recognize the legal validity of disclaimers on the grounds that they violate public policy. The disclaimer question with regard to used products is much more difficult. In a market with substantial elasticity where the consumer can and normally does bargain hard for price and quality, there is much to be said for permitting the disclaimer to have legal effect.

To date, the several cases that have dealt with the used-product question have not given clear guidelines so that we can predict how the courts will act. In *Cornelius v. Bay Motors, Inc.* [14] the question was raised whether strict liability would apply to a seven-year-old Valiant automobile with 50,000 miles on it. On the very day on which the car was purchased from the used car dealer, the plaintiff was involved in causing a rear-end collision owing to the failure of the car's brakes. The accident was caused because the "rubber-cups" in the master brake cylinder had become deteriorated and the brake fluid leaked out. The seller had contended that he had checked the car out and that there was no visible evidence of brake difficulty at the time of sale. A mechanic testified that, once rubber cups start to leak, their condition has so deteriorated that complete failure and loss of braking capacity occurs rapidly. It is thus probable in this case that liability would not attach if negligence must be made out, since the used car dealer may have acted reasonably in inspecting the car. Only under a strict liability theory does the plaintiff have any hope of recovery.

In *Cornelius* the court held that the jury instruction defining a product as "unreasonably dangerous" only if it failed to meet the expectations of the ordinary consumer was proper. The court thus held that the proper question was:

whether an ordinary purchaser of a seven year old used car would contemplate that the materials used in the construction of such a car could have crystallized [sic] or deteriorated to the point that such materials might break or collapse at any time.

Interestingly enough, the jury in this case found for the defendant. It thus gave emphasis to the consumer expectation aspect of products liability law, while denigrating the importance of the very real danger to the consumer arising from a car with defective brakes.

An intermediate position was taken by the court in *Realmuto v. Straub Motors* [15] in which the court avoided the question of whether strict liability ought to be applied against the seller of used cars. Instead the court applied strict liability for defective work repairs done by the dealer on the used vehicle prior to sale. This would suggest a general negligence standard for defects that were not repaired by the dealer and a strict liability standard for work done by the dealer on the car prior to sale.

Finally, in *Turner v. International Harvester Company* [16] the court took a clear stand in favor of strict liability for used product sales. Plaintiff in this case was killed when the cab of a truck, which he had purchased used, fell on him. It is not clear, from the opinion, whether the failure of the latch or counterbalance resulted from a production or design problem. The court held that it would be relevant to inquire whether the used product was unreasonably dangerous vis-à-vis this particular buyer. The court reasoned that:

Use of the "unreasonably dangerous" standard, whether viewed from the general statement of the rule or the definition of a dangerous condition, permits a court to look both at the sophistication of the injured purchaser and the reasonable expectations of the seller to determine whether the strict liability rule should be applied.

Looking at the used automobile situation, one can readily envision an antique car buff or "hot rod" enthusiast purchasing a car which is defective in many respects and where the relationship between the buyer and seller is such that both reasonably expect that all aspects of the automobile will be separately appraised and all defects corrected by the purchaser. . . .

Even with respect to the sale of a truck, the actual situation of the parties to the contract may present a question. A used truck purchased by a large trucking company known by both buyer and seller to have extensive repair facilities might be expected to undergo great scrutiny only by the buyer, while a similar truck purchased by a merchant to make his retail deliveries might not reasonably be expected to be so examined unless special circumstances exist. Thus, in some circumstances the relationship of the parties and apparent sophistication of the purchaser might indicate that the defect did not present an unreasonable danger to the particular purchaser as user of the product. In others the purchaser's conduct in not discovering or correcting a defect which a reasonable person of his background and experience should have corrected might warrant a finding that the defect was not unreasonably dangerous. . . . Thus, in these unusual cases the "unreasonably dangerous" qualification has a very practical use in stating the rule for strict liability in tort. With this "unreasonably dangerous" element intact, the Restatement rule is as applicable to the sale of a used product as to the sale of a new product.

It is clear that the courts are struggling with the role of strict liability with regard to used products. Much will depend on whether courts opt for a consumer expectation test or one based on unreasonable danger (safety test) as the predicate for products liability recovery. One can safely say that only the future will tell whether used products will be within the ambit of strict products liability.

8.4   THE INDUSTRIAL ACCIDENT

8.4.1   Common-Law Background

The industrial accident provides the background for an interesting interplay between accident compensation systems. It is necessary first to describe the plight of the employee who suffered a job-related injury at the turn of the century [17].

An employer at common law was held to several narrowly defined duties of care for the protection of his workers. An employer had to use reasonable care in providing both a safe place to work and adequate tools and appliances. He had a duty to warn his servants of those dangers with which they might conceivably be unacquainted and to promulgate and enforce rules in furtherance of employee safety. An employer also had an obligation to provide a suitable number of "fellow servants" (i.e., coemployees), although he was not held liable for the negligent conduct of an employee's fellow workers. The wrongdoing of a coemployee that led to an employee's injury operated to absolve the employer of liability. This is known as the "fellow-servant rule."

As an incontrovertible element of the employment contract an employee was held to have relieved his employer of liability for most work-related hazards not covered by the employer's common-law duties. Despite the lack of any conscious, voluntary choice on the part of an employee to subject himself to an occupational hazard, he had no right to collect for an injury arising from dangers normally inherent in his employment. An employee, by his decision to remain employed, despite knowledge of industrial hazards, implicitly absolved his employer of the common-law obligations to safeguard against such hazards.

Even when an employee's injury was clearly related to dereliction of his employer's common-law duty, there was no guarantee of compensation. The employee might find his recovery barred by the doctrine of contributory negligence, whereby his own negligence, however slight, destroyed his right to recover compensation from the more negligent employer. Or the employee's cause of action for his employer's violation of a duty could be defeated by the employer's defense of "voluntary assumption of the risk." Under this doctrine an employee was held to have "consented" to any negligence on the part of his employer—even that arising from breach of common-law duties—by choosing to remain employed.

The hardship on the workman was readily apparent. Even in cases where he had not been contributorily negligent, an employee had to overcome the presumption that he had impliedly consented to the injury by demonstrating that the employer had behaved willfully or wantonly or had created false illusions of safety on which the employee had relied. The three wicked sisters of the common law—the fellow-servant rule, contributory negligence, and voluntary assumption of the risk—effectively operated to shift the ultimate burden of a work-related injury from the employer to the party least able to bear the loss—the injured workman.

8.4.2 Workmen's Compensation

The proliferation of uncompensated occupational injuries mandated nothing short of a comprehensive solution. The reallocation of the burden of employee injury from the employee to the enterprise required a system of loss distribution whereby the economic burdens of such injury would be treated as a fixed cost of doing business and assimilated into the general costs of production. At the same time the distribution mechanism would have to strike a just balance between the workman, who had a right to some fair compensation for workplace injuries, and the employer, who had a right to pay only his fair share of work-related losses.

The solution settled upon was "workmen's compensation"—a system of no-fault compensation in which the employer would take out insurance coverage that would pay limited amounts to a worker who had sustained a "work-related" injury. No proof of employer negligence would be required; the payment of compensation would be determined by an evaluation of the employee's status at the time of his injury rather than an evaluation of the employer's fault. The existence of an employer-employee relationship, in the course of which a work-related injury was sustained, thus became the threshold determinant for payment of a workmen's compensation award.

For the employee the enactment of workmen's compensation statutes by the states was a welcome improvement over the private-law system that required an employee to affirmatively prove negligence on the part of his employer to recover. The long delays inherent in the private lawsuit as the mechanism for employee compensation were all but eliminated by the insurance claim provisions of the new statutes. These statutes also eliminated the three defenses—the fellow-servant rule, contributory negligence, and voluntary assumption of the risk—that had so effectively barred an employee's recovery under negligence theories, since degree of fault was no longer at issue.

In return for the speedy adjudication of claims and diminished proof of eligibility under the workmen's compensation statutes, the employee was forced to waive his common-law right to sue the employer for work-related injuries. A provision that workmen's compensation was to be the "exclusive remedy" for work-related injuries was incorporated in all the state statutes. Additionally, a ceiling was placed on the amount recoverable by the injured employee, the maximum recovery being fixed as a percentage of the average wage statewide, the percentage to be based on the degree of disability—an amount usually considerably less than a jury would have awarded as damages. The employee thus traded the possibility of a generous award after litigation for the assured recovery of a smaller amount under a workmen's compensation statute. The employer accepted the financial burden of a broadened statutory liability without proof of fault in exchange for a release from all common-law tort obligations of due care.

The workmen's compensation statutes in theory provide several practical advantages over the common-law system of recovery. The claim-recovery process, similar to that of private insurance contracts, avoids the cost and delay characteristic of the private lawsuit recovery mechanism. The funding for the loss distribution mechanism, accomplished by employers' periodic payments of premiums into a common fund from which compensation is paid, allows the cost of employee injuries to be figured into the ultimate cost of the product. The elimination of the possibility of a tort suit against an employer diminishes the friction that would normally occur between the adversary parties involved in a traditional lawsuit. Since the amount of the premium paid by the employer is related to the dollar value of the claims paid to his employees, the employer has, at least theoretically, a strong interest in providing a safe working environment. Moreover, the exclusiveness of the remedy against the employer generally does not preclude an employee's cause of action against a third party who in some way legally contributes to the employee's injury.

8.4.3   The Manufacturer as a Third-Party Defendant

Today the dissatisfaction with the workmen's compensation system is significant. First, the schedule of recovery for various kinds of injuries has been clearly recognized as inadequate. Second, the plaintiff at best recovers only a portion of his out-of-pocket losses. There is no recovery at all for the most significant dollar amount that normally graces a tort action—pain and suffering. This noneconomic, but very real, loss is totally uncompensated for in a workmen's compensation action.

In an industrial setting where a possible defective product is involved the focus naturally turns to the manufacturer of that product as a third-party defendant. Since the duty of the product manufacturer is separate and apart from that of the employer, there is no impediment to an action's being brought by an employee for products liability against the manufacturer. In this action the plaintiff would not be limited to workmen's compensation but would have available to him the full panoply of tort damages.

Where it is determined that the manufacturer did in fact sell a defective product that caused the plaintiff-employee's injury, recovery has been allowed. It is, however, important to note several possible problems that arise in these kinds of cases. First, it must be recognized that the product (defective or not) has been placed in the hands of the employer. It is often the case that employers take liberties with heavy industrial machinery to make them more efficient. Safety guards may be removed or not installed. The machinery may be changed significantly to meet the employer's particular needs. In each instance a court will have to determine whether there existed an original defect that was the cause-in-fact and the proximate cause of the harm. This element of the case has been discussed at length in Chapter 6. Note that courts are not prone to deciding that the acts of employers are superseding causes. Thus a defect that existed at the time of sale and that helped contribute to the injury will not be disregarded simply because the employer added to the injury potential of the machine.

Second, there has been a continuing concern about the proper allocation of damages between the third-party defendant (the product manufacturer) and the employer. Where the employer has been guilty of negligence and his negligence has combined with the defect of the defendant-manufacturer to cause injury, the question arose whether it was fair to require the third-party defendant to pay the entire damages. Courts have taken differing positions [18]:

1. *Employer Subrogation Rule*—The employer stands in the shoes of the employee and is reimbursed for his workmen's compensation payments. The net effect of this rule is that the manufacturer-defendant carried the full burden of an industrial accident even though the injury was caused by the combination of the employer's negligence and the defective product. This method provides for a free ride for the workmen's compensation system.

2. *Employer Shares in Cost to the Amount of Workmen's Compensation*— Under what has become known as the Pennsylvania rule the employer contributes as he normally would when an industrial accident takes place. If, however, the injury was due to the employer's negligence as well, the plaintiff's recovery against the defendant product manufacturer is reduced by the amount that plaintiff has already recovered under workmen's compensation. This means that the employer shares in the loss up to the amount of his workmen's compensation liability. The Pennsylvania rule has been extolled because:

[T]he Pennsylvania rule . . . (1) . . . preserves the economics of the workmen's compensation system; (2) . . . effectuates the policy of contribution . . . (3) . . . harmonizes the compensation law with the law of contribution and (4) . . . protects the non-employer tortfeasor from the possible gross inequity of carrying the whole liability for wrongs caused in perhaps major part by the employer tortfeasor [19].

3. *Fault Apportionment between the Defendants*—The most recent resolution of this problem has been to apply the principle of contribution between the third-party defendant and the employer. Thus, if the manufacturer were held liable for an employee's injuries, he would be able to recoup at least part of his losses from the negligent employer on the basis of an allocation of fault between the parties. Although this solution is fair, it does place the employer in a precarious position. He now is no longer under the safe umbrella of workmen's compensation for an industrial accident. If an accident results, in part, from the employer's fault, he will pay damages up to the percentage allocation of fault between himself and the manufacturer [20].

A study of the nuances that militate either in favor of or against any of these solutions is beyond this work. The three basic approaches do, however, indicate how the law has sought to deal with a most intractable problem. It also gives evidence of how an inadequate compensation system (workmen's compensation) can place enormous pressure for compensation on another system designed to compensate for tortious injury (products liability). Indeed some of the most far-reaching products liability decisions have occurred in the industrial accident setting. Clearly, the enactment of the Occupational Safety and Health Act (OSHA) in 1972 has added another dimension to the problem. Whether or not an employer has met the requisite OSHA standards and what effect this may have in regard to an employer's liability has not yet been extensively explored by the courts.

Courts, realizing that the plaintiff was without an adequate remedy against his employer, have stretched the law to provide an action against the manufacturer. Whether this is desirable or not is a matter of opinion. The phenomenon is very real and must give the reader pause when attempting to extrapolate principles from industrial accident cases to consumer product cases.

8.5 INDEMNIFICATION AND CONTRIBUTION

The potential liability of all members of the distributive chain in a products liability action based on implied warranty or strict liability has already been noted in this chapter. The umbrella of liability can cover component-parts manufacturers, assemblers, wholesalers, distributors, retailers, and in some cases suppliers of basic materials from which the product is made. In each instance it is necessary to prove that the product left the hands of the given defendant in a defective condition, unreasonably dangerous to the ultimate user or consumer. It should be clear, however, that in most instances the defect was created by one of these parties only. Thus, for example, if a component-parts manufacturer sold the part in a defective condition to the assembler and there was no way for the assembler to discover the defect by using normal inspection procedures, it is clear, simply as a matter of equity, where liability ought to lie. The law has not been insensitive to these equities, and where a defendant is required to pay the plaintiff for selling a defective product that has passed into his hands without any ability on his part to discover the defect, the defendant who was required to pay the plaintiff for his damages may seek full recovery from the party who sold him the product. This is known as indemnification. Ultimately, the bill will be paid by the defendant who was actually responsible for creating the defect in the product.

In some instances the plaintiff may suffer injury as a result of the combination of the action of a defective product and a negligent defendant. Thus, for example, when a plaintiff is injured by a speeding driver whose brakes failed when he attempted to stop, the plaintiff is entitled to recover the entirety of his damages from either the manufacturer of the car, if the defect in brakes was unreasonably dangerous, or from the driver of the car because of his negligence.

Where the liability of both parties is due to negligence, most jurisdictions will permit contribution between joint tortfeasors [21]. This means that, if one party has been compelled to pay the entire amount, the other negligent party is required to contribute a share of the damages. The exact formula for sharing differs among the states, but the rule of contribution generally governs. Where one party is liable for strict liability and the other for negligence, it is not yet clear that the normal rules for contribution will govern. Case law is as yet unclear about how this problem will be resolved [22]. The better view is, however, that the parties should share the losses and that the formula for apportionment should be based on some assessment of fault between them. To be sure, it is somewhat difficult to compare the fault of the "strict liability" (absence of fault) defendant with the fault of the negligent defendant. In our earlier discussion of comparative fault we indicated that, although equitable apportionment is somewhat awkward, it can be accomplished by assessing fault in proportion to the relative seriousness of each defendant's actions. That same resolution appears workable in the contribution cases [23].

CHAPTER 9

Proving a Products Liability Case— The Engineer's Perspective

9.1 DECIDING ON A LAWSUIT—THE EXPERT AS A RESOURCE

Whether a products liability lawsuit is even warranted is a decision that can be made intelligently by counsel only after the expert has identified and examined the evidence. Only in few instances does the surface appearance of the tangible evidence speak unambiguously to the attorney. Even then, only the expert can properly assess whether more detailed examination and testing are indicated.

While counsel must guide the expert concerning the feasible economic limits of his investigation, the expert must also guide counsel, especially in the initial stages of investigation, in regard to the reasonable degree of certainty concerning what may or may not be anticipated. This requires that the expert be considered a resource from the beginning of litigation rather than a tool to be used later in the trial to fill an evidentiary gap. A more appropriate view of the expert in products liability litigation is as a coequal partner with counsel from the moment they agree to undertake the lawsuit. Once this partnership is entered into, the expert's role should expand to encompass the direction that discovery procedures will take. He must synthesize all the evidence, nontechnical as well as technical, and he must appropriately control and care for the physical evidence.

If, for example, the issues of defect and causation hinge on whether a particular part of a product failed by fatigue or by the application of a single load, the physical evidence is crucial. But if the broken parts have been in a junk yard for three years, exposed to the elements, and the fracture surfaces have not only corroded but also have been knocked about, any probative value the evidence may have had has most certainly been lost. Such evidence leads only to the sort of speculation that serves *no* useful purpose for *either* side in confronting the real issues. It is only the careful expert who can guide counsel and provide the proper considerations for control and preservation of the physical evidence.

In very few instances, however, is the expert's judgment based solely on technical evidence. His conclusions, more often than not, are a composite judgment based on the physical evidence, the circumstances surrounding the incident, his understanding of the product and its use, and finally on his technologically grounded intuitive sense. In synthesizing a conclusion, the expert must not only reach the conclusion that is most probable, but he must also balance the conclusion against other possibilities that he considers less probable. This is the art form of the technologist.

For example, in a case centering around the design of a 30-year-old steel pickling machine, one issue was whether or not it was possible for a link on a partially corroded chain to have engaged a lug projecting from a rack. The rack had overturned during the operation of the machine and had killed an employee. At the time of the accident the machine had 16 chains. The 4 chains being used with the particular rack had not been identified, but all 16 were removed and stored in a garage for some years. The rack was never removed from service or identified. One of the plaintiff's experts, a safety expert, did not examine the chains but merely concluded, retrospectively, that the design was faulty because a man had been killed. The plaintiff's second expert examined only 1 of the 16 chains—not necessarily one of the ones on the rack—and concluded that one link of this chain had corroded to the point where it could have engaged a lug on a rack. If the experts had, at the very least, examined all the chains to determine how many oversized links there were, they might have been able to give some reasonable probabilities to reinforce the plaintiff's contention that an oversized link had caused the rack to tip. As it was, the limited evidence offered for the theory of faulty design—one link on one chain—could not be advanced as the most probable cause of the accident when balanced against the other possible explanations suggested by the defense. To compound the difficulty, the plaintiff's experts had not considered these other possible causes in reaching their conclusions. Needless to say, the plaintiff lost. It is our contention that the expert, the counsel, and the court must all agree that the appropriate role for the expert is to take a global view of the problems of identifying an unreasonably dangerous defect and establishing causation. Cases such as this one are improperly handled, in our opinion, not necessarily because of the incompetence of the expert, but rather because of the traditionally limited role that has been assigned to him.

9.2 BALANCING PROBABILITIES

Realistically speaking, the technological expert usually cannot bring an absolute sense of precision to his opinions. It must be recognized that any product is a compromise between quantifiable aspects of its design and specifications and the uncertainties of actual performance of the product in the environment of use. This gap is usually closed by the safety factor, but this focuses precisely on the inherent uncertainties in any design (see Figure 9-1). Thus, when a product is challenged as defective and unreasonably dangerous, the issue is often focused in this band of uncertainty between the quantifiable engineering parameters and the performance of the product in the environment of its use. This band of uncertainty is inherent in establishing a production defect just as it is in establishing a design defect, and it arises in the litigation of both the defect and causation issues. It is unreason-

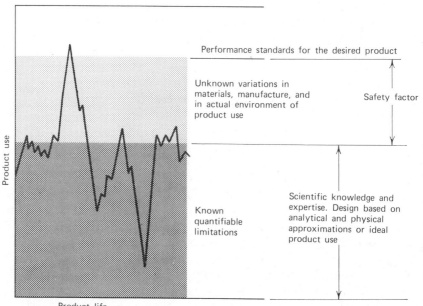

Figure 9-1.   Product design results from combining what can be quantified with the uncertainties in actual product use.

able to expect an expert to bring more certainty to his conclusions of defect and causation than existed in the original engineering of the product.

To shatter the myth of the absolute scientific certainty of the expert's conclusions, it is essential that counsel question the expert in such a way that his synthesizing process will be completely revealed to the jury. The function of the expert is to use his evaluative sense to assess complex issues. Thus the traditional practice of basing an opinion on an entire set of facts presented as if the probability of their truth were 100 percent raises a serious question about the validity of the expert's opinion. To counter, the opposing side asks the expert to discount one or more of the facts and thereby is assigning a zero percent probability of truth to those facts. This approach, rather than demonstrating the real-world probabilities that result in sensitively balanced intermediate positions inherent in a valid decision-making process, distorts the process by giving an aura of unreality to any opinion. Cross-examination under this unrealistic approach may result in the expert's having to draw the opposite conclusion when he is asked to discount a sufficient number of facts. This result has no firmer basis than the original conclusion if all facts are assumed at either zero percent or 100 percent certainty.

The problem just described is serious enough when one is faced with expert testimony from a single technical discipline. When the litigation necessarily involves the interrelationship between two or more technical disciplines, the failure to reveal the probabilistic nature of the decision-making process compounds the fault, for now each discipline builds on the conclusions of the other, using unrealistic probability levels in support of the other discipline's conclusions. Unless the synthesizing process is completely and coherently revealed in the courtroom, the jury may indulge in a process of evaluating the expert testimony, probably by half-believing some of the opinion and discarding the rest. The juries are then left to *their own devices* in conjuring up a scientific theory that lies somewhere between the theory of the plaintiff's expert and the theory of the defendant's expert. The implication of this process is that the truth rests somewhere between zero percent and 100 percent credibility, and the jury exercises the normal evaluative role that it undertakes when it evaluates any key testimony. This assumption must be resisted as inaccurate in cases involving expert testimony. The function of the expert is to evaluate the close case and bring *his evaluative sense* to difficult situations. The jury should then choose between the *competing expert evaluations* rather than formulate its own notion of the case as an amalgam of the testimony of the plaintiff's and the defendant's experts. If the jury is to assess the worth of testimony of competing experts, it *cannot* create its own theory of the case. Rather it should *evaluate* the competing expert evaluations and make an intelligent choice between them. This makes it all the more crucial that experts address themselves to real probabilities and to a sensitive evaluation of competing possibilities, rather than to the formulation of unrealistic positions. It should be carefully noted that what is suggested here is a refinement and an enhancement of the adversary system, rather than a weakening of its traditional role.

Juries are well equipped, as the triers of fact, to evaluate *human* behavior in judging the validity of testimony. When questions center around the *technological* behavior of a product, however, juries must rely on experts' interpretation of the evidence. This interpretation must be comprehensive enough to reveal how the expert reached his conclusions as well as demonstrate his perception of the probable certainties and uncertainties. Without a careful exposition of the process by which the expert reached his conclusions, it seems inevitable that the jury's evaluation will remain superficial and that the jury cannot probe the substantive questions that must be addressed in finding an unreasonably dangerous defect or establishing causation.

Yet regardless of how well an expert addresses himself to real probabilities and to sensitive evaluation of competing possibilities, there remains the major question of whether any layman can bring the necessary evaluative sense to the litigation process when complex technological data are involved. Both the legal and technological communities will have to give serious consideration to this problem. In a later section we suggest some changes in the litigation structure that can enhance the ability of the layman to focus on technological issues.

9.3   THE ROLE OF THE EXPERT

The role of the expert can be described as that of a resource, not a tool, as a coequal partner with counsel, not as a filler of an evidentiary gap. But who is the expert? He must understand the law sufficiently to permit his judgment of technical issues to reflect the proper perspective for advancing an opinion of unreasonably dangerous defect. He must be sufficiently expert to perceive the scope of the inquiry necessary during discovery as well as in further testing and evaluating of the evidence. The expert should not only provide guidance for counsel, but when necessary he must undertake self-education prior to trial in those aspects of the particular technology with which he is unfamiliar.

The expert in a products liability case must address the evidentiary elements necessary to establish or refute the defect and unreasonable-danger criteria and the causation issue. While a technological expert can often easily trace a product's failure or malfunction to either manufacture or design, this alone is generally insufficient to establish liability. Thus, in addition to purely technjcal matters, both parties' experts must weigh the general societal values reflected in risk and utility considerations. For example, if a production defect is alleged, experts must address the following elements:

1. Identification of the flaw or flaws relative to manufacturing or physical property standards.
2. Evidence that the product's failure or malfunction is directly attributable to the flaws.
3. The relationship of the failure or malfunction to the product's expected performance standards.
4. The causal link between the failure or malfunction and the injury.

Similarly, a design defect case would require that the experts consider the following:

1. The identification of the design flaw or flaws that occasioned the injury.
2. The enumeration of alternative design features proposed to reduce the danger.
3. The evaluation of these features relative to the expected performance standards of the product, as well as their effect on the product's subsequent usefulness and cost.
4. The comparison of this product with other similar products.
5. The causal link between the design deficiency and the injury.

Because of the scope of evidentiary material implicit in these delineations, a single expert may not possess the requisite expertise to evaluate each element properly. It is not unreasonable, therefore, to suppose that a number of individuals with distinct areas of expertise may address the individual evidentiary elements of proof. Each side must, however, employ at least one expert who is capable of synthesizing the diverse elements necessary to reach the ultimate legal conclusions. Whether or not the expert is permitted to explicitly state the conclusions of defect, unreasonable danger, and causation is not critical as long as the thrust and scope of his investigation and testimony reflect an understanding of the legal criteria.

Thus an expert who is called solely to testify that a proposed design alternative would have prevented an accident is not fulfilling the expert's critical role. Nonetheless, the authors' examination of trial transcripts [1] reveals that the view of an unreasonably dangerous and defective condition routinely employed by experts in products litigation has been narrow in focus. While a few courts have recognized that a risk-utility trade-off is not merely preferable but indispensable to adjudication of the strict liability question, the common approach has been the appraisal of a single factor, such as the availability of some alternative or the undisputed fact that the product caused the injury. Indeed, the area of expertise of the person who testifies limits the range of evidence that he can present and his role in the trial format. The arrival of a safety expert in the courtroom often foreshadows a statement that the product is defective and unreasonably dangerous solely because it caused an injury. All too often the metallurgist's presence heralds the discovery of "cracks" or "porous conditions," which the jury is invited to regard as sufficient evidence of defectiveness (with the further implication of unreasonable danger). And the too-frequent surfacing of the ubiquitous journeyman expert who will fashion his credentials as well as his conclusions "to fit the crime" is lamentably predictive of a superficial conclusion.

There is little indication that current practice encourages the selection of an expert who is capable of evaluating the risk-utility elements that constitute factors in the unreasonably dangerous and defective condition test. Yet among all possible witnesses, only the appropriate technological expert can speak to these broad questions.

9.4   IDENTIFICATION AND QUALIFICATION OF THE APPROPRIATE WITNESS

A determination of the expertise necessary for a given case should be based on the character of the elements of proof to be addressed. Certain elements may be primarily quantitative, for example, defining a production flaw as a deviation from manufacturing standards or isolating the absence of a guard as a design flaw. Some cases may progress from the more quantitative factors to those involving substantial qualitative value judgments, requiring a broader background for an expert judgment. For example, in judging the adequacy of a product's performance within the context of the consumer's justified expectations, the expert must demonstrate a capacity to define or delineate standards of performance that may encompass subjective as well as objective judgmental criteria. The expert's evaluation of economic and technological trade-offs would result in such standards. This expanded capability is also required of the expert who must testify in design defect cases about the effect of proposed design alterations on the product's usefulness and economic viability. As the qualitative dimension of the testimony increases, so does the need for an expert with a more extensive educational and experiential background.

Because the scope of the technological expert's testimony in addressing the unreasonably dangerous defect question ranges from quantitative matters of a purely technological nature to the more qualitative dimensions of risk and utility, the technological expert is fundamentally distinguished from, for example, the medical expert and thus is more difficult to identify. This difficulty is compounded by the broad range of technological expertise available. Depending on the issue, the appropriate expert may be selected from a range that includes auto mechanics, mechanical engineers, bakers, and home economists. The practice of using the medical expert as a prototype for establishing qualifications of experts arises from the widespread use of medical testimony in litigation. There is, however, no justification for using criteria appropriate only to the medical profession. Whether the medical expert speaks to questions of improper treatment procedures or to questions of medical cause of the injury, his qualitative judgments generally do not involve issues of broad social significance. The questions of an injured party's past trauma and prognosis are relevant only to the specific medical case at issue, and the expert opinion is therefore focused precisely on the variables of the individual case. Because the scope of the medical expert's testimony is more easily identifiable than that of the technological expert, qualifications of the appropriate technological expert are less readily categorized.

Rarely will there be a precise matching of the expert's prior education and experience and the particular expertise needed in a given situation. Consequently, the expert must be able and, if necessary, must have undertaken sufficient self-education to enable him to address the particular aspects of a given problem. The required special knowledge would ordinarily be acquired by ad hoc education undertaken for specific litigation. Such self-education may be the essential ingredient in establishing a given expert's qualifications to address the relevant questions.

The capacity for this training must be consistent with the expert's background. In determining whether a technological witness possesses the requisite capacity for self-education, the pervasive discipline underlying a given issue must be identified. If that discipline falls within the witness's general qualifications, the technologist may readily acquire the additional knowledge, data, and skill from qualified sources. Sources available to the technologist include such materials as drawings and specifications, methods of manufacturing a product, and literature pertinent to the particular product and similar products. Additionally, he would systematically observe the product and similar products in use and in the environment of use. To the extent necessary, he would acquire from other disciplines the additional information necessary to address adequately the questions of defect and causation. If, however, in the process of seeking self-education, the technologist discovers that the pervasive discipline involved is not within his basic qualifications, he would defer to someone more qualified.

The self-education requirement reveals another and perhaps more intrinsic difference between the technological expert and the medical expert: adaptability of expertise. For example, if an injury is associated with a neurological function, a physician whose principal experience has been in hematology would most likely be an inappropriate witness. On the other hand, an engineer with experience in the electromechanical machinery of steel plants may well be qualified to address the technical aspects of a carton-stacking machine in a soft drink bottling plant, because the basic principles underlying electromechanical machinery design inhere in both products. While the particular function of such components as shafts, bearings, gears, switches, controls, and hydraulic cylinders may differ, the basic considerations in the design of these elements are identical. More fundamentally, the principles of stress analysis, material behavior, heat transfer, fluid flow, electricity, and thermodynamics pervade the design of all technological devices. In contrast, the physician specializing in hematology would not be equally capable of addressing questions associated with a neurological injury, simply because no comparable unifying principles have yet been identified in human physiology. It is not suggested that a hematologist could not acquire the requisite expertise in neurological medicine, but the self-education necessary for such an undertaking would not be feasible. Therefore, qualification of the medical expert must of necessity generally be defined within the context of a narrow specialty. On the other hand, when the issue is the absence of a guard at the point of operation in a carton-stacking machine, the expert who is familiar with steel plant machinery (including safety features) may readily be capable of applying his expertise to a carton-stacking machine in a bottling plant. Having established his mastery of the underlying technological principles, the expert needs to demonstrate only his acquisition of special knowledge relating to the peculiarities of the particular product.

Thus, because of the necessarily broad scope of the technologist's testimony and the adaptability of technological expertise (which makes impossible a precise, readily discernible correlation between product type and appropriate expertise), the identification and qualification of the technological expert present difficulties. We have suggested, however, that the critical determinants of the expert's qualifications are in fact the *precise technical issues* in controversy in the litigation. The appropriate medical expert can be selected with relative ease because medical issues are generally specifically formulated. If technical issues are defined with comparable precision, technological experts can be identified and qualified with greater certitude than is presently possible. In part the necessity for exact delineation of the technical issue arises from the difficulty of assessing the appropriateness of the broad range of skills, education, and experience offered in support of the qualifications of a potential witness. Viewing the qualification of the expert from the perspective of precisely drawn technical issues, the court could more readily determine the relevance of a given expertise to the particular situation.

To continue with the illustration of the expert on steel plant machinery, in a case involving carton-stacking machines this expert need not qualify solely on the basis of specific experience in the design of carton-stacking machines if the issues are, for example: (a) the technical feasibility of a protective device at the machine's point of operation; (b) an evaluation of the protective device relative to the machine's expected performance standards; (c) the safety device's effect on the machine's subsequent usefulness and cost; and (d) the causal link between the design deficiency and the injury. Because of the generic similarity in considerations of the efficacy and feasibility of safety features a person with basic expertise in machine design may, upon demonstrating the appropriate self-education, qualify to speak to these issues. An essential element of this self-education would be familiarization with the operation of the bottling plant and the carton-stacking machine's role within the plant. This process should include an examination of the plant environment and of the employer's expectations of the machine operators and a determination of whether the machine is being used as anticipated.

Although this discussion has focused on experts in design defect cases, the considerations in identifying and selecting experts for production defect cases are substantially analogous. Additionally, this approach to establishing qualifications recognizes the variety of backgrounds, skills, and experience that potential witnesses will offer in support of their expertise in both production and design defect cases. Consequently, the suggested premises provide a viable basis from which to formulate more appropriate guidelines for the selection and qualification of the technological expert in products liability litigation.

9.5 ASKING THE RIGHT QUESTIONS

What follows will demonstrate that the foregoing suggestions for a comprehensive role for the expert in defining and shaping a products liability case are not merely theoretical. The following five examples demonstrate the searching inquiry that an expert must undertake before he can truly qualify himself to testify in a products liability action.

We begin with a case already examined in our discussion of defect and unreasonable danger in Section 4.4. The focus here is the identification of the proper expert for the case and the nature of the inquiry he has to make.

Example 1. A printer-slotter machine prints labels and cuts and scores pieces of corrugated cardboard, which are later assembled as boxes. There are two sets of printing rolls for two-color operations. These rolls and the knives and scores are driven by a single motor located at the feed end of the machine. The feed and exit ends of the machine can be separated to change the dies, exposing two vertical "walls" of rolls on either side of an open passageway 30 inches wide. The machine separation mechanically disconnects the motor from both the rolls and the knives and scores at the exit end of the machine, but the rolls at the feed end can continue to operate. At the time of the injury the plaintiff-employee was walking through the open passageway to obtain a tool from the other side of the machine. All employees worked on a pay incentive plan that paid a lower hourly rate during machine downtime than during production time. The plaintiff had left the motor running so that an automatic washing attachment could clean the set of rollers at the feed end of the machine while his coemployee reset the knives and scores on the inactive exit end of the machine. His arm caught in the rolls rotating on the feed side of the passageway.

Plaintiff alleged as a design flaw the absence of a switch that would automatically disconnect power to the machine motor whenever the feed and exit ends of the machine were separated. If the jury is to determine that this constitutes a design defect, the plaintiff's expert must address the following issues:

1. Is such a switch technically feasible?
2. Are there alternative design alterations, such as a guard enclosing the rotating rolls, that could have reduced the likelihood of this injury?
3. How do all proposed alternative designs compare, relative to the following broad questions:
    a. Is it necessary to open the machine to change dies?
    b. Are there conditions that necessitate operation of the feed end when the machine is open?
    c. What were the time sequences involved in setting up, cleaning, and operating the machine within the plant's pay incentive scheme?
    d. What would be the additional costs of each proposed alternative?
    e. Could the proposed alternatives be circumvented with comparative ease and thus their effect be obviated?
    f. Would usefulness of this machine in this plant environment be diminished by addition of the proposed design changes?
4. Are there other machines, performing the same or similar functions, that utilize any of the proposed design modifications?
5. If there are such machines, are they used in similar or different environments; for example, is a pay incentive plan employed?
6. The location and direction of the rolls' rotation being known, what is the probability that the accident happened as described by the plaintiff?

The knowledge necessary to answer these questions provides guidelines for the qualifications required of those called to give expert testimony. Ideally, the expert here would be a design engineer with substantial experience in designing a wide range of electromechanical production equipment and, in particular, prior success in designing, manufacturing, installing, and maintaining printer-slotter machines in all environments. Additionally, the prospective witness would have experience in production planning and scheduling and in establishing piece-part work rates. This expertise would be the product of formal education and practical experience.

It is highly doubtful that such a person can be found in the defendant's employ let alone in the open market of available experts. Realistically, therefore, the appropriate expert is one who can demonstrate competence in the design of electromechanical production equipment (not necessarily printer-slotter machines). He must also exhibit, through education or diversity of experience, the capacity to acquire knowledge germane to an understanding of the functioning of the printer-slotter machine and its use within its specific environment. In addition to the more usual industrial experience, diversity of experience can include the ability to communicate, through teaching, both principles and practice of machine design. The expert's capacity for self-education must include not only the ability to understand the functioning of the particular machine but also the ability to assess comparative costs of alternative design modifications and the effect of these modifications on the machine's utility. Finally, he must show that he has undertaken this self-education.

Example 2.   A one-year-old tractor-trailer truck that had traveled 90,000 miles collided with an automobile. Following a slight impact between the truck's right front end and the car's left rear end, the truck swerved off the right side of the road, struck an embankment, and overturned. The plaintiff-truck driver reported that the right front end of the truck "dropped down" prior to its impact with the car. Examination of the truck following the accident revealed that the right front leaf spring was completely broken just behind the front shackle connection. "Gouge marks" were discovered across the surface of the main leaf of the spring in the vicinity of the fracture surface. Additionally, the microstructure of the steel on the fracture faces near the leaf surface appeared to be significantly different from that of the remaining material in the leaf. The plaintiff contended that these two conditions were manufacturing flaws. He alleged that the gouge marks resulted from using a worn mandrel in fabricating the front eye of the spring and that the aberrant microstructure near the surface resulted from improper quenching of the spring leaf during the heat-treating operation.

Plaintiff claimed that either or both of these flaws would contribute to premature spring failure, which would cause the truck to go out of control. Thus he insisted that the spring was defective and unreasonably dangerous. If these flaws are ultimately to rise to the level of unreasonably dangerous defects, the plaintiff's experts must address the following issues:

1. Did the gouge marks result from an aberration in the manufacturing process, or do these marks routinely appear in the standard manufacturing process?
2. Was the variation in the microstructure caused by an aberration in the quenching process, or does this variation routinely appear as a result of normal and expected decarburization near the surface?
3. If either or both of these conditions can be characterized as flaws, measured by manufacturing and physical property standards, were they the principal or most probable cause of the spring failure, either by fatigue or single-load impact?
4. Can the fracture of a truck spring after 90,000 miles of use in one year be classified as premature failure?
5. What circumstances caused the truck to go out of control?
   a. At what point in the chain of events was it most probable that the spring failed; that is, prior to impact with the car, upon impact with the car, or as a result of impact with the embankment?
   b. Could the failure of the spring prior to impact with the embankment cause the truck to go out of control?
   c. To what extent did driver error contribute to loss of control and the ultimate accident?

To address the first three questions, the expert must possess a background in metallurgy with demonstrable skill in the mechanics of failure of ferrous materials. He must also exhibit an understanding, through either experience or self-education, of the spring manufacturing process, to diagnose whether the alleged deficiencies arose from the production process. A witness qualified to address the question of premature failure, in the absence of established standards for the lifetime of truck leaf springs, would be familiar with the historical performance of similar springs. This could be a person who has actually been engaged in truck maintenance for a reasonable period of time. Alternatively, such evidence could be gathered from several sources and introduced by an expert with the requisite capacity to comprehend the nature of the question and interpret the data.

The issue of causation should be addressed by a person with a background in those aspects of mechanical engineering that would enable him to understand prior metallurgical testimony and integrate it with eyewitness accounts of the truck's behavior; he should also be able to assess the effect of spring failure on the driver's ability to control the truck. Clearly relevant to this task are an understanding of vehicle dynamics and the ability to estimate impact and failure forces on the truck's spring system. The prospective witness must also bring to the role of synthesizing these diverse evidentiary elements a breadth of experience or education sufficient to permit him to address the issues of unreasonably dangerous defect and probable cause.

Example 3. The allegedly defective product was a baby carriage that would fold upon manual release of a latch mechanism on one side of the supporting structure. At the time of the injury a child under a babysitter's care occupied the carriage. The babysitter was seated next to the carriage, rolling it back and forth, with her foot resting on one of the carriage wheels. Her foot inadvertently engaged the latch mechanism, causing it to release. The carriage collapsed, injuring the child.

The plaintiff alleged that the latch was improperly designed. For the jury to find the latch defective, the plaintiff's expert must address the following issues:

1. What are the basic considerations in the design of this type of latch mechanism, with particular reference to the following?
   a. Location.
   b. The direction and magnitude of the force necessary to activate.
   c. The trade-offs among complexity, redundancy, ease of use, and safety.
   d. The effectiveness of a possible guard around the latch mechanism.
2. Within design constraints would any alternative designs be less dangerous than the one in question?
3. What effect would those alternative designs have on the cost and utility of the baby carriage?
4. Are there baby carriages marketed with features similar to the proposed alternative designs?
5. If one of the proposed design alternatives had been incorporated in the carriage, would the injury have been prevented?

The general background required of an expert in this case would include knowledge of the geometry of linkages and the capacity to calculate the forces that would be applied to the linkages from external loading. These skills are necessary to design such diverse products as typewriters, card tables, automobile hood release mechanisms, and the Apollo rocket docking mechanism. Those whose knowledge is based on devices other than the carriage release latch could apply it to the latch problem only after undertaking a regimen of self-education.

The requisite self-education would entail review of alternative linkage and latch designs, as described in patent literature as well as in open literature. Calculation of all forces that realistically could have been applied to the latch mechanism is also required. Within the context of these additional studies the expert must acquire a reasonable capacity to assess the trade-offs among complexity of design, ease of use, and cost increment.

Example 4. A child's toy, used exclusively for indoor play, contained a glass surface of more than 36 square inches. While playing with this toy, the child stumbled and fell on the glass surface, breaking it and injuring his arm near his elbow.

If it is reasonably foreseeable that a child within the class of anticipated users would carry the toy around without recognizing or guarding against the danger that it poses if he should trip and fall, the product's standard of performance should be one that avoids an unreasonable danger to the child-user who merely acts as expected. Thus the principal issue at trial would be the reasonably expected standard of performance of a piece of glass on the surface of a child's toy. The expert would then have to address the following:

1. What is the reasonable limit of impact loads that the material used for the toy's surface should withstand when the toy is dropped?
2. What is the reasonable limit of impact loads that the material should withstand upon contact with a child's body?
3. If standards for performance of glass under these conditions exist, are they consistent with the standards established in (1) and (2)?
4. Does the present design of the glass surface generally fall within the performance parameters indicated either in (1) and (2) or in (3)?
5. If the data found in (1) and (2) are offered as the requisite standard, can the design parameters of the glass be adjusted to meet the suggested level of performance?
6. Is there any material that could be substituted for the glass that would meet the impact-load criteria as well or better?
7. What would be the cost and utility effects of constructing the toy from a material, either glass or a substitute, that meets the expected impact-load standard of performance?

The general background of the appropriate expert in this case would include experience in the behavior of materials under a variety of loading conditions. He should demonstrate knowledge of the manner in which loads and forces would be transmitted to the glass. Additionally, he should be able to devise, implement, and interpret reasonable experiments to adduce the impact-load capacity of various materials.

The self-education required in this instance could be extensive. Absent any standard test procedures or standards for the impact load that glass should absorb before fracture, the expert would have to select a procedure that would simulate the reasonably foreseeable occurrence—a child carrying the toy, falling, and striking his elbow on the glass surface. The expert should demonstrate that there is sufficient weight and dimension data on children with which to calculate the force of a falling child and that this could be simulated in a drop test. Additionally, he would indicate the method used to simulate the padding effect of the flesh over a child's bone.

In establishing the scope of his self-education, founded on a general knowledge of the underlying scientific principles, the expert should not only demonstrate his ability to address the specific technical issues but also demonstrate his capacity to describe expected standards of product performance. Also required, however, is an expertise suitable to confront the issues of ultimate cost, based on the design changes necessary to meet the proposed performance standards. While this expertise could be furnished by one person, the background necessary to address these questions would include general experience in the design and production of consumer goods. This might require a second expert.

Example 5.   A carrier, fastened by a metal bracket over the rear fender of a single-seat motorcycle, was used to hold packages being transported by the driver. While riding a motorcycle with a load securely fastened to the carrier, the plaintiff was forced off the road, and the cycle collided with a tree. Upon impact, the carrier broke loose; the loaded carrier struck the driver's back, increasing the severity of his injuries.

Preliminary examination of the supporting bracket revealed apparently extreme porosity within the structure of the metal at the fracture surface. The plaintiff suggested that this flawed condition caused the bracket to break upon the motorcycle's impact. This contention raises the issue of "crashworthiness," or the appropriate standards of performance for the carrier bracket. The points at issue may be delineated as follows:

1. Did the observed porosity weaken the metal to a degree significant enough to cause the bracket's failure?
2. Is the observed porosity a true flaw or inherent in the nature of that particular material?
3. Regardless of whether or not the porosity was a flaw, should the bracket be expected to withstand the conditions of the accident?

4. Was the package load supported by the carrier, which was attached to the bracket, within the anticipated range of loadings?

5. If the material used in the bracket was not flawed, could the bracket failure have been prevented by a design alteration in either structure or material?

6. If bracket failure could have been prevented only by redesign, what would be the alteration's effect on the bracket's subsequent usefulness and cost?

Whereas it is obvious that a person with a background in metallurgy is needed to answer the first two questions, his methods of obtaining the necessary data are essential elements in establishing his qualifications. Subjective observations of the metallic surface are insufficient. They must be supported by other indicia, such as examination of similar parts constructed out of the same material. Unless it is obvious and generally uncontroverted that porosity weakens the material, experimental testing would be needed to establish the effect of porosity on the material's strength or impact resistance.

To address the questions on the effect of redesigning the bracket, the witness should demonstrate a background in machine design, though not necessarily carrier bracket design. This would require the ability to estimate dynamic loadings and an understanding of the response of materials to those loadings. The witness must also exhibit the capacity to make reasonable judgments concerning the incremental cost changes and to assess the effect thereof on the vehicle's utility. Possibly no single expert can address both the basic metallurgical questions and the design questions; thus two experts might be required. One of them, probably the latter, would address the aspects of crashworthiness, elicited in the third and fourth questions, as elements of the product's expected standard of performance.

It is not suggested that any expert can bring to these matters qualifications that give him a greater intrinsic ability to answer questions of ultimate social significance than are brought to the courtroom by the jurors who must ultimately answer them. Nonetheless, the expert should state for the jury's benefit his appraisal of whether the bracket should be expected to withstand this and similar accident conditions, given the frequency of vehicular collision. This exercise is designed, not to intrude upon the factfinding function of the jury, but rather to place the expert's technological evidence within a context appropriate to a determination of whether or not an unreasonably dangerous and defective condition existed in the product. Although there may not be specific qualifications for considering the social dimension of expected performance standards, only the expert qualified to address the related issues of the product's economic viability and usefulness should be permitted to provide the context testimony of standards of performance.

9.6 QUALIFYING THE EXPERT—A THREE-STEP PROCESS

The purpose of qualifying a witness as a technological expert is to demonstrate his capacity to address subject matter beyond the ordinary experience of the layman, whether judge or juror. The ultimate objective of his testimony is to raise the level of comprehension of remotely perceived technological material. The problems involved in qualifying the witness to give expert testimony arise both from the scope of evidentiary material that may have to be addressed and the diverse range of technological skills offered by potential witnesses.

An attempt to formulate a rule that addresses the multifaceted complexities of qualification of the expert witness is found in rule 702 of the Federal Rules of Evidence: "If scientific, technical, or other specialized knowledge will assist the trier of fact to understand the evidence or to determine a fact in issue, a witness qualified as an expert by knowledge, skill, experience, training, or education, may testify thereto in the form of an opinion or otherwise." This rule recognizes the broad scope of evidentiary material and the diversity of technological skills that may be involved but in so doing provides minimal guidance to the court in exercising its discretionary power to pass on the qualification of a witness.

It is not feasible to formulate a single rule that is at once sufficiently broad and adequately precise to afford any meaningful assistance to the trial court. Instead, we have enunciated what we consider to be the basic premise for qualification of the technological witness: the precise delineation of the technical issues must provide the focus for the evaluation of the expert's credentials. The parties, counsel, and prospective witnesses will identify the technical issues before the court, perhaps most appropriately at a pretrial hearing, as the initial step in the qualification procedure. Thereupon the witnesses must demonstrate that their education, background, and skills, together with the necessary self-education, would permit them to couple their basic expertise with the technical questions at issue. This task is not easy. The court must apply a three-stage qualification procedure to the prospective expert witness:

- The court must initially satisfy itself that the pervasive discipline, as identified by a given issue, is within the scope of the background skills of the witness.
- The prospective witness must then persuade the court that the self-education that he has undertaken involves a legitimate application of his basic skills.
- The witness must finally demonstrate that he has been sufficiently

thorough in acquiring this self-education to achieve a level of qualification consistent with the technical issues that he will address.

The court may, at any stage, find the expert's qualifications inadequate and may either limit the scope of his testimony or reject him as an inappropriate witness.

Some observations on the present state of the art of qualifying an expert are appropriate. The present emphasis is almost exclusively on examining paper credentials and relating them to the specific product at issue. This practice fails to fulfill the desiderata of even the first stated criterion. The capacity of the witness to undertake self-education and the extent to which he has actually done so receive almost no attention. Indeed, to the extent that the expert's self-education for particular litigation is introduced at all, it is used perversely, primarily as a weapon for discrediting the expertise of the witness rather than as a means for qualifying him. When a potential witness admits that he has undertaken special study to testify in specific litigation, he becomes fair game for derisive cross-examination, during which his self-education is dwarfed by his admitted lack of previous experience. It is difficult to understand why experience gained long ago enhances the credibility of a witness. In light of today's rapidly evolving technology, it seems illogical to place so much value on long past and possibly obsolete experience.

In practice the brunt of this phenomenon is borne by plaintiffs' witnesses. Most experts with experience in specific products are employed by institutional defendants. Plaintiffs are thus forced to seek out generalists such as consulting engineers, academicians, and technicians, whose only hope for qualification turns on the process of self-education for a particular case. The courts require expert testimony to establish a *prima facie* case, but at the same time they permit the opposition to attack the credibility of the witness by belittling his self-education, his only means for qualifying as an expert. This imposes a tremendous burden on the plaintiff. There may be valid reasons to distinguish between seasoned experience and recently acquired understanding, but courts should permit the question to be raised only if it is demanded by the scope of the technological issue. In short the courts should recognize the nature of technological expertise and acknowledge the need for appropriate self-education. Once self-education has been recognized as a legitimate basis for expert qualification, the courts have a duty to prevent its debasement by reckless cross-examination.

While no explicit criteria may be adduced for the suggested qualification procedures, incisive *voir dire* (i.e., a hearing to determine expertise, before the judge from which the jury is excluded) predicated upon the suggested framework should afford the court adequate bases for an informed judgment. This procedure can be more advantageously pursued in the pretrial period.

In some instances the technical issues may be so complex, or the range of qualifications offered by potential witnesses so diverse, that the court may find it advantageous to enlist the aid of independent technical consultants. These consultants could guide the court in isolating the relevant technical issues and in recognizing the general background needed to address the issues. The ultimate responsibility for judging the propriety of a witness's qualification will remain, of course, with the trial judge.

The very nature of the problem of qualifying potential witnesses as experts precludes a precise quantitative formulation and routine application of a formal check list to the great variety of technological issues and witness credentials. A basic premise for qualification of the witness has been presented, coupled with a suggested mechanism for providing the appropriate focus for the precisely defined technological issues. Together, they provide a viable basis for the selection and qualification of technological experts in products liability litigation.

9.7   PUTTING THE PRODUCT ON TRIAL

To focus this discussion, products cases will be characterized and analyzed according to the following elements: a description of product, accident, and defect; a description of the unreasonably dangerous nature of the product; the causal relationship between the defect and the resulting harm; and the issue of proximate cause.

The evidentiary flow relating to each of these elements in the actual trials forming the basis for the first two examples described in Section 9.5 is shown schematically in Figures 9-2 and 9-3. The width of each block is a measure of the time devoted in the trial at that evidentiary category. Hence the flow of evidence is shown as a horizontal time history of the elements presented by both the plaintiff and the defendant at various points in the trial. Where elements are addressed simultaneously, they are shown in the same vertical position in the figure.

Note in particular that the product description testimony was interspersed throughout the actual trials that afforded us these examples and that a substantial as well as factually important fraction of this testimony appears in the *defendant's case*. While a proper foundation for all the elements of a products case may be contained somewhere in the record and thus be available for purposes of appeal, the improper sequencing and intermingling of evidence relating to different elements of the cause of action not only militate against effective communication of evidence but corrupt the basic integrity of strict products liability litigation.

Since the manufacturer's conduct is no longer on trial in strict liability, the central issue in a products trial must be the product in the environment of its use. The product itself must ultimately be judged defective and unrea-

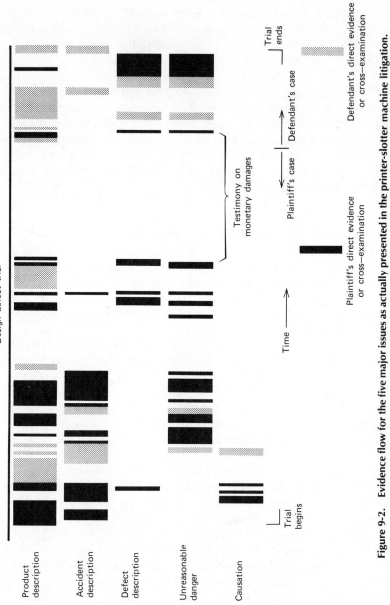

Figure 9-2. Evidence flow for the five major issues as actually presented in the printer-slotter machine litigation.

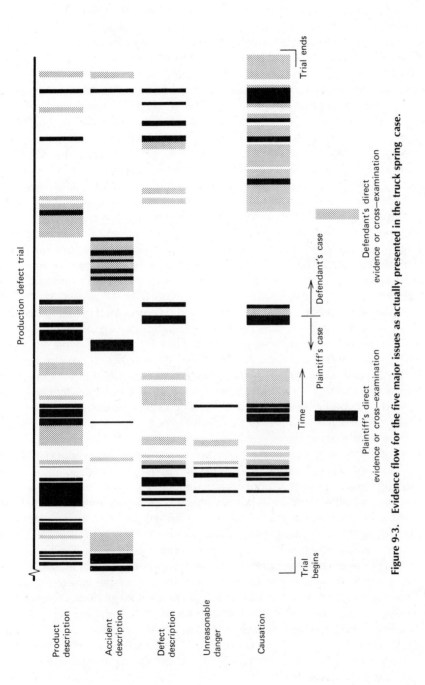

Figure 9-3. Evidence flow for the five major issues as actually presented in the truck spring case.

sonably dangerous. A comprehensive description of the product in the environment of its use should precede any other element of a products trial. If the product is not first understood in the environment of its use, the defect and causation issues can never be properly addressed. In a substantial number of cases this initial product description has been deficient. Difficulties encountered later in the trial are often directly attributable to an inadequate product description, a gap that compromises both the plaintiffs' and the defendants' cases. Inadequate product description at the outset of a trial can result in several serious distortions in the comprehension of the product. First, the product can be viewed primarily as an injury-producing instrument rather than as a useful, functioning device. Second, if descriptions of various aspects of a product are randomly interspersed among the various elements of the cause of action, they not only confuse the jury's perception of the product but also taint the ultimate comprehension of the product with value judgments derived from other elements of the lawsuit. Third, if the trial begins with a graphic description of the accident and injury, and the maimed plaintiff is present, it is difficult for the jury to overcome the bias that a product that could lead to this injury must indeed be unreasonably dangerous.

At the very outset of a trial, evidence should be provided to familiarize the court with the product. This product description can be accomplished in several ways. The product might be described by an expert who will later testify about defect and causation. A user of the product could also provide part or all of this description, since his experiences would focus attention on the product in its use environment. If necessary, this testimony could be offered in conjunction with movies or video tapes of the product in use. Mock-ups of salient features of the product could also be used to clarify its function and operation.

In addition to exploring the everyday operation of the product, its economics should be addressed as a critical part of the product description. This probing should include not only the manufacturer's costs in producing this product or viable alternatives but also the economic perceptions of the user of the product. For example, in the printer-slotter case described earlier, the plaintiff believed he was minimizing downtime by leaving the feed-end rollers running while walking through the open passageway. The reduction of downtime would augment his income since he was paid a higher hourly rate when the machine was in production. Indeed a large number of other trade-offs should have been considered to enhance the understanding of the product in its environment. Only after an adequate perception of the product in question has been communicated can the central issues of defect and causation be addressed.

So far, we have made suggestions for a more effective presentation of technological issues within the present format of products litigation. We now offer some suggestions for restructuring the trial format to focus sharply on the technological issues.

We propose a seriated trial, in which the first question before the jury is whether or not the product itself, apart from considerations arising from the injury-producing event, is defective and unreasonably dangerous. If the jury concludes that the product is defective, this trial would proceed by examining the issue of legal causation. At this stage the injury-producing event and the plaintiff's behavior are properly introduced. The jury is then asked whether the previously determined defective product was the most probable cause of the plaintiff's injuries. Finally, if the product has been adjudged both to be defective and to have caused the harm to the plaintiff, the issue of appropriate damages to be awarded is considered. Thus the seriated trial is a mechanism to be used to isolate and address, at trial inception, the risk-utility balancing of the product. Both plaintiff and defendant would address those factors that focus on the product within its environment of use and that would permit the jury to conclude that the product is reasonably safe or unreasonably dangerous.

To carry out this analysis in the courtroom, the product would first be extensively described as outlined previously. The alleged defect would then be identified. The design would next be tested against the indicia for unreasonable danger (see Section 4.4); this would allow viable alternatives to be examined for weighing the question of defect. These potential viable alternatives would be described in the same way as the product. After this presentation, with direct and cross-examination by both plaintiff's and defendant's counsel, the jury would be asked to make its initial determination of whether or not the product is defective and unreasonably dangerous. This format is particularly amenable to design defect cases. The absence of the plaintiff and injury-related evidence during this portion of the trial would reduce the possibility of elements' extraneous to the design problem interfering with the proper weighing of the defect issue, as intended under strict liability.

A seriated trial appears also to be feasible in many production defect cases, especially those in which the alleged defect can be clearly identified without recourse to inference. The product in these cases would again be thoroughly described, but it then would be tested for defect against performance standards developed during this first stage of the trial, by use of a risk-utility theory. In many cases this would require a description of performance standards not only at the time the product left the hands of the manufacturer but also after a reasonable period of ordinary use as well as foreseeable misuse.

The jury should be educated to the fact that all products contain certain levels of flaws. Only when a particular flaw is outside the limits of acceptable performance standards can a production defect be established. If the flaw lies within the norms of the manufacturer's quality spectrum but outside acceptable performance standards, the case can go forward only on a theory of generic defect or design defect, that is, that improper quality standards had been selected by the manufacturer. The climate of a products trial as currently litigated often prevents the defendant from providing a clear base line of normal average quality. To do this he must admit that he tolerates certain levels of flaws, a position that invites the attack of the plaintiff's counsel. Yet it is precisely this determination of normal average quality and permissible levels for flaws based on performance standards that is central to determining defect and unreasonable danger in a production defect case.

The issue of technical causation (Section 6.1) is intimately tied to the establishment of a production defect. Given the existence of a deviation from the manufacturer's standards, that is, a flaw, the technical causation question is simply, "Did this flaw cause this failure or malfunction of the product?"

In the litigation centering around the broken truck spring (see Section 3.6 and Example 2, Section 9.4), the technical causation issue is whether the flaws (gouge marks on the spring surface and allegedly imperfect microstructure) actually caused the spring to fail. Such issues are essentially technical and obviously must be addressed before any evidence is examined that establishes whether or not the product was unreasonably dangerous. If it is shown that the flaw could *not* cause the failure or malfunction, the only other products liability alternative would be to allege that the deficiency was the result of substandard product design. Too often this question of technical causation is bypassed at the initial stages of litigation. It surfaces, if at all, in the overall causation question, when the issue is whether the defect caused the injury-producing event. The effect of this unfortunate confusion of issues is that a truly technological issue that may be crucial to the determination of defect is lost in the morass of legal causation evidence that focuses on the whole panoply of events, including plaintiff's behavior, which links products failure to injury.

If insufficient attention is focused on the relationship of the flaw to the failure or malfunction of the product, then the pervasive effect is simply to create an aura of defect without the hard proof necessary to relate the failure to the flaw. The appropriate proof can take the form of physical examination, testing, engineering calculations, or whatever is needed to establish the technical causation link. Sometimes this detailed examination is compromised by the deterioration of evidence or the disciplinary bias of the expert. These difficulties are not, however, a rational basis for deflecting attention from the crucial technical causation issue. An earlier litigation of this issue is essential to avoid the cascading confusion that results from the introduction of evidence relating to subsequent events in the causal chain. The position of the technical causation issue in the seriated trial of a production defect case is shown in Figure 6-1, Section 6.2.

The subtleties of the technical issues may force an expansion of the seriated trial of a production defect case to include more than the defect issue. For example, to determine whether an actual failure occurred as the result of a single load or progressively by fatigue, the witness would have to draw upon some of the evidentiary elements of causation. The expert's analysis of a failure that potentially involves fatigue always proceeds by establishing the mode of failure first and then the defect, if any, that promoted this mode of failure. Since in these cases the issues of defect, technical causation, and causation in fact are inextricably intertwined technically, it appears appropriate to combine them in the seriated trial format as well.

By use of a seriated format the trial of the product can be conducted so that a jury will be given a coherent evidentiary basis for establishing defect and unreasonable danger. Although current litigation practice may lead to a trial record sufficient for appeal, the usual evidentiary sequencing fails to provide the clarity and direction required for the real task of trying the product itself. We recognize that there may be potential difficulties in implementing a truly seriated trial and securing a jury decision on the defect issue alone. As a first step, however, we propose that the evidentiary presentation be resequenced in the manner suggested.

The seriated trial format, which first isolates and examines the product in the environment of its use and subsequently examines causation, liability, and damages in that sequence, is offered as a viable means for achieving the goals of strict liability litigation, untainted by the irrelevancies of the manufacturer's conduct or unduly influenced by the injury-producing event.

CHAPTER 10

The Engineer
as a Designer—
Applying the Lessons

10.1 INTRODUCTION

In all of the material thus far we have dealt with the scope and substance of the law, including the subtle nuances and interrelationships of the many legal issues that pervade litigation. It is time now to reassess some of these issues as instruments of design.

Our premise is framed as two questions. If the courts dwell at length with concerns such as probability and gravity of harm, burden of precaution against the harm, foreseeable use, causation, duty, and warnings and standards of product performance, should not these same elements require open and honest consideration during the design process? Should not the process of developing product safety standards demand, prospectively, the same attention to the interaction of human behavior and product behavior as the courts use retrospectively after the injury has occurred? We suggest that the answers are "yes" to both questions and that no philosophy of product design or standards writing is complete without these considerations.

10.2 WHAT ARE THE LESSONS?

At the outset of this book we posed some searching questions. The purpose of the last nine chapters has been to provide the reader with the tools for formulating the answers to these questions. Although each manufacturer must answer the questions specifically within the context of his particular situation, it is instructive to set forth the boundaries of the legal responses to these questions.

We begin by reiterating a basic principle. Strict liability is *not absolute* liability. A manufacturer does not guarantee that his product will not cause injury. The requirement that a defect be established means that it is only the substandard product that may lead to liability.

Having said that the manufacturer does not guarantee that no injury will result from the use of his product, he does guarantee, however, that the product is not defective. We ought thus to acknowledge that the finest quality control extant will not save a manufacturer from liability when a product with a production defect comes off the assembly line.

For the manufacturer this is a bitter pill to swallow. Simply stated, the law tells him that his best is not good enough when a few of his products slip by with manufacturing mistakes. This does not mean, of course, that improved quality control is irrelevant as a practical matter, since the fewer bad products that escape, the less the chance of injury-producing events. Manufacturers will continue to make their decisions on instituting better quality control on the basis of cost effectiveness, but part of that equation must be the liability exposure for the improperly manufactured products.

When it comes to evaluating the design process for safety, the picture is more optimistic. The designer can plan for the total avoidance of liability. A product will not be declared defective in design merely because it caused an injury. A court will evaluate design safety by testing the reasonableness of the trade-offs that went into making the final design decisions. It is here that the manufacturer must be sensitive to the weight the courts have placed on the various factors in the risk-utility balancing process.

First and foremost the manufacturer must assess the actual environment in which the product will be used. The manufacturer will not be permitted to define either by marketing techniques or ineffectively worded communication with the user a use environment inconsistent with the real world. A product has a life of its own outside the walls of the design shop. A manufacturer must come to understand the real life of his product. Similarly, a manufacturer must know his user population, for they affect the scope and nature of product use.

The willingness of courts to account for frailties in human behavior and understanding explains why manufacturers have been singularly unsuccessful in persuading the courts that liability ought to be limited to the "intended" uses of products. It is for this reason that the law has insisted that foreseeable misuse be an important factor in the balancing process. It is the doctrine of *products* liability rather than *manufacturer's* liability that is the touchstone of the law.

Since the focus is truly on the product, it is necessary for the manufacturer to consider not only the adequacy of the buyer's specifications of the product and his desire to have certain equipment optional but also the ultimate user of the product. Ultimately the product becomes a functioning entity in the hands of the user, and the manufacturer's responsibility runs directly to him, regardless of the wishes and behavior of an intermediate purchaser. It is important not to overstate this premise. The needs of a purchaser may be so special and his expertise so unquestioned that responsibility can be shifted from the manufacturer to the purchaser. But as a general principle a manufacturer can no longer ignore responsibility for the product. He will be held accountable for its real use and user environment. It is for this reason that courts have viewed disclaimers between buyers and sellers with a jaundiced eye when the lives of innocent users are in danger. And it is also for this reason that courts have insisted that safety devices be built into the basic product and not left to the discretion of the purchaser.

Equally important for the manufacturer should be concern about the marketing of products. A safe product may be made unsafe by creating unrealistic expectations in the mind of the user through advertising representations. Finally it is clear that a manufacturer can take no solace from the fact that the defective product when combined with the negligence of an industrial employer caused injury to an employee. If the defect was present when the product left his hands, the manufacturer will still be liable, since the negligence of employers is foreseeable.

Perhaps the most important consideration in dealing with the real world of users and use environment is the balance that must be struck between designing out a hazard or warning against it. With the heavy emphasis that has been placed on warnings, it is understandable that manufacturers have seized on warnings as a panacea. There is a naive belief that, if the dangers attendant to product use have been warned against, the manufacturer is absolved of liability. Nothing could be further from the truth. Warnings will not reach or will be disregarded by a substantial fraction of the user population and cannot protect the user during a moment of inadvertence. If a reasonable design change can effect a substantial reduction in a hazard, then a warning will be deemed insufficient.

It is for this reason, too, that viewing a danger as open and obvious will not necessarily absolve a manufacturer from liability. The better approach is that designers will have the responsibility of creating safe rather than obviously dangerous products. An obvious danger is, after all, the poorest of warnings built into a product. When a design alteration is not possible or feasible for reducing risk, then effective warnings may be the only way to market an acceptably safe product. Such warnings must not only alert the user to the danger but must also tell him, appropriately, how to avoid injury.

The problem of rapidly evolving technology has yet to be resolved by the courts. It is yet unclear whether a manufacturer will be held liable for technological advances that were not available at the time of sale of the product. At the same time it is quite clear that reasonable conduct on the part of the manufacturer is not a defense to a products liability case. At the very least a manufacturer will be required to make available retrofit safety devices. What is crucial is the manner in which the retrofit devices are offered. A leading court has suggested that the manufacturer may have to bear the full cost of the retrofit. Although the burden may be onerous, it may be far cheaper than a single, serious products claim.

Fear of products liability exposure has caused some manufacturers to become cautious in upgrading the safety of new products. They are apprehensive that litigation concerning older products, without such safety features, will be unduly prejudiced against them. These fears are not unfounded, but they ought not to retard product evolution. Time does march on, and if a safety alternative is reasonable, it will inevitably surface in a trial. If, to demonstrate the impracticability of alternative safety devices, an entire industry colludes to prevent such safety improvements, it would face other liability problems every bit as onerous as the ones they sought to avoid. It is folly for the liability tail to wag the dog.

Manufacturers often seek refuge in their compliance with either industry or governmental standards. Adherence to such standards is not unimportant. It may go a long way toward establishing the reasonableness of the product. In certain instances, however, both industry and government standards have been held by courts to be inadequate. The willingness of courts to question these standards simply means that manufacturers must exercise their own best judgment about whether these standards are in fact adequate when the design trade-offs are confronted.

10.3 SAFETY BY DESIGN

The legal distinction between the reasonably safe product and the unreasonably dangerous one is fundamentally achieved by balancing the product's utility against the potential risks of harm stemming from its use. Simply put, the manufacturer's decision-making, before marketing a product, ought to reflect the firm's best judgment of the same balancing process.

In Section 4.4 we indicated the elements of the unreasonable-danger test, the bottom line in litigation for evaluating the efficacy of the product, after the fact. We suggest that these same indicia can form the basis of a manufacturer's design review process, before the product leaves the drawing board and emerges into the stream of commerce.

The preceding chapters have dealt with the broad scope of the duties courts are imposing upon manufacturers. Underlying these duties is the concept that products must be designed for *foreseeable* use, not solely *intended* use. This means that, once the functional aspects of a product are designed, a subjective, analytical process must begin. This process must articulate the types of use and misuse a product can suffer in the hands of all who may come in contact with it. This process must anticipate the hazards and risks of injury that are likely to be encountered by the users. Once this is done, the product design must be reviewed and decisions made concerning which design alterations, warnings, and instructions must be incorporated to minimize or eliminate the perceived risks of injury. The choice of materials as well as production and inspection methods for minimizing production flaws also becomes an intrinsic part of the process [1, 2, 3, 4, 5].

To apply these concepts in a more structured form, consider a reformulation of the seven indicia of Section 4.4, which is more suitable for use in design:

1. Delineate the scope of product uses.
2. Identify the environments within which the product will be used.
3. Describe the user population.
4. Postulate all possible hazards, including estimates of probability of occurrence and seriousness of resulting harm.
5. Delineate alternative design features or production techniques, including warnings and instructions, that can be expected to effectively mitigate or eliminate the hazards.
6. Evaluate such alternatives relative to the expected performance standards of the product, including the following:
   a. Other hazards that may be introduced by the alternatives.
   b. Their effect on the subsequent usefulness of the product.
   c. Their effect on the ultimate cost of the product.
   d. A comparison to similar products.
7. Decide which features to include in the final design.

This procedure should begin *after* the initial design has been formulated, which has incorporated the requirements of applicable standards. As noted, the courts generally view standards as floors, not ceilings, in judging a product's reasonableness.

The process begins by identifying the actual scope of product uses, where the product can be expected to be used, and who will be using it. Taken together, they set the boundaries of foreseeable use and foreseeable users.

For example, it is reasonable to expect that a hair dryer will be used to defrost refrigerators and thaw frozen water pipes and food, as well as to dry things other than hair. It will thus be used in humid environments and near water, as well as in locations with restricted air circulation or air supply. This is not to ignore, of course, its use for actually drying hair—but it would also consider that the user may be sitting in a bath tub. Users will be male and female, young and old. Users will thus have a broad range of manual dexterity, strength, and levels of understanding and awareness.

Once these product use and user situations are posited, the next task is to identify the hazards that are likely to arise from the interactions of product use, environment, and users. Thus short circuiting, overheating, user fatigue, entanglement, and limitations in understanding and appreciating warnings and instructions would be among the hazards that can lead to risks of injury for the user of the hair dryer.

The hazards having been identified and the probability and gravity of the harm that might result having been estimated, the question becomes, what changes in design, including warnings and instructions, can minimize or eliminate the risks of injury? It is at this point that the problem of design changes versus warnings to minimize a given risk must be carefully assessed. It is apparent that simply warning the user not to use the dryer near water may simply be inadequate in the light of the many foreseeable, water-related uses for which the product "invites" itself, particularly when the broad spectrum of users is considered. For each such alternative, some estimate should be made of the *reduction* in both probability and gravity of harm, since such reductions can have significant impact on the *ultimate* product cost.

Caution must be exercised, too, in recognizing that a cure may be worse than a disease. If a design alternative substitutes another set of hazards for the ones being eliminated, it may be that the original ones are less risky. A chilling example was the discovery that TRIS, a chemical flame retardant used for childrens' sleepwear, has a high probability of producing cancer. Another, perhaps less dramatic example of a questionable trade-off would be to enlarge the air inlets in a hair dryer to reduce the hazard of overheating and thus increase the chance of entangling the user's hair or of entraining water.

As each consideration is addressed, the effects on product usefulness and cost must obviously be introduced. But product cost is not based solely on materials, labor, marketing, overhead, and profit. Part of the product cost is that arising from possible injuries, either from the expected fraction of products marketed with production flaws or from hazards that the design did not minimize. Whether these costs are, in part, insurance premiums, settlements, judgments, or legal fees is not important. They are part of the real cost of the product and can significantly affect decisions about which safety features to incorporate in the final design. Certainly, some of these costs (e.g., settlement, judgments) are not factors for a court in deciding whether a product is unreasonably dangerous. A court performing a risk-utility analysis could not account for a manufacturer's settlement practice. Nonetheless, these considerations may weigh heavily on the manufacturer when it decides on its design or quality control standards.

If the manufacturer's risk-utility trade-offs are to be made realistically, they must be made with a full recognition of the potential risk of liability compared with the utility of marketing a product without safety design features that would raise the cost. Unquestionably competitive market position is important in decision-making and can influence the process. It should not, however, be the only consideration.

Admittedly, the safety design review procedure suggested here is highly subjective. Its success is predicated on the basic integrity and scope of the analysis undertaken. Procedures exist, such as fault-tree and failure-modes-and-effects analyses [6, 7], as well as others, that provide matrices for a structured analysis of hazards and risks. They are useful tools, particularly for complex products. But they are tools only. The results of such techniques only reflect the quality of the input. If, for example, the scope of anticipated product uses, users, and environments is restricted, the hazard and risk analysis will be also.

10.4 DOCUMENTATION—BENEFIT AND COST

Instituting a product safety design review procedure or a product safety audit is an investment in the future. Products liability litigation will not disappear overnight simply because a manufacturer's next generation of products is based on an intensive, honest, and balanced risk-utility decision-making process. Certainly there should result a reduction in hazards and risks, but the trade-off point between the reasonably safe product and the unreasonably dangerous one obviously cannot be made with precision. Our sensitized society will be alleging that even carefully designed products are still unreasonably dangerous.

It is important, then, that the legal forum be given an opportunity to assess the reasonableness of the manufacturer's risk-utility balancing process that defined the product in its final form. Thus the decision-making process needs to be supported with documentation that elucidates the considerations underlying the product design.

Such documentation can be categorized as:

1. Hazard and risk data—historical, field and/or laboratory testing, causation analyses.
2. Design safety formulation—fault-tree, failure modes, hazard analyses.

3. Warnings and instruction formulation—methodology for development and selection.
4. Standards—the use of in-house, voluntary, and mandated design or performance requirements.
5. Quality assurance program—methodology for procedure selection and production records.
6. Product performance—reporting procedures, complaint file, follow-up data acquisition and analysis, recall, retrofit, instruction and warning modification.
7. Decision-making—the "how," "who," and "why" of the process.

These are the necessary ingredients for an appropriate product safety design review. A comprehensive exposition of the basic data, coupled with the sensitivity of the decision-making process as illustrated through significant documentation, can provide the courts with the bench marks needed for judging a product's societal acceptability.

The hazard and risk data not only should be acquired from well-designed laboratory and field tests but also should include analyses of litigation, user complaints, and field failures. It may appear naive to suggest that product litigation can have a positive impact on product design. Yet careful scrutiny of both a given manufacturer's liability claims and reported appellate decisions for all products of the same type throughout the country can uncover problems or use patterns that are important for retrofit considerations as well as design review.

The existence and features of a quality assurance program are generally inadmissible under an action in strict liability if used to demonstrate the reasonableness of the production process or the improbability that the product was defective when it left the hands of the manufacturer [8]. But such a program, described within the context of the entire risk-utility balancing process, can highlight the attention paid by the manufacturer to all aspects of product formulation and can have persuasive impact on the court's understanding of the question of reasonable risk.

Learning about one's product is a crucial element in any decision-making process. Manufacturers are held to a standard of what they "should have known" about the product. Part of the design process that should be documented is what procedures were used to identify product problems as they emerge from actual use and how those data are used in subsequent changes, in addition to triggering recall and retrofit programs.

Ultimately, of course, it is how and why the trade-offs are made that will govern whether the product, as marketed, was a reasonable balance of risk and utility. That can be judged only if the decision-making process is clearly revealed as a sensitive balancing of competing considerations. Thus the "how," "who," and particularly the "why" of decisions all need to be documented.

Thorough documentation can be a two-edged sword, one edge of which could be viewed as being unreasonably dangerous to the manufacturer. The revelations of the trade-off and decision-making process may lead to an uncomfortable feeling of vulnerability. But a reasonably safe product is not required to be an absolutely safe one. Society must ultimately be sensitized to the concept that reasonable risk is a fact of life.

10.5   YET ANOTHER COMMITTEE

The implementation of a product safety program requires contributions from a variety of disciplines, as well as differing viewpoints within a given discipline. Judging the boundaries of human behavior and product behavior is too complex to be left in the hands of one person or discipline.

Certainly management, design, production, service, and marketing will bring differing perspectives to the problems. But together with those business, engineering, and science backgrounds, it is also clear that skills in communications, psychology, and the relevant law are just as necessary inputs. It may be argued that a product emerging from the deliberations of such a diverse group may resemble a camel, recognized as a committee's design of a horse.

The tasks of a design review group are, however, to elicit and evaluate data and to articulate the competing elements for the decision-making process, not to redesign the product. Included in the responsibilities of the group should be a review of all packaging, labeling, instructions, and advertising material, since the explicit representations are an essential dimension of the expected performance of a product.

Ultimately, the decisions for incorporating or eliminating design features, warnings, production techniques, and other elements must rest with responsible management. The actual procedures, check points, and personnel involved are a function of the organization and its structure, but the process should be clearly identified and integrated into the total management scheme.

10.6   A FINAL WORD

These few pages are meant to be only the outlines on a sketch pad. Applying the lessons requires a basic inquiry into the nature of the product and its use environment together with a review of existing procedures and techniques for design, production, and marketing before substance can be given to the form. The concerns will vary both in degree and kind for the individual product manufacturer. The primary materials supplier, the component-part fabricator, the assembler, and the distributor all have duties, some overlapping and some with differing emphases. We have suggested only the matrix of the important elements. Each organization must develop the procedures, techniques, documentation, and skills appropriate for itself and its product.

REFERENCES

One note concerning how to read these references is required. Cases, law review articles, and treatises on the law are all cited similarly. Following the case name, the article author and title, or the treatise author, is the volume number. The volume number is followed by the title of the particular case reporter, review, or treatise and by the page number. For example, 82 *Harvard Law Review* 1 is volume 82 of the *Harvard Law Review*, page 1.

Statutory material is referenced by the title of the statute and the section number. The symbol § indicates the section. Additional information is provided parenthetically. One asterisk indicates the case is included in Appendix A. Two asterisks indicate the statute is included in Appendix B.

Chapter 1

1. Final Report of the National Commission on Product Safety (June 1970) (available at U.S. Depository Libraries, document no. Y3.N 21/25: 1/970).

2. The President's Report on Occupational Safety and Health (May 1970) (available at U.S. Depository Libraries, document no. Pr 37.2:Oc 1).

3. Deparcq, "Law, Science and the Expert Witness," 24 *Tennessee Law Review* 166 (1956).

4. *Seely v. White Motor Company*, 63 California 2d 9, 403 Pacific 2d 145, 45 California Reporter 17 (1965). Also *Santor v. A. M. Karagheusian, Inc.*, 44 New Jersey 52, 207 Atlantic 2d 305 (1965).

5. *Dippel v. Sciano*, 37 Wisconsin 2d 443, 155 Northwestern 2d 55 (1967). Also *Berkebile v. Brantly Helicopter Corporation*, 462 Pennsylvania 83, 337 Atlantic 2d 893 (1975).

6. Terry, "Negligence," 29 *Harvard Law Review* 40 (1915).

7. **Restatement (Second) of Torts 1965 § 291.

8. *The T. J. Hooper*, 60 Federal 2d 737 (Second Circuit, Court of Appeals, 1932). Also Restatement (Second) of Torts 1965 § 295A, comment b.

9. *Marsh Wood Products Company v. Babcock and Wilcox*, 207 Wisconsin 209, 240 Northwestern 392 (1932).

10. *Berkebile v. Brantly Helicopter Corp.*, 219 Pennsylvania Superior 479, 281 Atlantic 2d 707 (1971).

11. *Metal Window Products Co. v. Magnusen*, 485 Southwestern 2d 355 (1972).

12. **Uniform Commercial Code 2-607.

13. **Uniform Commercial Code 2-316.

14. *Henningsen v. Bloomfield Motors, Inc.*, 32 New Jersey 358, 161 Atlantic 2d 69 (1960).

15. **Restatement (Second) of Torts 1965 § 402A, comment m.

16. *Crocker v. Winthrop Laboratories, Division of Sterling Drug, Inc.*, 514 Southwestern 2d 429 (1974).

17. *MacPherson v. Buick Motor Company*, 217 New York 382, 111 Northeastern 1050 (1916).

18. *Henningsen v. Bloomfield Motors, Inc.*, 32 New Jersey 358, 161 Atlantic 2d 69 (1960).

19. *Anderson v. Fairchild Hiller Corporation*, 358 Federal Supplement 976 (District Alaska 1973).

20. *Greenman v. Yuba Power Products, Inc.*, 59 California 2d 57, 27 California Reporter 697, 377 Pacific 2d 897 (1962).

21. **Uniform Commercial Code 2-607.

22. Uniform Commercial Code 2-715.

23. Prosser, *Handbook of the Law of Torts*, 4th edition, § 30 (1971).

24. **Uniform Commercial Code 2-316.

25. **Restatement (Second) of Torts 1965 § 402A, comment m.

Chapter 2

1. *Barry v. Manglass*, 389 New York Supplement 2d 870 (1976).

2. Prosser, *Handbook of the Law of Torts*, 4th edition, § 65 (1971).

3. **Restatement (Second) of Torts 1965 § 402A, comment n. Also Twerski, "Old Wine in a New Flask—Restructuring Assumption of Risk in the Products Liability Era," 60 *Iowa Law Review* 1 (1974).

4. *Dorsey v. Yoder Company*, 331 Federal Supplement 753 (Eastern District Pennsylvania 1971).

5. Frumer and Friedman, 2 *Products Liability* § 16.01|3| (1976).

6. Schwartz, *Comparative Negligence*, The Allen Smith Company, 1974; Fleming, "Foreword: Comparative Negligence at Last—by Judicial Choice," 64 *California Law Review* 239 (1976).

7. Twerski, "From Defect to Cause to Comparative Fault—Rethinking Some Product Liability Concepts," 60 *Marquette Law Review* 297, 1977. Also Twerski, "The Use and Abuse of Comparative Negligence in Products Liability," 10 *Indiana Law Review* 797 (1977).

8. Prosser, *Handbook of the Law of Torts*, 4th edition, § 53 (1971).

9. *Yania v. Bigan*, 397 Pennsylvania 316, 155 Atlantic 2d 343 (1959).

10. **Restatement (Second) of Torts 1965 § 402A, comments I and o.

11. *Codling v. Paglia*, 32 New York 2d 330, 298 Northeastern 2d 622, 345 New York Supplement 2d 461 (1973).

12. *Elliothorpe v. Ford Motor Company*, 503 Southwestern 2d 516 (Tennessee Supreme Court 1973).

13. *Evans v. General Motors Corp.*, 359 Federal 2d 822 (7th Circuit, Court of Appeals 1966); *Larsen v. General Motors Corp.*, 391 Federal 2d 495 (8th Circuit, Court of Appeals, 1968).

14. Hoenig and Getz, "A Rational Approach to 'Crashworthy' Automobiles: The Need for Judicial Responsibility," 6 *Southwestern University Law Review* 1 (1974).

15. *West v. Broderick and Bascom Rope Co.*, 197 Northwestern 2d 202 (1972).

16. *States Steamship Company v. Stone Manganese Marine, Ltd.*, 371 Federal Supplement 500 (District New Jersey 1973).

17. **Balido v. Improved Machinery Company*, 29 California Appeal 3d 633, 105 California Reporter 890 (1972); *Rios v. Niagara Machine and Tool Works*, 12 Illinois Appeals 3d 739, 299 Northeastern 2d 86 (1973).

Chapter 3

1. *Cronin v. J. B. E. Olson Corporation*, 8 California 3d 121, 501 Pacific 2d 1153, 104 California Reporter 433 (1972).

2. Prosser, *Handbook of the Law of Torts*, 4th edition, § 39 (1971); James, "Proof of the Breach in Negligence Cases," 37 *Virginia Law Review* 179 (1951).

3. *Escola v. Coca Cola Bottling Company*, 24 California 2d 453, 150 Pacific 2d 436 (1944).

4. **McCormack v. Hankscraft Company*, 278 Minnesota 322, 154 Northwestern 2d 488 (1967).

5. 5 Interagency Task Force on Product Liability, section C.b(3).

6. *Victorson v. Bock Laundry Machine Company*, 37 New York 2d 395, 335 Northeastern 2d 275, 373 New York Supplement 2d 39 (1975).

7. *Rosenau v. City of New Brunswick*, 51 New Jersey 130, 238 Atlantic 2d 169 (1968).

8. For example, Oregon Revised Statute 12.115(1) provides that no action for negligent injury can be commenced more than 10 years after the act or omission complained of; the Supreme Court of Oregon found this statute applicable to strict liability actions in *Johnson v. Star Machinery Company*, 530 Pacific 2d 53 (Oregon 1974). A Connecticut statute, Public Act number 76-293, enacted on June 4, 1976, provides that no action for strict products liability may be brought more than eight years after the date of sale, lease, or bailment.

9. *LaGorga v. Kroger Company*, 275 Federal Supplement 373 (Western District Pennsylvania 1967), affirmed, 407 Federal 2d 671 (3rd Circuit, Court of Appeals 1969).

10. *Muncy v. Magnolia Chemical Company*, 437 Southwestern 2d 15 (Court of Civil Appeals of Texas 1968).

11. *Tucson Industries, Inc. v. Schwartz*, 15 Arizona Appeals 166, 487 Pacific 2d 12 (1971).

Chapter 4

1. *Cronin v. J. B. E. Olson Corporation*, 8 California 3d 121, 501 Pacific 2d 1153, 104 California Reporter 433 (1972). As this book was going to press, the *Cronin* case was modified by *Barker v. Lull Engineering Co.* 2 Products Liability Reporter (Commerce Clearing House, Inc.) 18101 (California Supreme Court 1978).

2. Harper and James, 2 *The Law of Tort* § 28.5 (1966).

3. *Vincer v. Esther Williams All-Aluminum Swimming Pool Company*, 69 Wisconsin 2d 326, 230 Northwestern 2d 794 (1975).

4. Wade, "Strict Liability of Manufacturers," 19 *Southwestern Law Journal* 5 (1965).

5. For a comprehensive discussion of this case, see Weinstein et al., "Product Liability: An Interaction of Law and Technology," 12 *Duquesne Law Review* 425, appendix case A (1974).

6. *Cronin v. J. B. E. Olson Corporation*, 8 California 3d 121, 501 Pacific 2d 1153, 104 California Reporter 433 (1972).

7. *Ritter v. Narragansett Electric Company*, 109 Rhode Island 176, 283 Atlantic 2d 255 (1971).

8. *Magic Chef, Inc. v. Sibley*, 546 Southwestern 2d 851 (Court of Civil Appeals of Texas 1977).

9. *Berkebile v. Brantly Helicopter Corporation*, 462 Pennsylvania 83, 337 Atlantic 2d 893 (1975).

10. *Finnegan v. Havir Manufacturing Company*, 60 New Jersey 413, 290 Atlantic 2d 286 (1972).

11. Keeton, "Product Liability—Inadequacy of Information," 48 *Texas Law Review* 398 (1970).

12. *Green v. American Tobacco Company*, 391 Federal 2d 97 (1968), affirmed, 409 Federal 2d 1166 (5th Circuit, Court of Appeals 1969); *Davis v. Wyeth Laboratories, Inc.*, 399 Federal 2d 121 (9th Circuit, Court of Appeals 1968).

13. *Campo v. Scofield*, 301 New York 468, 95 Northeastern 2d 802 (1950).

14. *Micallef v. Miehle Company*, 39 New York 2d 376, 348 Northeastern 2d 571, 384 New York Supplement 2d 115 (1976).

15. *Berkebile v. Brantly Helicopter Corporation*, 219 Pennsylvania Superior 479, 281 Atlantic 2d 707 (1971).

Chapter 5

1. For a full discussion of the entire warning problem, see Twerski et al., "The Use and Abuse of Warnings in Products Liability—Design Defect Litigation Comes of Age," 61 *Cornell Law Review* 495 (1976).

2. *Phillips v. Kimwood Machine Company*, 525 Pacific 2d 1033 (Oregon 1974).

3. *Moran v. Faberge, Inc.*, 273 Maryland 538, 332 Atlantic 2d 11 (1975).

4. *Nissen Trampoline Co. v. Terre Haute National Bank*, 332 N.E. 2d 820. This case is still in litigation.

5. *Davis v. Wyeth Laboratories, Inc.*, 399 Federal 2d 121 (9th Circuit, Court of Appeals 1968).

6. *Borel v. Fibreboard Manufacturing Company*, 493 Federal 2d 1076 (5th Circuit, Court of Appeals 1973). For the opposing view, see *Jackson v. Coast Paint and Lacquer Company*, 499 Federal 2d 809 (9th Circuit, Court of Appeals 1974).

7. *Velez v. Craine and Clark Lumber Corporation*, 33 New York 2d 117, 305 Northeastern 2d 750, 350 New York Supplement 2d 617 (1973).

8. *Henningsen v. Bloomfield Motors, Inc.*, 32 New Jersey 358, 161 Atlantic 2d 69 (1960).

Chapter 6

1. *Chestnut v. Ford Motor Company*, 445 Federal 2d 967 (4th Circuit, Court of Appeals 1971).

2. *Garst v. General Motors Corporation*, 207 Kansas 2, 484 Pacific 2d 47 (1971).

3. *Jagmin v. Simonds Abrasive Company*, 61 Wisconsin 2d 60, 211 Northwestern 2d 810 (1973).

4. *Henningsen v. Bloomfield Motors, Inc.*, 32 New Jersey 358, 161 Atlantic 2d 69 (1960).

5. *Codling v. Paglia*, 32 New York 2d 330, 298 Northeastern 2d 622, 345 New York Supplement 2d 461 (1973).

6. *Rogers v. Unimac Company*, 2 Products Liability Reporter (Commerce Clearing House, Inc.) ¶ 7912 (Arizona Supreme Court 1977).

Chapter 7

1. *Velez v. Craine and Clark Lumber Corporation*, 33 New York 2d 117, 305 Northeastern 2d 750, 350 New York Supplement 2d 617 (1973).

2. *Codling v. Paglia*, 32 New York 2d 330, 298 Northeastern 2d 622, 345 New York Supplement 2d 461 (1973).

3. *Butaud v. Suburban Marine and Sporting Goods, Inc.*, 543 Pacific 2d 209 (Alaska 1976). For a full discussion, see Twerski, "The Use and Abuse of Comparative Negligence in Products Liability," 10 *Indiana Law Review* 797 (1977).

4. *Edwards v. Sears, Roebuck and Company*, 512 Federal 2d 276 (5th Circuit, Court of Appeals 1975); *Dippel v. Sciano*, 37 Wisconsin 2d 443, 155 Northwestern 2d 55 (1967).

5. **Bexiga v. Havir Manufacturing Corporation*, 60 New Jersey 402, 290 Atlantic 2d 281 (1972).

6. Restatement (Second) of Torts 1965 § 402A, comment n.

7. *Vernon v. Lake Motors*, 26 Utah 2d 269, 488 Pacific 2d 302 (1971).

8. For a full discussion, see Twerski, "Old Wine in a New Flask—Restructuring Assumption of Risk in the Products Liability Era," 60 *Iowa Law Review* 1 (1974).

9. *Codling v. Paglia*, 32 New York 2d 330, 298 Northeastern 2d 622, 345 New York Supplement 2d 461 (1973).

10. See generally Schwartz, *Comparative Negligence*, The Allen Smith Company, 1974.

11. The quotation is taken from the May 1, 1977, draft of the Uniform Comparative Fault Act, Section 1. An earlier version of the Act is discussed in Wade, "A Uniform Comparative Fault Act—What Should It Provide," 10 *University of Michigan Journal of Law Reform* 220 (1977). The proposed act was presented to the National Conference of Commissioners on Uniform State Law in 1977.

12. See Twerski, "From Defect to Cause to Comparative Fault—Rethinking Some Product Liability Concepts," 60 *Marquette Law Review* 297 (1977).

Chapter 8

1. *Velez v. Craine and Clark Lumber Corporation*, 33 New York 2d 117, 305 Northeastern 2d 750, 350 New York Supplement 2d 617 (1973).

2. *Clark v. Bendix Corporation*, 42 Appellate Division 727, 345 New York Supplement 2d 662 (1973).

3. Frumer and Friedman, 1 *Products Liability*, § 10 (1976).

4. Frumer and Friedman, 1 *Products Liability*, § 10 (1976).

5. *Barth v. B. F. Goodrich Tire Company*, 265 California Appeal 2d 228, 71 California Reporter 306 (1968); *Webb v. Zern*, 422 Pennsylvania 444, 220 Atlantic 2d 853 (1966).

6. *Carney v. Sears, Roebuck and Company*, 309 Federal 2d 300 (4th Circuit, Court of Appeals 1962); Restatement (Second) of Torts 1965 § 400.

7. *Vandermark v. Ford Motor Company*, 61 California 2d 256, 37 California Reporter 896, 391 Pacific 2d 168 (1964).

8. *Suvada v. White Motor Company*, 51 Illinois Appeals 201 318, 201 Northeastern 2d 313 (1964).

9. *Cintrone v. Hertz Truck Leasing and Rental Service*, 45 New Jersey 434, 212 Atlantic 2d 769 (1965).

10. *Francioni v. Gibsonia Truck Corporation*, 2 Products Liability Reporter (Commerce Clearing House, Inc.) ¶ 7911 (Pennsylvania Supreme Court 1977).

11. **Schipper v. Levitt and Sons, Inc.*, 44 New Jersey 70, 207 Atlantic 2d 314 (1965).

12. *Newmark v. Gimbel's, Inc.*, 54 New Jersey 585, 258 Atlantic 2d 697 (1969).

13. *Magrine v. Krasnica*, 94 New Jersey Superior 228, 227 Atlantic 2d 539 (1967), affirmed under the name *Magrine v. Spector*, 100 New Jersey Superior 223, 241 Atlantic 2d 637 (1968).

14. *Cornelius v. Bay Motors, Inc.*, 258 Oregon 564, 484 Pacific 2d 299 (1971).

15. *Realmuto v. Straub Motors, Inc.*, 65 New Jersey 336, 322 Atlantic 2d 440 (1974).

16. *Turner v. International Harvester Company*, 133 New Jersey Superior 277, 336 Atlantic 2d 62 (1975).

17. For a full discussion of the impact of workmen's compensation on product liability, see Mitchell, "Products Liability, Workmen's Compensation and the Industrial Accident," 14 *Duquesne Law Review* 349 (1976). Several pages in Section 8.4 have been adapted from that article with the author's permission.

18. For a complete discussion, see Davis, "Third-Party Tortfeasors' Rights Where Compensation-Covered Employers are Negligent—Where Do Dole and Sunspan Lead?" 4 *Hofstra Law Review* 571 (1976).

19. *Newport Air Park, Inc. v. United States*, 293 Federal Supplement 809 (District Rhode Island 1968).

20. *Dole v. Dow Chemical Company*, 30 New York 2d 143, 282 Northeastern 2d 288, 331 New York Supplement 2d 382 (1972).

21. Prosser, *Handbook of the Law of Torts*, 4th edition, § 50 (1971).

22. *Fenton v. McCrory Corporation*, 47 Federal Rules Decisions 260 (1969).

23. *Walters v. Hiab Hydraulics, Inc.*, 356 F. Supp. 1000 (M.D. Pa. 1973); *W.D. Rubright Co. v. International Harvester Co.*, 358 F. Supp. 1388 (W.D. Pa. 1973).

Chapter 9

1. See generally Weinstein et al., "Product Liability: An Interaction of Law and Technology," 12 *Duquesne Law Review* 425 (1974); also Donaher et al., "The Technical Expert: Who Is He?" 52 *Texas Law Review* 1303 (1974).

Chapter 10

1. Carrubba, Eugene R., *Assuring Product Integrity*, Lexington Books, Lexington, Massachusetts (1975).

2. Nixon, Frank, *Managing to Achieve Quality and Reliability*, McGraw-Hill Book Company, New York (1971).

3. Brook, R. H. W., *Reliability Concepts in Engineering Manufacture*, John Wiley & Sons, New York (1972).

4. Carter, A. D. S., *Mechanical Reliability*, John Wiley & Sons, New York (1973).

5. Enrick, Norbert, Lloyd, *Quality Control and Reliability*, Industrial Press, New York (1972).

6. *Reliability and Fault Tree Analysis*, Proceedings of Conference on Reliability and Fault Tree Analysis, University of California, Berkeley (1974). Published by Society for Industrial and Applied Mathematics, Philadelphia, Pennsylvania.

7. *Parts, Materials and Processes*, NASA, SP-6507, 1973 (ALERT Reports, two volumes).

8. *McKasson v. Zimmer Manufacturing Company*, 12 Illinois Appellate 3d 429, 299 Northeastern 2d 38 (1973); *Pulley v. Pacific Coca-Cola Bottling Company*, 68 Washington 2d 778, 415 Pacific 2d 636 (1966).

Appellate Court Opinions of Leading Cases

EDITING SYMBOLS

. . .	Omission of words within a sentence or of sentences at the start of a paragraph.
. . . .	Omission of a sentence or more within or at the end of a single paragraph.
. . . . .	Omission of consecutive sentences from two paragraphs or one or more full paragraphs.
(Citation)	Omission of a citation.
(Citations)	Omission of citations.
	All footnotes have been omitted from the cases.

The Appellate Court opinions of several leading cases in products liability are presented here. They have been edited to highlight the important elements of the legal and technological issues raised in the appeal.

These opinions are included for several purposes. First, they should be read for an understanding and appreciation of the scope of considerations brought by the judiciary to their resolution of the important societal questions raised by the legal issues. Second, it is instructive to trace the logic that leaves precedent together with present-day societal mores to arrive at a result that, it is hoped, secures justice for the litigants.

In the body of this book we have distilled what appear to be the principal thrusts of the legal issues. A given appellate opinion may, however, differ significantly from these positions. To assist the reader in focusing on the important considerations, we have formulated questions at the end of each opinion that look to the significant issues raised. Thus, by comparison and contrast with the discussion in the appropriate section of the book, together with the reader's own views, all the facets of each issue can be examined.

Finally, where appropriate, we have also included questions following each opinion that ask the reader to adopt the viewpoint of a manufacturer or designer in responding to technological issues concerning the product in question. The intent is to provide another mechanism for developing a perspective for the reasonably safe product.

LIST OF OPINIONS*

PRIVITY-STRICT LIABILITY

1. Greenman v. Yuba Power Products, Inc.

THE REASONABLY SAFE PRODUCT

2. Dreisonstok v. Volkswagenwerk, A. G.
3. Phillips v. Kimwood Machine Company.
4. McCormack v. Hankscraft Company.
5. Vincer v. Esther Williams All-Aluminum Swimming Pool Company.
6. Kaempfe v. Lehn & Fink Products Corporation.

THE DUTY QUESTION

7. Patten v. Logemann Brothers Company.
8. Micallef v. Miehle Company.
9. Mieher v. Brown.
10. Balido v. Improved Machinery, Inc.
11. Skyhook Corporation v. Jasper.
12. Schipper v. Levitt & Sons, Inc.

THE CAUSATION ISSUE

13. Technical Chemical Company v. Jacobs.
14. Berkebile v. Brantly Helicopter Corporation.
15. Leistra v. Bucyrus-Erie Company.

PROOF OF DEFECT

16. Friedman v. General Motors Corporation.
17. Ault v. International Harvester Company.
18. Brissette v. Milner Chevrolet Company, Inc.

DEFENSE

19. Dorsey v. Yoder Company.
20. Bexiga v. Havir Manufacturing Corporation.
21. Turner v. International Harvester Company.

ECONOMIC LOSS

22. Seely v. White Motor Company.

*The opinions are listed here by categories of their principal subject matter.

GREENMAN v. YUBA POWER PRODUCTS, INC.

59 Cal. 2d 57
377 P.2d 897
27 Cal. Rptr. 697
Supreme Court of California, In Bank
January 24, 1963

TRAYNOR, Justice.

Plaintiff brought this action for damages against the retailer and the manufacturer of a Shopsmith, a combination power tool that could be used as a saw, drill, and wood lathe. He saw a Shopsmith demonstrated by the retailer and studied a brochure prepared by the manufacturer. He decided he wanted a Shopsmith for his home workshop, and his wife bought and gave him one for Christmas in 1955. In 1957 he bought the necessary attachments to use the Shopsmith as a lathe for turning a large piece of wood he wished to make into a chalice. After he had worked on the piece of wood several times without difficulty, it suddenly flew out of the machine and struck him on the forehead, inflicting serious injuries. About ten and a half months later, he gave the retailer and the manufacturer written notice of claimed breaches of warranties and filed a complaint against them alleging such breaches and negligence.

After a trial before a jury, the court ruled that there was no evidence that the retailer was negligent or had breached any express warranty and that the manufacturer was not liable for the breach of any implied warranty. Accordingly, it submitted to the jury only the cause of action alleging breach of implied warranties against the retailer and the causes of action alleging negligence and breach of express warranties against the manufacturer. The jury returned a verdict for the retailer against plaintiff and for plaintiff against the manufacturer in the amount of $65,000. The trial court denied the manufacturer's motion for a new trial and entered judgment on the verdict. The manufacturer and plaintiff appeal. . . .

Plaintiff introduced substantial evidence that his injuries were caused by defective design and construction of the Shopsmith. His expert witnesses testified that inadequate set screws were used to hold parts of the machine together so that normal vibration caused the tailstock of the lathe to move away from the piece of wood being turned permitting it to fly out of the lathe. They also testified that there were other more positive ways of fastening the parts of the machine together, the use of which would have prevented the accident. The jury could therefore reasonably have concluded that the manufacturer negligently constructed the Shopsmith. The jury could also reasonably have concluded that statements in the manufacturer's brochure were untrue, that they constituted express warranties, and that plaintiff's injuries were caused by their breach.

The manufacturer contends, however, that plaintiff did not give it notice of breach of warranty within a reasonable time and that therefore his cause of action for breach of warranty is barred by section 1769 of the Civil Code. Since it cannot be determined whether the verdict against it was based on the negligence or warranty cause of action or both, the manufacturer concludes that the error in presenting the warranty cause of action to the jury was prejudicial.

Section 1769 of the Civil Code provides: "In the absence of express or implied agreement of the parties, acceptance of the goods by the buyer shall not discharge the seller from liability in damages or other legal remedy for breach of any promise or warranty in the contract to sell or the sale. But, if, after acceptance of the goods, the buyer fails to give notice to the seller of the breach of any promise or warranty within a reasonable time after the buyer knows, or ought to know of such breach, the seller shall not be liable therefor."

Like other provisions of the uniform sales act (Citation), section 1769 deals with the rights of the parties to a contract of sale or a sale. It does not provide that notice must be given of the breach of a warranty that arises independently of a contract of sale between the parties. Such warranties are not imposed by the sales act, but are the product of common-law decisions that have recognized them in a variety of situations. (Citations.). . . .

The notice requirement of section 1769, however, is not an appropriate one for the court to adopt in actions by injured consumers against manufacturers with whom they have not dealt (Citations). "As between the immediate parties to the sale [the notice requirement] is a sound commercial rule, designed to protect the seller against unduly delayed claims for damages. As applied to personal injuries, and notice to a remote seller, it becomes a booby-trap for the unwary. The injured consumer is seldom 'steeped in the business practice which justifies the rule.' (James, Product Liability, 34 *Texas L. Rev.* 44, 192, 197) and at least until he has had legal advice it will not occur to him to give notice to one with whom he has had no dealings." (Prosser, Strict Liability to the Consumer, 69 *Yale L.J.* 1009, 1130, footnotes omitted.). . . . We conclude, therefore, that even if plaintiff did not give timely notice of breach of warranty to the manufacturer, his cause of action based on the representations contained in the brochure was not barred.

Moreover, to impose strict liability on the manufacturer under the circumstances of this case, it was not necessary for plaintiff to establish an express warranty as defined in section 1732 of the Civil Code. A manufacturer is strictly liable in tort when an article he places on the market, knowing that it is to be used without inspection for defects, proves to have a defect that causes injury to a human being. Recognized first in the case of unwholesome food products, such liability has now been extended to a variety of other products that create as great or greater hazards if defective (Citations).

Although in these cases strict liability has usually been based on the theory of an express or implied warranty running from the manufacturer to the plaintiff, the abandonment of the requirement of a contract between them, the recognition that the liability is not assumed by agreement but imposed by law (Citations), and the refusal to permit the manufacturer to define the scope of its own responsibility for defective products (Citations) make clear that the liability is not one governed by the law of contract warranties but by the law of strict liability in tort. Accordingly, rules defining and governing warranties that were developed to meet the needs of commercial transactions cannot properly be invoked to govern the manufacturer's liability to those injured by their defective products unless those rules also serve the purposes for which such liability is imposed.

We need not recanvass the reasons for imposing strict liability on the manufacturer. They have been fully articulated in the cases cited above (Citations). The purpose of such liability is to insure that the costs of injuries resulting from defective products are borne by the manufacturers that put such products on the market rather than by the injured persons who are powerless to protect themselves. Sales warranties serve this purpose fitfully at best (Citation). In the present case, for example, plaintiff was able to plead and prove an express warranty only because he read and relied on the representations of the Shopsmith's ruggedness contained in the manufacturer's brochure. Implicit in the machine's presence on the market, however, was a representation that it would safely do the jobs for which it was built. Under these circumstances, it should not be controlling whether plaintiff selected the machine because of the statements in the brochure, or because of the machine's own appearance of excellence that belied the defect lurking beneath the surface, or because he merely assumed that it would safely do the jobs it was built to do. It should not be controlling whether the details of the sales from manufacturer to retailer and from retailer to plaintiff's wife were such that one or more of the implied warranties of the sales act arose (Citation). "The remedies of injured consumers ought not to be made to depend upon the intricacies of the law of sales" (Citations). To establish the manufacturer's liability it was sufficient that plaintiff proved that he was injured while using the Shopsmith in a way it was intended to be used as a result of a defect in design and manufacture of which plaintiff was not aware that made the Shopsmith unsafe for its intended use. . . . .

The judgment is affirmed.

□   □   □

1. Is this case a design or production defect case? Does the court distinguish between production and design defects in this far-reaching opinion?

2. The last sentence quoted from the opinion states that the manufacturer is liable if the product was being used as *intended* when the defect caused the injury. This suggests that a manufacturer's duty exists only for the prescribed uses of the product. Does the rest of the opinion support this narrow interpretation?

3. Consider fully the reasoning of the court in rejecting both warranty and representation theories as a basis for adopting strict liability.

4. Can we isolate those considerations, either stated or implied by the court, necessary to establish defect in strict liability?

5. Formulate the design and/or production considerations to minimize loosening of the tail stock screws under foreseeable use conditions of this product.

DREISONSTOK v. VOLKSWAGENWERK, A. G.

489 F.2d 1066
United States Court of Appeals, Fourth Circuit
January 14, 1974

DONALD RUSSELL, Circuit Judge.

The plaintiff, along with her mother, sues a car manufacturer for so-called "enhanced" injuries sustained by her when the Volkswagen microbus in which she was riding crashed into a telephone pole. The microbus had passed the crest of a small hill and was proceeding down the grade at the time of the accident. When the vehicle passed the crest of the hill, the driver noted that his speed was about 40 miles per hour. As the vehicle continued down the hill, the bus began "picking up some speed, a little too much." To reduce his speed, the driver attempted to downshift the vehicle. Because he had some difficulty in locating the gearshift lever, the driver took his "eyes off the road" and in some way "pulled the steering wheel" causing the vehicle to veer to "the right" into "the driveway." The plaintiff screamed, causing the driver to look up. As the driver did, he "saw a telephone pole headed right toward us." He tried to cut back into the road but there "was an oncoming vehicle the other way, so it was either the telephone pole or another vehicle." He chose the telephone pole. The bus hit the pole on its right front. The plaintiff was seated in the center of the seat, next to the driver, with her left leg under her. As a result of the impact, her right leg was caught between the back of the seat and the dashboard of the van and she was apparently thrown forward. She sustained severe injuries to her ankle and femur. She seeks to recover for her injuries, and her mother for medical expenses, from the vehicle manufacturer, contending that the latter was guilty of negligent design in the location of the gearshift in its vehicle and in the want of crashworthiness of its vehicle. The action was tried without a jury. The District Court dismissed the claim relating to the gearshift but concluded that the defendant manufacturer had been guilty of negligence in failing to use due care in the design of its vehicle by providing "sufficient energy-absorbing materials or devices or 'crush space,' if you will, so that at 40 miles an hour the integrity of the passenger compartment would not be violated," and that, as a result, the injuries of the plaintiff were enhanced "over and above those injuries which the plaintiff might have incurred." From judgment entered on the basis of that conclusion in favor of the plaintiff and her mother, the defendants have appealed. We reverse.

The correctness of the finding by the District Court that the defendant manufacturer was guilty of negligent design in this case depends on the determination of what extent a car manufacturer owes the duty to design and market a "crashworthy" vehicle, one which, in the event of a collision, resulting accidentally or negligently from the act of another and not from any defect or malfunction in the vehicle itself, protects against unreasonable risk of injury to the occupants. The existence and nature of such a duty is a legal issue, for resolution as a matter of law. So much all the authorities agree. There are, however, two fairly definite lines of conflicting authority on whether there is such a duty. One group . . . holds that no such duty rests on the manufacturer, since the "intended use" of an automobile does not extend to collisions. The other, while relieving the manufacturer of any duty to design an accident-proof vehicle, would impose a duty to use reasonable care in the design and manufacture of its product so as "to eliminate any unreasonable risk of foreseeable injury" as a result of a collision, for which the manufacturer may not be responsible. . . .

The key phrase in the statement of the . . . rule is "*unreasonable* risk of injury in the event of a collision". . . . It would patently be unreasonable "to require the manufacturer to provide for every conceivable use or unuse of a car." Nader & Page, Automobile Design and the Judicial Process, 55 *Cal. L. Rev.* 645, 646. Liability for negligent design thus "is imposed only when an unreasonable danger is created. Whether or not this has occurred should be determined by general negligence principles, which involve a balancing of the likelihood of harm, and the gravity of harm if it happens against the burden of the precautions which would be effective to avoid the harm." (Citation.). . . . The likelihood of harm is tied in with the obviousness of the danger, whether latent or patent, since it is frequently stated "that a design is not unreasonably dangerous because the risk is one which anyone immediately would recognize and avoid" (Citation). The purposes and intended use of the article is an even more important factor to be considered. After all, it is a commonplace that utility of design and attractiveness of the style of the car are elements which car manufacturers seek after and by which buyers are influenced in their selections. In every case, the utility and purpose of the particular type of vehicle will govern in varying degree the standards of safety to be observed in its design. This was recognized in the Traffic and Motor Vehicle Safety Act, which undertakes "to establish motor vehicle safety standards for motor vehicles." 15 U.S.C. 1381 *et seq.* In prescribing such standards, the Secretary is directed to "consider whether any such proposed standard is *reasonable, practicable and appropriate for the particular type of motor vehicle.* . . ." Section 1392(f)(3). (Italics added.) Stated somewhat differently, the safety of every type of vehicle is to be evaluated under this Act in connection with what is "reasonable, practicable and appropriate" for its special type. And this is the same rule that has been judicially applied . . . Thus, in *Dyson v. General Motors Corporation* (D.C. Pa. 1969) 298 F. Supp. 1064, 1073, the Court emphasized that design safety must take account of "differentiation between various models of automobile" and involves "a recognition of the inherent characteristics of each." It pointed out that a convertible could not be made "as safe in roll-over accidents as a standard four-door sedan with center posts and full-door frames." The convertible was only required to be as reasonably safe as its intended use would allow and "not appreciably less safe than other convertibles." Price is, also, a factor to be considered, for, if a change in design would appreciably add to cost, add little to safety, and take an article out of the price range of the market to which it was intended to appeal, it may be "unreasonable" as well as "impractical" for the Courts to require the manufacturer to adopt such change. Of course, if an article can be made safer and the hazard of harm may be mitigated "by an alternate design or device at no substantial increase in price," then the manufacturer has a duty to adopt such a design but a Cadillac may be expected to include more in the way of both conveniences and "crashworthiness" than the economy car. Moreover, in a "crashworthy" case, it is necessary to consider the circumstances of the accident itself. As *Dyson* puts it, "it could not reasonably be argued that a car manufacturer should be held liable because its vehicle collapsed when involved in a head-on collision with a large truck, at high speed. In summary, every case such as this involves a delicate balancing of many factors in order to determine whether the manufacturer has used ordinary care in designing a car, which, giving consideration to the market purposes and utility of the vehicle, did not involve unreasonable risk of injury to occupants within the range of its "intended use."

Applying the foregoing principles to the facts of this particular case, it is clear that there was no violation by the defendant of its duty of ordinary care in the design of its vehicle. The defendant's vehicle, described as "a van type multipurpose vehicle," was of a special type and particular design. This design was uniquely developed in order to provide the owner with the maximum amount of either cargo or passenger space in a vehicle inexpensively priced and of such dimensions as to make possible easy maneuverability. To achieve this, it advanced the driver's seat forward, bringing such seat in close proximity to the front of the vehicle, thereby adding to the cargo or passenger space. This, of course, reduced considerably the space between the exact front of the vehicle and the driver's compartment. All of this was readily discernible to any one using the vehicle; in fact, it was, as we have said, the unique feature of the vehicle. The usefulness of the design is vouchsafed by the popularity of the type. It was of special utility as a van for the transportation of light cargo, as a family camper, as a station wagon and for use by passenger groups too large for the average passenger car. It was a design that had been adopted by other manufacturers, including American. . . . There was no evidence in the record that there was any practical way of improving the "crashability" of the vehicle that would have been consistent with the peculiar purposes of its design. The only theory on which the plaintiffs posited their claim of negligent design was, to quote the language of their brief in this Court, that "[T]he 1968 Volkswagen station wagon did not provide the protection for the front seat passengers as did the 'normal' or standard passenger car." The "normal or standard passenger car" to which, under the plaintiff's argument, the vehicle was required to conform if it was to meet the test of reasonable design, was defined by the plaintiff on one occasion as "a standard American made vehicle, which is a configuration with the passengers in the middle and the motor in the front" and on another as "a passenger car with an engine in front and with a long hood. . . ." And all of their expert testimony was to this point. These experts offered by the plaintiffs concededly made no attempt to compare for safety of design or for any other purpose defendant's special type of vehicle with similar types made by other manufacturers or indicated any way in which safety in such vehicles could have been improved, given the peculiar purpose of the vehicle. They completely disregarded the rule developed in *Dyson, supra,* and the standards developed by Congress in the Traffic and Motor Vehicle Safety Act, which would compare vehicles of the same type in determining safety standards. These experts contented themselves with arriving at the reasonable design of the defendant's vehicle by one test and that was by comparing it with the 1966 midsized Ford passenger car. In short, the plaintiff's theory of negligent design and the thrust of all their expert testimony on such point was that, to meet the test of ordinary care in design so as to avoid "unreasonable risk" of injury, the vehicle of the defendant had to conform with the configuration of the standard American passenger car, vintage 1966, i.e., its motor must be in front, not in the rear; its passenger compartment must be "in the middle"; and the space in front of the passenger compartment must be. approximately the same as that in a "standard American passenger car." Under this standard, any rear engine car would be "inherently dangerous"; any microbus or front-end tractor—both in wide use in 1968 and now—would be declared "inherently dangerous." To avoid liability for negligent design, no manufacturer could introduce any innovative or unique design, even though reasonably calculated to provide some special advantage such as greater roominess. . . . It is entirely impermissible to predicate a conclusion of negligent design simply because a vehicle, having a distinctive purpose, such as the microbus, does not conform to the design of another type of vehicle, such as a standard passenger car, having a different nature and utility. As a matter of fact, the defendant offered evidence—unrefuted in the testimony—that its design, at least so far as "crash space" between the front and the passenger compartment, was equal to or superior to that of other vehicles of like type.

The District Court, however, seems to have accepted plaintiffs' theory, though expressing it somewhat differently from the standard stated by the plaintiffs in their brief. It stated the standard of ordinary care in design to require that a vehicle be able to withstand a "head-on" collision at 40 miles an hour without a violation of "the integrity of the passenger compartment," and held that the defendant had "violated" its duty in failing to meet this standard. Accepting the principle that a manufacturer must anticipate that its product will likely at some point in its use be involved in a collision, does ordinary care demand that, in taking precautions, it must provide against impacts at a speed of 40 miles per hour? Is this the "reasonable risk," as it has been defined in the authorities quoted *supra*, against which the manufacturer must provide protection? And why "40 miles an hour" as the standard anyway? This standard was adopted, it seems clear from the District Court's order, because the plaintiff contended that a "standard American passenger car" had sufficient "crash space" that its passenger compartment would not have been invaded in a 40-mile impact. This conclusion rests on some measurements made by the plaintiffs' experts in comparing the "crashability" of a microbus and that of a 1966 Ford passenger car. No tests were made by these experts to confirm experimentally these conclusions. The plaintiffs' experts merely measured the distance from the exact front of the microbus and the point where the plaintiff had collided with the interior of the van and compared that distance with the distance between the front and passenger seat of a 1966 Ford passenger car; and because the distance in the latter instance was greater than in the former, they concluded that, had the plaintiff been riding in a 1966 Ford passenger car, she would have escaped injury. But, as we have already seen, in determining whether a vehicle has been negligently designed so far as safety is concerned, the special purpose and character of the particular type of vehicle must be considered, and a microbus is no more to be compared with a standard 1966 passenger type car than the convertible instanced in *Dyson* is to be compared with a standard hard-top passenger car. Both the plaintiffs and the District Court employed an improper standard in determining whether the defendant had been guilty of negligent design.

Reversed and remanded with directions to the District Court to enter judgment in favor of the appellants-defendants.

□   □   □

1. Can one isolate the factors that this court considers important in establishing whether product users are subject to unreasonable risk of injury? Are these factors

both necessary and sufficient? How should they be weighed in arriving at a conclusion of whether or not a product is unreasonably dangerous?

2. The court adopted the rule that a manufacturer has a duty to market "crashworthy" cars. Do you agree with this rule? Why?

3. The district court accepted the plaintiffs' argument, rejected by the appellate court, that the microbus should at least be as crashworthy as the 1966 Ford passenger car. If you agree that the plaintiffs' standard was inappropriate, what standard should have been used to measure the crashworthiness of the microbus?

4. The court suggests that the buyer of a microbus trades off reduced occupant protection for increased cargo capacity and maneuverability. Is this trade-off obvious during purchase? Should there be some minimum standard for the crashworthiness of every vehicle? If so, what should the criteria and limits be for such a standard?

5. The plaintiffs' experts were criticized for inadequate testing of their conclusion. On the assumption that you support the plaintiffs' contention that the microbus was not crashworthy, what should have been the scope and content of an adequate investigation?

6. On the assumption that the manufacturer of the microbus wished to explore the possibility of improving the crashworthiness of the vehicle, what considerations, test requirements, and design requirements would you, as the design engineer, propose?

PHILLIPS v. KIMWOOD MACHINE COMPANY

525 P.2d 1033
Supreme Court of Oregon, In Banc
September 6, 1974
(In the lower court, a verdict was directed for the manufacturer,
and the plaintiff appealed to the Supreme Court of Oregon.)

HOLMAN, Justice.

Plaintiff was injured while feeding fiberboard into a sanding machine during his employment with Pope and Talbot, a wood products manufacturer. The sanding machine had been purchased by Pope and Talbot from defendant. Plaintiff brought this action on a products liability theory, contending the sanding machine was unreasonably dangerous by virtue of defective design. At the completion of the testimony, defendant's motion for a directed verdict was granted and plaintiff appealed.

... The machine in question was a six-headed sander. Each sanding head was a rapidly moving belt which revolved in the direction opposite to that which the pieces of fiberboard moved through the machine. Three of the heads sanded the top of the fiberboard sheet and three sanded the bottom. The top half of the machine could be raised or lowered depending upon the thickness of the fiberboard to be sanded. The bottom half of the machine had powered rollers which moved the fiberboard through the machine as the fiberboard was being sanded. The top half of the machine had pinch rolls, not powered, which, when pressed down on the fiberboard by use of springs, kept the sanding heads from forcefully rejecting it from the machine.

On the day of the accident plaintiff was engaged in feeding the sheets of fiberboard into the sander. Because of the defective operation of a press, a large group of sheets of extra thickness was received for sanding. These sheets could not be inserted into the machine as it was set, so the top half of the sander was adjusted upwards to leave a greater space between the top and bottom halves to accommodate the extra thick fiberboard sheets. During the sanding of the extra thick sheets, a thin sheet of fiberboard, which had become mixed with the lot, was inserted into the machine. The pressure exerted by the pinch rolls in the top half of the machine was insufficient to counteract the pressure which the sanding belts were exerting upon the thin sheet of fiberboard and, as a result, the machine regurgitated the piece of fiberboard back at plaintiff, hitting him in the abdomen and causing him the injuries for which he now seeks compensation.

Plaintiff asserts in his complaint that the machine was defective in its design and unreasonably dangerous because (1) "it . . . could not be operated in the manner and for the purpose for which it was manufactured and sold without throwing back towards the operator panels of material being sanded . . . ," and (2) " . . . it did not . . . contain . . . any guards, catches, shields, barricades or similar devices to protect the operator of said machine from being struck by panels of material thrown back out of the sanding machine. . . ." The two allegations assert substantially the same thing, the first one in general terms, and the second one in particular terms. In effect, they allege the machine was defective and was unreasonably dangerous because there were no safety devices to protect the person feeding the machine from the regurgitation of sheets of fiberboard.

While we do not here attempt to recount all of the testimony presented by plaintiff concerning the defective design of the machine, there was evidence from which the jury could find that at a relatively small expense there could have been built into, or subsequently installed on, the machine a line of metal teeth which would point in the direction that the fiberboard progresses through the machine and which would press lightly against the sheet but which, in case of attempted regurgitation, would be jammed into it, thus stopping its backward motion. The evidence also showed that after the accident such teeth were installed upon the machine for that purpose by Pope and Talbot, whereupon subsequent regurgitations of thin fiberboard sheets were prevented while the efficiency of the machine was maintained. There was also evidence that defendant makes smaller sanders which usually are manually fed and on which there is such a safety device.

It was shown that the machine in question was built for use with an automatic feeder and that the one installed at Pope and Talbot is the only six-headed sander manufactured by defendant which is manually fed. There also was testimony that at the time of the purchase by Pope and Talbot, defendant had automatic feeders for sale but that Pope and Talbot, did not purchase or show any interest in such a feeder. Pope and Talbot furnished a feeding device of their own manufacture for the machine which was partially automatic and partially manual but which, the jury would find, at times placed an employee in the way of regurgitated sheets.

There was testimony that at the time defendant's employee inspected the installation of the machine purchased by Pope and Talbot, which inspection was required by their contract, the inspecting employee became aware that the machine was being manually fed. There was no testimony of any warning given by defendant of the danger concerning regurgitated sheets to a person manually feeding the machine. Neither was there any evidence that Pope and Talbot was told that the machine was built for use with a fully automatic feeder and that it was not to be fed manually, nor was the recommendation made to plaintiff's employer that if the machine was to be used without a fully automatic feeder, some sort of safety device should be used for the protection of anyone who was manually feeding the machine. There was evidence that one of Pope and Talbot's representatives was told that the top of the machine should not be raised while sanding was taking place, but there was no evidence of the danger from doing so ever being mentioned. . . . .

In defense of its judgment based upon a directed verdict, defendant contends there was no proof of a defect in the product, and therefore strict liability should not apply. This court and other courts continue to flounder while attempting to determine how one decides whether a product is "in a defective condition unreasonably dangerous to the user." It has been recognized that unreasonably dangerous defects in products come from two principal sources: (1) mismanufacture and (2) faulty design. Mismanufacture is relatively simple to identify because the item in question is capable of being compared with similar articles made by the same manufacturer. However, whether the mismanufactured article is dangerously defective because of the flaw is sometimes difficult to ascertain because not every such flaw which causes injury makes the article dangerously defective.

The problem with strict liability of products has been one of limitation. No one wants absolute liability where all the article has to do is to cause injury. To impose liability there has to be something about the article which makes it dangerously defective without regard to whether the manufacturer was or was not at fault for such condition. A test for unreasonable danger is therefore vital. A dangerously defective article would be one which a reasonable person would not put into the stream of commerce *if he had knowledge of its harmful character*. The test, therefore, is whether the seller would be negligent if he sold the article *knowing of the risk involved*. Strict liability imposes what amounts to constructive knowledge of the condition of the product.

On the surface such a test would seem to be different than the test of 2 Restatement (Second) of Torts § 402A, comment i, of "dangerous to an extent beyond that which would be contemplated by the ordinary consumer who purchases it." This court has used this test in the past. These are not necessarily different standards, however. As stated in *Welch v. Outboard Marine Corp.* [481 F.2d 252 (5th Cir. 1973)], where the court affirmed an instruction containing both standards:

We see no necessary inconsistency between a seller-oriented standard and a user-oriented standard when, as here each turns on foreseeable risks. They are two sides of the same standard. A product is defective and unreasonably dangerous when a reasonable seller would not sell the product if he knew of the risks involved or if the risks are greater than a reasonable buyer would expect.

To elucidate this point further, we feel that the two standards are the same because a seller acting reasonably would be selling the same product which a reasonable consumer believes he is purchasing. That is to say, a manufacturer who would be negligent in marketing a given product, considering its risks, would necessarily be marketing a product which fell below the reasonable expectations of consumers who purchase it. The foreseeable uses to which a product could be put would be the same in the minds of both the seller and the buyer unless one of the parties was not acting reasonably. . . .

While apparently judging the seller's conduct, the test set out above would be actually a characterization of the product by a jury. If the manufacturer was not acting reasonably in selling the product, knowing of the risks involved, then the product would be dangerously defective when sold and the manufacturer would be subject to liability.

In the case of a product which is claimed to be dangerously defective because of misdesign, the process is not so easy as in the case of mismanufacture. All the products made to that design are the same. The question of whether the design is unreasonably dangerous can be determined only by taking into consideration the surrounding circumstances and knowledge at the time the article was sold, and determining therefrom whether a reasonably prudent manufacturer would have so designed and sold the article in question had he known of the risk involved which injured plaintiff. The issue has been raised in some courts concerning whether, in this context, there is any distinction between strict liability and negligence. The evidence which proves the one will almost always, if not always, prove the other. We discussed this matter recently in the case of *Roach v. Kononen*, 99 Or. Adv. Sh. 1092, 525 P.2d 125 (1974), and pointed out that there is a difference between strict liability for misdesign and negligence. We said:

> However, be all this as it may, it is generally recognized that the basic difference between negligence on the one hand and strict liability for a design defect on the other is that in strict liability we are talking about the condition (dangerousness) of an article which is designed in a particular way, while in negligence we are talking about the reasonableness of the manufacturer's actions in designing and selling the article as he did. The article can have a degree of dangerousness which the law of strict liability will not tolerate even though the actions of the designer were entirely reasonable in view of what he knew at the time he planned and sold the manufactured article. [A] way of determining whether the condition of the article is the requisite degree of dangerousness to be defective (unreasonably dangerous; greater degree of danger than a consumer has a right to expect; not duly safe) is to assume that the manufacturer knew of the product's propensity to injure as it did, and then to ask whether, with such knowledge, something should have been done about the danger before it was sold. In other words, a greater burden is placed on the manufacturer than is the case in negligence because the law assumes he has knowledge of the article's dangerous propensity which he may not reasonably be expected to have, had he been charged with negligence. 99 Or. Adv. Sh. at 1099, 525 P.2d at 129.

To some it may seem that absolute liability has been imposed upon the manufacturer since it might be argued that no manufacturer could reasonably put into the stream of commerce an article which he realized might result in injury to a user. This is not the case, however. The manner of injury may be so fortuitous and the chances of injury occurring so remote that it is reasonable to sell the product despite the danger. In design cases the utility of the article may be so great, and the change of design necessary to alleviate the danger in question may so impair such utility, that it is reasonable to market the product as it is, even though the possibility of injury exists and was realized at the time of the sale. Again, the cost of the change necessary to alleviate the danger in design may be so great that the article would be priced out of the market and no one would buy it even though it was of high utility. Such an article is not dangerously defective despite its having inflicted injury.

In this case defendant contends it was Pope and Talbot's choice to purchase and use the sander without an automatic feeder, even though it was manufactured to be used with one, and, therefore, it was Pope and Talbot's business choice which resulted in plaintiff's injury and not any misdesign by defendant. However, it is recognized that a failure to warn may make a product unreasonably dangerous. . . . .

It is our opinion that the evidence was sufficient for the jury to find that a reasonably prudent manufacturer, knowing that the machine would be fed manually and having the constructive knowledge of its propensity to regurgitate thin sheets when it was set for thick ones, which the courts via strict liability have imposed upon it, would have warned plaintiff's employer either to feed it automatically or to use some safety device, and that, in the absence of such a warning, the machine was dangerously defective. It is therefore unnecessary for us to decide the questions that would arise had adequate warnings been given. . . . .

It is necessary to remember that whether the doctrine of negligence, ultrahazardousness, or strict liability is being used to impose liability, the same process is going on in each instance, i.e., weighing the utility of the article against the risk of its use. Therefore, the same language and concepts of reasonableness are used by courts for the determination of unreasonable danger in products liability cases. . . .The difference between the three theories of recovery is in the manner in which the decisional functions are distributed between the court and the jury. The following language, we believe, is appropriate:

> In an action for negligence it is normally the function of the jury to determine whether the defendant was negligent, subject, of course, to the authority of the judge to direct a verdict for the defendant if he finds that the jury could not reasonably find for the plaintiff. On the other hand, in an action based on strict liability . . . for an abnormally dangerous activity, the determination as to whether strict liability will be imposed for the activity is held to be one for the judge, not the jury—for the reason that the decision involves issues of general social policy. In the products cases the courts seem not to have approached the problem in this fashion. Instead, they seem to have assumed that strict products liability is like negligence in this respect, so that a plaintiff, in order to recover, must convince the jury that the product was 'defective' or 'unreasonably dangerous' or 'not duly safe,' or whatever test is used. This generally works quite satisfactorily when the question is whether the product was unsafe because of an error in the manufacturing process so that it was not in the condition in which it was intended to be. The issue then seems more factual of the kind the jury is accustomed to handling. The difficulty comes when it is not just the single article which is to be classed as unsafe because something went wrong in the making of it, but a whole group or class or type which may be unsafe because of the nature of the design. It is here that the policy issues become very important and the factors . . . must be collected and carefully weighed. . . . It is here that the court—whether

trial or appellate—does consider these issues in deciding whether to submit the case to the jury. If a plaintiff sues the manufacturer of a butcher knife because he cut his finger, on the sole ground that the knife was so sharp that it was likely to cut human flesh, the court would probably take the case out of the hands of the jury and not give it the opportunity to find that the knife was unsafe. Similarly with an aspirin manufacturer, when an ordinary tablet stuck to the lining of the plaintiff's stomach and caused a hemorrhage, or the manufacturer of the Pasteur treatment for rabies, when there were untoward reactions. The problem in these cases is likely to be called one of law and decided by the court. Court control of jury action is more extensive here than in the ordinary negligence action. And yet, of course, if the court decides that it would be reasonable to allow the jury to find for the plaintiff, the issue of lack of due safety will be submitted to the jury even in these cases. (Footnotes omitted.)

It is important to point out, as indicated in the above quotation, that while the decision is made by the court whether an activity is abnormally dangerous and strict liability ... is to be applied, the determination of whether a product is dangerously defective and strict liability is to be applied has been treated as one primarily for the jury, similar to the manner in which negligence is determined. . . . If such a case has been made out, then it is submitted to the jury for a determination under instructions as to what constitutes a "dangerously defective" product, much in the same manner as negligence is submitted to the jury under the "reasonable man" rule. . . . .

Defendant calls to our attention that one of the principal rationales behind the imposition of strict liability upon the manufacturer for injuries caused by dangerously defective products is that the manufacturer is in the position of distributing the cost of such risks among all users of the product. Defendant then argues that in the present situation Pope and Talbot would normally bear the responsibility for the injury to its employee and that because Pope and Talbot is just as capable of spreading the cost of injury by the sale of its product as is defendant, there is no logic in imposing liability without fault upon defendant for the purpose of distributing the risk. . . .

While the enterprise liability theory may be indifferent as to whether the defendant or plaintiff's employer should bear this loss, there are other theories which allow us to make a choice.

Where a defendant's product is adjudged by a jury to be dangerously defective, imposition of liability on the manufacturer will cause him to take some steps (or at least make calculations) to improve his product. Although such inducement may not be any greater under a system of strict liability than under a system of negligence recovery, it is certainly greater than if the liability was imposed on another party simply because that other party was a better risk distributor. We suspect that, in the final analysis, the imposition of liability has a beneficial effect on manufacturers of defective products both in the care they take and in the warning they give.

The case is reversed and remanded for a new trial.

□   □   □

1. The court, here, views the distinction between negligence and strict liability as one that defines the judge's role. What is this role? What functions would the jury serve in strict liability in contrast to negligence?
2. The court indicates that the manufacturer should have warned the purchaser

either to buy an automatic feeder or use the "finger" device. From the viewpoint of risk-utility considerations, consider the efficacy of warning versus incorporating the "fingers" as a standard feature of the product.

McCORMACK v. HANKSCRAFT COMPANY

278 Min. 322
154 N.W. 2d 488
Supreme Court of Minnesota
November 17, 1967
Rehearing Denied December 12, 1967

ROGOSHESKE, Justice.

Plaintiff appeals from the judgment entered upon an order of the district court granting judgment n.o.v. and a conditional new trial in favor of defendant, Hankscraft Company, Inc.

Plaintiff, Andrea McCormack, brought this action for damages by Donald McCormack, her father and natural guardian, alleging that defendant's negligence and breach of implied and express warranties in the manufacture and sale of a steam vaporizer caused her to suffer substantial personal injuries. . . . The court submitted the case to the jury on the questions of negligence and breach of express warranties, refusing to instruct on implied warranties. The jury returned a verdict against defendant, awarding plaintiff $150,000 damages.

Defendant's motion for judgment n.o.v. [notwithstanding the verdict] and in the alternative for a new trial was granted. . . . .

[T]he jury reasonably could have found the following facts.

In October 1957, Andrea's father, Donald McCormack, purchased from a retail drugstore an electric Hankscraft steam vaporizer manufactured by defendant. It was purchased pursuant to the advice of a doctor to be used as a humidifier for Andrea, then 8 months old, who had just returned from being hospitalized for croup and pneumonia. After unpacking the vaporizer, Andrea's parents read the instruction booklet accompanying the unit from "cover to cover." Then, following defendant's printed instructions, they put the vaporizer to use in the treatment of Andrea. Thereafter, from time to time as the need arose, it was used for the young children of the family in the prescribed manner, including the use of it unattended throughout the night, without any problem. . . . .

In the spring of 1960, the children had colds and Mrs. McCormack desired to use the vaporizer but found it "wasn't working." She went to the same self-service drugstore and purchased another Hankscraft vaporizer similar to the first unit. She personally selected it without the aid or recommendation of any clerk because it was a Hankscraft, knowing defendant to be a manufacturer of a number of products for children and relying upon defendant's prior representations contained in the booklet accompanying the first vaporizer that its vaporizers were "safe" and "practically foolproof," as well as advertisements representing them to be "tip-proof." This second vaporizer, purchased in a sealed carton, was known as Model 202A, and its general appearance as to size and shape and its method of operation were identical with the first unit. It was accompanied by an instruction booklet substantially identical to that furnished with the first vaporizer, which Mrs. McCormack again completely read.

This second vaporizer had been used about a half dozen times without incident when, on November 20, 1960, it was again set up for use in a small bedroom in the northwest corner of the house, occupied by Andrea, then 3 years and 9 months old, and her baby sister, Alison, 1 year and 10 months old. Andrea slept in a regular single bed. . . .Andrea's mother set up the vaporizer at about 8 p.m. on a seat-step-type metal kitchen stool about 2½ feet high. . . .The stool was about 4 feet from the foot of Andrea's bed. When steam started coming from the hole in the top of the unit, Mrs. McCormack left the room. After visiting a neighbor until about 11 p.m., she did some ironing, and at about 1:30 a.m., she returned to the room to replenish the water supply in the vaporizer. Using some type of "mitt," she lifted the cap and poured water from a milk bottle into the jar. She then went to bed.

At about 2:30 a.m., Mrs. McCormack heard a terrible scream and got out of bed. She found Andrea lying on the floor of her bedroom, screaming. The metal stool was upright, but the vaporizer was on the floor and the water had come out of the jar. The vaporizer had separated into its three component parts—a glass jar, a metal pan, and a plastic top-heating unit. The electric cord was still plugged into the electric outlet. In some manner, Andrea, while intending to go to the bathroom, had tipped over the vaporizer and caused the water in the jar to spill upon her body.

Andrea was rushed to the hospital for treatment. More than 30 percent of her body had severe burns; she was suffering from shock; and her condition was critical for some time. She had third-degree burns on her chest, shoulders, and back. Skin-graft surgery was performed on her twice. She was hospitalized for 74½ days. Ten days later she was admitted to the Kenny Institute for treatment. She remained there 102 days and thereafter was taken to the Mayo Clinic, where she had further surgery in August 1961. At the time of the trial, Andrea had heavy scar tissue on her chest, stomach, legs, arms, and neck; a deformed jaw; restricted movement of her head; an irregular posture; and the prospect of 6 to 12 more surgical procedures during her lifetime. Her condition is largely permanent.

The "automatic-electric" vaporizer in question is of normal design and consists of three component parts—an aluminum pan which serves as a base, a 1-gallon glass jar or water reservoir which is inserted into the pan, and a black plastic cap to which is fastened a black plastic heating-chamber tube. . . . .

The cap and heating chamber assembly, by its own weight, rests loosely upon the glass jar with the black tube extending down into the jar. There are no threads inside the plastic cap or any other means provided to fasten the cap to the threaded neck of the jar. This design and construction were intended by defendant to serve as a safety measure to avoid any buildup of steam in the glass jar, but it also has the result of allowing the water in the jar to gush out instantaneously when the vaporizer is tipped over. This unit can be tipped over easily by a child through the exertion of about 2 pounds of force.

To operate the vaporizer in accordance with the instructions contained in defendant's booklet, the "entire plastic cover" is removed, the glass jar is filled to the filling marker with tap water containing minerals, and the cord is plugged into an electric outlet, whereupon "[t]he vaporizer will produce a gentle cloud of steam within a few minutes." The heating unit is designed so that it automatically turns off whenever the water in the jar decreases to a certain level. As the booklet pictorially illustrates, the water from the jar enters the lower section of the heating chamber through the small hole at the bottom. Here it is heated until it boils and is vaporized into steam, which passes out of the unit through the hole in the cap.

Tests made of the unit established that after about 4 minutes of operation the water in the heating chamber reaches 212 degrees Fahrenheit and steam emanates from the steam port. Although the water in the jar outside the heating chamber does not reach the boiling point, the upper portion of this water does reach 211 degrees within 35 minutes of operation and the middle portion reaches 211 degrees within 3 hours. The temperature of the outside of the jar ranges from 172 degrees after about 1 hour to 182 degrees after 5 hours. Thus, during most of the 6- to 8-hour period in which the unit is designed to operate without refilling, the water in the reservoir is scalding hot, since water of 145-degree temperature will burn and 182-degree water will cause third-degree burns on a child 5 years old.

By touch, a user can determine that the water in the jar outside the heating unit, as well as the jar and the plastic cap, becomes hot during the operation of the vaporizer. However, there is no movement of the water in the jar and no means by which a user could discern by sight or touch that this reserve water in the jar became and remained scalding hot. Plaintiff's parents, relying upon their understanding of what defendant represented in its instruction booklet, were reasonably led to believe up to the time of plaintiff's injury that, since steam was generated only in the heating unit, the temperature of the water in the jar during the entire operation of the vaporizer remained the same as when put in. At all of the times when replenishing the water in either the first or second vaporizer, plaintiff's mother followed the routine of removing the entire plastic cover by using some "glove" or "mitt" as a precaution against the steam. She would leave the cord plugged in, add water to the jar, replace the cover, wait until steam appeared, and then leave the unit unattended in the room. As her testimony implied, she at no time discovered by touching or handling the unit when it was in use that the temperature of any part of the water in the jar became hot.

The instruction booklet furnished by defendant did not disclose the scalding temperatures reached by the water in the jar, nor was any warning given as to the dangers that could result from an accidental upset of the unit. While plaintiff's mother realized that the unit could be tipped over by a sufficient external force, she justifiably relied upon defendant's representations that it was "safe," "practically foolproof," and "tip-proof." She understood this to mean that the unit "was safe to use around [her] children" and that she "didn't have to worry" about dangers when it was left unattended in a child's room since this was the primary purpose for which it was sold.

In its booklet and advertising, defendant in fact made the representations relied upon by plaintiff's mother. In addition to the simple operating instructions and a pictorial "cut-away" indicating how the steam is generated by the electrodes in the heating chamber, the booklet stated:

WHY THE HANKSCRAFT VAPORIZER IS SUPERIOR TO OTHERS IN DESIGN.

Your vaporizer will run all night on one filling of water, directing a steady, gentle flow of medicated steam exactly where it is needed. No attention is necessary.

It's safe, too, and practically foolproof. Since the water itself makes the electric contact, the vaporizer shuts off automatically when the water is gone. The electric unit cannot burn out.

The booklet also had a picture of a vaporizer sending steam over a baby's crib. . . .

Defendant's officers realized that the vaporizers would be primarily used in the treatment of children and usually would be unattended. They had knowledge that the water in the jar got scalding hot; that this water would cause third-degree burns on a small child; that the water in the jar would gush out instantaneously if the unit were tipped over; that the unit was not "tip-proof"; that the combination of the unsecured top and the hot water in the jar was dangerous because of the possibility that a child might tip it over during operation; and that, prior to plaintiff's injury, at least 10 to 12 children had been burned in this manner. Furthermore, defendant's officers realized that the fact the water in the jar got hot was not discernible during operation except by touching or handling the unit and that a user could conclude from their booklet that steam was generated in the plastic core and be led to believe that the reserve water in the jar did not itself become scalding hot.

Plaintiff called two expert witnesses, whose qualifications in the field of product design were unquestioned. Both testified that the design of the vaporizer was defective principally in that it failed to provide a means for securing the plastic cover to the jar in a manner which would prevent the water in the jar from instantaneously discharging when the unit was tipped over. In the opinion of both, the unit could be tipped over with little force and this defective design created a risk of bodily harm to a child if the unit were left operating and unattended in the room. This defect could have been eradicated by the adoption of any one of several practical and inexpensive alternative designs which utilized simple and well-known techniques to secure the top of the jar. Any of these alternative designs could have been employed by defendant prior to its production of the second vaporizer by the application of sound product-design principles current at that time. Among these alternative designs was that of making threads on the inside of the plastic top so it could screw onto the jar and the putting of two or three small holes in the top, which would take care of any danger that steam would build up inside the jar. Both witnesses stated that such a change in design was essential to make the unit safe for its intended use because the presence of near-boiling water in the jar was not discernible by sight or touch and no warning of the risk of harm was contained in defendant's instruction booklet.

Plaintiff contends that the evidence not only raised jury issues as to negligence, breach of warranties, and causation but also is more than sufficient to support the jury's finding of liability on the two theories submitted. Defendant contends the evidence presented was so deficient to establish its liability on any ground that it is entitled to a judgment on the merits as a matter of law.

At this late date in the development of the law relating to the tort liability of manufacturers of all types of products for injuries caused by their products, there can be no doubt that a manufacturer is subject to liability for a failure to use reasonable care in the design of its product to any user or consumer, including any person who may reasonably be expected to be in the vicinity of its use, to protect against unreasonable risk of physical harm while the product is used for its intended purpose. Such liability may equally be predicated upon a failure to use reasonable care in giving adequate and accurate instructions as to the use of the product and a warning as to any dangers reasonably foreseeable in its intended use (Citation).

Plaintiff urges that defendant was negligent both in its failure to give any warning of the dangers inherent in the use of the vaporizer and in its adoption of an unsafe design. . . . Defendant concedes it gave no such warning but vigorously argues that a warning was not necessary since the fact that the water in the jar becomes and remains hot should be obvious to any user. . . . .

We have little difficulty in reaching the conclusion that the evidence justified the jury in finding that defendant failed to exercise reasonable care to inform users, including plaintiff's parents, of the scalding temperatures of the water and to warn of the dangers unreasonably foreseeable in the use of the vaporizer (Citation). Surely the evidence does not as a matter of law compel a conclusion that the true nature and gravity of the dangers which could result from the scalding water in the jar were sufficiently obvious to most potential users as to preclude the jury from finding that due care required an appropriate warning. . . .

We similarly conclude and hold that the evidence is also sufficient to support the jury's verdict of liability on the ground that defendant was negligent in adopting an unsafe design. It is well established that a manufacturer, despite lack of privity of contract, has a duty to use reasonable care in designing its product so that those it should expect will use it are protected from unreasonable risk of harm while the product is being used for its intended use. A breach of such duty renders the manufacturer liable (Citation). Clearly, such a duty was owed to plaintiff for defendant admitted that the primary, intended use of the vaporizer was for the treatment of children's colds and croup.

The proof is sufficient to support plaintiff's claim of defective design in that, among other defects, defendant failed to exercise reasonable care in securing the plastic cover to the jar to guard against the reasonably foreseeable danger that a child would tip the unit over when it was in use and be seriously burned by coming in contact with the scalding water that would instantaneously gush out of the jar. . . . .

We also find no merit in defendant's contention that it was not negligent because any defect caused by its failure to secure the heating unit to the jar was obvious. Clearly the jury could have justifiably found that users, particularly children such as plaintiff who was a mere child of 3 years of age, are incapable of meaningfully comprehending the true nature and gravity of the risk to them that results from a product's design and of effectively acting so as to avoid the danger. . . .

We also conclude that the evidence was sufficient to support a finding of liability upon a breach of an express warranty.

We are persuaded that whether the previously quoted language of the booklet, particularly in combination with the picture of a vaporizer sending steam over a baby's crib, amounted to an express warranty that it was "safe" for a user to let this vaporizer run all night in a child's room without attention was a jury question. No particular words are required to constitute an express warranty, and the representations made must be interpreted as an ordinary person would understand their meaning, with any doubts resolved in favor of the user. Since parents instinctively exercise great care to protect their children from harm, the jury could justifiably conclude that defendant's representations were factual (naturally tending to induce a buyer to purchase) and not mere "puffing" or "sales talk. . . . ."

Reversed with directions to enter judgment upon the verdict.

□ □ □

1. Before technology developed vaporizers, a teakettle on a hot plate set up in the bedroom did the job. Under strict liability would such a steam generator be considered defective? If so, what would be required to make it reasonably safe, on the assumption that the teakettle-hot plate system was marketed as a vaporizer?
2. The court viewed the vaporizer as defective because it lacked either a threaded cap or a warning. Could a warning have just as effectively reduced the danger as a secure cap? Consider these alternatives from the viewpoint of the expected users and the use environment.
3. Discuss the inconvenience of having to disconnect the plug and twist off a screw-on cap with an electric wire attached as against the ease of removing a simple lift-off cap. Why was this not considered in this case?
4. How much safety is enough? At what point should consumers have free choice of the safety features they buy? How should a basic level of safety for each product be established?

VINCER v. ESTHER WILLIAMS ALL-ALUMINUM SWIMMING POOL COMPANY

69 Wisc. 2d 326
230 N.W. 2d 794
Supreme Court of Wisconsin
June 30, 1975

This is a products liability case. The second amended complaint alleges that Curt Vincer, the injured plaintiff-appellant, who was two years old at the time of the July 13, 1970, incident, fell into a swimming pool in the backyard of the home of his grandparents, whom he was visiting. The complaint alleges that a retractable ladder to the above-ground pool had been left in the down position, that the pool was unsupervised, and that Curt climbed the ladder, fell into the water and remained there for an extended period of time, resulting in severe brain damage causing permanent and total disablement. . . .

The complaint states causes of action based upon . . . strict liability due to the defendants' failure to equip the pool with a self-closing gate. . . .

To state a cause of action for strict liability, the complaint alleges, in part:

(a) That the swimming pool was defective and unreasonably dangerous because they failed to take the reasonable and low-cost precaution of building the swimming pool so that the fencing extended across the deck at the top of the ladder opening with a self-closing, self-latching gate on the deck of the swimming pool so as to prevent access to the swimming pool area by children of the age of Curt Vincer, even when the ladder from the deck to the ground was in that down position. . . .

CONNOR T. HANSEN, Justice.

The sole issue on this appeal is whether the complaint states a cause of action against the Esther Williams All-Aluminum Swimming Pool Company and the Banner Builders, Inc. . . . We conclude that it does not. Therefore, we affirm the trial court in its decision. . . .

In *Dippel v. Sciano* (Citation), this court adopted sec. 402A of Restatement, 2 Torts 2d, pertaining to strict liability in tort. Under this section, where the plaintiff proves he was injured by a product "in a defective condition unreasonably dangerous to the user" and establishes the other requisite elements listed in the section, he is relieved of the burden of proving specific acts of negligence by the manufacturer who is then deemed negligent per se. . . .

Comment g to sec. 402A of Restatement, 2 Torts 2d, defines "defective condition" in part as follows:

g. *Defective condition.* The rule stated in this Section applied only where the product is, at the time it leaves the seller's hands, in a condition not contemplated by the ultimate consumer, which will be unreasonably dangerous to him.

The particular defect in the design of the swimming pool, as alleged in the complaint, is the absence of a self-latching and closing gate to prevent entry to the pool. We are satisfied that the swimming pool is not defective in this respect because, as a matter of law, the swimming pool was as safe as it reasonably could be since it did contain a retractable ladder, which unfortunately was allegedly left down and led to the injury of the small child.

Even if a product is defective, it must be shown to be unreasonably dangerous to the user or consumer. Comment i to sec. 402A of the Restatement defines "unreasonably dangerous" in part as follows:

i. *Unreasonably dangerous.* The rule stated in this Section applies only where the defective condition of the product makes it unreasonably dangerous to the user or consumer. Many products cannot possibly be made entirely safe for all consumption, and any food or drug necessarily involves some risk of harm, if only from over-consumption. . . . *The article sold must be dangerous to an extent beyond that which would be contemplated by the ordinary consumer who purchases it, with the ordinary knowledge common to the community as to its characteristics.* (Emphasis supplied.). . . . .

Thus, the test, in Wisconsin of whether a product contains an unreasonably dangerous defect depends upon the reasonable expectations of the ordinary consumer concerning the characteristics of this type of product. If the average consumer would reasonably anticipate the dangerous condition of the product and fully appreciate the attendant risk of injury, it would not be unreasonably dangerous and defective. This is an objective test and is not dependent upon the knowledge of the particular injured consumer, although his knowledge may be evidence of contributory negligence under the circumstances. In *Schuh v. Fox River Tractor Co.* (Citation), for example, the court held that the positioning of the clutch lever on a crop blower machine constituted an unreasonably dangerous defect because a potential user might be misled as to its function. However, the court held the particular injured plaintiff's contributory negligence greater than any negligence of the manufacturer because the plaintiff was an experienced operator of the machine and knew of the potential dangers, yet failed to exercise due care.

Based upon the principles discussed above, we conclude that the swimming pool described in plaintiff's complaint does not contain an unreasonably dangerous defect. The lack of a self-latching gate certainly falls within the category of an obvious rather than a latent condition. Equally important, the average consumer would be completely aware of the risk of harm to small children due to this condition, when the retractable ladder is left in a down position and the children are left unsupervised. We conclude, therefore, that plaintiffs second amended complaint fails to state a cause of action.

Judgment and order affirmed.

WILKIE, Chief Justice (dissenting).

The first problem I find in the majority opinion is that it holds that there was no defect here as a matter of law. I would hold that this was a factual determination to be tried out by the trier of fact. There is a question here for the trier to determine whether the swimming pool (which did not have a self-latching and closing gate) was unavoidably unsafe as, for example, knives, baseball bats, alcohol, small foreign cars, and, therefore, not defective. Then, too, it would be a question of fact whether rendering the product safe by incorporating other safety features would destroy the usefulness of the product, or would be far too costly. On this the defective swimming pool manufacturer would have the burden of proof.

The additional holding of the majority ruling out liability where the defect is obvious and apparent—as here—is really based upon the concept of assumption of risk which *Dippel, supra*, held was not an absolute bar to recovery but rather a matter of contributory negligence. I would, therefore, drop the requirement that a product must be affirmatively shown to be unreasonably dangerous and I would regard the introduction of this element as a factor of contributory negligence to be compared with the negligence on the part of the manufacturer.

The requirement of showing "unreasonable danger" was dropped by the California Supreme Court in . . . *Cronin v. J. B. E. Olson Corp.* (Citation.) . . . In *Cronin* the court held that a plaintiff no longer need show that the product injuring him was unreasonably dangerous, but rather merely that it was defective. . . . .

There is an additional difficulty here that the small child is less than seven years of age and therefore incapable of negligence on his own. In swimming pools of this type, which are obviously intended for adult use, their use by children is anticipated but always under the immediate supervision of adults. In a products liability case, as here, I would therefore consider the negligence on the part of the parents for improper supervision as a matter of contributory negligence to be imputed to the child, and accordingly offset against the negligence of the manufacturer.

Further, the manufacturer here would still have the additional defense of showing that its negligence in producing a defective product was not causal.

But in any event, the complaint does state a cause of action . . . and the defendants [should have been] ordered to answer. . . .

□   □   □

1. The majority opinion suggests that the consumer expectation test for the existence of defect in this case consists solely of the obviousness of the danger and appreciation of risk by the average consumer. The dissenting opinion suggests a risk-utility balancing approach. Is the test by the majority adequate, in your opinion? Consider, in contrast, the result of using the risk-utility approach in deciding the issues here.

2. The dissenting opinion indicates that a defective condition can be demonstrated without establishing unreasonable danger. What criteria would be necessary to establish defect if unreasonable danger is not essential? Consider the elements for establishing that the lack of a self-latching gate was a defect?

3. The majority opinion decided, as a matter of law, that the plaintiff did not state a cause of action in strict liability. Were the issues of obviousness of the danger and the consumer's appreciation of the risk ones that a jury should have answered? Why or why not?

KAEMPFE v. LEHN & FINK PRODUCTS CORP.

21 A.D. 2d 197
249 N.Y.S. 2d 840
Supreme Court, Appellate Division, First Department
May 21, 1964

EAGER, Justice.

The plaintiff, in a suit against the manufacturer of the spray deodorant "Etiquet," has recovered judgment for a severe case of dermatitis resulting from an allergic reaction in the use of the product. The action was tried and submitted to the jury on the theory that the defendant-manufacturer was negligent in its alleged failure to give adequate warning to the very few persons who might possibly suffer some allergic reaction in the use of the product.

The plaintiff, a 19-year-old woman, had purchased at a local drug store two containers of the product labeled "Etiquet Spray-On Deodorant," which was prepared, sold and used for the purpose of preventing body perspiration and odor. The label on the container read as follows: "Easy to use A quick squeeze—it sprays Stops underarm odor Checks perspiration Safe for normal skin Harmless to clothes." The container also was marked with the statement, "Contains Aluminum Sulphate."

Aluminum sulphate, the essential ingredient in the preparation, when applied to the skin, has the effect of closing the pores, stopping perspiration and eliminating odor. According to the testimony, practically all of the deodorants on the market contain aluminum sulphate.

After her purchase of the product, the plaintiff, following the directions thereon, applied the spray in the area of both armpits. Thereafter, during that day, she detected an itching sensation and observed an inflammation where the spray had been applied. Subsequently, a rash or dermatitis developed which spread to adjacent parts of her body. It was accompanied by burning, blistering and itching. Although permanent injury was not claimed, the sequelae persisted for sometime until it was fully healed. This was plaintiff's first allergic reaction to this or any other product.

The plaintiff's medical expert testified that the aluminum sulphate in the product was the cause of plaintiff's dermatitis. By his testimony, it was established that a few persons may be sensitive to products containing this particular ingredient. The doctor stated, however, that the chemical agent aluminum sulphate, which is used in almost all deodorants, is not normally harmful to skin; that it is in fact safe for "normal skin" as claimed.

This is the typical case where a peculiar reaction to a product in common use was due solely to an allergy possessed by the user. Plaintiff's medical expert testified that her rash was due to an allergy, and, in this connection, he described an allergy as "the reaction of the skin to a substance which, as a rule, does not bother normal people but which in people who are susceptible, sensitized, makes them react differently from normal people." The plaintiff is apparently one in a multitude of persons who has an allergy to the ingredient aluminum sulphate. Here, as measured by defendant's sales figures for this product for the year 1956 (the year in which plaintiff used this preparation) and the number of complaints it received therefrom, it appears that some sensitivity was experienced in the ratio of about one to 150,000 customers. . . . .

In light of the foregoing, the plaintiff attempted to make out a case against the defendant on the theory that the defendant was negligent in failing to give due warning of an alleged danger in the use of the product. It is true that, where a particular product, though not poisonous or inherently dangerous, may become unreasonably dangerous in its use, a seller or manufacturer may be required to give directions or warning on the container as to the proper use thereof. In the case of the non-poisonous and reasonably safe product in general use, the duty to warn depends upon whether or not it was reasonably foreseeable by the supplier that a substantial number of the population may be so allergic to the product as to sustain an injury of consequences from its use (Citation). "If the danger of such an allergy is known or should be known to the maker, and if the consequences of the idiosyncrasy are serious enough, reasonable care may well require the taking of some precaution such as warning and instructions for making tests." (Harper and James, *The Law of Torts,* § 28.8, p. 1551.)

The fundamental test of negligence—reasonable foreseeability of harm and reasonable care to guard against same—is applicable in these cases. The manufacturer or seller may be held liable where he knows or with reasonable diligence should anticipate that the normal use of his product may result in substantial harm and where he fails to exercise reasonable care to warn of such danger. On the other hand, it is clear that the manufacturer or seller should not be held bound to anticipate and warn against a remote possibility of injury in an isolated and unusual case. The law requires a person to exercise reasonable care to guard against probabilities, not mere remote possibilities. A supplier of a product in daily use ought not to be placed in the position of an insurer. We have not yet reached the point where the manufacturer is under the absolute duty of making a product, useful to many, free from all possible harm to each and every individual; nor the point where the manufacturer is to be held under an absolute duty of giving special warning against a remote possibility of harm due to an unusual allergic reaction from use by a miniscule percentage of the potential customers. "Every substance, including food which is daily consumed by the public, occasionally becomes anathema to him peculiarly allergic to it. To require insurability against such an unforeseeable happenstance would weaken the structure of common sense, as well as present an unreasonable burden on the channels of trade." (Bennett v. *Pilot Products Co.,* 120 Utah 474, 478, 235 P.2d 525, 527, 26 A.L.R. 2d 958, 961; *Gerkin v. Brown & Sehler Co.,* 177 Mich. 45, 143 N.W. 48.)

So, according to the prevailing authority, the existence of a duty on the part of a manufacturer to warn depends upon whether or not, to his actual or constructive knowledge, the product contains an ingredient "to which a substantial number of the population are allergic" (see Tentative Draft No. 7, Restatement of the Law, Torts, Second, *supra*), or an ingredient potentially dangerous to an identifiable class of an appreciable number of prospective customers. (Citations.). . . .

Knowledge or constructive notice of an unreasonable danger to users of a particular product may impose upon the manufacturer a duty of warning. But, in the case of a useful and reasonably safe product, in general use, the supplier owes no special duty of warning to the unknown few who constitute a mere microscopic fraction of potential users who may suffer some allergic reaction not common to the ordinary or normal person (Citations).

In light of the foregoing, the plaintiff, as the basis for imposing upon defendant a special duty of warning, was bound at the very least to show (1) that she was one of a substantial number or of an identifiable class of persons who were allergic to the defendant's product, and (2) that defendant knew, or with reasonable diligence should have known of the existence of such number or class of persons. There was, however, a failure of proof as to both of these requirements. Furthermore, it does not appear that a special warning here would have been effective for any purpose. . . . .

Furthermore, the defendant did give notice, by statement on the container, of the presence of aluminum sulphate in the deodorant. If, as further stated on the container, the product was "safe for normal skin"—and there was no credible evidence to the contrary—what special warning would the defendant, acting reasonably, be expected to give to the very exceptional few who, unknown even to themselves, might have an allergy to the aluminum sulphate expressly stated to be contained in the product. This is left solely to a matter of speculation because there is not one iota of evidence in the record as to any customary or adequate mode of warning or as to known or proper tests to be suggested for use by the unknown few who might possibly suffer an allergic reaction.

. . . Specific words of caution would be meaningless as to those, such as the plaintiff, who did not know of their allergy to the particular sulphate. The plaintiff's prior use of deodorants containing the particular ingredient did not yield any manifestations of sensitivity and she expected none when she applied the defendant's product. So, it is difficult to see that a special warning in general terms of danger to the infinitesimal few with an allergy would be of any help or have persuaded plaintiff here from the purchase and use of defendant's merchandise. Under the circumstances, the special warning would have been wholly ineffective (Citation). And the defendant should not be held negligent in failing to give a warning which would have served no purpose.

The conclusion we reach is that the plaintiff failed as a matter of law to establish that the defendant was derelict in any duty of warning to plaintiff. This conclusion is supported by the reasoning underlying the decisions which have denied recovery in these cases on theory of breach of implied warranty. . . . .

Determination unanimously reversed, on the law, with costs to the appellant in this Court and in the Appellate Term, the judgment for plaintiff vacated and the complaint dismissed.

All concur.

□   □   □

1. Was the deodorant spray in this case unreasonably dangerous?
2. The court suggested a two-part test for imposing a duty to warn: (a) that the plaintiff be one of a substantial number of persons allergic to the product and (b) that the defendant knew or should have known of this class of persons. Consider what a "substantial number" might be. Would these requirements be the same if the cases were tried under strict liability? How would the test be formulated? Would this plaintiff have recovered under strict liability? Why?
3. Suppose the plaintiff in this case had sustained permanent scars or had died as a result of her reaction. Would the fact that only 1 in 150,000 customers experienced a reaction be enough to preclude the manufacturer's liability?

PATTEN v. LOGEMANN BROTHERS COMPANY

263 Md. 364
283 A.2d 567
Court of Appeals of Maryland
November 10, 1971

BARNES, Judge.

In *Blankenship v. Morrison Machine Co.*, 255 Md. 241, 257 A.2d 430 (1969), we held that the manufacturer of a machine was not an insurer and was under no duty to make an accident-proof product, a cause of action by a person injured by the machine being dependent upon the allegation and proof that his injury was caused by a latent defect not known to the plaintiff or by a danger not obvious to him which was attendant on proper use of the machine. We deliberately adhered to the "latent-patent" test as previously established in *Myers v. Montgomery Ward & Co.*,

Inc., 253 Md. 282, 252 A.2d 855 (1969) and in prior Maryland cases, notwithstanding the adverse criticism of the rule in 2 Harper and James, *The Law of Torts,* § 28.5, p. 1544 (1956) that it is a vestigial carry over from pre-*MacPherson* days (*MacPherson v. Buick Motor Co.,* 217 N.Y. 382, 111 N.E. 1050 (1916) when deceit was needed for recovery. . . .

We are asked by the appellant, Joshua Patten, to modify the latent-patent rule or, at least, to engraft an exception upon it, so that he might recover damages from the appellee, Logemann Brothers, Inc. (Logemann), for severe injuries to his left fingers and hand when his left hand went into an oil lubrication hole on the side of a paper baling machine manufactured by Logemann while he was using the machine as an employee of the Washington Rag & Bag Company, Inc. (Washington Rag), at its plant at Seat Pleasant, Prince George's County. Patten contends that inasmuch as the danger in the machine did not occur at the *point of the operation* of the machine, the latent-patent test does not—and should not—apply.

Patten had worked for Washington Rag with the baling machine as a paper baler for approximately five years prior to his injury on May 10, 1967. There is a lubrication and maintenance opening about seven or eight inches wide in the baling machine, 25 inches above the floor. Inside the opening the sliding piston that compresses the paper into bales passes by the opening within one inch of the inside wall of the machine. This piston does not move constantly but moves automatically when the paper in the compaction chamber reaches a predetermined level. Patten, in his deposition, indicated that prior to the accident, he knew that there was a piston passing by the hole and saw it as it passed. On May 10, 1967, he tripped on a bundle of paper baling wire lying loose on the floor next to the baling machine; and, as he fell, his left hand went into the lubrication hole. He was able to turn the machine off by pressing a button with his right hand. As a result of the piston engaging his left hand, however, he lost his middle, ring and little fingers on that hand and also suffered damages to the hand itself. His medical expenses are large and his damages substantial.

Patten's job was to feed the wire to bale the paper. He would push the wire in at the proper time and then go around the machine to push it back so that it could be tied. He tripped on the loose wire on the floor which he did not see. He did not purposely put his hand in the hole because he knew it would hurt his hand. . . . . .

After oral argument, Judge Bowen rendered an oral opinion in which he concluded that *Blankenship* was controlling and inasmuch as the alleged defect in the machine was clearly patent and known to Patten, there was no legal duty to Patten breached by Logemann so that summary judgment in favor of Logemann for costs should be granted. From the judgment entered for the defendant, Logemann, for costs on February 1, 1971, Patten took a timely appeal to this Court.

We agree with Judge Bowen that our decision in *Blankenship* is dispositive of the case and we will affirm the judgment.

The Safety Code for Mechanical Power-Transmission Apparatus, mentioned above—and in effect when the accident occurred—does provide for certain guards and shields, except at the "point of operation" for the safeguarding of all connecting rods, cranks, gears, etc., of equipment used for the mechanical transmission of power. "Point of operation" is defined as "that point at which cutting, shaping or forming is accomplished upon the stock and shall include such other points as may offer a hazard to the operator in inserting or manipulating the stock in the operation of the machine."

Patten contends that these provisions are at least evidence of negligence in not providing a mesh or guard over the lubrication hole which he contends is not at the "point of operation." The provisions of Code (1969 Replacement Volume) Art. 89, §§ 1–63 in regard to the Department of Labor and Industry and especially §§ 28 to 49 in regard to Occupational Safety apply to the *relationship between employer and employee* and not to persons *manufacturing equipment*. . . . .

Factually, the present case is quite similar to the facts in *Blankenship* in which an employee in a bleach and dye mill got his arm caught and injured in a sanforizing machine when he slipped on the wet floor. He sued the manufacturer, alleging negligence in the failure to install protective shields or guards in the area of the squeeze roller and drum where his arm was caught. No point was made that the accident happened at the "point of operation" and the reasoning underlying the latent-patent rule would not make Patten's attempted distinction meaningful. In the absence of any modification of the rule by statute, we deem our holding in *Blankenship* to control our decision in the present case.

Logemann also raises the point that the injury in the present case was not attendant upon a proper use of the machine—a necessary prerequisite for recovery in negligence from the manufacturer of a machine under the latent-patent rule—in that Patten or someone in the Washington Rag plant had allowed baling wire to spread out on the floor beside the baling machine over which Patten tripped, fell and stuck his hand into the lubricating hole as he fell. There is much force in this argument; but in view of our conclusion that there is no recovery under the latent-patent rule without regard to this prerequisite to recovery, we do not find it necessary to pass upon this contention.

Judgment affirmed, the appellant to pay the costs.

□   □   □

1. Was the paper baling machine with the open lubricating hole unreasonably dangerous? Did the court inquire whether the design was a reasonable one?

2. Did the plaintiff assume the risk?

3. Was the plaintiff contributorily negligent?

4. Is there any justification for the machine manufacturer's not covering the lubricating hole? If not, what considerations prompted the court to grant the defendant a directed verdict?

5. Formulate all the design considerations for safety of a paper baling machine from the context of the environment of use described in this case.

MICALLEF v. MIEHLE CO.

39 N.Y. 2d 376
348 N.E. 2d 571
384 N.Y.S. 2d 115
Court of Appeals of New York
April 8, 1976

COOKE, Judge.

The time has come to depart from the patent danger rule enunciated in *Campo v. Scofield*, 301 N.Y. 468, 95 N.E. 2d 802.

This action was initiated to recover damages for personal injuries, allegedly resulting from negligent design and breach of an implied warranty. Paul Micallef, plaintiff, was employed by Lincoln Graphic Arts at its Farmingdale plant as a printing-press operator. For eight months he had been assigned to operate a photo-offset press, model RU 1, manufactured and sold by defendant Miehle-Goss Dexter, Inc., to his employer. The machine was 150 feet long, 15 feet high and 5 feet wide and was capable of printing at least 20,000 sheets an hour. Then, while working on January 22, 1969, plaintiff discovered that a foreign object had made its way onto the plate of the unit. Such a substance, known to the trade as a "hickie," causes a blemish or imperfection on the printed pages. Plaintiff informed his superior of the problem and told him he was going to "chase the hickie," whereupon the foreman warned him to be careful. "Chasing a hickie" consisted of applying, very lightly, a piece of plastic about eight inches wide to the printing plate, which is wrapped around a circular plate cylinder which spins at high speed. The revolving action of the plate against the plastic removes the "hickie." Unsuccessful in his first removal attempt, plaintiff started anew but this time the plastic was drawn into the nip point between the plate cylinder and an ink-form roller along with his hand. The machine had no safety guards to prevent such occurrence. Plaintiff testified that while his hand was trapped he reached for a shut-off button but couldn't contact it because of its location.

Plaintiff was aware of the danger of getting caught in the press in "chasing hickies." However, it was the custom and usage in the industry to "chase hickies on the run," because once the machine was stopped, it required at least three hours to resume printing and, in such event, the financial advantage of the high speed machine would be lessened. Although it was possible to have "chased the hickie" from another side of the machine, such approach would have caused plaintiff to be in a leaning position and would have increased the chances of scratching the plate. Through its representatives and engineers, defendant had observed the machine in operation and was cognizant of the manner in which "hickies were chased" by Lincoln's employees.

Samuel Aidlin, a professional engineer, had inspected the machine subsequent to the mishap. In his opinion, based upon the custom in the printing industry, it would have been good custom and practice to have placed guards near the rollers where plaintiff's hand entered the machine, the danger of human contact being well known. Moreover, he testified that at least three different types of guards were available, two for over 30 years, that they would not have impeded the practice of "chasing hickies," and that these guards would have protected an employee from exposure to the risk. Based upon the foregoing, both causes of action, negligence and breach of warranty, were submitted to the jury. . . . .

We are confronted here with the question as to the continued validity of the patent-danger doctrine of *Campo v. Scofield*, 301 N.Y. 468, 95 N.E. 2d 802. . . .

Directing our attention to the cause of action for negligence in design, defendant asserts, citing *Campo v. Scofield* (*supra*), that the action must be dismissed because the danger created by the absence of safeguards on the machine was open and obvious and, therefore, as the manufacturer it was under no duty to protect plaintiff from such a patent defect. *Campo* set forth the following principles (301 N.Y. p. 471, 95 N.E. 2d p. 803): "The cases establish that the manufacturer of a machine or any other article, dangerous because of the way in which it functions, and patently so, owes to those who use it a duty merely to make it free from latent defects and concealed dangers. Accordingly, if a remote user sues a manufacturer of an article for injuries suffered, he must allege and prove the existence of a latent defect or a danger not known to plaintiff or other users." It was then declared (p. 472, 95 N.E. 2d p. 804): "If a manufacturer does everything necessary to make the machine function properly for the purpose for which it is designed, if the machine is without any latent defect, and if its functioning creates no danger or peril that is not known to the user, then, the manufacturer has satisfied the law's demands. We have not yet reached the state where a manufacturer is under the duty of making a machine accident proof or foolproof. Just as the manufacturer is under no obligation, in order to guard against injury resulting from deterioration, to furnish a machine that will not wear out (Citation), so he is under no duty to guard against injury from a patent peril or from a source manifestly dangerous."

The requirement that a latent defect be proved, before there could be a recovery against a manufacturer in a negligence action, has retained its vitality (Citations). The underlying rationale of the court's decision in *Campo* apparently is founded on the notion that it should be the task of the Legislature, not the judiciary, to compel manufacturers to install possible safety devices (*Campo v. Scofield, supra,* 301 N.Y. p. 472, 95 N.E. 2d p. 804; see Marschall, An Obvious Wrong Does Not Make a Right: Manufacturers' Liability For Patently Dangerous Products, 48 *N.Y.U.L. Rev.* 1065, 1081). *Campo* has been the subject of sustained attack (Citations). The major thrust of criticism stems from the belief that, in our highly complex and technological society, we fall victim to the manufacturer who holds himself out as an expert in his field. It is argued that the *Campo* doctrine is "a vestigial carryover from . . . days when deceit was needed for recovery" (2 Harper & James, *Torts,* § 28.5).

More specifically, it is contended that the application of *Campo* amounts to an assumption of risk defense as a matter of law "with the added disadvantage that the defendant was relieved of the burden of proving that plaintiff had subjectively appreciated a known risk" (Rheingold, Expanding Liability of the Product Supplier: A Primer, 2 *Hofstra L. Rev.* 521, 541). *Campo* is viewed as inconsistent because, on the one hand, it places a duty on the manufacturer to develop a reasonably safe product yet eliminates this duty, thereby granting him immunity from answering in damages, if the dangerous character of the product can be readily seen, irrespective of whether the injured user or consumer actually perceived the danger. As Professors Harper and James succinctly assert: "The bottom does not logically drop out of a negligence case against the maker when it is shown that the purchaser knew of the dangerous condition. Thus if the product is a carrot-topping machine with exposed moving parts, or an electric clothes wringer dangerous to the limbs of the operator, and if it would be feasible for the maker of the product to install a guard or safety release, it should be a question for the jury whether reasonable care demanded such a precaution, though its absence is obvious. Surely reasonable men might find here a great danger, even to one who knew the condition; and since it was so readily avoidable they might find the maker negligent." (2 Harper & James, *Torts,* § 28.5.)

Other jurisdictions have taken a more liberal position. For example, in *Palmer v. Massey-Ferguson*, 3 Wash. App. 508, 476 P.2d 713, *supra*, the plaintiff brought an action against the manufacturer of a hay baler for injuries sustained while adjusting a drawbar. In response to the defendant's allegations that the patent peril precluded liability, the court said (p. 517, 476 P.2d p. 719): "The manufacturer of the obviously defective product ought not to escape because the product was obviously a bad one. The law, we think, ought to discourage misdesign rather than encouraging it in its obvious form" (Citations). Another case, *Bexiga v. Havir Manufacturing Co.*, 60 N.J. 402, 412, 290 A.2d 281, 286, forcefully stated: "The asserted negligence of plaintiff—placing his hand under the ram while at the same time depressing the foot pedal—was the very eventuality the safety devices were designed to guard against. It would be anomalous to hold that defendant has a duty to install safety devices but a breach of that duty results in no liability for the very injury the duty was meant to protect against." We find the reasoning of these cases persuasive. *Campo* suffers from its rigidity in precluding recovery whenever it is demonstrated that the defect was patent. Its unwavering view produces harsh results in view of the difficulties in our mechanized way of life to fully perceive the scope of danger, which may ultimately be found by a court to be apparent in manufactured goods as a matter of law. As this court itself recently observed: "Today as never before the product in the hands of the consumer is often a most sophisticated and even mysterious article. Not only does it usually emerge as a sealed unit with an alluring exterior rather than as a visible assembly of component parts, but its functional validity and usefulness often depend on the application of electronic, chemical or hydraulic principles far beyond the ken of the average consumer. Advances in the technologies of materials, of processes, of operational means have put it almost entirely out of the reach of the consumer to comprehend why or how the article operates, and thus even farther out of his reach to detect when there may be a defect or a danger present in its design or manufacture. In today's world, it is often only the manufacturer who can fairly be said to know and to understand when an article is suitably designed and safely made for its intended purpose. Once floated on the market, many articles in a very real practical sense defy detection of defect, except possibly in the hands of an expert after laborious and perhaps even destructive disassembly." (*Codling v. Paglia*, 32 N.Y. 2d 330, 340, 345 N.Y.S. 2d 461, 468, 298 N.E. 2d 622, 627, *supra*.) Apace with advanced technology, a relaxation of the *Campo* stringency is advisable. A casting of increased responsibility upon the manufacturer, who stands in a superior position to recognize and cure defects, for improper conduct in the placement of finished products into the channels of commerce furthers the public interest. To this end, we hold that a manufacturer is obligated to exercise that degree of care in his plan or design so as to avoid any unreasonable risk of harm to anyone who is likely to be exposed to the danger when the product is used in the manner for which the product was intended (Citations) as well as an unintended yet reasonably foreseeable use (Citations).

What constitutes "reasonable care" will, of course, vary with the surrounding circumstances and will involve "a balancing of the likelihood of harm, and the gravity of harm if it happens, against the burden of the precaution which would be effective to avoid the harm" (Citations). Under this approach, "the plaintiff endeavors to show the jury such facts as that competitors used the safety device which was missing here, or that a 'cotter pin costing a penny' could have prevented the accident. The defendant points to such matters as cost, function, and competition as narrowing the design choices. He stresses 'trade-offs.' If the product would be unworkable when the alleged missing feature was added, or would be so expensive as to be priced out of the market, that would be relevant defensive matter" (Citations). In this case, there was no evidence submitted at trial to show the cost of guards that could have been attached in relation to the entire cost of the machine.

Also relevant, but by no means exclusive, in determining whether a manufacturer exercised reasonable skill and knowledge concerning the design of the product is whether he kept abreast of recent scientific developments (Citations) and the extent to which any tests were conducted to ascertain the dangers of the product (Citations). This does not compel a manufacturer to clothe himself in the garb of an insurer in his dealings (Citations) nor to supply merchandise which is accident proof (Citations). It does require, however, that legal responsibility, if any, for injury caused by machinery which has possible dangers incident to its use should be shouldered by the one in the best position to have eliminated those dangers.

We next examine the duty owing from a plaintiff or, in other words, the conduct on a plaintiff's part which will bar recovery from a manufacturer. As now enunciated, the patent-danger doctrine should not, in and of itself, prevent a plaintiff from establishing his case. That does not mean, however, that the obviousness of the danger as a factor in the ultimate injury is thereby eliminated, for it must be remembered that in actions for negligent design, the ordinary rules of negligence apply (Citations). Rather, the openness and obviousness of the danger should be available to the defendant on the issue of whether plaintiff exercised that degree of reasonable care as was required under the circumstances. . . . .

The order of the Appellate Division should be reversed and a new trial granted, with costs to abide the event. . . . .

□   □   □

1. Is assumption of the risk a valid defense to a patent danger case? If so, what has been accomplished by abolishing the patent-danger rule?

2. The court suggested a test for an unreasonably dangerous product. Is the test adequate? Is it possible to manufacture a reasonably dangerous product? Consider the issues from the viewpoints of both plaintiff and defendant.

3. The court alluded to the worker's lack of choice in carrying out a task as mitigating or eliminating contributory negligence. Should the design of a product reflect the social or economic pressures motivating the worker or user of that product, if the manufacturer can have knowledge of these conditions?

4. Contrast the design issues in this case with those involved in the *Patten v. Logemann* case (Case No. A-7).

MIEHER v. BROWN

54 Ill. 2d 539
301 N.E. 2d 307

Supreme Court of Illinois
June 4, 1973
Rehearing Denied September 27, 1973

RYAN, Justice.

Kathryn Mieher, while driving east on State Highway 140 near Old Ripley, Illinois, collided with the right rear corner of an International Harvester truck which was also going east and which was making a right turn off of the highway. Kathryn Mieher died as a result of injuries received in the accident. The plaintiff, Esther Mieher, as administrator of Kathryn Mieher's estate, filed a two-count action in the circuit court of Montgomery County against Kenneth L. Brown, the driver of the truck. Later, the plaintiff amended her complaint and added counts III and IV claiming damages against International Harvester Company (hereinafter defendant) for the wrongful death of the decedent, and for funeral, hospital and medical bills, alleging that the truck with which the decedent collided was negligently designed. . . .

The amended complaint alleged that the defendant had negligently designed the truck in that it did not attach to the rear of it a bumper, fender or shield. The plaintiff argued that the absence of a bumper, fender or shield made the truck unsafe in that a vehicle colliding with the rear of it would be allowed to proceed unimpeded under the bed of the truck. From the allegations, it appears that the plaintiff's decedent sustained fatal injuries when her automobile ran under the rear of the truck and the truck bed penetrated the windshield of the car which she was driving.

The amended complaint had been considered by both parties in the trial court and in the appellate court as being based on the theory of strict liability. However, the appellate court held that it did not state a cause of action on the theory of strict liability in that it did not allege that the truck was in the same condition when it left the possession of the defendant as it was at the time of the accident which caused decedent's death (Citation). The appellate court held, however, that the amended complaint did state a cause of action based on common-law negligence on the basis of the allegation of negligent design and it reversed the trial court's dismissal.

The appellate court correctly concluded that the amended complaint failed to state a cause of action for strict liability. We shall therefore examine the amended complaint as one based on common-law negligence. In doing so we must test the amended complaint by the traditional requirements of such an action: the existence of a duty owed by the defendant to the decedent, the breach of that duty and the injury proximately resulting from this breach (Citation). The determination of the question of duty—whether the defendant and the decedent stood in such a relationship to one another that the law imposed upon the defendant an obligation of reasonable conduct for the benefit of the decedent—is an issue of law for the determination of the court (Citations). Since we are here determining the propriety of the trial court's dismissal of the amended complaint, we are concerned only with that question of law presented by the pleading.

In concluding that under the facts alleged in the amended complaint the defendant owed the plaintiff's decedent the duty to exercise reasonable care in designing its motor vehicle, the appellate court placed substantial reliance on *Larsen v. General Motors Corp.* (8th cir. 1968), 391 F.2d 495, and other cases which followed the

Larsen rationale (Citations). The reasoning in this line of cases, as stated in *Larsen,* is: "While automobiles are not made for the purpose of colliding with each other, a frequent and inevitable contingency of normal automobile use will result in collisions and injury-producing impacts." (391 F.2d at 502.) These cases finding that such injury-producing impacts are foreseeable conclude that the manufacturer is under a duty to design its vehicle to avoid subjecting the user to an unreasonable risk of injury in the event of collision.

The appellate court acknowledged that there is a considerable amount of authority to the contrary. The leading case supporting the contrary view is *Evans v. General Motors Corp.* (7th cir. 1966), 359 F.2d 822, cert. denied 385 U.S. 836, 87 S.Ct. 83, 17 L.Ed. 2d 70. . . . This line of cases holds that the intended use of an automobile does not include its participation in collisions despite the manufacturer's ability to foresee the possibility that such collisions may occur. These cases hold that the manufacturer's duty extends only to insure that the vehicle is reasonably safe for its intended use. . . . .

Both the *Larsen* cases and the *Evans* cases involve so-called "second collision" injuries by the occupants of the alleged defective vehicles. In these cases, after the original collision, the occupants were injured due to an alleged defect in the vehicle in which they were riding. Recovery was sought against the manufacturer of the vehicle in which the injured party was riding. Our case differs substantially, although it may be, in fact, a "second collision" case to the extent that the plaintiff claims that the decedent received fatal injuries occasioned by the defective design in the truck after the original collision with the truck had been brought about by other means. The question in *Larsen* and *Evans* concerned the duty of the manufacturer to design a vehicle in which it was safe to ride. The question in our case involves the duty of the manufacturer to design a vehicle with which it is safe to collide.

The plaintiff insists that the distinction is of no importance. She contends that under the rationale of *Larsen,* the defendant should have foreseen that its truck would be struck in the rear and should have taken the necessary precautions to prevent an automobile from running under the bed of the truck. We do not believe, however, that the foreseeability rule applied in *Larsen* is intended to bring within the ambit of the defendant's duty every consequence which might possibly occur. In a sense, in retrospect almost nothing is entirely unforeseeable.

Professor Leon Green discusses foreseeability in distinguishing between the judge's role in determining the duty owed and the jury's role in determining the violation of the duty by stating:

[H]owever valuable the foreseeability formula may be in aiding a jury or judge to reach a decision on the negligence issue, it is altogether inadequate for use by the judge as a basis of determining the duty issue and its scope. The duty issue, being one of law, is broad in its implication; the negligence issue is confined to the particular case and has no implications for other cases. There are many factors other than foreseeability that may condition a judge's imposing or not imposing a duty in the particular case, but the only factors for the jury to consider in determining the negligence issue are expressed in the foreseeability formula. Green, Foreseeability in Negligence Law, 61 Colum. L. Rev. 1401, 1417–18. . . .

Section 435 (2) of the Restatement (Second) of Torts provides: "The actor's conduct may be held not to be a legal cause of harm to another where after the event and looking back from the harm to the actor's negligent conduct, it appears to the court highly extraordinary that it should have brought about the harm." Dean Prosser observed that this provision of the Restatement recognizes the basic idea "that liability must stop somewhere short of the freakish and the fantastic." (Palsgraf Revisited, 52 *Mich. L. Rev.* 1, 27.) The court in *Larsen* stated that the duty of the manufacturer was only to "use reasonable care to avoid subjecting the user of the product to an *unreasonable risk* of injury." (Emphasis added.) (391 F.2d at 502.) "Liability is imposed only when an unreasonable danger is created." 391 F.2d 495, 502 n. 3.

It is apparent that the concept of duty in negligence cases is very involved, complex and indeed nebulous. The term is so ill defined and its boundaries so indistinct that one commentator has observed: "There is a duty if the court says there is a duty." And he concluded that the court's pronouncement often reflects the policy and social requirements of the time and community (Citation).

Although the injury complained of may have been, in a sense, foreseeable, we do not consider that the alleged defective design created an unreasonable danger or an unreasonable risk of injury. In the words of section 435 (2) of the Restatment (Second) of Torts, "looking back from the harm to the actor's negligent conduct, it appears to the court highly extraordinary that it should have brought about the harm" for which recovery is now sought. Public policy and the social requirements do not require that a duty be placed upon the manufacturer of this truck to design his vehicle so as to prevent injuries from the extraordinary occurrences of this case.

Counts III and IV of the amended complaint do not state a cause of action against the defendant on the theory of common-law negligence.

The judgment of the appellate court is reversed and the judgment of the circuit court of Montgomery County is affirmed.

Appellate court reversed; circuit court affirmed.

GOLDENHERSH, Justice (dissenting):

The majority have correctly concluded that the rationale of *Larsen* and the cases which follow it is that since injury-producing impacts are foreseeable "the manufacturer is under a duty to design its vehicle to avoid subjecting the user to an unreasonable risk of injury in the event of collision." The question in this case, however, does not, as stated by the majority, involve the duty of the manufacturer to design a vehicle "with which it is safe to collide." The question involved is the extent of the duty of the manufacturer to design its vehicle so as to avoid the unreasonable risk of injury in the event of collision, whether the injured be a passenger in that vehicle, another vehicle, a pedestrian, or a bystander.

Upon a close reading of the opinion it appears to me that the majority recognize that the duty owed by the manufacturer is to design his vehicle so as to avoid the unreasonable risk of injury in the event of collision irrespective of whether the injured is within or without the particular vehicle, and insofar as the opinion so holds, I concur. I do not agree, however, that the amended complaint, upon the facts alleged, fails to state a cause of action against the manufacturer, and I would affirm the judgment of the appellate court.

□   □   □

1. Was the design of the International Harvester truck unreasonably dangerous? Was that the question in the case?
2. Was the reasonableness of the design a factor in deciding the duty issue? Should it be?
3. What other factors may have gone into the duty determination?
4. Was there any justification for the court to conclude that the facts as alleged did not make out a case for strict liability? If there was a design defect, could it have originated other than in the hands of the manufacturer?

BALIDO v. IMPROVED MACHINERY, INC.

29 Cal. App. 3d 633
105 Cal. Rptr. 890
Court of Appeal, Second District, Division 2
December 26, 1972
As Modified January 8, 1973
Hearing Denied March 8, 1973

FLEMING, Associate Justice.

In 1965 Juana Balido's right hand was crushed when a plastic injection molding press closed as she was adjusting an insert. Balido brought an action for negligence, breach of warranty, strict liability, and intentional misconduct against the manufacturer of the press, Improved Machinery, Inc. (Improved); against the former owner of the press, Paper Mate Manufacturing Company (Paper Mate); and against her employer and owner of the press at the time of the accident, Olympic Plastics Company, Inc. (Olympic). After the presentation of plaintiff's case, the trial court entered judgment of nonsuit in favor of all defendants. Balido appeals. . . . .

Improved designed and manufactured the plastic injection molding press in New Hampshire in 1950–1951 and sold it to Paper Mate in California in 1953. Paper Mate sold the press to Olympic in 1958. As originally designed and manufactured, the press contained a lift safety gate which when fully closed covered the operating area of the press. As the safety gate turned on its pivot in closing, it triggered an electric limit switch near the gate's pivot point, and the switch in turn activated the press and permitted its platens to close. The electric limit switch, a standard item of equipment procured from another manufacturer, was adjustable, and an improper adjustment of the switch could allow the press to activate while the gate was open as much as 10 degrees, an opening that amounted to five inches at the far end of the gate. In the opinion of two industrial safety engineers the lift gate and electric limit switch as originally designed and installed did not provide adequate safety for the operator of the press.

After the press had been sold to Paper Mate, Improved learned that operators of similar presses were being injured and that a California industrial safety order in effect since 1949 required more comprehensive safety devices for plastic molding presses than Improved had originally installed. Specifically, the industrial safety order required that plastic presses be equipped with either a sliding gate or dual hand controls. (A sliding gate would alleviate the problem of untimely activation, while dual hand controls would keep both operator's hands away from the press during its closing cycle.) Starting in 1954 Improved incorporated into its new presses a package of additional safety devices, which it then offered for sale with free installation to owners of its earlier model presses. The package included a sliding gate, an additional gate-activated switch that limited the hydraulic system, and a metal bar that held the press platens apart while the gate was open. Paper Mate added the hydraulic limit switch to the press but did not install the other devices. It subsequently sold the press to Olympic.

On several occasions a sales-and-service representative of Improved notified Olympic that the press did not meet California's industrial safety standards and suggested that Olympic purchase Improved's package of additional safety devices for $500. Improved also sent two letters to Olympic pointing out the safety deficiencies of the press and calling attention to the California industrial safety order. . . .

Olympic did not install any additional safety devices on the press.

On January 25, 1965, Balido was operating the plastic molding press on her job at Olympic. She reported to her supervisor the press was working faster than usual, and the latter told her to be sure the insert did not fall out. During one of the molding operations the insert began to fall out, and Balido opened the gate and put her right hand in the press to adjust the insert. The press closed, crushing her hand with 175 tons of pressure and causing her to lose three fingers and part of the fourth on her right hand.

Subsequently, Balido obtained permanent disability benefits for her injuries under workmen's compensation.

At the trial an industrial safety engineer and a state safety engineer testified that in their opinion the accident occurred because the safety devices on the press were inadequate and ineffective. . . . . .

There remain for consideration the negligence, warranty, and strict liability counts against Improved. The theory of these counts is that Improved negligently and deficiently designed, manufactured, and sold a press whose inadequate safety devices made it unreasonably dangerous to operate. Although separate counts for negligence, warranty, and strict liability have been pleaded, we view them as stating a single cause of action, in that the complaint seeks damages for personal injuries caused by deficiencies in the design of a manufactured product. As Professor Wade has pointed out, the manufacturer is not an insurer of the safety of its product, and the test for strict liability is the same as that for negligence, except for the element of scienter. (Wade, Strict Liability of Manufacturers, 19 *Sw. L.J.* 5, 15–17.) Strict liability for deficient design of a product (as differentiated from defective manufacture or defective composition) is premised on a finding that the product was unreasonably dangerous for its intended use, and in turn, the unreasonableness of the danger must necessarily be derived from the state of the art at the time of design (Citation). A danger is unreasonable when it is foreseeable, and the manufacturer's ability, actual, constructive, or potential, to forestall unreasonable danger is the measure of its duty in the design of its product. A manufacturer's failure to achieve its full potential in design and thereby forestall unreasonable danger forms the basis for its strict liability in tort. It is a liability whose essence parallels the lack of due care that is the essence of its liability for negligence. It may be seen, therefore, that in cases involving deficient design, foreseeability is merely scienter under another name. Since the issue is whether Improved designed and put into circulation a product unreasonably dangerous for use and since the unreasonableness of the danger must be determined by the potential available to the designer at the time of design, it is apparent that the strict liability and negligence claims merge. The same is true of the warranty claim, for in personal injury product-liability actions not involving a commercial relationship between manufacturer and injured person, the warranty formulation adds nothing to that of strict liability and negligence. (Rest. 2d Torts, § 402A, comment m.) Consequently, we treat plaintiff's three counts as stating a single cause of action.

For purposes of nonsuit Improved conceded the existence of deficient design, a concession that would ordinarily make the question of its liability for an unreasonably dangerous product one for the trier of fact. Improved's concession was neither misguided nor inadvertent, for the press as designed in 1950–1951 did not meet the standard of a 1949 California industrial safety order that required plastic presses to be equipped with sliding gates or with dual hand controls. Noncompliance with a standard set out in an industrial safety order furnishes probative evidence of deficient design, even though the order is directed at the user of equipment and not at its manufacturer (Citation). Nevertheless, the trial court concluded that two factors relieved the manufacturer from liability for deficient design and compelled the nonsuit: (1) the long interval of time between the deficient design and the injury, and (2) the multiple warnings of safety deficiency given the owner of the press by the manufacturer. We consider the weight and effect of these two factors. . . . .

At bench, the circumstances in no wise appear extraordinary. For purposes of nonsuit Improved conceded deficient design of the press. Moreover, from the first year of manufacture Improved had been put on notice that this model press might be causing injuries attributable to inadequate safety controls. The product was an item of capital equipment sold to a small market and a limited number of customers, and its continuing superintendence did not present the difficulties associated with such mass consumer products as automobiles, refrigerators, and washing machines. To the contrary, Improved kept track of this particular press at all times through repair and maintenance records. We cannot say this is one of those extreme cases that would require a trial court to rule as a matter of law that passage of time had broken the causation between deficiency and injury and terminated the manufacturer's liability. We conclude, therefore, that passage of time did not justify the nonsuit but rather presented a question for the trier of fact.

The second factor relied upon by the trial court to support the nonsuit was the series of warnings given the owner of the press by its manufacturer. The court viewed the owner's disregard of these warnings as a superseding cause of the injury that legally relieved Improved from liability for its antecedent deficient design. The court concluded that Olympic's continued use of the press after it had been warned of the press's safety deficiencies constituted a superseding cause of the injury that cut off Improved's liability for deficient design. In familiar legal terminology Improved's deficient design ceased to be a proximate cause of Balido's injury and receded to a remote cause of the injury. Olympic's knowing disregard of the industrial safety order, the trial court said introduced an unforeseeable element that amounted to a legally superseding cause of the accident.

In this second aspect of the case the . . . question is whether as a matter of law the obligation of the original wrongdoer has been replaced by that of a third-party wrongdoer. On the shift of responsibility from one wrongdoer to another, Restatement 2d Torts, section 452(2), comment f, has this to say:

"It is apparently impossible to state any comprehensive rule as to when such a decision [shift of duty] will be made. Various factors will enter into it. Among them are the degree of danger and the magnitude of the risk of harm, the character and position of the third person who is to take the responsibility, his knowledge of the danger and the likelihood that he will or will not exercise proper care, his relation to the plaintiff or to the defendant, the lapse of time, and perhaps other considerations. The most that can be stated here is that when, by reason of the interplay of such factors, the court finds that full responsibility for control of the situation and prevention of the threatened harm has passed to the third person, his failure to act is then a superseding cause, which will relieve the original actor of liability."

On the specific issue before us, whether Olympic's failure to heed the warnings of inadequate safety devices amounted as a matter of law to a superseding cause of the injury, we consider the following propositions relevant:

a. The extent to which third-party neglect supersedes deficient design as the legal cause of an injury depends on the foreseeability of the third-party neglect (Citation).

b. The degree of foreseeability charged to the designer of a product depends on the degree of danger involved in its use.

c. A molding press is a highly dangerous piece of machinery.

d. In other instances involving the use of comparable dangerous machinery the extent of the designer's duty to anticipate safety neglect by the owners of the machinery has been ruled a question of fact.

The basic question is whether the court should pass on superseding cause as matter of law or the jury should do so as matter of fact. From our reading of the cases we conclude that the extent to which designers and manufacturers of dangerous machinery are required to anticipate safety neglect presents an issue of fact. . . . .

Thus far we have examined the issue of superseding cause largely on the assumption that deficient design creates a static element not susceptible to later change. But the specific issue at bench involves the liability of a manufacturer initially deficient in the design of its product, who later attempted to correct its initial deficiency. Is such a manufacturer required to anticipate a particular kind of third-party neglect—the failure of an owner to respond to a specified warning of danger?

As a general proposition it can be said that a manufacturer who has taken all reasonable steps to correct its error may succeed in absolving itself from future liability. An example of the manufacturer's ability to terminate its liability for deficient design is found in the leading case of Ford Motor Co. v. Wagoner (1946), 183 Tenn. 392, 192 S.W. 2d 840, 842, 164 A.L.R. 371, where an automobile manufacturer discovered a defect in a hood catch and distributed an auxiliary catch to its dealers with instructions to install the catch on defective automobiles at no cost. The owner of an automobile with the defective catch refused to have the auxiliary catch installed, and a subsequent owner of the vehicle was injured in an accident caused by the defect. The court held that the original owner's refusal to accept free repair of the defect amounted to an independent superseding cause of the accident that cut off the manufacturer's liability. (See, Rest. 2d Torts, §452, illustration 10.) Similarly in *Rekab, Inc. v. Frank Hrubetz & Company* (1971) 261 Md. 141, 274, A.2d 107, the court found that a manufacturer of Ferris wheels did all that was reasonably possible to correct a deficiency in the design of one of his products when he notified the customer of the deficiency, shipped free replacement parts, and offered free installation of the new parts.

The inifinite variety of factual situations arising out of corrective efforts highlights the factual nature of an inquiry as to whether the manufacturer has done what it could reasonably be expected to do to correct an earlier design deficiency. Central to the inquiry here is the question whether under the particular circumstances the manufacturer could have reasonably foreseen that the neglect of third persons to respond to the manufacturer's warnings of danger would frustrate its corrective efforts. Insofar as machinery dangerous to life and limb is involved, we think it a question of fact whether a manufacturer would reasonably anticipate that a wholesaler, a dealer, a retailer, an owner, or a user, may not positively respond to warnings of the need to correct a design deficiency (Citations). It is also a question of fact whether the manufacturer of a deficiently designed product could reasonably foresee that a purchaser of the product would not spend additional money to correct the deficiency. Undoubtedly, the manufacturer of a deficiently designed product finds itself in a difficult position when in good faith it attempts to correct a deficiency. Yet its position is not impossible, and the trier of fact may not necessarily decide the issue adversely to the conscientious manufacturer. In *Rekab*, for example, the trier of fact, concluding that the manufacturer had taken all reasonable steps to correct its design deficiency, entered judgment in the manufacturer's favor.

Improved relies heavily on *E. I. Du Pont De Nemours & Co. v. Lander* (1954) 221 Miss. 378, 73 So. 2d 249, and *Nishida v. E. I. Du Pont De Nemours & Co.* (5th Cir. 1957) 245 F.2d 768, two cases involving a chemical manufacturer's warning to a processor of soybean meal that use of the manufacturer's chemical in the processing of soybean meal made the meal dangerous for cattle. In spite of this explicit warning the soybean processor continued to sell its existing stock of soybean meal as cattle feed, and dairy herds of purchasers of the cattle feed were injured. In both cases the court viewed the conduct of the soybean processor as a superseding cause of the injury to the dairy herds and absolved the chemical manufacturer from liability. We find these cases readily distinguishable from that at bench in that the hazards they presented did not involve danger to human life and limb.

In the present case a trier of fact might have concluded that Improved had not done everything reasonably within its power to prevent injury to Balido (Citation). Improved warned Olympic on several occasions that the press did not meet California industrial safety standards, but offered to conform the press to those standards only at a cost of $500. Quere: Should Improved have reasonably anticipated that a purchaser of a second-hand press would ignore its warnings of inadequate safety devices and refuse to spend money to purchase additional safety equipment? In our view this question remained open for decision by the trier of fact, and hence the judgment of nonsuit was improper.

The judgment for Olympic and Paper Mate is affirmed. The judgment for Improved is affirmed on the fourth cause of action for willful misconduct and reversed on the first, second, and third cause of action. . . . .

1. What was the court's rationale in deciding that the issue of whether the duty had shifted from Improved to Olympic was for the jury rather than the court? Were there any other actions that Improved could have undertaken, apart from the letters to Olympic, that might have caused the court to decide the shifting-duty issue in their favor?

2. What general policies should be adopted by a manufacturer who, after a product is marketed, discovers the need for a safety retrofit? How should such policies be implemented?

SKYHOOK CORPORATION v. JASPER

CCH Products Liability Reports ¶ 7913
New Mexico Supreme Court
March 11, 1977

OMAN, Chief Justice.

. . . . .

This is an action for claimed wrongful death brought by plaintiff (Jasper), as administrator of the estate and personal representative of Malvin Mack Brown, deceased . . . Decedent was employed by Electrical Products Signs, Inc. (Signs, Inc.) as an apprentice sign installer. On January 11, 1973, he was assisting a journeyman installer of signs (Pulis), also employed by Signs, Inc., to install a Phillips 66 sign at a service station near Springer, New Mexico.

A hole had been dug in the ground in which to place the heavy signpost, a metal pipe, in an upright position. Pulis and decedent were using a 100-foot telescoping crane rig to lift and place the signpost in the hole. This crane was manufactured by Skyhook and sold by it to Signs, Inc., in January 1968. A clearly visible written warning appeared on the boom. In this warning it was stated: "All equipment shall be so positioned, equipped or protected so no part shall be capable of coming within ten feet of high voltage lines."

Pulis was aware of and had read the warning, and the evidence is to the effect that decedent also had seen and was aware of the warning, since it was clearly visible and decedent had previously worked on and had operated the rig. Both Pulis and decedent knew of the presence of overhead high voltage lines, since they had been warned of the presence of these lines by the operator of the Phillips 66 station at which the sign was being installed. The station operator had warned them that they should operate the equipment ten feet from these high voltage lines.

Pulis and decedent positioned the crane so that, in the judgment of Pulis, the crane was ten or twelve feet from the power lines. However, no measurements were made to assure that the positioned distance of the crane from the power lines was sufficient to prevent any portion of the equipment from coming within ten feet of these lines, even though a tape measure was kept in the cab of the rig for the purpose of making these measurements. Pulis then hoisted the signpost with the crane and began swinging it toward the hole in which it was to be positioned. As he was swinging the signpost toward the hole, he heard decedent scream. Decedent, who was guiding the signpost by hand toward the hole, was electrocuted when the lift cable came in contact with the overhead power line. A "tag line" or "guide rope," which was not an effective conductor of electricity and which decedent could have used to guide the signpost to the hole, was available, but was not ordinarily used by the helper in setting a post. There were also other measures commonly known, and known at least to Pulis, which could have been taken to avert the electrocution of decedent.

Decedent had been warned by his father of the dangers in operating a crane too near high voltage lines. The rig had been used by Signs, Inc. for the purpose of erecting signs for a period of five years, and no such accident or incident had ever previously occurred. . . .

Plaintiff sought recovery from Skyhook on the theory of strict tort liability for failing to equip its crane, at the time of its sale to Signs, Inc. in January 1968, with either an "insulated link" or a "proximity warning device." An insulated link is a device installed on a crane to isolate the lifting hook from the lifting line or cable, so that there is no electrical continuity between the crane boom or lifting cable and the load being lifted. In January 1968, no crane manufacturer installed insulated links as standard equipment, but they were available to a purchaser of a crane at an additional cost of $300 to $400, depending on the size of the link.

A proximity warning device is an alarm warning system activated by the electrostatic field of overhead power lines. The use of this device requires that the crane be positioned at the minimum distance desired from the power line and the device then set for operation. If properly set, it will warn the operator by sound and lights when the equipment encroaches on the minimum pre-set distance from the power line. At the time of the sale of the crane to Signs, Inc., no crane manufacturer offered this device as either standard or optional equipment, but it could be purchased for approximately $700. . . . .

Since Skyhook was the seller, as well as the manufacturer of the crane involved in this case, we need only consider whether the evidence adduced at trial required the submission to the jury by the trial court of the issue of Skyhook's liability under section 402A. . . . As stated above, plaintiff sought recovery under section 402A, and we have heretofore adopted as the law of New Mexico the concept of liability set forth therein (Citations).

Thus, the question to be resolved is whether the evidence created an issue of fact as to liability of Skyhook under section 402A, which should have been submitted to the jury. . . . .

There is no question about the sale of the rig by Skyhook to Signs, Inc.; no question that Skyhook was engaged in the business of selling these rigs; no question that decedent was using the crane rig at the time of his death; and no question about any substantial change having been effected in the rig from the day of its sale to Signs, Inc. in January 1968 to January 11, 1973, the date of the unfortunate accident. Therefore the only issue under section 402A which must be determined is whether the crane was in a defective condition which made it unreasonably dangerous to the user. . . .

First, we must decide whether the failure of a seller to include an optional safety device as a part of the product may be considered as a sale of the product in a "defective condition." It would serve no useful purpose to try to reconcile the authorities on this point. However, we are of the opinion that a failure to incorporate into a product a safety feature or device may constitute a defective condition of the product. Obviously, the test of whether or not such a failure constitutes a defect is whether the product, absent such feature or device, is unreasonably dangerous to the user or consumer or to his property. . . . .

The crane rig had been used by Signs, Inc. for five years, had performed well, and no injury had resulted. Obviously, it was not unreasonably dangerous within the contemplation of the ordinary consumer or user of such a rig when used in the ordinary ways and for the ordinary purposes for which such a rig is used. See section 402A, comment I. Furthermore, even though Skyhook had knowledge that the rig might be used in areas where overhead high voltage lines were present, it placed on the boom a clearly visible written warning that "all equipment shall be so positioned, equipped or protected so that no part shall be capable of coming within ten feet of high voltage lines." There is no contention that this warning was inadequate, had it been heeded. Skyhook, as the seller, could reasonably assume that the warning would be read and heeded. And had it been heeded, the crane rig was not in a defective condition nor unreasonably dangerous. See section 402A, comment j.

The above reasons are sufficient in themselves to dispose of this case, but we have more here. Both Pulis and decedent had the presence of the high voltage lines called to their attention, both knew the dangers of high voltage electricity—as does every ordinary adult in this present day society in New Mexico in which electricity is used so commonly for so many purposes—and together they positioned the crane rig away—but not far enough away—from these high voltage lines. There is no duty to warn of dangers actually known to the user of a product, regardless of whether the duty rests in negligence or on strict liability under section 402A (Citation).

Since there was no defect in the crane rig unreasonably dangerous to the decedent within the contemplation of the strict liability concept enunciated in section 402A, there was no culpable conduct on the part of Skyhook which could have proximately caused the accident and the resulting death. . . . .

The decision of the Court of Appeals is reversed and this cause is remanded to that court with directions to affirm the judgment of the district court.

IT IS SO ORDERED. . . . .

□   □   □

1. The court considered the warning, if heeded, was adequate to establish that the crane was not unreasonably dangerous. The manufacturer offered an optional insulated link as a safety device to minimize the same risk that the warning addressed. If a warning was adequate, why should there be an optional safety device? Why should there be a market for the proximity device?

2. Are there conditions under which the crane would be unreasonably dangerous with the warning but reasonably safe with the insulated link? If so, how should the courts distinguish these cases? What burden or duty would be placed on the manufacturer in selling optional safety features?

3. What guidelines can be offered on when a safety device should be standard equipment or when it should be optional?

4. The court found that, since the crane had been used for five years without a prior electrocution, it was "obviously" not unreasonably dangerous. What role does incident-free life play in the establishment of defect? What are the effects on the defect question of the cost of the insulated link and the fact that no manufacturer offered an equivalent device as standard equipment?

SCHIPPER v. LEVITT & SONS INCORPORATED

44 N.J. 70
207 A.2d 314
Supreme Court of New Jersey
Argued December 1, 1964
Decided February 10, 1965

JACOBS, Justice.

The plaintiffs sued for damages suffered as a result of the severe scalding received by the infant plaintiff Lawrence J. Schipper, II when he came in contact with excessively hot water drawn from the faucet in the bathroom sink. The trial court dismissed the proceeding at the close of the plaintiff's case. They appealed to the Appellate Division and we certified before argument there.

The defendant Levitt & Sons, Inc. is a well-known mass developer of homes, specializing in planned communities. Its homes are generally sold on the basis of advertised models constructed in accordance with Levitt's specifications. One of its communities is at Levittown (now known as Willingboro), New Jersey, where it built thousands of homes, including the home at 81 Shawmont Lane purchased in 1958 by the Kreitzers. This home was evidently built for the Kreitzers after they had selected a model, for Mrs. Kreitzer testified that "we watched the complete building of our home as it was going up." The Kreitzers moved in during November 1958 and received a "Homeowner's Guide" from Levitt which contained a message of welcome to Levittown and various informational items. Under the caption "Heating System" it advised that the "system consists of a gas-fired boiler supplying heating coils imbedded in the concrete floor beneath the tile" and that "as heated water is pumped through these heating coils, the coils warm the concrete in which they are imbedded and the entire floor becomes warm." There was a cautionary note against any attempts at "adjustments" of the heating unit and instructions to call Public Service Electric and Gas Company "for emergency service." Under the caption "Hot Water," the Homeowner's Guide had the following to say:

You will find the hot water in your Levittown home much hotter than that to which you are accustomed. Hot water such as this is desirable for clothes washing as well as other uses.

We have provided at each fixture, mixing type faucets so that you adjust the water temperature to suit. The proper procedure at any faucet is to first open the cold water tap part way, and then turn on the hot water. This avoids wasting hot water and yields properly tempered water for bathing and dishwashing.

Mr. Kreitzer testified that he found the domestic hot water to be really hot and that he was burned on several occasions. He complained to Levitt's representatives but was told that they could not reduce the temperature except through "the installation of a mixing valve" in the heating unit. Mr. Kreitzer also complained to the Public Service representatives but they told him that they could make no significant reduction in the temperature of the water. Mrs. Kreitzer testified that the water "was exceptionally hot coming out of the bathroom faucets." She was burned mildly on several occasions and a house guest was "burned pretty badly" when she "didn't have a chance to warn her." Thereafter Mrs. Kreitzer put a handwritten note in the bathroom reading: "Caution. Water Hot. Turn on cold water first." She did not recall whether the note was in the bathroom when the Kreitzers leased their house to the Schippers.

The plaintiff Mr. Lawrence J. Schipper testified that in July 1960 he leased the house at 81 Shawmont Lane from the Kreitzers for a term of one year. He did not recall that his lessors had mentioned anything about the hot water and he did not read the Homeowner's Guide until after the scalding of his son Lawrence J. Schipper, II. When he and his family moved in on August 13, 1960, he turned on the control switch in the closet which contained the gas-fired heating unit and waited for the gas to "cycle through." He then tried the hot water faucet in the bathroom adjacent to the closet and noticed that the water coming from the tap "gave a sort of spitting noise and seemed to be a mixture of gas and steam." He examined the heating unit to see whether it had any mechanism to control the temperature of the water and found none. He cautioned his wife and children that the water was "extremely hot" and that they would have to be careful until he "could find a means of regulating it." He spoke to the realtor through whom he had negotiated his lease and, on the realtor's recommendation, he decided to call Public Service on Monday morning August 15th when he "next expected their services to be available." He did call Public Service at about 8:30 on Monday morning and, in response, its representative made a service call later that morning but found the heating unit to be operating in normal fashion and could make no adjustment which would appreciably affect the temperature of the domestic hot water.

During the morning of August 15th and apparently before the Public Service representative had arrived, the scalding of the infant plaintiff (Larry), who was then sixteen months old, had occurred. Mrs. Schipper testified that she was upstairs when she heard Larry crying. She came downstairs, heard the water running, found the hot water faucet in the bathroom sink turned on, and realized that Larry had been scalded. He was taken immediately to the doctor's office and then to the Cherry Hill Hospital where he remained for seventy-four days. Thereafter he was hospitalized on three separate occasions and during two of these, skin grafting operations were performed.

In 1961 the plaintiffs filed a complaint against Levitt & Sons, Inc. and York Shipley, Inc., the company which manufactured the heating unit, and another complaint against Builders Supply Corporation, Levitt's wholly owned subsidiary which had purchased the heating unit from York. Thereafter the matters were consolidated and amendments and other pleadings were duly filed. The plaintiffs charged that, in the construction of the Levittown homes, Levitt had directed and ordered the installation of a gas-fired hot water boiler and water distribution system which was so defectively designed and equipped "that it produced without notice or warning scalding hot water at a temperature that was dangerously high for ordinary domestic use" and that it "knew or should have known of the highly dangerous condition created by it, which involved an unreasonable risk of bodily harm to children of immature years and others, who had no means of discovering the condition or realizing the risks." Similarly, the plaintiffs charged that York had manufactured the improperly designed system and that it knew or should have known of the highly dangerous condition created by it which involved unreasonable risk of harm. The plaintiffs sought damages from Levitt and its wholly owned subsidiary Builders Supply and from York for the injuries sustained by the infant plaintiff as the result of his scalding and also sought consequential damages suffered by his father Lawrence J. Schipper.

In support of their complaints, the plaintiffs introduced expert and other testimony which dealt extensively with the installation and operation of the heating and hot water system. Mr. Witt testified that he was an experienced mechanical engineer, had been employed by Levitt for nine years, and was responsible for the design of the heating and hot water system in the New Jersey Levittown homes as well as in Levittown homes elsewhere. He described the prime component of the system as a boiler manufactured by York to supply both hot water for heating and domestic purposes through the use of an instantaneous hot water coil immersed in the boiler. He recognized that the temperature of the water as it came from the boiler (at 190 degrees Fahrenheit and upward) would be excessively high for domestic use and that since the heating closet in the plaintiffs' home was only six feet away from the bathroom sink, the water coming from the hot water tap on initial draw would be almost at the same temperature as that in the boiler. He acknowledged that York had recommended that a mixing valve be installed at the outside of the boiler to avoid excessively hot water for domestic use and that Levitt had deliberately not followed the recommendation. Instead, Levitt had merely provided bathroom and sink fixtures which supplied hot and cold water through combination spigots and had cautioned purchasers in its Homeowner's Guide that the proper procedure at any faucet was first to open the cold tap part way and then turn on the hot water.

Mr. Snyder testified that he had been in the employ of York for fourteen years and was now the chief design engineer for "residential and Jackson & Church Products," a division of York. He was responsible for the design of York's heating units including those sold to Builders Supply for installation in Levittown homes in New Jersey and elsewhere. He testified that several thousand units had been furnished for the New Jersey Levittown homes and that seventeen thousand units of similar design had been furnished for the Pennsylvania Levittown homes. He stated that the normal range for hot water which would come in contact with the person was around 140 degrees and he acknowledged that, on initial draw, water drawn from the boiler might be 190 degrees and higher. It was for this reason that his company strongly recommended to Levitt that it install "a mixing valve which would limit the temperature delivery to the faucets at 140 degrees." In fact, York recommended a particular valve known as Taco although "there are other makes on the market that are normally supplied through plumbing supply houses as a standard animal in the plumbing trade."

Mr. Snyder stated that all manufacturers recommend the use of this type of valve which is a marketed item "normally installed by the installer" and "not an inherent piece of the equipment." When asked why he considered the valve to be not inherently part of its heating unit, he testified that it is a normal trade item such as a circulator or thermostat and that it is unusual for an original heating equipment manufacturer to merchandise items of this type. He stressed that the mixing valve is normally applied to the unit at the time of installation, that "the valve itself has sweat fittings that are normally applied with heat and solder" to the exterior of the boiler, and that it "would not be practical in present known designs" to install the mixing valve in the original manufacture of the boiler.

Mr. Snyder stated further that his company buys mixing valves for about $3.60 each, that they probably retail at $9 or $10, and that they are not expensive to install. The plaintiff Lawrence J. Schipper testified that after the scalding of his son, he installed a mixing valve at a total cost of $18 for parts and labor. Mr. Lightner, administrative assistant to the president of York, testified that he had participated in the negotiations for the purchase and sale of the heating units, that William Levitt of the Levitt organization represented it in the negotiations, and that ultimately the purchase order came from Builders Supply, Levitt's purchasing corporation. He estimated that two or three thousand units were sold for the Levittown homes in New Jersey and sixteen or seventeen thousand units for the Levittown homes in Pennsylvania. He stated that his company recommended the use of a mixing valve but that "Levitt was not interested in buying the mixing valve from us for either Pennsylvania or Jersey" although it had purchased mixing valves for its homes at Levittown, Long Island.

Three engineers who testified as experts for the plaintiffs all agreed that while temperatures ranging from 190 degrees and upward were necessary for house heating purposes, temperatures above 140 degrees for domestic purposes involving contacts with the person would be highly dangerous. They all referred to the mixing valve as one of the recognized devices for reducing the temperature of the domestic hot water to acceptable limits. Mr. Baccini testified that for this type of burner a mixing valve "can be either furnished with the unit or it is made available in a piping harness which is sold with the unit." He acknowledged that the plans set up by Levitt for its New Jersey homes did not call for any mixing valves and that Levitt could decide for itself whether to purchase heating units from any particular manufacturer without also purchasing mixing valves from him. Mr. Lerner testified that mixing valves are made by many companies and are available in plumbing supply houses, and that some manufacturers of tankless heaters such as those furnished by York will include mixing valves "as part of their package boiler" while "other manufacturers will not if they feel they don't know where the unit is going." He also testified that if the unit is to be installed in a home "engineering practice is definitely that a mixing valve must be on." When asked about the combination spigots which Levitt had installed, he testified that they were not "a substitute for a mixing valve in the line itself" but were simply used as a means of manually controlling temperature below the 140-degree acceptable standard. Professor Edgar testified that he would not accept the combination spigot as a substitute for the mixing valve and that he would consider it "highly unsafe" to have a unit which supplied hot water to the tap at a temperature ranging from 190 degrees upward.

After the plaintiffs had completed their presentation, the defendants moved for dismissal and their motions were granted. Insofar as Levitt was concerned, the trial court considered itself bound by the holdings in *Sarnicandro v. Lake Developers, Inc.,* 55 N.J. Super. 475, 151 A.2d 48 (App. Div. 1959), and *Levy v. C. Young Construction Co., Inc.,* 46 N.J. Super. 293, 134 A.2d 717 (App. Div. 1957), aff'd on other grounds, 26 N.J. 330, 139 A.2d 738 (1958). In *Sarnicandro,* the court held that a builder vendor is not liable for injuries suffered by a lessee of the vendee when she fell on steps which had been improperly constructed by the builder vendor. In *Levy,* a divided Appellate Division held that a builder vendor was not liable to the purchaser for damages resulting from latent defects "in the absence of express warranties in the deed or fraud of concealment." In dealing with Builders Supply, the trial court described it as an *alter ego* of Levitt and said that it could find no evidence that it had violated any duty "either by way of negligence or by way of breach of warranty" which it owed to the plaintiffs or others. And in dealing with York it said that it could find no evidence of "any duty to the plaintiffs" or for that matter to anyone else concerned.

Under the first point in their brief the plaintiffs contend that Levitt should be liable for "negligence causing injury to the infant plaintiff." They point out that Levitt was not just an ordinary vendor of a house but was "also the architect, the engineer, the planner, the designer, the builder and the contractor." Under the proofs, the decision to install the hot water distribution system without a mixing valve was a deliberate one by Levitt in disregard of York's explicit recommendations to the contrary. The common spigots installed by Levitt were no substitute for the mixing valve and the cautionary instruction in the Homeowner's Guide was insufficient to advise of the serious dangers attendant upon bodily contact with the water heated to 190–210 degrees. Furthermore, it was entirely foreseeable that the Guide would never come to the attention of many persons who would come in contact with the heated water such as invited guests, and indeed the infant plaintiff himself (Citation). If ordinary negligence principles are applied, it may readily be found that in view of the likelihood and gravity of the danger and the ease with which it could have been avoided, Levitt had failed to exercise reasonable care in the design and installation to avoid unreasonable risk of harm. See 2 Harper and James, Torts § 28.3 (1956). The fact that Messrs. Kreitzer and Schipper may have known of the dangerous condition would not, as a matter of law, preclude a finding of negligence; Harper and James, *supra,* § 28.5 at p. 1543 have put it this way:

Today, however, the negligence principle has been widely accepted in products liability cases; and the bottom does not logically drop out of a negligence case against the maker when it is shown that the purchaser knew of the dangerous condition. Thus if the product is a carrot-topping machine with exposed moving parts, or an electric clothes wringer dangerous to the limbs of the operator, and if it would be feasible for the maker of the product to install a guard or a safety release, it should be a question for the jury whether reasonable care demanded such a precaution, though its absence is obvious. Surely reasonable men might find here a great danger, even to one who knew the condition; and since it was so readily avoidable they might find the maker negligent. Under this analysis the obviousness of a condition will still preclude liability if the obviousness justifies the conclusion that the condition is not unreasonably dangerous; otherwise it would simply be a factor to consider on the issue of negligence.

(Citations.)

In fulfillment of the deliberate design of its system for distributing hot water for domestic use, Levitt assembled the ingredients, including the heating unit from York, and directed their installation. In this respect it was not unlike the manufacturers of automobiles, airplanes, etc., whose products embody parts supplied by others. When their marketed products are defective and cause injury to either immediate or remote users, such manufacturers may be held accountable under ordinary negligence principles (*MacPherson v. Buick Motor Co.*, 217 N.Y. 382, 111 N.E. 105), as well as under expanding principles of warranty or strict liability (Citations). The plaintiffs urge that the MacPherson principle, imposing liability for negligence, should be applied to a builder vendor such as Levitt. We consider their point to be well taken for it is clear to us that the impelling policy considerations which led to MacPherson and its implementations are equally applicable here. (Citations.)...

... Dean Prosser... noted that the reasons which had earlier been advanced against holding general contractors liable in negligence actions by third persons were reminiscent of those which had been advanced in actions against manufacturers of goods and had been rejected in MacPherson; and he concluded that the earlier approach is now in full retreat and that the majority rule now imposes responsibility to third persons for negligence "not only as to contractors doing original construction work, but also as to those doing repair work or installing parts, as well as supervising engineers and architects." Prosser [Torts § 85] at p. 695 (3d ed. 1964).....

Professor Noel has noted that a definite requirement that the defect or danger be latent would appear to be a reversion to the earlier concept that the chattel must be inherently dangerous whereas now the accepted concept is that the creation of any unreasonable danger is enough to establish negligence; and he has taken the approach set forth in Harper and James that "even though the absence of a particular safety precaution is obvious, there ordinarily would be a question for the jury as to whether or not a failure to install the device creates an unreasonable risk." 71 *Yale L.J.*, at p. 838.....

... Earlier in this opinion, we questioned that requirement and indicated our support of the position that the obviousness of a danger does not necessarily preclude a jury finding of unreasonable risk and negligence; in any event the danger here was not patent... in the sense of the reference in Levitt's brief to the potential sources of danger to children which may be found in all homes, "ranging from stoves and ovens to electrical appliances, stairways, second-story windows and porches without railings." Those dangers are generally incident to normal living, they generally create no unreasonable risks, and there are admittedly no obligations on builder vendors to make their houses danger-proof or fool-proof. However, here the hot water faucet had a special and concealed danger far beyond any danger incident to contact with normally hot water; certainly no one, whether he be adult or child, would have suspected from its appearance that the water drawn from it would be at the dangerously high temperature of 190–210 degrees. Even the Homeowner's Guide gave no true indication of the serious scope of the danger when it simply described the water as much hotter than customary.

While the evidence may indicate that Messrs. Kreitzer and Schipper had become aware of the absence of a mixing valve, they may not have fully appreciated the extraordinary nature of the risk and, in any event, any omissions or contributory fault on their part would not preclude a finding that Levitt had been negligent and was to be held responsible to others who foreseeably might be injured as a result of its negligence. . . .

Under the second point in their brief, the plaintiffs contend that Levitt should be held liable "for a breach of warranty of habitability where a dangerous condition causes injury to a subsequent occupant." They point to the developing law in the products liability field. . . . The plaintiffs acknowledge that in the realty field there has thus far been no comparable movement in our State, but they suggest that it may no longer justly be put off since there is, in today's society, no reason for differentiating mass sales of homes from advertised models, as in the Levitt operation, from mass sales of automobiles from advertised models, as in the Chrysler operation. . . . .

The law should be based on current concepts of what is right and just and the judiciary should be alert to the never-ending need for keeping its common law principles abreast of the times. Ancient distinctions which make no sense in today's society and tend to discredit the law should be readily rejected. . . . We consider that there are no meaningful distinctions between Levitt's mass production and sale of homes and the mass production and sale of automobiles and that the pertinent overriding policy considerations are the same. That being so, the warranty or strict liability principles . . . should be carried over into the realty field, at least in the aspect dealt with here. Incidentally, recent reference to the sweep of Levitt's mass production approach may be found in the July 1963 issue of American Builder at pages 42–45 where the president of Levitt, in response to an inquiry as to whether its policy of "no changes" would be applied in the building of its more expensive homes at Long Island, had this to say: "We intend to hold to our mass production approach in Long Island. People buy Cadillacs, don't they, and they're mass produced" (Citation).

When a vendee buys a development house from an advertised model, as in Levitt or in a comparable project, he clearly relies on the skill of the developer and on its implied representation that the house will be erected in reasonably workmanlike manner and will be reasonably fit for habitation. He has no architect or other professional adviser of his own, he has no real competency to inspect on his own, his actual examination is, in the nature of things, largely superficial, and his opportunity for obtaining meaningful protective changes in the conveyancing documents prepared by the builder vendor is negligible. If there is improper construction such as a defective heating system or a defective ceiling, stairway and the like, the well-being of the vendee and others is seriously endangered and serious injury is foreseeable. The public interest dictates that if such injury does result from the defective construction, its cost should be borne by the responsible developer who created the danger and who is in the better economic position to bear the loss rather than by the injured party who justifiably relied on the developer's skill and implied representation.

The arguments advanced by Levitt in opposition to the application of warranty or strict liability principles appear to us to lack substantial merit. Thus its contention that *caveat emptor* should be applied and the deed viewed as embodying all the rights and responsibilities of the parties disregards the realities of the situation. *Caveat emptor* developed when the buyer and seller were in an equal bargaining position and they could readily be expected to protect themselves in the deed. Buyers of mass produced development homes are not on an equal footing with the builder vendors and are no more able to protect themselves in the deed than are automobile purchasers in a position to protect themselves in the bill of sale. Levitt expresses the fear of "uncertainty and chaos" if responsibility for defective construction is continued after the builder vendor's delivery of the deed and its loss of control of the premises, but we fail to see why this should be anticipated or why it should materialize any more than in the products liability field where there has been no such result.

Levitt contends that imposition of warranty or strict liability principles on developers would make them "virtual insurers of the safety of all who thereafter come upon the premises." That is not at all so, for the injured party would clearly have the burden of establishing that the house was defective when constructed and sold and that the defect proximately caused the injury. In determining whether the house was defective, the test admittedly would be reasonableness rather than perfection. As was pointed out in *Courtois v. General Motors Corp.*, 37 N.J. 525, 182 A.2d 545 (1962), the comparable warranty of merchantability in the sale of goods means only that the article is reasonably fit for the purpose for which it is sold and does not imply "absolute perfection." 37 N.J., at p. 543, 182 A.2d 545. See *Jakubowski v. Minnesota Mining and Manufacturing*, 42 N.J. 177, 185, 199 A.2d 826 (1964). And as Professor Noel has indicated, though the imposition of warranty or strict liability principles to a case of defective design, as alleged against Levitt here, would render unnecessary any allegation of negligence as such, it would not remove the plaintiff's burden of establishing that the design was "unreasonably dangerous" and proximately caused the injury. *Noel, supra*, 71 *Yale L.J.*, at pp. 877–878 (Citation).

Levitt relies on the traditional rule that warranties in the sale of real estate are not to be implied (4 Williston, Contracts § 926 (Rev. ed. 1936)) and seeks to distinguish recent out-of-state cases which have limited the rule or departed from it (Citations). Whether or not the cases may be differentiated, they undoubtedly evidence the just stirrings elsewhere towards recognition of the need for imposing on builder vendors an implied obligation of reasonable workmanship and habitability which survives delivery of the deed. . . . .

[I]t seems hardly conceivable that a court recognizing the modern need for a vendee occupant's right to recover on principles of privity, which is fast disappearing in the comparable products liability field, to preclude a similar right in other occupants likely to be injured by the builder vendor's default. Issues of notice, time limitation and measure of proof, which have not really been discussed in the briefs, would seem to be indistinguishable from those which have been arising in the products liability field and are there being dealt with by developing case law and occasional statutory enactment. (Citations.). . . .

In the case against Levitt we need not at this stage concern ourselves with these issues for, under the plaintiff's proofs, the design was a deliberate one, its special danger was not observable on sight, specific notice and complaint with respect to it were brought early to Levitt's attention by the original vendee, injury foreseeably occurred later to an unaware member of a family which had leased the premises from the original vendee, and suit was instituted shortly after the injury. All in all, the time expiration from the original conveyance by Levitt to the date of suit was less than three years. We are satisfied that, in the particular situation here, the plaintiffs may rely not only on the principles of negligence set forth under their first point but also on the implied warranty or strict liability principles set forth under their second point. We note, however, as indicated earlier in this opinion, that even under implied warranty or strict liability principles, the plaintiffs' burden still remains of establishing to the jury's satisfaction from all the circumstances that the design was unreasonably dangerous and proximately caused the injury (Citation).

Under the third point in their brief the plaintiff's contend that Builders Supply should be held liable for Levitt's negligence and breach of warranty and they quote from *Mueller v. Seaboard Commercial Corp.*, 5 N.J. 28, 73 A.2d 905 (1950), where reference is made to cases holding that the corporate cloak may in proper circumstances be disregarded in order to avoid injustice. 5 N.J., at pp. 34–35, 73 A.2d 905. Here there is no indication that the corporate cloak is being used to achieve injustice and there is no showing of any reason for disregarding it. The allegedly dangerous design and installation was not that of the subsidiary corporation Builders Supply but was that of the parent corporation Levitt. So far as appears, Builders Supply simply acted as Levitt's purchasing agent, followed Levitt's orders, exercised no discretion of its own, and did not participate at all in the design and installation. There is no suggestion that there would be difficulty in obtaining satisfaction of any judgment rendered against Levitt nor is there reference to any practical purpose which would be served by continuing Builders Supply in this proceeding. The lower court's judgment of dismissal as to Builders Supply is sustained.

Under the final points in their brief the plaintiffs contend that, as the manufacturer of the heating unit, York should be held accountable under negligence and warranty or strict liability principles. . . . York did no assembling or installation at the Levittown houses but simply sold and delivered heating units which met Levitt's specifications. These heating units were not defective when they were delivered to Levitt and functioned strictly as they were intended to. The defect alleged by the plaintiffs arose not from the heating unit as such but from the later installation which did not include any mixing valve or other tempering device at the boiler. York had furnished suitable installation instructions which "strongly recommended that a mixing valve be installed between the hot and cold domestic water lines." Levitt deliberately disregarded York's recommendation and decided upon its own design and installation which included common spigots and cautionary remarks in the Homeowner's Guide. It is evident from the plaintiff's proofs that neither Levitt nor anyone else placed any reliance on York's judgment or skill in connection with the over-all design of the system and its installation; that being so there would appear to be no sound basis for invoking principles of implied warranty or strict liability against York. (Citations.). . . .

It must be borne in mind that York was dealing with Levitt as a highly responsible development company which had extensive experience in the field and which had selected York's heating units for installation in its development houses. Those units were standard in the trade as were the separate mixing valves which were obtainable either from York or from plumbing supply houses generally. According to the testimony, it would not have been practical for York to have installed mixing valves in the initial manufacture of its units nor would it have been feasible to attach the valves to the boilers other than at the time of installation. In any event, Levitt had specifically decided that it did not want mixing valves with the heating units and its purchase order did not include them. Its engineer testified that Levitt had not followed York's recommendation with respect to the valves because Levitt believed that its system of combination spigots and cautionary instructions had operated with sufficient success in the past and that the attachment of mixing valves would present unnecessary service problems. In the developing steps toward higher consumer and user protection through higher trade morality and responsibility, the law should view trade relations realistically rather than mythically. Thus viewed, it is difficult to see how York could reasonably have been expected to do anything other than fill Levitt's purchase order while expressing its recommendation in clear and strong terms as it did. Conceivably it might have refused to sell its heating units unless Levitt also purchased the valves but then Levitt could readily have purchased comparable heating units without valves from other manufacturers. And even if Levitt had purchased the valves from York, there was nothing York could do to compel their attachment or to prevent Levitt from pursuing its own chosen design and mode of installation. All in all, it would appear evident that York had not acted unreasonably, that no defaulting action on its part had proximately caused the injuries, and that no just purpose would be served by affixing responsibility to it in addition to Levitt for the injuries allegedly resulting from Levitt's defective design and installlation

The judgment of dismissal as to the defendant Levitt & Sons, Inc. is reversed and the cause is remanded for trial, costs to abide the event; the judgment of dismissal as to the other defendants is affirmed, without costs. . . .

□   □   □

1. Courts, in general, have held the manufacturer of equipment (e.g., presses) liable for not installing safety devices as part of the equipment. There is also support for the conclusion of the inadequacy of a warning to a purchaser that safety devices should be installed. How can the court's dismissal of York be consistent with these points of view?

2. Would York's position in this case have been altered by the court had the builder-vendor been a small contractor instead of Levitt? Of what relevance is the relative bargaining position of the parties?

3. Levitt apparently installed mixing valves as a standard item in at least one development. Would this fact be germane in deciding liability? If so, in what ways?

TECHNICAL CHEMICAL COMPANY v. JACOBS

Supreme Court of Texas
April 26, 1972
Rehearing Denied June 7, 1972

POPE, Justice.

W. T. Jacobs instituted this suit against Technical Chemical Company and Joe Bain for damages he sustained when a can of freon exploded. The freon had been processed and canned by Technical Chemical and sold to Jacobs by Bain. Jacobs tried the case as one of consumer protection and relied only upon the defendants' failure to warn him about the danger of attaching the can to the wrong side of an automobile air conditioning compressor. The trial court rendered judgment for the defendants on the jury verdict, but the court of civil appeals reversed that judgment and rendered judgment that Jacobs recover damages in the sum of $24,000.00. The intermediate court also rendered judgment in favor of Bain against Technical Chemical by way of indemnity (Citation), but that question is not before us. The issue presented by this case is one of causation.

Jacobs' action is grounded upon strict liability as enunciated in Restatement (Second) of Torts § 402A (1965), and the problem arises out of the jury answers to the first three special issues. The jury found that (1) Technical Chemical's failure to warn Jacobs on July 11, 1966, of the danger of connecting the freon can to the high pressure side of the compressor exposed him to an unreasonable risk of harm, and (2) it was reasonably foreseeable by Technical Chemical that users of its product might attempt to charge air conditioners by connecting the freon to the high pressure side of the compressor; but, the jury refused to find that (3) such failure to warn was a producing cause of the injuries and damages sustained by Jacobs. The court of civil appeals ruled that the third special issue was irrelevant in a case in which the only defect asserted was the defendant's failure to warn a user who foreseeably would use the product as Jacobs did. In our opinion, the court of civil appeals erred in that conclusion. . . . .

The court of civil appeals identified the defect in the product as the danger of connecting the can to the high pressure side of the compressor. Because the can was so connected and the explosion resulted, the court held that Jacobs proved causation as a matter of law. Technical Chemical, on the other hand, says that the only defect upon which Jacobs sued and submitted his case to the jury was the defendant's failure to give a warning that the can should not be connected to the high side of the compressor, and that the jury was entitled to conclude from the evidence that such a warning would have made no difference.

In strict liability cases, proof of negligence is excused; but, neither Section 402A, *supra*, nor our former decisions have excused proof that the defect in the product was the cause of the injuries. . . .

Proof of causation is a necessary element of a strict liability case (Citations).

The issue now before the court is narrower than that suggested by the cited cases. The product itself was neither defective nor unreasonably dangerous. The danger was the failure to warn consumers of an improper use of the product. It is defendant's contention that a proper warning would not have avoided Jacobs' wrong installation procedure because he would not have read a label with full and adequate warnings. This precise question has not been previously presented to this court and little has been written on the subject. Dean W. Page Keeton has carefully examined and analyzed the problem of warning and causation, and we find his several articles helpful. Keeton, Products Liability—Inadequacy of Information, 48 *Texas L. Rev.* 398 (1970); Keeton, Private Law—Torts, Annual Survey of Texas Law, 24 *Sw. L.J.* 3, 12 (1970); Keeton, Products Liability—Problems Pertaining to Proof of Negligence, 19 *Sw. L.J.* 26, 33–34 (1965). Dean Keeton divides defective products into three categories: (1) those which are unreasonably dangerous due to safety legislation prohibiting the sale of the product under the circumstances; (2) those which are unreasonably dangerous since the ordinary man, knowing the risks and dangers involved in the use of the product, would not have marketed the product; (3) those which are unreasonably dangerous since the same ordinary man would not have marketed the product without supplying warnings as to the risks and dangers involved in using the product as well as instructions as to how to avoid those risks and dangers. The first two categories may be said to describe products which are defective per se; their mere presence in the marketplace is enough to impose liability if the product is the source of the injuries. This result occurs because the product and the defect are inseparable. An example of liability under a product defective per se would be for an injury caused by the use of Thalidamide. When the defect is due to inadequate labeling, however, there is a difference; the defect and the product are separable. In the words of Dean Keeton, when a product is defective due to inadequate labeling, "the aspect of the defendant's conduct that made the sale of the product unreasonably dangerous [i.e., the label] must be found to have contributed to the plaintiff's injury." 48 *Texas L. Rev.* at 413. This means that it is incumbent upon the plaintiff to secure a jury finding that the faulty labeling was a cause of the injury. It is this finding that Jacobs failed to secure. . . . .

We recognize the problems of proving causation in such a case as this. If the user of a product dies from its use, testimony whether he did or did not read the label may be impossible. If the label is inadequate, whether he would or would not have read an adequate label may be speculative. On the other hand, proof that the defect was the cause of the injuries should, on logic, be required as it is in other cases.

It has been suggested that the law should supply the presumption that an adequate warning would have been read. "Where warning is given, the seller may reasonably assume that it will be read and heeded." Restatement (Second) of Torts § 402A, Comment j (1965). See Note, 50 *Texas L. Rev.* 577 (1972). Such a presumption works in favor of the manufacturer when an adequate warning is present. Where there is no warning, as in this case, however, the presumption that the user would have read an adequate warning works in favor of the plaintiff user. In other words, the presumption is that Jacobs would have read an adequate warning. The presumption, may, however, be rebutted if the manufacturer comes forward with contrary evidence that the presumed fact did not exist (Citations). Depending upon the individual facts, this may be accomplished by the manufacturer's producing evidence that the user was blind, illiterate, intoxicated at the time of the use, not responsible or lax in judgment or by some other circumstance tending to show that the improper use was or would have been made regardless of the warning.

The jury in this case refused to find that Technical Chemical's failure to warn was a producing cause of Jacobs' injuries, and we are unable to say that Jacobs established as a matter of law that it was a producing cause. . . . There was left in the record Jacobs' own statements that he did not read the label before the explosion. Jacobs at one time testified he had previously installed freon in his car about four dozen times, but later said he had done so a few times. From this unsatisfactory state of Jacobs' testimony and all the circumstances, the jury could have concluded that the warning, whatever it might have contained and however it might have been displayed, would have been disregarded by Jacobs.

The court of civil appeals reversed the take nothing judgment of the trial court and rendered judgment that Jacobs recover as damages the amount found by the jury. The court then made an alternative holding that, in the event it should be held that

Jacobs did not prove causation as a matter of law, nevertheless, the jury's refusal to find for Jacobs on the causation issue was against the great weight and preponderance of the evidence. We reverse the judgment of the court of civil appeals which rendered judgment for Jacobs. We remand the cause to the trial court in accord with the alternative holding of the intermediate court.

□　　□　　□

1. Did the Texas Supreme Court respond to the appellate court's argument that causation is not a factor in a failure to warn case?
2. What was the defect in the product in this case? How can defining the defect affect the determination of causation?
3. When the defect is failure to warn, can it ever be shown with certainty that the injured person would have read it? How are warnings usually presented on a can?
4. Has anyone ever been injured by a failure to warn?

BERKEBILE v. BRANTLY HELICOPTER CORPORATION

462 Pa. 83
337 A.2d 893
Supreme Court of Pennsylvania
May 19, 1975

JONES, Chief Justice.

This case is before us on a grant of allocatur. The Superior Court reversed a verdict for the defendant-appellant in the trial court. We affirm.

Cloyd Berkebile was killed on July 9, 1962, when the helicopter he was piloting crashed while in climbing flight. The executrix wife brought this wrongful death and survival action against Brantly Helicopter Corporation, the manufacturer of the helicopter. The plaintiff relied upon the theory of strict liability. Restatement (Second) of Torts, § 402A. Several significant issues of importance in the growing area of strict liability recovery are presented in this multifaceted appeal. To avoid further confusion we find it necessary to clarify the concepts of strict liability under Pennsylvania law.

Brantly manufactured the small, two-person, B-2 model helicopter in October of 1961. Addressing itself to the general aviation market, the advertising described the helicopter as "safe, dependable," not "tricky to operate," and one that "beginners and professional pilots alike agree . . . is easy to fly." Brantly had experienced some difficulties in designing its rotor blades and autorotation in the development stage and modified the system to some degree prior to its distribution. In January 1962, Mr. Berkebile, a businessman, purchased the helicopter from defendant's distributor. Mr. Berkebile flew alone on July 9, and while in climbing flight the seven-foot outboard section of one of the three main rotor blades separated. The helicopter crashed on a wooded hillside, killing Mr. Berkebile.

Plaintiff proposed four grounds for recovery at the second trial: (1) The design of the rotor system of the helicopter was defective because the average pilot had insufficient time to place the helicopter in autorotation in an emergency power failure in climbing flight; (2) The rotor blade was defectively manufactured and designed; (3) The defendant rendered the helicopter defective as a result of the inadequate warnings regarding the possible risks and inherent limitations of one of the systems of the helicopter; and (4) The defendant misrepresented the safety of the helicopter in its advertising brochures.

The defendant, denying the existence of any defective condition in its product, theorized that the helicopter's rotor blade had fractured due to an abnormal use brought about by power failure resulting from fuel exhaustion, followed by a failure on decedent's part to push down the collective pitch in time to go into autorotation and to effect a proper emergency landing.

Plaintiff contends on appeal that the trial court erred in charging the jury on the law to be applied to these facts and erred in several of its evidentiary rulings. A review of the record and of the court's charge in particular, when taken as a whole, demonstrates a basic confusion concerning the principles of strict liability in torts. . . .

The law of products liability developed in response to changing societal concerns over the relationship between the consumer and the seller of a product. The increasing complexity of the manufacturing and distributional process placed upon the injured plaintiff a nearly impossible burden of proving negligence where, for policy reasons, it was felt that a seller should be responsible for injuries caused by defects in his products. *See* Restatement (Second) of Torts § 402A, comment c. . . . We emphasized the principle of liability without fault most recently by stating that the seller is "effectively the guaranter of his product's safety," in *Salvador v. Atlantic Steel Boiler Co.*, 457 Pa. 24, 32, 319 A.2d 903, 907 (1974).

Our courts have determined that a manufacturer by marketing and advertising his product impliedly represents that it is safe for its intended use. We have decided that no current societal interest is served by permitting the manufacturer to place a defective article in the stream of commerce and then to avoid responsibility for damages caused by the defect.

Strict liability requires, in substance, only two elements of requisite proof: the need to prove that the product was defective, and the need to prove that the defect was a proximate cause of the plaintiff's injuries. Thus, the plaintiff cannot recover if he proves injury from a product absent proof of defect, such as developing diabetic shock from eating sugar or becoming intoxicated from drinking whiskey. Neither can plaintiff recover by proving a defect in the product absent proof of causation, as where plaintiff sustains eye injury while not wearing defective safety glasses. Also, plaintiff must prove that the defect causing the injury existed at the time the product left the seller's hands; the seller is not liable if a safe product is made unsafe by subsequent changes (Citations).

The crucial difference between strict liability and negligence is that the existence of due care, whether on the part of seller or consumer, is irrelevant. The seller is responsible for injury caused by his defective product even if he "has exercised all possible care in the preparation and sale of his product." Restatement (Second) of Torts, § 402A(2)(a). As we declared in *Salvador, supra,* 457 Pa. at 32, 319 A.2d at 907, the seller "may not preclude an injured plaintiff's recovery by forcing him to prove negligence in the manufacturing process." What the seller is not permitted to do directly, we will not allow him to do indirectly by injecting negligence concepts into strict liability theory. In attempting to articulate the definition of "defective condition" and to define the issue of proximate cause, the trial court here unnecessarily and improperly injected negligence principles into this strict liability case.

Section 402A recognizes liability *without fault* and properly limits such liability to defective products. The seller of a product is not responsible for harm caused by such inherently dangerous products as whiskey or knives that despite perfection in manufacture, design or distribution, can cause injury. See Restatement (Second) of Torts, § 402A, comment i. At first glance, however, it would appear that the section does impose a contradictory burden of proof in that the defect also be "unreasonably dangerous." An examination of comment i indicates that the purpose of the drafters of the clause was to differentiate those products which are by their very nature unsafe but not defective from those which can truly be called defective. The late Dean Prosser, the reporter of the Restatement (Second) of Torts, has suggested that the only purpose for the clause was to foreclose any argument that the seller of a product with inherent possibilities for harm would become "automatically responsible for all the harm that such things do in the world" (Citation). Commentators and courts, attempting to define "defective condition" have suggested tests based upon the negligence-oriented "reasonable man" that have further diluted the strict liability concept. The purpose of the "unreasonably dangerous" clause would appear to be best served by its inclusion in the issue of proximate cause. Those courts in the vanguard of products liability law, in doing away with this distinction, have adopted this analysis. . . .

We hold today that the "reasonable man" standard in any form has no place in a strict liability case. The salutary purpose of the "unreasonably dangerous" qualification is to preclude the seller's liability where it cannot be said that the product is defective; this purpose can be met by requiring proof of a defect. To charge the jury or permit argument concerning the reasonableness of a consumer's or seller's actions and knowledge, even if merely to define "defective condition" undermines the policy considerations that have led us to hold in *Salvador* that the manufacturer is effectively the guarantor of his product's safety. The plaintiff must still prove that there was a defect in the product and that the defect caused his injury; but if he sustains this burden, he will have proved that as to him the product was unreasonably dangerous. It is therefore unnecessary and improper to charge the jury on "reasonableness" (Citations).

The trial court further confused the standards of strict liability in its charge on proximate cause. The court charged that, in order for it to be said that a defect caused plaintiff's injury, "such a consequence, under all the surrounding circumstances of the case, *must have been foreseeable by the seller.* To require foreseeability is to require the manufacturer to use due care in preparing his product. In strict liability, the manufacturer is liable even if he has exercised all due care. Restatement (Second) of Torts, § 402A(2)(a). Foreseeability is not a test of proximate cause; it is a test of negligence (Citation). Because the seller is liable in strict liability regardless of any negligence, whether he could have foreseen a particular injury is irrelevant in a strict liability case. In either negligence or strict liability, once the negligence or defective product is shown, the actor is responsible for all the unforeseen consequences thereof no matter how remote, which follow in a natural sequence of events (Citation).

The trial court further erred in charging the jury separately on the issue of "abnormal use." On this issue the court charged in part:

> The defendant is not liable if the product is used in an abnormal manner, or in a way in which it was not designed to be used. . . . If you take a helicopter and use it abnormally . . . , and such improper use was the proximate cause of the accident, that does not make the helicopter defective. . . . It must be used normally and properly in order for it to be defective and dangerous. . . . If you push the collective lever down and go into autorotation within the necessary time, then you are using it normally, but if you do not do it then you are not using it normally.

On plaintiff's theory that the helicopter was designed defectively in that there was not enough time for the average pilot to effect autorotation safely, the question of "necessary time" to go into autorotation was the plaintiff's entire case. Under this theory, plaintiff agreed that the decedent did not achieve autorotation but argued that this was because of the defect in that system's design. When the trial judge drew the factual and legal conclusions for the jury that if plaintiff's decedent did not place the helicopter in autorotation there could be no recovery, it was tantamount to his directing a verdict against plaintiff on this theory. Such charge was error.

The evidence such as was introduced by the defense in this case under the guise of "abnormal use" was admissible but for a different purpose. Plaintiff must prove a defect existing in the product at the time the product left the seller's hands and he must prove proximate cause. If the seller can prove the defect arose from use after sale he would not be liable. Plaintiff contended that the blade fractured because of a defect in manufacture; defendant's contention that the blade fractured from impact with the "stops" rebutted the contention of this defect. Plaintiff contended the autorotation system was defective because it gave a pilot insufficient time to activate it. The autorotation system is a safety device existing for the sole purpose of preventing a crash in the event of engine failure *for any reason.* The reason the engine failed is irrelevant. Even defendant's argument that decedent was flying without gas, would be no "abnormal use." The autorotation system only comes into use in the event of engine failure for whatever reason it may be. Nor can it be said that the failure of decedent to go into autorotation "within the necessary time" rebuts the contention that the autorotation system was defective in not allowing sufficient time for its activation. What constitutes "necessary time" is the key to the issue of the defect. For example, if defendant showed that an average pilot required one second to achieve autorotation and also showed that this helicopter gave decedent one second to achieve autorotation in climbing flight, he would rebut the contention of this defect. Whether decedent actually attempted autorotation is relevant to the issue of causation. If the jury were to conclude, for example, that a non-defective system would allow two seconds for autorotation and that the decedent did not attempt autorotation for three seconds; even if a defect was shown, it could not have been the proximate cause of the crash. In conclusion, evidence which would be admissible in a negligence case to prove "abnormal use" is admissible in a strict liability case only for the purpose of rebutting the plaintiff's contentions of defect and proximate cause. It is not properly submitted to the jury as a separate defense.

The trial court's charge on "abnormal use" permitted the jury to conclude that an alleged failure on decedent's part to determine the amount of gas available for flight precluded plaintiff's recovery on any theory. A plaintiff cannot be precluded from recovery in a strict liability case because of his own negligence. He is precluded from recovery only if he knows of the specific defect eventually causing his injury and voluntarily proceeds to use the product with knowledge of the danger caused by the defect (Citations). Furthermore, a finding of assumption of risk must be based on the individual's own subjective knowledge, not upon the objective knowledge of a "reasonable man." See *Dorsey v. Yoder*, 331 F. Supp. 753, 765 (E.D. Pa., 1971); Restatement (Second) of Torts, § 496D, comment c. Such a defense can be charged upon by the court only if there is evidence introduced by defendant that the decedent knew of the specific defect causing his death and appreciated the danger it involved before using the aircraft (Citation).

A "defective condition" is not limited to defects in design or manufacture. The seller must provide with the product every element necessary to make it safe for use. One such element may be warnings and/or instructions concerning use of the product. A seller must give such warning and instructions as are required to inform the user or consumer of the possible risks and inherent limitations of his product (Citation). If the product is defective absent such warnings, and the defect is a proximate cause of the plaintiff's injury, the seller is strictly liable without proof of negligence. . . .

In the instant case, the warnings of the dangers and instructions for flying the B-2 are contained in the Rotorcraft Flight Manual and in the cockpit placard. There is no specific warning as to the time needed to get into autorotation, and there is no direction or warning with respect to "Engine Failure in Climbing Flight." There are, however, directions to the pilot to lower the collective pitch lever in case of engine failure; that autorotation should be implemented at no less than 300 rotor RPM; and that failure to comply "may result in damage to the rotor blades."

The question for the jury concerning warnings was whether the warnings appearing in the flight manual and the cockpit placard were sufficient to make Mr. Berkebile aware of the dangers of power failure and delayed autorotation, and whether said warnings adequately conveyed the urgency of the situation and the need to react almost instantaneously. If the jury determines that the helicopter was in a defective condition by the failure to provide sufficient warnings and directions for use, the seller is liable for all harm caused thereby.

It must be emphasized that the test of the necessity of warnings or instructions is not to be governed by the reasonable man standard. In the strict liability context we reject standards based upon what the "reasonable" consumer could be expected to know, or what the "reasonable" manufacturer could be expected to "foresee" about the consumers who use his product (Citations). Rather, the sole question here is whether the seller accompanied his product with sufficient instructions and warnings so as to make his product safe. This is for the jury to determine. The necessity and adequacy of warnings in determining the existence of a defect can and should be considered with a view to all the evidence. The jury should view the relative degrees of danger associated with use of the product since a greater degree of danger requires a greater degree of protection (Citation). In this case, plaintiff argued that the most serious emergency in the event of power failure was in climbing flight, since there would be the greatest rotor decay and thus least amount of time available for activating the autorotation system. In cruise flight, rotor decay upon engine failure is the least serious emergency and thus gives the greatest amount of time in which to achieve autorotation. In hovering flight, rotor decay is in an intermediate amount. Defendant's flight manual for the helicopter's operation gives the maximum detailed warnings in regard to the minimum emergency (cruise) and the minimum warnings (none) in the maximum emergency situation (climb). One study done by defendant and specifically excluded by the trial court showed a concern on the part of defendant's chief test pilot regarding rapid rotor decay in climbing flight. If the jury determined this was an insufficient warning, the product would be defective even if the product had been perfectly designed and manufactured. The jury would have to go on to conclude that the defective condition was the proximate cause of decedent's death before there would be recovery. As an example, the failure of a seller of ordinary knives to warn of dangerous propensities cannot be considered the proximate cause of a consumer's cutting his finger since the potentiality of its danger is generally known and recognized. It is sometimes necessary to consider whether any warnings are required. Here the only issue was the adequacy of warnings since FAA regulations and the defendant's own inclusion of some warnings in regard to the autorotation system demonstrated the necessity of warnings. The issue of necessity and adequacy of warnings and instructions for use must also be considered in light of any contradictory promotional activities on the part of the seller (Citation).

Where warnings or instructions are required to make a product non-defective, it is the duty of the manufacturer to provide such warnings in a form that will reach the ultimate consumer and inform of the risks and inherent limits of the product. The duty to provide a non-defective product is non-delegable. (Citation.). . . . .

The order of the Superior Court is affirmed. . . . .

□   □   □

1. The court here holds that the manufacturer is the guarantor of his product's safety but the plaintiff must prove the product was defective. If the plaintiff sustains the burden of proving defect, then the product is "unreasonably dangerous" to him. This paraphrase of the court's argument appears to be a "Catch 22" situation. How would you resolve the apparent burden the court has placed on the plaintiff in proving a defect in the product?

2. The issue of the time available for placing the helicopter in autorotation was raised both as failure to design a sufficient time lapse period for the action (FAA standard) and as a failure to warn of the inherent limitations of the system. Can both arguments be correct? Discuss the issues involved here in the interplay of design and warnings for a given hazard.

3. If strict liability demands (as this court says it does) that foreseeability be banished from the test of unreasonable danger, then must it not also be banished from the proximate-cause test (i.e., was the harm appropriately assignable to the identified

defect?) If so, then what mechanism is available for limiting liability when the plaintiff uses the product in a nonforeseeable manner, or should liability be limited in such a case?

LEISTRA v. BUCYRUS-ERIE COMPANY

443 F.2d 157
United States Court of Appeals, Eighth Circuit
May 25, 1971
Rehearing En Banc Denied
July 20, 1971
Rehearing Denied July 20, 1971

BRIGHT, Circuit Judge

Donald Leistra, as plaintiff, brought this diversity action under Nebraska law to recover for injuries he sustained in an industrial accident. He attributed his injuries to negligence in the design of a large crawler-type crane, manufactured by Bucyrus-Erie Company, about which he worked as an employee of building contractor Peter Kiewit Sons Company of Omaha, Nebraska. A jury awarded Leistra $70,000 in damages, but the federal district court, Judge Robinson presiding, granted defendant Bucyrus-Erie judgment notwithstanding the verdict. Leistra brings this timely appeal. We agree with the district court's decision that Leistra, as a matter of law, established no proper basis for a claim against Bucyrus-Erie.

The facts surrounding the accident are not in dispute. Leistra served as an oiler or assistant to the operator of the fifty-ton load capacity Bucyrus-Erie 30-B Series Three Supercrane. On April 22, 1966, the crane was being used to lift and transport freshly made concrete from truck mixers to the top of a bridge under construction. The operator of the crane, Donald Cronkhite, after moving the machine from one location to another at the bridge site, discovered that a portion of the steel cable used to raise and lower the load had spilled out beyond the confines of its drum, the front drum, and had become wedged between the drum and an adjacent circular chain called the power-down chain. The power-down chain and its sprocket operate as a brake in controlling the downward movement of the load. Apparently, the movement of the crane caused the cable to unwind and jump over the drum flange. This, in turn, prevented the ball and hook at the end of the boom from being lowered to pick up another load.

The front drum and power-down unit are housed in a recessed compartment at the center-front of the cab and above the machinery deck. Though recessed, the unit is, nevertheless, unshielded at its exterior part. It is thus accessible to contact by a person located at or near this point. . . .

Operator Cronkhite called Leistra's attention to the wedged cable. Leistra climbed onto the machine and first attempted to free the cable by hand. When this effort failed, he tried to dislodge the cable by prying it with a crowbar. During these efforts, the master clutch which transfers power from the engine to the front drum was disengaged. When Leistra was unable to pry the cable free, Cronkhite advised plaintiff that he would assist him by moving the drum slightly back and forth. As Leistra continued his attempts to pry the cable from the chain, Cronkhite engaged the master clutch, rotating the drum twice back and forth. With this additional force, the power-down chain snapped and struck Leistra in the face, causing his injuries, including the loss of an eye.

Leistra brought suit against Bucyrus-Erie Company, claiming negligent design and manufacture of the crane in two respects: (1) failure to install a small metal shield, called a rope-guard, which allegedly permitted the cable to become wedged; and (2) failure to provide a shield over the power-down unit, which allegedly permitted the broken chain to hit plaintiff. The district court rejected the jury award on the basis that the plaintiff failed, as a matter of law, to establish that any such negligence on the part of Bucyrus-Erie caused his injuries. The court stated, in part:

> The problem that is bothersome to the Court is the matter of causation, whether it be termed as a duty owed, proximate cause, foreseeability or a superseding intervening cause. Choosing first to speak mainly in terms of a superseding intervening cause, the Court believes, and so holds, that some conduct by either the plaintiff, other employees, or his employer, or a combination thereof, superseded any pre-existing negligence on the part of the defendant thereby relieving defendant of liability.

We shall likewise consider the matter of causation, mindful, however, that such consideration requires an examination of aspects of negligence, foreseeability and duty. (Citations.). . . .

Although a rope-guard was not present on the crane at the time of the accident, no evidence of probative force suggests that its absence is chargeable to Bucyrus-Erie (Citations). On the contrary, the manufacturer's records disclosed that such a guard, which was designed to prevent loose cable from spilling over the drum flange and contacting the power-down unit had been specially manufactured and installed on this particular crane prior to its leaving the factory. Moreover, plaintiff's expert witness testified that a rope-guard will not always prevent the cable from jumping over the flange of the drum. On the basis of this evidence, we cannot attribute the crane's malfunction, which was caused by entanglement of the cable and the power-down chain, to any negligent conduct on the part of Bucyrus-Erie. Plaintiff's claim for recovery must, therefore, rest solely upon the manufacturer's failure to provide a shield over the power-down unit.

Upon reviewing the evidence on this issue, we conclude, as did the district court, that any negligence on the part of Bucyrus-Erie did not operate as a legal cause of plaintiff's injuries. In so holding, we rely in part upon the rules of the Restatement of Torts, Second. The Nebraska Supreme Court has often cited the Restatement with approval in considering causation (Citations).

Section 281 of the Restatement of Torts, Second, sets forth the elements of a cause of action for negligence. The following comment and illustration from that section apply to the facts of this case:

> f. *Harm beyond the risk.* Where the harm which in fact results is caused by the intervention of factors or forces which form no part of the recognizable risk involved in the actor's conduct,

the actor is ordinarily not liable. This is subject, however, to the qualification that where the harm which has resulted was itself within the risk created, the fact that it has been brought about in a manner which was not to be expected, or by the intervention of forces which were not within the risk, does not necessarily prevent the actor's liability. . . .

Illustration:

3. A gives loaded pistol to B, a boy of eight, to carry to C. In handing the pistol to C the boy drops it, injuring the bare foot of D, his comrade. The fall discharges the pistol, wounding C. A is subject to liability to C, but not to D.

Thus, for Bucyrus-Erie to be liable for plaintiff's injuries, the resulting harm must be within the recognizable risk, if any, created by Bucyrus-Erie. Appellant charges the manufacturer with failing "to guard the power-down chain." He fails to distinguish between shielding against the risk of human contact with the power-down unit and shielding against the risk of parts flying from the unit. Leistra sustained his injuries, not from contact with the moving power-down chain, but rather from being hit by a part of the chain when it broke.

The record is devoid of any evidence indicating that Bucyrus-Erie, in failing to provide a shield, created a risk of the power-down chain breaking, flying and hitting a workman. The plaintiff produced evidence that industry standards require the shielding of sprockets, drums and chains as well as other moving parts of equipment. The basic purpose of machine guarding, according to the evidence, is to prevent injuries from the following sources: (1) direct contact with moving parts; (2) work in process; (3) mechanical failure; (4) electrical failure; and (5) human failure. Plaintiff's expert witness, a safety consultant, only briefly commented upon mechanical failure, as follows:

The next one is to guard against mechanical failure. Breaks. If it flies out, it is contained. It doesn't fly. A grinding wheel that breaks, a belt that breaks, it isn't allowed to fly out and strike people in the proximity or send fragments out like missiles.

While the expert opined generally that the crane in question did not comply with the standards of the industry since the power-down unit was "not guarded for contact . . . [or] from parts flying from it," he made no comment on the location of the power-down unit within the recessed compartment, the chain's strength, or the risk of it flying out of the compartment and striking a workman.

We note the following other evidence: (1) the power-down chain was designed to handle three times the normal operating load; (2) a basic rule of safety, here taught by plaintiff's employer, is that no repairs, adjustments or lubrication should be made while a machine is in operation; and (3) the power-down chain and sprocket were located in a recessed compartment. On the basis of this evidence, we conclude that the resulting harm to Leistra was not within any recognizable risk created by the manufacturer.

Even if it were, however, the undisputed facts establish that other human conduct intervened to insulate the defendant from liability. Although we find no Nebraska case factually similar to this one, Nebraska courts have frequently held that an independent intervening force severs the chain of causation flowing from the original tortfeasor. (Citations.). . . .

These cases speak in terms of the defendant creating a passive condition which is operated upon by another active moving force, a concept not readily adaptable to a products liability case against a manufacturer since the latter's conduct almost always requires activation by another force to produce an injury. We deem the real question to be whether "the forces set in operation by the defendant have come to rest in a position of apparent safety, and some new force intervenes" (Citations).

As mentioned above, the absence of the rope-guard may have permitted the entanglement of the steel cable with the power-down chain, forcing the chain out of its normal position. But, once the crane had become disabled, the absence of a shield over the power-down unit did not pose a hazard to the workman. The power-down chain broke and hit plaintiff as a result of the following: (1) plaintiff applying a force by his prying action, further stressing the chain; and (2) the crane operator's movement of the drum back and forth, producing the necessary additional force to break the chain. We think these events must be characterized as superseding the failure of Bucyrus-Erie to place a shield over the particular drum and chain unit. We, therefore, hold that any negligence on the part of Bucyrus-Erie in failing to shield was not the legal cause of plaintiff's injuries. . . .

We find no proper basis to support the verdict for the plaintiff. Accordingly, we affirm.

LAY, Circuit Judge (dissenting).

I respectfully submit that the majority opinion misapplies Nebraska law. In *Rose v. Buffalo Air Services,* 170 Neb. 806, 104 N.W. 2d 431, 444 (1960), the Nebraska Supreme Court announced the rule to be followed in Nebraska relating to a manufacturer's liability for a defective product:

A vendor and the manufacturer or supplier of a chattel who know or have reason to know that it is likely to be dangerous when used and which is purchased as safe for use in good faith reliance upon their professions or representations of safety, competence, and care, are subject to liability to the purchaser or to others whom they should expect to share in or be in the vicinity of its use, for damages proximately caused by their failure to exercise reasonable competence and care to supply the chattel in a condition safe for use.

The trial court correctly instructed the jury on proximate cause under Nebraska law as follows:

'Proximate Cause'—An injury or damage is proximately caused by an act, or a failure to act, whenever it appears from the evidence in the case, that the act or omission played a substantial part in bringing about the injury or damage; and that the injury or damage was either a direct result or a natural or probable consequence of the act or omission.

This does not mean that the law recognizes only one proximate cause of an injury or damage, consisting of only one factor or thing, of the conduct of only one person. On the contrary, many factors, or the conduct of two or more persons, may operate at the same time, either independently or together, to cause injury or damage; and in such a case, each may be a proximate cause. . . .

It is not necessary that the defendant might or should have foreseen the likelihood of the particular injury or harm, the extent of the harm or the manner in which it occurred, but it is only necessary that he should have anticipated that some injury or harm might result from his conduct.

The majority opinion now holds that the actions of the plaintiff in attempting to pry the cable loose and the operator in rotating the drum constituted a superseding cause. Thus, although this case was submitted to the jury under general definitions of proximate cause, we sustain the judgment n.o.v. by applying different principles of causation. The defendant did not try its case on the theory of an intervening or superseding cause. Defendant's motion for directed verdict did not even raise this issue. No jury instruction on this issue was requested by the defendant and no such instruction was given.

The majority opinion borrows a principle of causation from Nebraska cases which are not related to the facts before us. . . . In each of these cases the Nebraska Supreme Court found that the alleged negligence of the original tortfeasor had *come to rest* and was not a *substantial factor* in the cause of the accident. This is not true here. In the instant case, if the manufacturer's negligence had not still been contributive, that is, *had it placed* the protective shield around the drum containing the chain, plaintiff would not have been injured when the operator rotated the drum resulting in the chain flying loose. On the facts presented a jury could reasonably determine that the action of the operator in rotating the drum *acted on* and *in conjunction with* the absence of the shield. . . .

To hold that the negligence of the manufacturer, to-wit, the failure to safety guard the chain and drum, has come to rest, totally misconceives the events that took place. The majority's statement that the plaintiff confuses the manufacturer's duty to place a shield to guard against snagging one's clothing or hands with a duty to guard against flying parts escapes me. The industry safety standards anticipate both protections.

The majority opinion stresses that the breakdown of the machine interrupts the natural and probable sequence of events because the manufacturer could not reasonably anticipate the malfunction and the events which followed. To so hold as a matter of law ignores the favorable evidential inferences to which a verdict holder is entitled. Under the evidence, the jury could consider that: (1) the defendant knew or should have known that the cable could jump the flange and wedge against the chain, with or without a rope guard; (2) the defendant could anticipate such a malfunction, since the defendant knew the rope guard is often discarded once the crane is put in actual use; (3) the defendant's own testimony reveals that once the malfunction occurs the flange could not be removed without unwinding the full cable drum, an impossibility here because the cable was wedged tight against the chain and the drum would not turn; (4) loosening the master link of the chain would not serve to release the chain where the chain was otherwise wedged and taut by reason of the cable; (5) alternative methods to loosen the chain, according to the testimony of defendant's own engineer, would be to *rotate the drum, pry the chain loose,* or use a torch to cut the chain; (6) the breaking of a taut chain would be hazardous to people in the vicinity; (7) according to plaintiff's expert, there existed an industry-wide practice to shield or guard the drum containing the chain in order to protect those in the vicinity from flying parts; (8) plaintiff's expert gave an opinion that the unshielded chain on the first drum was in violation of safety codes and the industry-wide practice.

A manufacturer has the duty to reasonably anticipate harm that may arise from a foreseeable emergency. This is particularly true where the evidence demonstrates the manufacturer's awareness of such potential emergencies. Judge Gibson, speaking for this court in *Larsen v. General Motors Corp.*, 391 F.2d 495, 501 (8th Cir. 1968), said:

> Generally, as noted in 76 A.L.R. 2d 93, Anno: Products Liability—Duty As To Design, the manufacturer has a duty to use reasonable care under the circumstances in the design of a product but is not an insurer that his product is incapable of producing injury, and this duty of design is met when the article is safe for its intended use and when it will fairly meet any "emergency of use" which is foreseeable. [Citation omitted.] *This doctrine has even been extended to cover an unintended use where the injury resulting from that unintended use was foreseeable or should have been anticipated.* (My emphasis.)

See also *Ford Motor Co. v. Zahn,* 265 F.2d 729, 733 (8th Cir. 1959).

We are all agreed that failure of a plaintiff to fully appreciate the risk of attempting to loosen the chain and cable was clearly an issue of fact for the jury under Nebraska comparative negligence law (Citations).

We are also agreed that the plaintiff produced sufficient evidence of negligence, to-wit, the failure to properly guard a hazardous area. This was disputed, but the jury resolved the conflicting facts in favor of the plaintiff. In interpreting Nebraska law, Judge Van Oosterhout wrote for this court in *Chicago B. & Q. R. R. v. Beninger,* 373 F.2d 854, 858 (8th Cir. 1967):

> An accident may be proximately caused by separate and distinct acts of negligence of different parties which concur in producing the accident. *Where negligence is established, the issue of probable cause is usually one of fact for the jury.* (My emphasis.)

I submit that the evidence here was sufficient to take the issue of proximate cause to the jury. A jury is much better equipped to offer a composite expertise to resolve issues which bear on what is a foreseeable harm and on what is a natural and probable consequence of an act or omission. Jurors bring with them community standards and understandings to resolve issues of fact in areas where judges should hesitate to pronounce doctrine. Mr. Justice Hunt observed years ago:

> It is assumed that twelve men know more of the common affairs of life than does one man, that they can draw wiser and safer conclusions from admitted facts thus occurring than can a single judge. *Railroad Co. v. Stout,* 84 U.S. 657, 664, 21 L.Ed. 145 (1873).

A judge's role should be confined to viewing the record to ascertain whether there exists sufficient evidence to sustain a verdict. Simply because we might personally disagree as to what inferences may be taken from the evidence, we are not justified in setting aside a jury verdict which finds to the contrary. In *Tennant v. Peoria & P. U. Ry. Co.,* 321 U.S. 29, 35, 64 S.Ct. 409, 412, 88 L.Ed. 520 (1944), the Supreme Court admonished:

Courts are not free to reweigh the evidence and set aside the jury verdict merely because the jury could have drawn different inferences or conclusions or because judges feel that other results are more reasonable.

I adhere to that principle. I would affirm the verdict of the jury below.

□   □   □

1. The majority opinion concluded that the act of attempting to free the drum was a new "force" that superseded and intervened to relieve the defendant of any negligence in not providing guards or shields. The dissent finds that the plaintiff's act could be viewed as foreseeable and flowing from the defendant's acts. Consider this issue from the viewpoint of duty, proximate cause, and foreseeable use.
2. Would the majority opinion be any different if the case had been tried under strict liability rather than negligence?
3. The evidence suggests that the "rope guard" is often discarded once the crane is in use. With the assumption that such a device is necessary, what design considerations should be prompted by the manufacturer's knowledge of the widespread removal of the device?

FRIEDMAN v. GENERAL MOTORS CORPORATION

43 Ohio St. 2d 209
331 N.E. 2d 702
Supreme Court of Ohio
July 23, 1975

On May 8, 1967, Mr. and Mrs. Morton Friedman, their son, Sheldon, and their daughter, Susan, were driving east on Lake Road in Lorain County. Their automobile, a 1966 Oldsmobile Toronado, had been purchased some 17 months previously from A. D. Pelunis Oldsmobile, Inc., Lakewood.

As Mr. Friedman drove through the city of Avon Lake, he observed that his gasoline gauge registered near empty. Accordingly, he pulled into a gasoline station on the north side of the highway, stopped behind a Rambler which was being serviced at the forward pump of the gasoline pump island, and, after waiting for a short period, turned off the ignition. Some minutes later, after the Rambler had been serviced, a gasoline attendant instructed Friedman, by word or gesture, to pull ahead to the forward set of pumps.

As Friedman turned on the ignition key and started the engine, the Toronado moved forward. It "peeled" away from the gasoline pumps, bounced off the Rambler and a telephone pole, careened across the street into the steel support posts of a large sign. The front end of the Toronado was heavily damaged. The transmission linkages under the hood were jammed so that the gear selector lever could not be shifted into Neutral, Reverse, or Park. All four occupants of the car sustained injuries.

Thereafter, Friedman, his wife, and his two children filed suit, in the Court of Common Pleas of Cuyahoga County, against General Motors Corporation, manufacturer of the automobile, and A. D. Pelunis Oldsmobile, Inc., which had sold it. The complaint alleges that when Friedman started the automobile at the Sohio station, "the gear shift selector was actually in Drive position, and the engine should not have started. The engine nevertheless did start, and the car leaped forward, and so startled the driver that he could not regain control before the automobile ran wild. . . ." The complaint alleges further that the collisions which followed ". . . were directly caused by defective mechanisms in the car sold by the defendants; and by the misrepresentations of the defendants that the car could not be started in Drive position". . . . .

A. D. Pelunis, President of A. D. Pelunis Oldsmobile, Inc., testified that the 1966 Toronado was delivered to the Friedmans on December 10, 1965. From that date to the date of the accident, no adjustment was made to the neutral start switch, the gear shift indicator needle, or the transmission linkage. Neither the shift tube itself, the neutral start switch, nor the gear shift indicator were damaged in the collision. Further, according to Pelunis, no post-accident repairs were made until the automobile had been inspected by representatives of both the plaintiffs and the defendants.

Charles E. English, a metallurgist, testified that he examined the damaged Toronado on two occasions. On May 26, 1967, a Pelunis mechanic connected jumper cables from another car to activate the Toronado's electrical circuits. The gear shift indicator on the damaged auto was in Drive position. English turned the ignition key on the ignition lock a number of times. Twice the starter kicked and the car lurched with a forward-backward vibration as the starter engaged. At this time, the engine would not fire and run because of interference by the crushed radiator grill and fan.

On June 19, 1967, English conducted another investigation. The gear shift indicator was still in Drive. By this time, the radiator grill and engine fan had been removed, and the front end raised onto blocks so as to permit front wheel rotation. On the 29th or 30th try, the automobile started. The front wheels started rotating rapidly, accelerating to 30 miles per hour in five seconds. The acceleration of the front wheels was so rapid, according to English, that ". . . in my opinion, if these were on the ground, the car would move forward."

At all times during his two investigations, English testified, the gear shift indicator on the Toronado remained in Drive position, a position from which it could not be dislodged.

John Isenhath, the service representative of General Motors called as a witness by the plaintiffs, examined the damaged Toronado on August 17 and September 1, 1967. He, too, started the automobile with the gear shift indicator in Drive position. This indicated, according to Isenhath, that the neutral start switch was either in Neutral or Park, regardless of whether such position was reflected on the gear shift indicator. This was true, according to Isenhath, because the only factor which determines whether the ignition key will start the engine is the position of the contacts inside the neutral start switch. If the contacts are in Neutral, even though the transmission gears and gear shift indicator are in Drive, the ignition key will start the car, in which case the front wheels would immediately rotate. . . . .

Friedman, his wife Selma, and his son Sheldon each testified as to their past experience in driving the Toronado, and as to their recollection of the accident. None of the Friedmans had ever attempted to start the Toronado with the gear shift indicator in any position other than Park. None had encountered a problem shifting gears, and each stated that the gear shift indicator was always accurate. Both Mr. Friedman and Sheldon stated that, when Friedman started the automobile in the Sohio station, it began to move rapidly immediately upon ignition. . . . .

Morton Friedman was questioned extensively as to his actions immediately before the accident. According to his testimony, he believed the automobile was in Park. "I turned my key on the car like I normally do and the car just went off, just like a jet, at such great speed that I felt—I slammed my foot on the brakes and I was hysterical—I mean, in other words, I just got shook up." Friedman was positive and explicit that at no time after he turned the ignition key did he make a change in the position of, or touch, the gear shift lever. Friedman admitted that although he thought he had put his foot on the brake, he could have hit the accelerator at the same time.

Friedman also testified that the Toronado had never been serviced at an independent garage or gasoline station, that only mechanics from Pelunis Oldsmobile had ever worked on it.

During plaintiffs' case-in-chief, their causes of action against A. D. Pelunis Oldsmobile, Inc., were voluntarily dismissed. At the close of plaintiffs' case, a motion by the defendant, General Motors Corporation for a directed verdict was granted. The trial court concluded that ". . . upon the issue of alleged product defect, reasonable minds could come to but one conclusion upon the evidence submitted, that conclusion being adverse to the plaintiffs."

Upon appeal to the Court of Appeals the judgment of the Court of Common Pleas was reversed. The journal entry filed by the Court of Appeals stated, in part. . . . .

"It was the claim of the plaintiffs that the subject car was defective when it left the factory in that the 'neutral safety switch' was malconnected or maladjusted so that the engine could start upon turning the ignition switch when the transmission gears were in a Drive position. This fact had never come to the attention of the plaintiffs before the occurrence described in the complaint because the engine had always been started when the indicator had shown Park and the transmission gears were in the Park position.

"The defendant denied the contentions of the plaintiffs as to the defective condition of the car and the cause of the action. It contended that there is no evidence from which the jury could find that a defective condition was present in the car. . . . .

"Under the law of Ohio the jury has the right to make any logical and immediate inferences from facts which have been established by the evidence. An inference is a reasonable deduction of fact which logically follows from other facts established by the evidence and which the jury may, but is not required to make. . . . .

"We hold that the jury had the right to infer, if it found the facts to be as testified to by the plaintiffs, that the 'neutral safety switch' was either malconnected or malaligned by General Motors when it built the car and that the car was, therefore, defective in a respect which was the proximate cause of injuries to and damages to the plaintiffs. . . . .

"The trial court, therefore, erred to the substantial prejudice of the plaintiffs in granting the General Motors' motion to dismiss. The judgment of the trial court is, therefore, overruled and the action, therefore, remanded to the trial court for further proceedings according to law". . . . .

PAUL W. BROWN, Justice.

The single issue presented by this appeal is whether the evidence introduced by the plaintiffs was of sufficient quality to overcome the defendant's motion for a directed verdict. . . .

To sustain their allegation against General Motors, the plaintiffs were required to prove that the Oldsmobile Toronado, manufactured and sold by the defendant, was defective; that the defect existed at the time the product left the factory; and that the defect was the direct and proximate cause of the accident and injuries (Citations). A defect may be proven by circumstantial evidence, where a preponderance of that evidence establishes that the accident was caused by a defect and not other possibilities, although not all other possibilities need be eliminated (Citations).

In our judgment, the evidence presented by the plaintiffs established a prima facie case of defect for which defendant General Motors would be liable. . . . .

[W]e believe the jury might reasonably have concluded that the defendant was guilty of manufacturing a defective automobile, which directly and proximately caused the accident. For that reason, the judgment of the Court of Appeals is affirmed.

Judgment affirmed. . . .

STERN, Justice (dissenting). . .

No direct physical evidence was presented that any part was defective, and, in fact, there was evidence that the safety switch itself was properly aligned and that the transmission worked properly as indicated. The plaintiffs' case is that from this evidence one can infer a defect in the car, in that the car could be started in Drive, and that this defect existed at the time of manufacture.

In products liability cases, proof that a defect existed is often difficult and complex. Frequently the product in dispute will have been destroyed, beyond any possibility of analysis, or be so complex that a plaintiff would have a greater difficulty in determining the presence of a defect than would the manufacturer. In most cases, proof of the defect must necessarily be by circumstantial evidence and inference. No general rule can adequately apply to the wide range of such cases, each involving a different mixture of fact and inference, but fundamental to any such case is that some defect must be proved. . . .

Although plaintiff's evidence may be sufficient to permit an inference that something was wrong with the car, that alone is not sufficient to establish a defect, except perhaps in cases, analogous to res ipsa loquitur, in which ordinary human experience tells us that the event could not happen without a defect. The instant case is not such a case, for driver error, failure of some part, accidental or unwitting damage to the car, and other possibilities do provide other explanations (Citation). In this case, the fact that something went wrong is not sufficient to support an inference that a defect caused the accident.

The particular defect that plaintiff alleges is that the indicator and the transmission gear linkages were both malaligned in a similar fashion, relative to the neutral start switch, so that the car as manufactured could start in Drive rather than, as intended, only in Park and Neutral. There are various ways in which that particular fact could be proved, by means of several types of evidence. Keeton, Manufacturer's Liability: The Meaning of Defect in the Manufacture and Design of Products, 20 *Syracuse L. Rev.* 559, for example, suggests five ways by which the particular fact could be proved. (See, also, Rheingold, Proof of Defect in Product Liability Cases, 38 *Tenn. L. Rev.* 325.)

1. Plaintiff might introduce evidence by an expert based upon an examination of the product in question following the happening of the damaging event. Expert evidence would be direct evidence of an identifiable defect. In the instant case, two expert witnesses testified, and neither was able to point out an identifiable defect. Both testified that the car could be started in an indicated Drive position, but neither identified a cause for that based upon their examination. The only explanation, offered by one of the experts, was that the pointer was probably damaged.

2. There may simply be evidence of a damaging event occurring in the course of or following use of a product, whether by the testimony of the user or otherwise. This may be sufficient in the case where, as a matter of common knowledge, a defect is the probable cause. As already indicated, the instant case is not one involving such common knowledge.

3. A plaintiff may produce both evidence of a damaging event occurring in the course of or following the use of a product and expert evidence that the most likely probable cause was attributable to a defect in the product being used at the time.

In the instant case, the only expert who was qualified to state such an opinion, the company expert called as a witness by the plaintiff, was not asked to state whether a defect was the probable cause, and in fact made clear in his testimony that he believed it probable that there was no defect and that the apparent starting of the car in Drive was probably caused by damage from the accident to the indicator. He stated only that it was possible for various components to be malaligned as plaintiffs' theory required.

4. In addition to evidence of an accident and the probable cause of such accident, evidence could be introduced to negate the existence of "probable causes" not attributable to the maker.

This type of evidence was not introduced in the instant case, except with respect to the issue of maintenance on the car in the 17 months after delivery.

5. In some cases, the physical evidence of the actual condition of the product after the accident would be such that a layman could infer that it was defective.

No such physical evidence was introduced in the instant case.....

In the instant case, the most exact method of determining whether there was in fact a malalignment of the transmission parts would have been actual examination of those parts, which were under the control of plaintiffs for several months after the accident. The examination actually made was incomplete. No identifiable defect was found; nor was the testimony of the mechanics who repaired the automobile offered. Failing such examination, even by a nonexpert, plaintiffs could have introduced expert testimony that the probable cause of the accident was a defect. This was not done, and the expert testimony was only to the effect that a malalignment was possible, but according to one expert, was not probable. The sum of the evidence is thus only that something unusual happened in the car, and that a possible explanation of that happening is a defect. I believe plaintiffs could have and should have done more in order to make a case for the jury, for the essential link of actual proof, between the accident and any possible explanation, is missing.

The same difficulty arises with regard to the issue of whether the claimed defect existed at the time the car left the hands of the defendant. Plaintiffs introduced evidence that the transmission had not been serviced or tampered with, and that the family's method of starting the car could have permitted a defect to remain undiscovered. But this, again, is only evidence of the possibility of a defect. Here, the car was 17 months old, there was no expert testimony that the claimed defect was one which would probably have existed at the time the car was manufactured, and common experience does not permit any such inference. . . . In the instant case, plaintiffs' negative evidence indicates the possibility that the claimed defect could have existed at the time of manufacture; but this possibility remains only a theory, for there is lack of any positive evidence which would overcome the inference arising from the long-continued use of the car.

At the center of plaintiffs' case, which is made up of evidence of an unusual event and a possible explanation thereof, there should be some positive proof that the possible malalignment was something more than a theory. Such proof was not presented and remains a matter of speculation. For that reason, I agree with the trial judge that plaintiffs failed to submit sufficient evidence from which it could be inferred that a defect existed in the Friedman car at the time it left the hands of the defendant.

□   □   □

1. The dissenting opinion takes issue with whether sufficient evidence was introduced to establish defect. The majority opinion discusses inference of defect, while the dissent asks for the precise flaw that led to the malfunction. Was there sufficient evidence to establish defect? What role does the age of the car have in establishing the defect in this case?

2. Was the investigation by the plaintiffs' expert adequate? If not, describe in detail the scope of an appropriate investigation for this case.

3. On the basis of the distillation of the evidence given in the opinion, would it be appropriate to have let the jury decide this case? If not, what level of evidence should have been presented to permit more than mere speculation?

AULT v. INTERNATIONAL HARVESTER COMPANY

13 Cal. 3d 113
528 P.2d 1148

117 Cal. Rptr. 812
Supreme Court of California, In Banc
December 12, 1974
As Modified on Denial of Rehearing
January 23, 1975

MOSK, Justice.

Plaintiff was injured in an accident involving a motor vehicle known as a "Scout," manufactured by defendant. He brought an action alleging that the accident was caused by a defect in the design of the vehicle, asserting that he was entitled to recovery under theories of strict liability, breach of warranty, and negligence.

The gear box of the Scout involved in the accident was manufactured of aluminum 380, a material which plaintiff asserts was defective for that purpose. At the trial evidence established that after the accident defendant changed from aluminum 380 to malleable iron in the production of the gear box. A jury returned a verdict of $700,000 in plaintiff's favor. . . .

On the morning of November 8, 1964, plaintiff was riding as a passenger in the Scout on Nine Mile Canyon Road near Mojave, California, when the vehicle plunged 500 feet to the bottom of the canyon, injuring him seriously. The road was 20 feet wide and dry. Just prior to the accident, the Scout was traveling at a speed of only 10 to 15 miles an hour. The owner and driver of the vehicle had traversed Nine Mile Canyon Road on two prior occasions in the Scout without difficulty. Both the driver and plaintiff developed retrograde amnesia and were unable to testify as to the circumstances of the accident.

After the accident, it was discovered that the gear box on the Scout had broken. Plaintiff contended that the break occurred while the Scout was traveling on the highway, causing the vehicle to go out of control, whereas defendant asserted that the gear box broke on impact as the vehicle hurtled down into the canyon and that the accident was caused either by driver negligence or the collapse of the roadway.

It was plaintiff's contention that the gear box broke because the aluminum 380 out of which it was made suffered from metal fatigue, and he produced a number of expert witnesses in support of this theory. Plaintiff's witnesses also testified that aluminum 380 was an unsuitable material out of which to build the gear box, that malleable iron was stronger than aluminum 380, that a gear box made of malleable iron would have been less likely to fail, and that in 1967, three years after the accident, defendant substituted malleable iron for aluminum 380 in the manufacture of the Scout's gear box.

Defendant asserts that the admission of the evidence it changed from aluminum 380 to malleable iron after the accident violated the prescription of section 1151. . . .

Section 1151 by its own terms excludes evidence of subsequent remedial or precautionary measures only when such evidence is offered to prove negligence or culpable conduct. In an action based upon strict liability against a manufacturer, negligence or culpability is not a necessary ingredient. The plaintiff may recover if he establishes that the product was defective, and he need not show that the defendants breached a duty of due care. (*Greenman v. Yuba Power Products, Inc.* (1963) 59 Cal. 2d 57, 61–63, 27 Cal. Rptr. 697, 377 P.2d 897.). . . . .

The history and purpose of section 1151 compel our conclusion that it was not intended to apply to cases founded on the theory of strict liability in a products liability action. According to its draftsmen, section 1151 was intended merely to codify "well-settled law." (Law Revision Com. comment to Evid. Code, § 1151.) The rule excluding evidence of subsequent repairs originally rested on the notion that such repairs were completely *irrelevant* to the issue of defendant's *negligence* at the time of the accident. Thus, the first case to adopt this rule in California, *Sappenfield v. Main St., etc., R. R. Co.* (1891) 91 Cal. 48, 62, 27 P. 590, 593, stressed that "The negligence of the employer, which renders him responsible for the accident, depends upon what he did and knew before the accident, and must be established by facts and circumstances which preceded it, and not by acts done by him after the occurrence" (Citation).

On the other hand a number of more recent cases have recognized several exceptions to the rule of exclusion in negligence cases. For example, several decisions acknowledge that evidence of subsequent repairs is relevant to the issue of negligence, for if the changes occur closely in time they may well illustrate the feasibility of the improvement at the time of the accident, one of the normal elements in the negligence calculus (Citations).

Nevertheless, courts and legislatures have frequently retained the exclusionary rule in negligence cases as a matter of "public policy," reasoning that the exclusion of such evidence may be necessary to avoid deterring individuals from making improvements or repairs after an accident has occurred. Section 1151 rests explicitly on this "public policy" rationale. In explaining the purpose of the section, the draftsmen's comment states: "The admission of evidence of subsequent repairs *to prove negligence* would substantially discourage persons from making repairs after the occurrence of an accident." (Emphasis added.) (Law Revision Com. comment to Evid. Code, § 1151.)

While the provisions of section 1151 may fulfill this anti-deterrent function in the typical negligence action, the provision plays no comparable role in the products liability field. Historically, the common law rule codified in section 1151 was developed with reference to the usual negligence action, in which a pedestrian fell into a hole in a sidewalk (Citation) or a plaintiff was injured on unstable stairs (Citation); in such circumstances, it may be realistic to assume that a landowner or potential defendant might be deterred from making repairs if such repairs could be used against him in determining liability for the initial accident.

When the context is transformed from a typical negligence setting to the modern products liability field, however, the "public policy" assumptions justifying this evidentiary rule are no longer valid. The contemporary corporate mass producer of goods, the normal products liability defendant, manufactures tens of thousands of units of goods; it is manifestly unrealistic to suggest that such a producer will forego making improvements in its product, and risk innumerable additional lawsuits and the attendant adverse effect upon its public image, simply because evidence of adoption of such improvement may be admitted in an action founded on strict liability for recovery on an injury that preceded the improvement. In the products liability area, the exclusionary rule of section 1151 does not affect the primary conduct of the mass producer of goods, but serves merely as a shield against potential liability. In short, the purpose of section 1151 is not applicable to a strict liability case and hence its exclusionary rule should not be gratuitously extended to that field.

This view has been advanced by others. It has been pointed out that not only is the policy of encouraging repairs and improvements of doubtful validity in an action for strict liability since it is in the economic self interest of a manufacturer to improve and repair defective products, but that the application of the rule would be contrary to the public policy of encouraging the distributor of mass-produced goods to market safer products. (Note, Products Liability and Evidence of Subsequent Repairs, 1972 *Duke L.J.* 837, 845–852.). . . . .

Defendant assigns numerous other evidentiary rulings of the trial court as error. It complains that the trial court allowed expert witnesses to testify regarding an accident occurring prior to the present one, as well as one occurring subsequently, in which gear boxes made of aluminum 380 in Scout vehicles had allegedly failed. . . .

Evidence of other accidents is admissible to prove a defective condition, knowledge, or the cause of an accident, provided that the circumstances of the other accidents are similar and not too remote (Citations). Here, the expert witnesses had been retained in other litigation to analyze the properties of the gear boxes involved in the other accidents, and had reached the conclusion that they had failed because of metal fatigue. In the trial of the present case, they described the tests they performed, and testified that in their opinion the physical properties of all three gear boxes were similar and that the failure in the present case was also due to metal fatigue. The expert who testified regarding the first accident compared the damaged gear box involved in that accident with the box in the present case, and stated that a blow to the gear box would not have caused the failure in either accident. The other witness' testimony consisted largely of an account of the scientific tests he had performed on aluminum 380 to determine its properties, and the conclusions he had reached from those tests.

Thus, although the purpose of the testimony was to indicate that all three accidents occurred because of the failure of the gear box, the focus was not on the accidents themselves but upon the inherent similarity in the physical and mechanical properties of the three gear boxes, all of which purportedly contained similar defects. Since there was no dispute that all three instruments were manufactured out of aluminum 380, we cannot conclude that the evidence was erroneously admitted. . . .

The judgment is affirmed. . . .

CLARK, Justice (dissenting).

I

I dissent.

Section 1151 of the Evidence Code excludes evidence of subsequent remedial modifications when offered to prove "culpable conduct." Culpable conduct includes conduct breaching a legal duty. Because a plaintiff seeking recovery on a product liability theory must prove the defendant breached his legal duty not to place a defective product in the stream of commerce, section 1151 is applicable to the case before us. . . . .

A manufacturer placing a product in the stream of commerce has a legal duty to prevent defects causing injury. (Greenman v. Yuba Power Products, Inc. (1963) 59 Cal. 2d 57, 63, 27 Cal. Rptr. 697, 377 P.2d 897.) And before a plaintiff may recover on a theory of product liability, he must prove the defendant breached this duty. Thus, by definition, the plaintiff must prove the defendant's conduct "culpable," and in proving such culpability, section 1151 clearly prohibits using evidence of subsequent remedial measures.

The important policy underlying prohibiting evidence of subsequent change is applicable to product liability actions as to negligence actions.

The basis for the exclusion in negligence cases is that the jury may unjustifiably view the change as an admission of fault. Following an injury, modifications will frequently be made which would have rendered the injury less likely. While these modifications might be the result of some feeling of responsibility, it is at least as probable the change was made because it was the socially desirable or humane thing to do. Such conduct is not probative of an admission that the modification was the required standard of conduct prior to the injury. It may have been thought to be the standard required only after the injury is known. Or, the defendant may have desired to rise above the required standard (Citation). Finally, the change may not be a safety measure at all but rather a change made for functional, aesthetic or economic reasons.

Acknowledging the lack of probative value, this court many years ago held that an admission of negligence may not be founded on evidence of change following an accident and that when such evidence is relevant only to prove admission it must be excluded (Citations). Lack of probative value is the basis for the exclusionary rule according to Professor Wigmore, although he recognizes that some courts have also relied on public policy to avoid discouraging persons from making repairs following an accident. (2 Wigmore on Evidence (3rd ed. 1940) pp. 151–159.)

There is even less probative value when evidence of subsequent change is offered to prove an admission in product liability cases. Change in a product is frequently made for reasons unrelated to the remedial nature of the change. Among the motivations for change are the desires to decrease production cost or to increase efficiency or salability. The most striking illustration of lack of probative value is supplied by the automobile industry. Each year hundreds of changes are made in a new model. It is absurd to suggest that each change reflects an admission the modification was made to remedy a defect.

Notwithstanding the lack of probative value, juries, in the heat of negligence or product liability trials—learning only of a single change—may conclude the change reflects an admission of negligence or defect and may give great and decisive weight to the perceived admission. The danger of such misuse of evidence is at least as great in product liability cases as in negligence cases.

The lack of probative value and the danger of misuse of evidence of subsequent change are not cured when the issue before the jury is defect rather than negligence, and no reason exists for refusing to give the word "culpable" its common meaning. Accordingly, I conclude that section 1151 should be applicable in product liability cases.

II

The remaining issue is the application of section 1151 to the evidence that International Harvester changed from aluminum 380 to malleable iron. Section 1151 excludes evidence only when used to prove negligence or culpable conduct. Case law allows evidence of subsequent change to prove issues other than negligence or culpable conduct. For example, evidence of subsequent precautions may properly be admitted when it tends to impeach the testimony of a witness (Citations).

Despite relevance to a proper purpose, the danger of a jury improperly viewing the evidence as an admission of legal fault is apparent, and the danger of misuse may well outweigh probative value of the evidence. Not only is such misuse contrary to the express prohibition created by the Legislature, but also the misuse is manifestly unfair to defendant. To alleviate the potential unfairness and to implement the legislative prohibition, the trial court must carefully balance the need for the evidence against the dangers of its use. . . . .

The primary dispute in this case was whether the aluminum steering gear box caused the injury. Feasibility was not a contested issue and, even if contested, could have been proven by evidence other than International Harvester's subsequent replacement of the aluminum steering gear box. Accordingly, the evidence should have been excluded.

The record reveals improper introduction of the subsequent modification was highly prejudicial to defendant. The evidence on the critical issue—whether the aluminum steering gear box *actually caused* the injury—was closely balanced. In the first trial, the jury was unable to reach a verdict. During the second trial, plaintiff's trial tactics included constant emphasis of the subsequent change in the steering gear box, resulting in a plaintiff's verdict. Under these circumstances, it must be concluded the improper admission of evidence substantially affected the verdict, constituting reversible error. . . .

□   □   □

1. Strict liability focuses on the product in the environment of its use, while negligence gauges the conduct of the defendant. Does this basic distinction offer any rationale for concluding that evidence of subsequent modifications is irrelevant in an action in negligence but relevant in strict liability?

2. The majority opinion concludes that postaccident product modifications are admissible from "public policy" considerations. The dissenting opinion argues that such evidence can be misused by the jury, even in a strict liability action, since the defendant's conduct must still be shown to be culpable. Consider arguments that would either admit or exclude such evidence on the basis of the "relevance" (question 1) and/or "public policy" rationales.

3. On the assumption of the admissibility of evidence of subsequent modifications, what arguments can be raised by the defendant manufacturer regarding its significance? Consider the reasons offered by the dissent arguing against admissibility.

4. On the basis of the available technical, mechanical, and metallurgical evidence

in the literature, consider the use of "aluminum 380" and "malleable iron" as materials for the gear box. Formulate the design criteria for material selection.

5. Consider the effect on your own process of design modification that this decision may have. Is the court correct in its assumption that manufacturers will disregard the liability potential if they should introduce new design parameters?

BRISSETTE v. MILNER CHEVROLET COMPANY, INC.

479 S.W. 2d 176
Missouri Court of Appeals
March 28, 1972

SIMEONE, Judge.

This case is one of first impression in this State. It presents unique issues in the expanding field of products liability. The principal issues raised are: (1) whether the failure to produce the tire in a products liability case is essential in the proof of the plaintiff's case; (2) whether the plaintiff-appellant may be permitted to introduce expert testimony regarding an alleged defect in an automobile tire which is claimed to have failed, causing the plaintiff's injuries, when the plaintiff is unable to produce the allegedly defective tire for examination; and (3) whether a directed verdict, under the circumstances, at the close of the plaintiff's opening statement was proper.

Following the plaintiff's opening statement, the trial court granted defendants' motion for a directed verdict, ruling that the plaintiff's offer of proof, made during the course of argument on defendants' motion, was rejected "first, because the object was not made available to the defendants, and secondly, that a case could not be made even in the absence of this, by expert testimony."

According to the record, on July 25, 1964, the plaintiff-appellant went to Milner Chevrolet Co., Inc. (hereinafter Milner) and advised the company that he wanted to purchase a two-door Impala hardtop with certain accessories, including four-ply tubeless tires. He was informed that he could have the four-ply tires but at an extra charge, and that the company did not have the car in stock but that one would be located.

On July 29, 1964, the automobile was delivered to the plaintiff. It was equipped with two-ply tires with four-ply rating. According to the plaintiff, the automobile was driven carefully and almost exclusively by him and the auto had only about 900 miles on it as of August 29, 1964.

On that date, as plaintiff alleged in his pleadings, he was driving the automobile on Highway 61 in Ste. Genevieve County when the left front tire "did then and there fail and collapse" causing the automobile to skid and spin across the highway eventually landing in a ditch. As a result, plaintiff suffered various injuries which required hospitalization.

Some three years later, on September 14, 1967, plaintiff filed his petition in the Circuit Court of the City of St. Louis seeking damages against Milner; General Motors

Corporation, the manufacturer of the automobile (hereinafter General Motors); and General Tire and Rubber Company, the alleged manufacturer of the tire (hereinafter General Tire). The petition was framed on both theories of negligence and breach of warranty.

During the pre-trial stage of the proceedings in April 1968, the plaintiff testified in a deposition that after the accident he had possession of the tire for a period of time but turned it over to his insurance company, Covenant Security Insurance Company, in connection with his claim for property damage. Subsequently, interrogatories and supplemental interrogatories were filed upon plaintiff, and in answer to General Tire's supplemental interrogatories, plaintiff indicated that the tire had "no physical tests," that the tire had been in the possession of the insurance adjuster and then in the possession of Covenant. Plaintiff's answers to General Tire's second supplemental interrogatories later filed, indicated that the tire had been examined by Rip's Garage and Service. Later, and on the date of trial, March 15, 1971, the plaintiff, by way of amended answers to General Tire's second supplemental interrogatories, indicated that the tire had been examined by plaintiff, his father Louis Brissette, Mr. Adrian Meyer and Bernell Ruebsam of Rip's Garage, and that they made an examination within two weeks after August 29, 1964.

Prior to the trial in October 1970, General Tire filed a motion to produce the tire. Plaintiff, however, was unable to comply with the motion.

The cause ultimately came to trial in the circuit court on March 15, 1971.

The following then occurred on the opening statement:

Mr. Kirby (plaintiff's counsel): The evidence will show that as far as the automobile was concerned, up until August 29, 1964, it had approximately nine hundred miles on it; that he had not run into any curbing with the automobile; that he had not hit any chug [sic] holes with the tires on the car or he hadn't struck any rocks or obstacles with it to where there might be bruising or damaging of the tires at all. . . .

At that point the attorney for General Tire objected to the plaintiff's attorney "making any mention or anything about any inspection of the tire" on the basis that the plaintiff was "unable to produce the tire for inspection by General Tire" and hence the plaintiff is "foreclosed from putting on any evidence regarding any inspection they may have had of the tire."

After a discussion out of the hearing of the jury, the court discharged the jury following which the attorney for General Tire elaborated on his earlier motion to preclude plaintiff's attorney from "mentioning in his opening statement that he will produce evidence of expert witnesses to show a defect existed in the tire. . . ." The plaintiff then made an offer of proof. His offer showed that if permitted to make an opening statement that the plaintiff, under the provisions of his insurance policy to cooperate, delivered the tire to the adjuster for the Covenant Security Insurance Company in November 1964, and that since that time he has not had the tire in his possession; that some three years later a letter was sent to Covenant attempting to locate the tire and any reports of inspection but that no answer was ever received. He stated also that the tire was not "destroyed for the purpose of destroying evidence" and that this information was given when his deposition was taken on April 19, 1968. He also stated that the plaintiff, his father, one Adrian Meyer and Bernell Ruebsam the owner of Rips Garage, saw the tire and that Mr. Ruebsam "has had experience in handling, selling, changing, repairing tires since 1938; that he is thoroughly familiar with the construction of tubeless tires; that he examined this tire and he is in a position to describe the condition of the beads of the tire; that it would be his opinion that the condition of the bead . . . would be a defect that cause [sic] the tire to come off of the rim. . . ." As far as the other witness, Adrian Meyer, is concerned, the offer of proof showed that he also had examined the tire while still at the garage. Mr. Meyer had worked one year in a service station and had repaired and changed over two thousand tires, of which one thousand had gone flat or had some type of defect of blowout—or something similar, and that he had examined the tire and that it was his opinion that the defect was due to a defect in manufacture. . . .

The attorneys for the defendants objected to the offer of proof and moved for a directed verdict.

The court then rejected the offer of proof ". . . first, because the object was not made available to the defendants, and, secondly, that a case could not be made even in the absence of this, by expert testimony. It follows that I will sustain the Motion for a Directed Verdict.". . .

The question next to be considered, is whether the object—the tire—not being available to the defendants for inspection precludes the plaintiff from having an opportunity to prove a case. On this issue there are no Missouri decisions. . . . .

While the tire on the Brissette automobile was not available for discovery or for evidentiary purposes, the testimony of several persons is available, subject to the right of cross-examination. If plaintiff's witnesses are permitted to testify concerning the examination of the tire, plaintiff may establish the defect and causation essential to his cause. . . .

The plaintiff has the burden of proving (1) a defect in the tire, (2) that the defect existed when the tire left the manufacturer's control and entered the stream of commerce and (3) that the defect was the proximate cause of the injuries suffered by the plaintiff. But such proof may be made by either direct or circumstantial evidence. The object is not, under the circumstances here, essential to such proof. It is sufficient if there is testimony, subject to cross-examination which may tend to show these essentials. The lack of the object—the tire—is a matter going to the weight of the evidence rather than to a complete failure of proof when there is sufficient testimony to indicate what defects existed.

It is true, as our Supreme Court has said, that "the destruction of written evidence without a satisfactory explanation gives rise to an inference unfavorable to the spoliator. . . . 'This court has several times given effect to the rule that where a party to a suit has been guilty of spoliation of documentary evidence, he is held thereby to admit the truth of the allegation of the opposite party. . . .'" Garrett v. Terminal R. Ass'n of St. Louis, Mo. Sup., 259 S.W. 2d 807, 812; Gaugh v. Gaugh, 321 Mo. 414, 11 S.W. 2d 729; Beckman v. Raines, 210 Mo. App. 253, 243 S.W. 192; Pomeroy v. Benton, 77 Mo. 64. However, to give rise to such an admission it must appear that the "circumstances of the act must manifest bad faith. Mere negligence is not enough." McCormick, Evidence, 538. "[I]t is at least necessary that the document be in the party's power to produce. . . ." 2 Wigmore on Evidence 185. Where the evidence is not in the plaintiff's possession it is not within the rule that evidence must be produced or considered against his interest. See *Arnold v. Brotherhood of Locomotive Firemen and Engineermen,* 231 Mo. App. 508, 101 S.W. 2d 729, 731.

The judgment is reversed and the cause remanded.

□   □   □

1. Is the defendant adequately protected in its defense of the case by having the right to cross-examine witnesses?
2. Given the pivotal role of the product in a product liability case, should the court impose a higher burden than lack of bad faith upon the possessor of the physical evidence? If so, how can that be done?

DORSEY v. YODER COMPANY

331 F. Supp. 753
United States District Court, E. D. Pennsylvania
September 9, 1971

MASTERSON, District Judge.

. . . . .

James T. Dorsey began operating metal slitting machines in 1945. Sometime in 1950, he came to work for General. Except for an absence of about 4 years between 1956 and 1960 due to an unrelated illness, he worked continuously for General up until the date of the accident, August 23, 1965.

At that time Dorsey was operating a slitter machine manufactured by Yoder and delivered to General in 1958. Yoder's representatives visited General's plant twice and recommended the machine they felt best suited to General's requirements. The particular model involved in the case was built by Yoder especially for General. It is clear that General relied heavily upon the expertise of Yoder's engineers in providing the proper machine for the job orders General had to perform. The machine cost $8375.00.

When the new metal slitter arrived at General, it was not functioning properly. To understand the nature of the problem, it is necessary to explain briefly how this machine works. As indicated by its name, the basic function of a metal slitter is to cut sheet metal into strips of varying widths according to customers' orders. The operator accomplishes this by feeding sheet metal from a roll which rests on an arbor through rotary cutters which slit the metal into desired widths. As the strips of metal exit from the cutters, they are wound up into take-up reels. To prevent the slitted metal from becoming entangled or wound around the cutter shaft, the operator inserts small pieces of wood called "stripper fingers" into the open spaces between the rotary blades after he positions the blades for the particular width desired. The uncoiler, which holds the metal sheets on an arbor, sits about 18 feet from the entrance to the cutters. Since there is no table between the uncoiler and these rotary blades, the machine has guides located about nine inches from the cutters in order to help feed the metal.

Soon after the machine arrived, employees who operated it complained to Mr. Tanseer, General's president and treasurer, that the metal tended to buckle up near the entrance to the cutter and would not stay within the guides. Mr. Tanseer complained to Yoder, and the manufacturer sent an engineer to examine the machine. The engineer's subsequent report contained a notation that the guides were inadequate, and Yoder recommended installation of a hold-down bar to prevent the metal from buckling up or rising over the entry guides. General agreed to purchase the bar and it was immediately installed on the Yoder machine.

Aside from the hold-down bar supplied by Yoder, two additional modifications were made by the plaintiff himself on the machine. First, he fashioned a pair of auxiliary guides, but these did not solve the problem of the metal riding out of the original guides. Secondly, when the original stripper fingers which were made from hard maple wood became worn out from continued use, plaintiff replaced them with duplicates fashioned from scraps of soft pine. Although the duplicates were made from cracked wood, nevertheless they served the purpose for which they were intended, i.e., stripping the metal away from the cutter shaft. Yoder's instructions authorized the making of duplicate stripper fingers but did not specify that they be made of hard maple. Plaintiff's expert testified that even if the duplicates were fashioned from maple, the stripper fingers still might have fractured and allowed plaintiff's hand to enter the cutter area. In any event, nothing in the Yoder instruction booklet indicated that the stripper fingers served a safety purpose.

When the accident occurred, plaintiff was not using the hold-down bar mentioned above because it scratched the metal, bounced around and sometimes struck his elbow. However, since the soft copper he was slitting was buckled because of annealing, it became necessary for plaintiff to put his right hand on the metal (applying downward pressure) in order to keep the metal from riding over the guides. Downward pressure with his hand was the only method of solving the problem since any other material would scratch the surface or collect dirt. Because of plaintiff's 20-year accident-free experience in bearing down on metal with his hand he considered it safe to do so on the day of the accident. On this particular occasion, his right hand was four inches from the edge of the roll and nine inches from the cutters.

As the sheet moved into the machine, a sliver of metal that extended outward from the roll caught the soft part of the palm of his hand and pulled it into the stripper fingers. The force of his hand striking the stripper fingers caused them to be sucked through the rollers and into the cutters along with plaintiff's right hand and arm causing severe injuries.

At the time of the accident, the machine had no guard whatsoever in front of the cutters. The point at which the rotary blades are located on this machine creates an "in-running nip point." That term is applied to the point of contact between a fixed piece of equipment and rotating part where the tendency is for the material to be sucked or pulled into the machinery. The Yoder machine had other in-running nip points which had guards as standard equipment to prevent injury to persons who might come in contact with these mechanisms.

After plaintiff's hand and arm entered the machine, he immediately turned it off with his left hand. But as plaintiff describes it, his arm was already a piece of "bloody meat." Miraculously, a surgeon sewed the arm back on, even though a mere slice of skin held the extremity in place. Needless to say, plaintiff has suffered greatly over the past five years with numerous operations and out patient treatments. In addition, he has difficulty performing trivial acts such as tying his shoes or shaving. He will not work again. . . . .

Pennsylvania law recognizes that a manufacturer may be liable under Section 402A for a design which creates an unreasonable risk of danger to the user (Citation). Since liability is imposed even though the product is manufactured exactly as intended, the bad design itself constitutes the defect. But the design is considered defective only if it (the design) makes the product unreasonably dangerous. Hence the focal issue in this case becomes whether or not the absence of a guard or other device on Yoder's metal slitter to prevent the operator from coming in contact with the rotary blades created an *unreasonable danger* to the operator.

Section 402A of the Restatement, 2d, Comment (i) states that a product is unreasonably dangerous if:

The article sold [is] *dangerous to an extent beyond which would be contemplated by the ordinary consumer* who purchases it, with the ordinary knowledge common to the community as to its characteristics (emphasis supplied).

Similarly comment (g) explains that a defective condition exists:

[W]here the product is, at the time it leaves the seller's hands in a condition *not contemplated by the ultimate consumer* which will be unreasonably dangerous to him (emphasis supplied).

Again, as to when warnings of the manufacturer are necessary, comment (j) states, in part:

But a seller is not required to warn with respect to products . . . when the danger or the *potentiality of danger, is generally known* (emphasis supplied).

Defendant summarizes the import of these comments as follows:

In short, as the Restatement intended, an *obvious danger,* known to the average person as such, is not an 'unreasonable danger' and hence there is no liability on the manufacturer if one encounters it. . . . .

To complete the syllogism, defendant then concludes that the Yoder machine was not unreasonably dangerous because the danger created by unguarded blades is patently obvious, especially as to an experienced operator such as the plaintiff. As persuasive as this argument seems, it contains one fatal flaw.

In essence, the defendant advocates the so-called "latent defect" rule, i.e., the injured party must have been unaware of the defect in order to recover. According to this view, the danger must be hidden and consequently not reasonably contemplated by the average user. . . . .

[S]kepticism of the latent defect rule places Pennsylvania in keeping with the modern trend which recognizes that manufacturers ought to make safer not more dangerous products.

For example, in *Palmer v. Massey-Ferguson, Inc.*, 3 Wash. App. 508, 476 P.2d 713 (1970) the Washington Supreme Court held that the trial court properly refused defendant's requested instruction that a manufacturer has no duty to provide guards to prevent injury from a patent peril or source manifestly dangerous:

The rule excusing the duty of safe design because of a patent peril has come under criticism in treatises. See Frumer & Friedman, Products Liability § 7.02 (1968). It seems to us that a rule which excludes the manufacturer from liability if the defect in the design of his product is patent but applies the duty if such a defect is latent is somewhat anomalous. The manufacturer of the obviously defective product ought not to escape because the product was obviously a bad one. The law, we think, ought to discourage misdesign rather than encouraging it in its obvious form. *Id.* at 718–719. . . . .

Therefore, we hold that even though the *danger of unguarded rotary blades* was obvious to plaintiff, this does not *ipso facto* preclude recovery.

It does not follow from this holding that the manufacturer of every obviously defective or dangerous product owes an automatic duty to an injured party. Although a knife qualifies as an obviously dangerous instrumentality, a manufacturer need not guard against the danger that it presents. "[Nor is it] necessary to tell a zookeeper to keep his head out of the hippopotamus' mouth" (Citations). The point is that to preclude absurd results the obviousness of the danger must constitute but *one* of the factors that determines whether the danger is unreasonable.

The proper test of "unreasonable danger" is whether a reasonable manufacturer would continue to market his product in the same condition as he sold it to the plaintiff *with* knowledge of the potential dangerous consequences the trial just revealed (Citations).

To answer this question one must:

[balance the] likelihood of harm to be expected from a machine with a given design and the gravity of harm if it happens against the burden of precaution which would be effective to avoid harm. 2 Harper and James, The Law of Torts § 28.4 (1956 ed), cited with approval in Pike v. F. G. Hough Co., supra.

And in measuring the likelihood of harm one may consider the obviousness of the defect since it is reasonable to assume that the user of an obviously defective product will exercise special care in its operation, and consequently the *likelihood* of harm diminishes.

In a persuasive article, Dean Wade has enumerated the specific factors that enter into the final balance as follows:

(1) the usefulness and desirability of the product, (2) the availability of other and safer products to meet the same need, (3) the likelihood of injury and its probable seriousness, (4) the obviousness of the danger, (5) common knowledge and normal public expectation of the danger (particularly for established products), (6) the avoidability of injury by care in use of the product (including the effect of instructions or warnings), and (7) the ability to eliminate the danger

without seriously impairing the usefulness of the product or making it unduly expensive (J. Wade, Strict Liability of Manufacturers, 19 Sw. L.J. 5 (1965) at 17.)

Taking the Harper and James formulation as expanded by Dean Wade, it becomes understandable why the plaintiff accidentally injured by a knife does not recover from the manufacturer. The product is not *unreasonably* dangerous and no duty arises because (1) everyone realizes the dangers; (2) by definition a guard over the blade (the part that causes danger) would eliminate its utility; (3) the cost of a "safe" knife might be prohibitive. Balancing the likelihood and gravity of harm against the burden of protection, a manufacturer should not be liable for a slip of the knife.

But consider the Yoder machine. Certainly Dorsey knew the danger of unguarded cutters. On the other hand, a guard would not eliminate the machine's usefulness, nor would the cost of $200 to $500 on an $8,000 machine be unreasonable. Moreover, the seriousness of the potential harm was great. Ultimately, all of these facts were questions to be weighed by the jury in making their ultimate determination as to whether, under all of the circumstances, the machine was "defective." The jury found the balance tipped in favor of plaintiff. Considering the evidence in this case, this court could not possibly rule otherwise.

Defendant advances the abnormal use of the machine as an additional reason for concluding as a matter of law that the metal slitter was not unreasonably dangerous to the plaintiff. According to the Restatement of Torts, 2d, a manufacturer assumes no responsibility for injuries that occur during an unforeseeable use or manner of use. Comment h to Section 402A explains:

A product is not in a defective condition when it is safe for normal handling and consumption.

And comment j to Section 395 explains the rationale behind this rule:

The liability stated in this Section is limited to persons who are endangered and the risks which are created in the course of uses of the chattel which the manufacturer should reasonably anticipate. In the absence of special reason to expect otherwise, the maker is entitled to assume that his product will be put to a normal use, for which the product is intended or appropriate; and he is not subject to liability when it is safe for all such uses, and harm results only because it is mishandled in a way which he has no reason to expect, or is used in some unusual and unforeseeable manner. . . . .

In this case, Yoder contends that it could not reasonably foresee use of the machine either without a guard or manually, because it reasonably expected both (1) that *General* would install a guard over the cutter and (2) that the machine would be operated *automatically* without the operator ever using his hands to hold down the metal. . . . .

[N]one of the evidence indicates that Yoder had any reason whatsoever to expect that General would install any guards. Mr. Tanseer, the president and treasurer of General, testified that he had no engineering background, knew nothing about the operation of the slitter and consequently relied exclusively upon Yoder to supply him with the proper machine. Moreover, Yoder never discussed safety features with General nor did its representative indicate to Mr. Tanseer that the machine required a safety device over the cutters. In sum, the jury's implicit conclusion that Yoder had no reason to expect General to install the guards meshes perfectly with the weight of the evidence.

Yoder also asserts that it could not reasonably foresee the possibility that plaintiff would place his hand on or over the metal just 9 inches from the cutters. Defendant points out that the slitter was designed to operate *automatically* and the instruction booklet so indicated. Manual feeding, so its argument goes, constituted an abnormal manner of operation. . . . .

Dorsey did not place his hand *into* the machine, rather he placed it over the metal 9 inches from the cutters. A jury could reasonably find that Yoder should have expected that an operator on occasion might have to use his hand in such a manner (Citation).

Yoder is a large manufacturer of metal slitters doing business throughout the country. As such, it is held to the standards of an expert.

Uncontroverted testimony of the plaintiff established that some rolls of sheet metal are defective and this cannot be ascertained until the slitting process begins; the Yoder machine did not feed properly when this occurred; an operator would nevertheless continue to cut the metal because the defect did not normally affect the salability of the final product; and, as a result, an operator has to use his hand to feed the metal properly into the blades. This evidence indicates that manual operation constituted a not unusual or abnormal means of operation and Yoder should have known about it.

Moreover, the jury could reasonably conclude that Yoder should have known about the inadequacy of the hold-down bar which it hoped would correct the problem. Plaintiff testified that it bounced up and down occasionally striking his elbow, and scratched the metal because it was unpolished. The jury could reasonably conclude from this evidence that Yoder should have realized the uselessness of the device. . . .

Another element of strict liability requires that:

[the product] is expected to and does reach the user or consumer without *substantial change* in the condition in which it was sold. Restatement of Torts, 2d § 402A (emphasis added).

Defendant asserts that it expected the machine to undergo substantial change because General was to install guards over the cutters. Whether or not the addition of a guard constitutes a "substantial change," this contention lacks merit since Yoder's expectation of the addition by General was unreasonable (Citation).

Yoder cites the substituted stripper fingers made of soft pine rather than hard maple as another "substantial change." Comment (p) to Section 402A explains that a substantial change involves situations where the product itself will undergo processing or substantial modification such that the product originally sold is not *itself* in a final or remotely usable state *viz.* the ultimate consumer. Thus, the comment presents the following example:

[T]he manufacturer of pigiron, which is capable of a wide variety of uses, is not so likely to be held to strict liability when it turns out to be unsuitable for the child's tricycle into which it is finally made by a remote buyer.

In this case, the mere use of soft pine rather than hard maple in making substitute stripper fingers did not constitute a substantial change. The new fingers served the same function as the old ones, i.e., to keep the cut metal from becoming tangled in the cutter shaft. The machine still operated in the same way and performed the same function. Moreover, the stripper fingers were not designed to operate as a guard. In short, the jury could reasonably conclude that the change was insubstantial. . . .

Defendant's other basis for judgment n.o.v. against the plaintiff asserts that "the knowledge of the plaintiff and General of the alleged defect and its obvious danger would make the negligent acts of General (in failing to install a guard), and plaintiff in operating the machine 'intervening superseding' causes relieving defendant from any liability." This contention has no merit.

First, as to General, the jury found that company free from any negligence; therefore no negligent act on their part exists to intervene. And as to Dorsey, even assuming he acted negligently, such an act or omission will relieve Yoder only if it:

... was so extraordinary as not to have been reasonably foreseeable, and ... whether the act was reasonably foreseeable [is] to be determined by following retrospectively the sequence of events and looking back from the harm to the negligent act rather than by considering whether the defendant should prospectively have envisaged the events which unfolded and caused the accident. Wilson v. American Chain and Cable Co., 364 F.2d 558, 562 (3rd Cir. 1966) (Citation).

There is nothing in the record that indicates to us that as a matter of law Dorsey's act of using an unguarded machine was so unforeseeable that it possibly constituted an "intervening superseding cause." Further, even if the test were a prospective one, there was abundant evidence for the jury to conclude that Yoder should have anticipated that occasional feeding problems might cause the operator to put his hand on the metal and that if the metal caught his hand, the stripper fingers would not act as an adequate guard. . . .

Although a duty arose between Dorsey and Yoder, nevertheless, under Pennsylvania law, the defendant is relieved of liability if plaintiff voluntarily assumed the risk (Citation). On that issue the jury was charged as follows:

Assumption of risk is walking into a dangerous situation with your eyes open, not inadvertently and testing a known danger.

For example, in my view—and this of course is not binding on you—but in this case, if Mr. Dorsey had consciously put his hand into the machine, you might find that he assumed the risk.

But if you believe the testimony here that he put his hand on the copper simply to feed it into the machine and then it was picked up by a splinter and taken into the machine, I do not believe that you could find him guilty of assumption of risk, because there is no evidence that he had consciously assumed the risk of injury (Citation).

Defendant excepts to this charge because:

The distinction is not one of putting a hand into a machine as described by the trial judge, but knowing the danger (or "defect") and voluntarily doing an act which exposed him to the danger, i.e., putting his hand in proximity to the danger . . . The mere fact that the judge charged the jury on assumption of the risk is unimportant in light of his further instruction that on the evidence in this case he did not believe the defense existed. This was prejudicial, fundamental error.

As to the law on assumption of the risk, defendant ignores one vital aspect. In addition to realizing the existence of the defect or danger and voluntarily doing an act which exposes himself to it; the plaintiff must *perceive and appreciate the risk* involved, i.e., the *probability* of harm. In other words, although Dorsey knew about the *existence* of a danger and although he voluntarily (i.e., without inadvertence) put his hand *on the metal;* under the circumstances, he may not have appreciated the *risk* of his actions.

Section 496D of the Restatement, 2d, states this often overlooked contour of assumption of the risk:

§ 496D. *Knowledge and Application of Risk.*
Except where he expressly so agrees, a plaintiff does not assume a risk of harm arising from the defendant's conduct unless he then knows of the existence of the risk and appreciates its unreasonable character.

Moreover, as Comment (c) explains, the question is not whether he *should have realized* the risk that putting his hand on the metal created, but *whether in fact,* plaintiff *did realize* the risk involved.

The standard to be applied is a subjective one, of what the particular plaintiff in fact sees, knows, understands and appreciates. In this it differs from the objective standard which is applied to contributory negligence. (See §§ 464, 289, 290.)......

[I]t is quite likely that, in light of twenty years' prior experience, Dorsey did *not in fact* appreciate the *risk* of his actions. It cannot be said as a matter of law that the jury could reach such a conclusion......

We have considered all other alleged errors cied by counsel for the defendant and find them either without merit or harmless.

□   □   □

1. Two of the issues raised by the defendant were the obviousness of the danger of the unguarded slitters and the plaintiff's assumption of the risk. (See Appendix B, Restatement (Second) of Torts, Section 402A, comment n.) Consider these two issues within the context of an unreasonably dangerous product. How should these two concepts operate within an industrial setting? How should they be treated for a consumer product?

2. What should a manufacturer be held responsible to foresee concerning the unintended use of a product? Must every conceivable accident be envisioned?

3. For what reasons is any guard, shield, or safety device provided on a product? More often than not, such devices protect the user from what would otherwise be an obvious danger. Is there any inconsistency then in providing protection against obvious dangers?

4. Under what circumstances could a manufacturer expect an owner to supply appropriate safety devices? If there are such circumstances, how could this duty be appropriately delegated?

BEXIGA v. HAVIR MANUFACTURING CORP.

60 N.J. 402
290 A.2d 281
Supreme Court of New Jersey
Decided April 24, 1972

PROCTOR, J.

This is a products liability case. Plaintiff John Bexiga, Jr., a minor, was operating a power punch press for his employer, Regina Corporation (Regina), when his right hand was crushed by the ram of the machine, resulting in the loss of fingers and deformity of his hand. His father, John Bexiga, Sr., brought this suit against Havir Manufacturing Corporation (Havir), the manufacturer of the machine, for damages in behalf of his son and individually *per quod.* The action was grounded in negligence, strict liability in tort and breach of warranty of fitness of purpose. The trial court dismissed the action at the close of the plaintiffs' case. The Appellate Division affirmed (Citation), and this Court granted plaintiffs' petition for certification (Citation).

The machine which caused the injuries was a 10-ton punch press manufactured by Havir in 1961 and sold that same year to J. L. Lucas & Sons, Inc., a dealer, and, at its direction, shipped to Regina. With the exception of a guard over the flywheel there were no safety devices of any kind on the machine when it was shipped. Plaintiffs do not contend that the accident resulted from defective materials, workmanship or inspection. Rather, their theory is that the punch press was so dangerous in design that the manufacturer was under a duty to equip it with some form of safety device to protect the user while the machine was being operated.

In June of 1966, plaintiff John Bexiga, Jr., 18 years of age and a junior in high school, had been employed by Regina at its Rahway plant for about two months, working nights after school. During his employment he operated punch presses and drilling machines for 40 hours per week.

On June 11, 1966, John, Jr., reported for work at 5:00 P.M. and was assigned to operate a drilling machine. He worked on this machine until the 9:30 break, after which the foreman directed him to work on the Havir punch press (which he had never before operated) and instructed him in its use. Thereafter he operated the machine unattended. He testified that the punch press was approximately six or seven feet high with a ram, die and foot pedal.

The particular operation John, Jr., was directed to do required him to place round metal discs, about three inches in diameter, one at a time by hand on top of the die. Once the disc was placed on the die it was held there by the machine itself. He would then depress the foot pedal activating the machine and causing the ram to descend about five inches and punch two holes in the disc. After this operation the ram would ascend and the equipment on the press would remove the metal disc and blow the trimmings away so that the die would be clear for the next cycle. It was estimated by John, Jr., that one cycle as described above would take approximately 10 seconds and that he had completed about 270 cycles during the 40 minutes he operated the machine. He described the accident as follows:

> Well, I put the round piece of metal on the die and the metal didn't go right to the place. I was taking my hand off the machine and I noticed that a piece of metal wasn't in place so I went right back to correct it, but at the same time, my foot had gone to the pedal, so I tried to take my hand off and jerk my foot off too and it was too late. My hand had gotten cut on the punch, the ram.

Plaintiff's expert, Andrew Gass, a mechanical engineer, testified that the punch press amounted to a "booby trap" because there were no safety devices in its basic design and none were installed prior to the accident. He added that the accident would probably never have occurred had the machine been properly designed for safety. The only literature accompanying the sale of the machine was a service manual which made no mention of safety devices in the operation of the machinery with the exception of a reference to the guard on the flywheel which was unrelated to the accident. He said there should have been more stress put on the factor of safety but that he did not know what recommendations should be made.

Gass described two "basic types" of protective safety devices both of which were known in the industry at the time of the manufacture and sale. One was a push-button device with the buttons so spaced as to require the operator to place both hands on them away from the die area to set the machine in motion. The other device was a guard rail or gate to prevent the operator's hands from entering the area between the ram and die when the machine was activated. These and other safety devices were available from companies specializing in safety equipment.

On cross-examination Gass conceded that, in accordance with the custom of the trade, presses like the one in question were not equipped with safety devices by the manufacturer. Rather, he said safety devices were to be installed by the ultimate purchaser. However, in his opinion the custom of the trade was improper in that the machine was defectively designed for safety and that purchasers "almost never" provided safety devices. Further, he said the large presses were generally equipped by the manufacturer with the push-button device. He said that smaller presses like the one in question were as dangerous to the user as the larger ones. He concluded that the press here involved should have been equipped with a two-hand push-button device as are the larger presses. On cross-examination he was not asked to explain why push-button devices were installed by the manufacturer on the large presses but not on the small ones.

While pointing out that guard rails or gates might have to be "modified" to suit the particular die or part used with the press, Gass stated that the push-button device would not have to be "modified" no matter what die was used. In other words, the push-button device would be appropriate for any of the machine's normal uses. On cross-examination he admitted that if the press were employed to punch holes in a 4-foot pipe a guard rail or gate would impede entry of the pipe into the die area and would have to be removed. He said that in such a case the guard rail or gate would not be needed because in holding the pipe the operator would be standing away from the machine. Further, when questioned as to the suitability of guard rails or gates, or other devices such as magnetic lifters or vacuum tubes to the varied uses of the machine, he stated that the particular operation of the press could dictate which of these devices would be appropriate.

The Appellate Division in affirming the trial court's dismissal held that plaintiffs failed to make out a *prima facie* case under strict liability, breach of warranty or negligence principles.... The court reasoned that since it was the custom of the trade that purchasers, rather than manufacturers, provide safety devices on punch presses like the one in question, Havir "had no reason to believe that the press would be put to use without some additions, i.e., the installation by Regina of protective devices suitable to whatever manufacturing process the press was to be devoted" (Citation). It also stated that N.J.S.A. 34:6–62, in effect at the time of the sale, required the factory owner to equip its power presses with proper guards (Citation). It held liability could not be imposed under the Restatement rule because the manufacturer did not expect the product to reach the user without substantial change. (Citation). . . . .

Taking as true all evidence supporting plaintiffs' position and according them the benefit of all inferences which can reasonably be drawn therefrom, as we are required to do on a motion for involuntary dismissal at the close of plaintiffs' case (Citation), we cannot agree with the Appellate Division's application of the law on either negligence or strict liability on the evidence presented. We have concluded that on either theory the proofs were sufficient to withstand a motion for dismissal.

There is no question but that the punch press here without any safety devices was dangerous to the user. From the evidence as to the guardrails or gates mentioned above we agree with the Appellate Division that it would be impracticable for the manufacturer to equip his presses with all of these protective devices, and therefore improper to place the responsibility for their installation upon the defendant. However, the expert testified that the alternative basic safety device, the push-button guard, would not have to be "modified" to suit the die used with the press and there was no evidence that that device would have to be changed for any of the varied uses of the machine. He was not cross-examined as to whether the push-button device would be inappropriate when the machine was employed to cut holes in a 4-foot pipe or when it was employed for any other operation. Even assuming the two-hand push-button device would be inappropriate if the machine were used to cut a length of pipe, there is nothing in the record which shows that the device could not be partially or completely inactivated on such an occasion.

On the basis of Gass' testimony the jury could infer that the two-hand device was appropriate for every normal operation of the machine and, thus, that it was not impracticable for Havir to equip its machine with such a device. Moreover, as noted above, the expert pointed out that larger punch presses are equipped by the manufacturer with push-button devices; that smaller presses, such as the one in question, were just as dangerous as the larger ones; and that they should be prepared for safety in the same manner. The jury could infer that the two-hand device was appropriate for all of the operations performed on the larger presses and, since the expert was not cross-examined as to why there should be a difference as to the safety devices provided on the two types of presses, it could also infer that the push-button device was equally appropriate for the normal uses of the smaller presses.

As we previously said on the issue of strict liability, the Appellate Division applied the rule set forth in the Restatement. To the extent that that rule absolves the manufacturer of liability where he may expect the purchaser to provide safety devices (Restatement, *supra,* § 402A(1)(b)), it should not be applied. Where a manufacturer places into the channels of trade a finished product which can be put to use and which should be provided with safety devices because without such it creates an unreasonable risk of harm, and where such safety devices can feasibly be installed by the manufacturer, the fact that he expects that someone else will install such devices should not immunize him. The public interest in assuring that safety devices are installed demands more from the manufacturer than to permit him to leave such a critical phase of his manufacturing process to the haphazard conduct of the ultimate purchaser. The only way to be certain that such devices will be installed on all machines—which clearly the public interest requires—is to place the duty on the manufacturer where it is feasible for him to do so.

We hold that where there is an unreasonable risk of harm to the user of a machine which has no protective safety device, as here, the jury may infer that the machine was defective in design unless it finds that the incorporation by the manufacturer of a safety device would render the machine unusable for its intended purposes. As we have said, the jury could infer from plaintiffs' evidence that it was feasible for Havir to install the push-button device. Therefore, it was error for the trial court to dismiss the strict liability claim at the close of plaintiffs' case.

Of course the question of whether one is negligent depends on whether he acted reasonably under the circumstances of a particular case. Thus, aside from the question of the practicability of Havir's installation of a safety device on the press here involved as to negligence, we must consider whether Havir could reasonably foresee that Regina would not install a safety device. On this issue the custom of the trade—that the manufacturer did not install safety devices but relied on the purchaser to do so—while ordinarily evidential, is not conclusive (Citation). Nor would it be conclusive that N.J.S.A. 34:6-62 imposed the duty on the purchaser. While Havir may have thought that Regina would have taken adequate precautions to protect its employees or that it would be required to do so by statute, we do not think in view of the circumstances here that Havir had a right as a matter of law to assume such devices would be provided (Citation). As to negligence, we hold that a jury question was presented, and that it was error for the trial court to dismiss the action at the close of plaintiffs' case.

If the jury should find for the defendant on the issue of the defective or negligent design of the machine, the next question for it should be whether the defendant was negligent in failing to attach to the machine a suitable warning to the operator of the danger of using it without a protective device. See *Schipper v. Levitt & Sons, Inc.,* 44 N.J. 70, 98–99, 207 A.2d 314 (1965).

Because of our disposition of the case it is necessary to consider defendant's contention that John, Jr. was contributorily negligent as a matter of law. Neither court below decided this issue. Contributory negligence may be a defense to a strict liability action as well as to a negligence action (Citations). However, in negligence cases the defense has been held to be unavailable where considerations of policy and justice dictate. See, e.g., *Soronen v. Olde Milford Inn, Inc.*, 46 N.J. 582, 218 A.2d 630 (1966). And . . . this Court said that undoubtedly the defense will be unavailable in special situations within the strict liability field (Citation). We think this case presents a situation where the interests of justice dictate that contributory negligence be unavailable as a defense to either the negligence or strict liability claims.

The asserted negligence of plaintiff—placing his hand under the ram while at the same time depressing the foot pedal—was the very eventuality the safety devices were designed to guard against. It would be anomalous to hold that defendant has a duty to install safety devices but a breach of that duty results in no liability for the very injury the duty was meant to protect against (Citations). We hold that under the facts presented to us in this case the defense of contributory negligence is unavailable.

The judgment of the Appellate Division is reversed and the cause is remanded for a new trial.

□   □   □

1. A press can be considered a multifunctional device. The court here believed that a two-hand control would provide safe operation for most normal press uses but expressed some concern over whether it would be suitable for other possible uses. This issue is perhaps related to whether the manufacturer, purchaser, or both have the duty to provide or install safety devices. What are the factors fundamental to resolution of this question and what policies could be recommended to make certain that appropriate devices are installed on every machine? What role should industry custom play in this process?

2. The court indicated that contributory negligence could not be available as a defense to either negligence or strict liability. Why? What policy issues underlie this conclusion? What concerns are being expressed by the court about the environment of the workplace and the role of the worker?

3. The court felt that at the very least the manufacturer should have warned the operator about the need for safety devices on the machine. Consider this as a viable alternative to actually having a safety device on the machine both from its effectiveness in reducing risk and as a manufacturer's defense.

4. Is it sufficient that the defendant meet the "state of the art" at the time this punch press was manufactured? Should manufacturers be held responsible for the new safety consciousness when their products were manufactured in the previous era? What role should retrofit play in this question?

5. See Appendix B, Restatement (Second) of Torts, Section 402A, comment n. Will the plaintiff's behavior in this case bar his recovery under the requirements of comment n?

TURNER v. INTERNATIONAL HARVESTER COMPANY

133 N.J. Super. 277
336 A.2d 62

Superior Court of New Jersey, Law Division
March 7, 1975

DREIER, J. D. C., Temporarily Assigned.

. . . . .

On or about December 2, 1969, plaintiff's decedent, Thomas W. Turner, acquired a 1967 IHC tractor-truck manufactured by defendant International Harvester Company. . . .

The truck was of the type where the engine is located beneath the cab; to work on the engine the cab must be raised and propped or counter-balanced. Two years and four days after taking delivery of the truck, that is, on or about December 6, 1971, plaintiff's decedent was working on the engine. While he was under the cab (which was in its raised position) the cab suddenly collapsed and fell upon him. He died from the ensuing injury. Plaintiff, his widow, sues on behalf of herself and their children for the death on the theories of (a) strict liability, (b) negligence and (c) breach of warranty.

The bill rendered by Hall & Fuhs, Inc. to plaintiff's decedent for the truck in question stated that the sale encompassed:

USED TRACTOR SOLD AS IS
One (1) used 1967 IHC model C04000D
Serial G226064

The price was $14,000 plus sales tax. . . .

Therefore, the real questions on this motion are the effect of the sale of used goods and of the words "as is" upon the three causes of action alleged by plaintiff.

I

We will first consider the third claim, that of breach of warranty, for it is the easiest to dispose of. The Uniform Commercial Code in N.J.S.A. 12A:2-316 covers the subject of exclusion or modification of warranties. One subsection reads as follows:

(2) Subject to subsection (3), to exclude or modify the implied warranty of merchantability or any part of it the language must mention merchantability and in case of a writing must be conspicuous, and to exclude or modify any implied warranty of fitness the exclusion must be by a writing and conspicuous. Language to exclude all implied warranties of fitness is sufficient if it states, for example, that "There are no warranties which extend beyond the description on the face hereof."

The next subsection, however, covers the situation now before the court and states:

(3) Notwithstanding subsection (2)

(a) unless the circumstances indicate otherwise, all implied warranties are excluded by expressions like "as is," "with all faults" or other language which in common understanding calls the buyer's attention to the exclusion of warranties and makes plain that there is no implied warranty; and . . .

Circumstances here did not indicate other than the normal statutory exclusion of warranties. The New Jersey Study Comment number 3, citing prior New Jersey case law, shows that this section merely restated the then existing law of the State as of the date the Code was enacted. It therefore appears that plaintiff's claim for breach of warranty must be dismissed, because the sale was for used goods explicitly noted "as is."

II

. . . The court will assume for the purpose of this motion either that a specified defect existed which caused the cab to fall, or sufficient circumstantial proofs could be shown to substantiate the existence of some defect. There is no question that such defect, if it existed, manifested itself over two years after the truck had been purchased by plaintiff's decedent. Whether this delay exceeded the time within which it was reasonable to expect the cab catch or counter-balance not to be defective is a jury question and will not be decided here. (Citation.). . . . There also is little question but that a dealer in used equipment is strictly liable for defective work repairs or replacement that such dealer has performed on the vehicle before the sale. *Realmuto v. Straub Motors*, 65 N.J. 336, 344–345, 322 A.2d 440 (1974). What is before this court, however, is the very question left open in *Realmuto*, where the Supreme Court stated:

. . . The strict liability in tort rule is of course, grounded in reasons of public policy. Restatement, Torts (2d) § 402A, comment c. *It may well be that these policy reasons are not fully applicable to the seller of a used chattel—for example, the buyer cannot be said to expect the same quality and durability in a used car as in a new one and so the used car dealer should not be held to the same strict liability as the seller of new automobiles. We need not reach that broad question here,* for we are of the view that a used car dealer ought to be subject to strict liability in tort with respect to a mishap resulting from any defective work, repairs or replacements he has done or made on the vehicle before the sale and we so hold. That in essence is the instant case, at least as it was set forth in the pleadings as a "defect" case [at 344–345, 322 A.2d at 444: emphasis supplied].

The germinal statement of the rule of strict liability in tort is found in the Restatement, Torts 2d, § 402A, although the New Jersey courts have expanded the rule beyond these limits. . . . . As the Supreme Court in *Realmuto* noted, quoting from 2 Frumer and Friedman, Products Liability, § 16A[4][b][iv], at 3-282 to 3-283, no case in New Jersey has yet applied the rules of strict liability in tort to the seller of a used product. Both the Supreme Court and the authors of the text note that the strict liability rules have been applied in *Cintrone v. Hertz Truck Leasing & Rental Service*, 45 N.J. 434, 451–453, 212 A.2d 769 (1965), where a defect in a leased motor vehicle was held to be a sufficient basis for applying the rule of strict liability in tort. In New Jersey it appears that the *Cintrone* case and the recent *Realmuto* case are the closest that our courts have come to applying this rule to a seller of a used chattel.

Nationally, the cases are collected in Annotation, "Products Liability—Used Products," 53 A.L.R. 3d 337 (1973).

... [C]ourts may consider as a liability-limiting factor the requirement that the used product be unreasonably dangerous, by applying the test of whether an ordinary purchaser of the particular product, considering its age and condition, would regard it as unreasonably dangerous when sold [Comment at 340].

In Pennsylvania, for example, plaintiff buyer purchased a ten-year-old car from a dealer. Within 15 minutes after leaving the dealer's place of business in the car, brake failure caused an accident in which plaintiff sustained injury. As plaintiff had not altered the condition of the car since taking delivery, a good cause of action was found under § 402A of the Restatement. *Lewis v. E. F. Moore, Inc.,* 87 Montg. Cty. L.R. 379 (Pa. 1967). A similar cause of action went to the jury in *Grady v. Kenny Ross Chevrolet Co.,* 332 F. Supp. 689 (D.C. Pa. 1971), applying Pennsylvania law where plaintiff's decedent had died of carbon monoxide poisoning allegedly resulting from a defective tail pipe assembly in a used car purchased from defendant dealer. But see *Cornelius v. Bay Motors, Inc.,* 258 Or. 564, 484 P.2d 299 (Sup. Ct. 1971), wherein the court expressly reserved ruling on whether strict liability under § 402A applied to sellers of used cars, while upholding a jury verdict for defendent dealer who had sold a seven-year-old car whose brakes failed on the day of purchase. The concurring opinion in that case suggests that a used-car dealer should not be regarded as making any implied representations since that is not the expectation or understanding of either the buyer or seller in such a transaction. See also, *Ikerd v. Lapworth,* 435 F.2d 197 (7 Cir. 1970), in which strict tort liability was held inapplicable to a new car dealer who sold a car to a used-car dealer, who thereafter sold it to the injured plaintiff, because the first dealer had sold the car along with several others, all "as is," and was found to have relied upon the second dealer to inspect and discover any defects before resale to third parties. In *dictum* the court noted:

> Plaintiffs cite numerous cases in which automobile manufacturers and dealers have been held liable for injuries resulting from the sale of an automobile in a defective condition to a consumer customer. They conclude from these cases that the seller of a used-car is negligent, or accountable under the doctrine of strict product liability if he sells the used car in a defective condition to one who he should know will use or resell it without first remedying the defect....[at 201].

This court must therefore come to grips with the underlying policy considerations and determine what should be the rule when applied to the case at bar. Three questions appear relevant: (1) In a sale of used goods, should the seller be held strictly liable in tort for defects, unknown at time of sale, that affect the safety (as opposed to economic value of the bargain) of ordinary buyers (and third persons)? Expressed in terms of the Restatement, are safety defects, by their very nature, unreasonably dangerous to ordinary consumers? (2) If so, should an "as is" disclaimer effectively insulate the seller of used goods from such liability to buyers (and third persons) by transferring the burden of all risks to the buyer? (3) If not, should such a disclaimer effectively insulate the seller of used goods from strict liability where the *particular* buyer was knowledgeable and in as good a position as the seller (or better), to guard against all risks of the product? That is, as to *this* buyer, was the product unreasonably dangerous?

We will first consider whether this is the type of case for the application of strict liability in tort. An economic analysis of enterprise liability, which includes direct as well as indirect costs, would charge those in the business of selling a defective product with responsibility for all harms, physical and economic, which result from its use (Citations). To a considerable extent—with respect to *new* goods—the manufacturer bases the cost of his product on his expenses, which include damages caused by the product and insurance to cover those damages. This cost is spread among all the customers for that product; it reflects the justifiable expectations of customers regarding safety, quality and durability of new goods. Sellers of used goods may similarly distribute their costs of doing business which, in turn, will reflect what is considered by the public to be justifiable expectations regarding safety, quality and durability of used goods.

As suggested by the court in *Realmuto* and the A.L.R. annotations, realistic expectations of quality and durability will be lower for used goods, commensurate with their age, appearance and price. However, safety of the general public demands that when a used motor vehicle, for example, is sold for use *as a serviceable motor vehicle* (and not as junk parts), absent special circumstances, the seller be responsible for safety defects whether known or unknown at time of sale, present while the machine was under his control. Otherwise, the buyer and the general public are bearing the enterprise liability stemming from introduction of the dangerously defective used vehicle onto the public highways. Public policy demands that the buyer receive a used chattel safe for the purpose intended (where no substantial change will occur prior to reaching the buyer or foreseeable consumer. See discussion in 2 Frumer & Friedman, Products Liability, *supra:*

> . . . It is conceded that a buyer of a used car, for example, cannot expect it to last as long as a new one. But it can be argued that he is entitled to expect that there is no latent defect in the brakes or other parts of the car [§ 19.03[5] at 5-129].

Justifiable expectations for safety run to ordinary parts expected to receive regular maintenance and replacement, e.g., brake shoes and linings, steering linkage, exhaust system, etc. On the other hand, surface dents, rust or metal fatigue resulting from mere old age would be defects the risk of which a buyer reasonably may be expected to absorb without undue threat to the public at large.

It is also significant in this case that the safety defect seemingly had nothing particular to do with the truck *qua* motor vehicle. Unlike virtually all of the cases dealing with the topic of dealer liability for used motor vehicles, this defect did not involve the ordinary use of the truck insofar as its operation on the highway was concerned. The "defect," if any, in the cab latch was collateral; it could just as well have been a defective latch on an overhead garage door or a piece of stationary machinery (Citation). It is clear, therefore, that this is an "ordinary" product liability problem, not affected by theories of motor vehicles as "dangerous instrumentalities," and special only in that it deals with reasonable expectations of buyers of used goods.

That there is room for further definition of the "unreasonably dangerous" standard of the Restatement rule, and of its application to used products in our society (which

increasingly sets a premium on recyclability of resources) is demonstrated by the
A.L.R. annotation comment quoted earlier (53 A.L.R. 3d at 340), as well as by further
discussions in recent New Jersey and out-of-state products liability opinions. . . . .

The Restatement rule within the "unreasonably dangerous" qualification has been
criticized as creating a trial situation "too imprecise for judicial application." (Citation.). . . . The Restatement, comment (g), states that such is a condition "not contemplated by the ultimate consumer, which will be *unreasonably dangerous* to him."
It is only where there is an unreasonable danger of personal injury in the defective
product that recovery can be founded on the rule of strict liability in tort, and this
should be especially so when dealing with used goods. Only by this word "unreasonable" is the court or jury permitted an inquiry into the nature of the product, its age
and condition, and thus able to set a standard against which the defect can be
measured.

Should a simple "as is" disclaimer effectively insulate the dealer from a claim of
strict liability in tort following an accident resulting from a *safety* defect present in the
vehicle when it was in the control of the dealer? When selling to the ordinary
consumer, the answer must be No. Bargaining power and ability to protect one's
interests are generally disproportionate as between the buyer of used goods and one
in the business of selling them. While freedom to contract need not be impaired if a
buyer wishes to contract away his right to protection, an unequivocal waiver of safety
defects must be shown (see the discussion with respect to waiver of tort claims under
section III of this opinion, *infra*). Otherwise, when the additional indirect costs will be
borne by the public through insurance costs, a decent regard for the public safety
requires the thumb of the State to be on the buyer's side of the scale (Citation).

The third question also raises a jury issue. It may be found that the buyer in this
case was (or represented himself to be) knowledgeable about this product because of
his background or experience. This will not necessarily result from the transaction
being denominated "commercial" (Citation). Also, the effect upon plaintiff and her
family, and upon injured persons in general, is no less because the injury occurred in
a nonconsumer atmosphere. In fact, the pleadings and affidavits submitted here
suggest that plaintiff's decedent may have been personally familiar with the particular truck he bought. The goods should be viewed, not in the abstract, but as they
affect a particular seller, purchaser or user, and the circumstances of the sale.

Use of the "unreasonably dangerous" standard, whether viewed from the general
statement of the rule or the definition of a dangerous condition, permits a court to
look both at the sophistication of the injured purchaser and the reasonable expectations of the seller to determine whether the strict liability rule should be applied.

Looking at the used automobile situation, one can readily envision an antique car
buff or "hot rod" enthusiast purchasing a car which is defective in many respects and
where the relationship between the buyer and seller is such that both reasonably
expect that all aspects of the automobile will be separately appraised and all defects
corrected by the purchaser. . . .

Even with respect to the sale of a truck, the actual situation of the parties to the
contract may present a question. A used truck purchased by a large trucking company known by both buyer and seller to have extensive repair facilities might be
expected to undergo great scrutiny only by the buyer, while a similar truck purchased

by a merchant to make his retail deliveries might not reasonably be expected to be so examined unless special circumstances exist. Thus, in some circumstances the relationship of the parties and apparent sophistication of the purchaser might indicate that the defect did not present an unreasonable danger to the particular purchaser as user of the product. In others the purchaser's conduct in not discovering or correcting a defect which a reasonable person of his background and experience should have corrected might warrant a finding that the defect was not unreasonably dangerous. . . . Thus, in these unusual cases the "unreasonably dangerous" qualification has a very practical use in stating the rule for strict liability in tort. With this "unreasonably dangerous" element intact, the Restatement rule is as applicable to the sale of a used product as to the sale of a new product. The failure of the Supreme Court to use the "unreasonably dangerous" standard in its statements of the rule of strict liability in tort (Citation), should not be taken as a negation of its usefulness in the appropriate case.

On the record before this court, defendant dealer has not shown that special circumstances of this sale constituted either an express or implied waiver of *this* buyer's reasonable expectations, regarding the absence of *safety* defects. Thus, summary judgment must be denied on the strict liability claim.

III

With respect to the claim for negligence, the court in *Realmuto v. Straub Motors, supra,* set forth the standards to be applied:

There is no doubt of the applicability of the negligence theory; a used car dealer has the *duty of reasonable inspection, testing and warning of any defects,* as well as that of reasonable care with respect to any repairs or replacements he may make to the vehicle [65 N.J. at 344, n. 3, 322 A.2d at 444; emphasis supplied].

An annotation, 6 A.L.R. 3d 12, § 10 at 43–47, deals with this matter also, commenting that:

. . . [a] seller of a used or second-hand product—especially, but not exclusively, a motor vehicle—has often been held to have a duty to test or inspect it, and to be liable for injuries resulting from the omission of proper tests or inspections.

A current model, low-mileage automobile purchased by a consumer from a dealer in such automobiles is subject to nearly all of the expectations on the part of the public as is a new motor vehicle purchased under similar circumstances. As the vehicle's age increases, however, such expectations will tend to decrease. So, too, with other products. This is true especially where the sale of motor vehicles is concerned, considering the tremendous volume of sales evidenced by even the most casual perusal of the used car sections of a newspaper. . . . To preclude recovery merely because of the used nature of a product would, therefore, be to defeat the interests of the public. A dealer in used trucks is subject to similar expectations. Of course, there are additional elements that must be proven in the negligence claim that need not be proven under the strict liability in tort cause of action described above, but a cause of action has been stated in the complaint.

The "as is" notation, however, adds an additional element to the negligence aspects of this case. . . . In section I of this opinion the warranty disclaimer has been held to have its statutory effect. In section II, it was noted that an unequivocal waiver was necessary to defeat a claim of strict liability in tort. But, does a disclaimer of statutory warranties also act as a waiver of both tort claims in strict liability and negligence? Without any language of waiver, and without any evidence before this court that the "as is" language was meant to serve as an intentional relinquishment of a known right, such effect will not be implied. . . .

This determination, however, does not fully answer the question of the effect of the "as is" statement, for it will have a very real evidentiary effect at the trial. What conditions did the "as is" designation disclaim? A jury must eventually determine what was reasonable with respect to any proven danger present in a product sold "as is." Did the parties understand that the "as is" designation applied only to body damage, gas mileage, worn tires or other such problems that could be discerned by a reasonable inspection or test drive? Was it limited to performance rather than safety defects? Was the designation intended to cover all defects? (Citations).

Defendant Hall & Fuhs, Inc. alleges that the cause of the accident was a design defect, and thus is the responsibility of the manufacturer. Whether this is so and whether a reasonable inspection, testing or warning of the defect had or had not been accomplished is not now before the court, but as a matter of law, from the affidavits and supporting documents, this court cannot say that the defendant dealer is free from negligence.

Plaintiff's attorney should present an order denying summary judgment on the issues of strict liability in tort and negligence, and granting summary judgment on the issue of breach of warranty, pursuant to R. 4:42-1.

□   □   □

1. With the assumption that the cab latch contained a flaw that precipitated its failure after four years, can the unreasonable-danger question be argued without reference to the capabilities of the buyer of the used truck? If so, how can the court's discussion of unreasonable danger be measured relative to user sophistication be rationalized?

2. The court attaches significance to the fact that the latch problem was unrelated to the use of the truck on the road; that is, it was an " 'ordinary' product liability problem." Does this distinction have any bearing on the principal issue of whether a used vehicle dealer should be held strictly liable for defects?

3. Consider the various types of latch flaws or conditions that could have led to its failure after four years. For each of the hypothesized flaws, who should bear the burden: manufacturer, used vehicle dealer, and/or plaintiff?

4. Under what conditions should a dealer in used products be strictly liable for defects? Under what conditions or by what means could such a dealer disclaim all liability for defects? Of what significance would the buyer's characteristics be in addressing the question?

SEELY v. WHITE MOTOR COMPANY

45 Cal. Rptr. 17
403 P.2d 145
Supreme Court of California, In Banc
June 23, 1965
Rehearing Denied July 21, 1965

TRAYNOR, Chief Justice.

In October 1959 plaintiff entered into a conditional sales contract with Southern Truck Sales for the purchase of a truck manufactured by defendant, White Motor Company. Plaintiff purchased the truck for use in his business of heavy-duty hauling. Upon taking possession of the truck, plaintiff found that it bounced violently, an action known as "galloping." For eleven months after the purchase, Southern, with guidance from White's representatives made many unsuccessful attempts to correct the galloping. On July 22, 1960, when slowing down for a turn, plaintiff found that the brakes did not work. The truck overturned, and plaintiff, who was not personally injured, had the damage repaired for $5,466.09. In September 1960, after paying $11,659.44 of the purchase price of $22,041.76, plaintiff served notice that he would make no more payments. Southern thereafter repossessed the truck and resold it for $13,000.

Plaintiff brought this action against Southern and White seeking (1) damages, related to the accident, for the repair of the truck, and (2) damages, unrelated to the accident, for the money he had paid on the purchase price and for the profits lost in his business because he was unable to make normal use of the truck. During the trial plaintiff dismissed the action against Southern without prejudice. The court found that White breached its warranty to plaintiff and entered judgment for plaintiff for $20,899.84, consisting of $11,659.44 for payments on the purchase price and $9,240.40 for lost profits. It found that plaintiff had not proved that the galloping caused the accident and therefore denied his claim for $5,466.09 for the repair of the truck. Both plaintiff and White appeal from the judgment.

Defendant contends that the trial court erred in awarding damages for lost profits and for the money paid on the purchase price of the truck. We do not agree with this contention. The award was proper on the basis of a breach of express warranty.

Defendant included the following promise in the printed form of the purchase order signed by plaintiff: "The White Motor Company hereby warrants each new motor vehicle sold by it to be free from defects in material and workmanship under normal use and service, its obligation under the warranty being limited to making good at its factory any parts or parts thereof...." This promise meets the statutory requirement for an express warranty: "Any affirmation of fact or any promise by the seller relating to the goods is an express warranty if the natural tendency of such affirmation or promise is to induce the buyer to purchase the goods, and if the buyer purchases the goods relying thereon" (Citations). The natural tendency of White's promise was to induce buyers to rely on it, and plaintiff did so rely in purchasing the goods. The reliance on the warranty, and the warranty itself, are manifested by plaintiff's continued efforts to have the truck repaired, and by defendant's acceptance of the responsibility to correct the galloping. The statute requires only that plaintiff rely on the warranty. It does not additionally require that he be aware that it was made by the manufacturer instead of the dealer to reach the one who in fact made it. Surely if plaintiff sought to have a part replaced that was covered by the warranty, White could not escape its obligation by showing that plaintiff thought the warranty White made was made by the dealer.

Defendant contends that its limitation of its obligation to repair and replacement, and its statement that its warranty "is expressly in lieu of all other warranties, expressed or implied," are sufficient to operate as a disclaimer of responsibility in damages for breach of warranty. This contention is untenable. When, as here, the warrantor repeatedly fails to correct the defect as promised, it is liable for the breach of that promise as a breach of warranty (Citations). Since there was an express warranty to plaintiff in the purchase order, no privity of contract was required (Citation). Plaintiff also gave reasonable notice of the defect (Citations).

The damages awarded by the trial court, "the loss directly and naturally resulting in the ordinary course of events from the breach of warranty" (Citations), can properly include lost profits (Citations) as well as the amount paid on the purchase price. . . .

Defendant also contends that the damages awarded are excessive since the rental value of the truck was not offset against plaintiff's claim for lost profits. Plaintiff replies that, in estimating that 60 percent of the lost gross earnings was lost profits, the trial court deducted a reasonable rental value for the truck. We cannot say that the trial court failed to take rental value into account when it evaluated the estimates of profit percentage that ranged from 25 percent to 77 percent. Since defendant failed to request a finding on the issue of an appropriate rental value, it cannot complain that a specific finding was not made.

It is contended that the foregoing legislative scheme of recovery has been superseded by the doctrine of strict liability in tort set forth in *Greenman v. Yuba Power Products, Inc.* (Citations). We cannot agree with this contention. The law of sales has been carefully articulated to govern the economic relations between suppliers and consumers of goods. The history of the doctrine of strict liability in tort indicates that it was designed, not to undermine the warranty provisions of the sales act or of the Uniform Commercial Code but, rather, to govern the distinct problem of physical injuries.

An important early step in the development of the law of products liability was the recognition of a manufacturer's liability in negligence to an ultimate consumer without privity of contract. (*MacPherson v. Buick Motor Co.* (1916) 217 N.Y. 382, 389, 111 N.E. 1050.) About the same time, the courts began to hold manufacturers liable without negligence for personal injuries. Over a score of theories were developed to support liability (Citation), and the one that was generally accepted was borrowed from the law of sales warranty (Citation). "Only by some violent pounding and twisting," however, could the warranty doctrine be made to serve this purpose (Citations). Final recognition that "[t]he remedies of injured consumers ought not to be made to depend upon the intricacies of the law of sales" (Citations) caused this court to abandon the fiction of warranty in favor of strict liability in tort (Citations).

The fact that the warranty theory was not suited to the field of liability for personal injuries, however, does not mean that it has no function at all. In *Greenman* we recognized only that "rules defining and governing warranties that were developed to meet the needs of commercial transactions cannot properly be invoked to govern the manufacturer's liability to those injured by its defective products unless those rules also serve the purposes for which such liability is imposed" (Citation). Although the rules governing warranties complicated resolution of the problems of personal injuries, there is no reason to conclude that they do not meet the "needs of commercial transactions." The law of warranty "grew as a branch of the law of commercial transactions and was primarily aimed at controlling the commercial aspects of these transactions" (Citations).

Although the rules of warranty frustrate rational compensation for physical injury, they function well in a commercial setting (Citations). These rules determine the quality of the product the manufacturer promises and thereby determine the quality he must deliver. In this case, the truck plaintiff purchased did not function properly in his business. Plaintiff therefore seeks to recover his commercial losses; lost profits and the refund of the money he paid on the truck. White is responsible for these losses only because it warranted the truck to be "free from defects in material and workmanship under normal use and service." The practical construction of this language by both parties during the eleven months that repairs were attempted establishes that plaintiffs use of the truck was a normal use within the meaning of the warranty. White's failure to comply with its obligation to make "good at its factory any part or parts" of the truck after ample opportunity was given it to do so entitles plaintiff to recover damages resulting from such breach. Had defendant not warranted the truck, but sold it "as is," it should not be liable for the failure of the truck to serve plaintiff's business needs.

Under the doctrine of strict liability in tort, however, the manufacturer would be liable even though it did not agree that the truck would perform as plaintiff wished or expected it to do. In this case, after plaintiff returned the truck, Southern resold it to Mr. Jack Barefield, an experienced trucker. Mr. Barefield used the truck "to pull a 40-foot band" over state highways. After driving the truck 82,000 miles, he testified that he had no unusual difficulty with it. Southern replaced two tires, added a new fifth wheel, and made minor alterations to the truck before reselling it to Mr. Barefield, so that it is possible that it found a cure for the galloping. Southern, however, replaced the tires five times, adjusted the fifth wheel, and made many other changes on the truck during the eleven months plaintiff drove it. Thus, it is more likely that the truck functioned normally when put to use in Mr. Barefield's business because his use made demands upon it different from those made by plaintiff's use. If under these circumstances defendant is strictly liable in tort for the commercial loss suffered by plaintiff, then it would be liable for business losses of other truckers caused by the failure of its trucks to meet the specific needs of their businesses, even though those needs were communicated only to the dealer. Moreover, this liability could not be disclaimed, for one purpose of strict liability in tort is to prevent a manufacturer from defining the scope of his responsibility for harm caused by his products (Citation). The manufacturer would be liable for damages of unknown and unlimited scope. Application of the rules of warranty prevents this result. Defendant is liable only because of its agreement as defined by its continuing practice over eleven months. Without an agreement, defined by practice or otherwise, defendant should not be liable for these commercial losses.

In *Santor v. A & M Karagheusian, Inc.,* 44 N.J. 52, 207 A.2d 305, the plaintiff purchased from a retailer carpeting that soon began to develop unusual lines. The court held the manufacturer liable for the difference between the price paid for the carpet and its actual market value on the basis of strict liability in tort. We are of the opinion, however, that it was inappropriate to impose liability on that basis in the Santor case, for it would result in imposing liability without regard to what representations of quality the manufacturer made. It was only because the defendant in that case marketed the rug as Grade #1 that the court was justified in holding that the rug was defective. Had the manufacturer not so described the rug, but sold it "as is," or sold it disclaiming any guarantee of quality, there would have been no basis for recovery in that case. Only if someone had been injured because the rug was unsafe for use would there have been any basis for imposing strict liability in tort.

The distinction that the law has drawn between the tort recovery for physical injuries and warranty recovery for economic loss is not arbitrary and does not rest on the "luck" of one plaintiff in having an accident causing physical injury. The distinction rests, rather, on an understanding of the nature of the responsibility a manufacturer must undertake in distributing his products. He can appropriately be held liable for physical injuries caused by defects by requiring his goods to match a standard of safety defined in terms of conditions that create unreasonable risks of harm. He cannot be held for the level of performance of his products in the consumer's business unless he agrees that the product was designed to meet the consumer's demands. A consumer should not be charged at the will of the manufacturer with bearing the risk of physical injury when he buys a product on the market. He can, however, be fairly charged with the risk that the product will not match his economic expectations unless the manufacturer agrees that it will. Even in actions for negligence, a manufacturer's liability is limited to damages for physical injuries and there is no recovery for economic loss alone (Citations). The Restatement of Torts similarly limits strict liability to physical harm to person or property (Citation).

The law of warranty is not limited to parties in a somewhat equal bargaining position. Such a limitation is not supported by the language and history of the sales act and is unworkable. Moreover, it finds no support in *Greenman.* The rationale of that case does not rest on the analysis of the financial strength or bargaining power of the parties to the particular action. It rests, rather, on the proposition that "[t]he cost of an injury and the loss of time or health may be an overwhelming misfortune to the person injured, and a needless one, for the risk of injury can be insured by the manufacturer and distributed among the public as a cost of doing business" (Citation). That rationale in no way justifies requiring the consuming public to pay more for their products so that a manufacturer can insure against the possibility that some of his products will not meet the business needs of some of his customers. Finally, there was no inequality in bargaining position insofar as the damages plaintiff recovered in this case are concerned. Unlike the defendant in *Henningsen v. Bloomfield Motors, Inc.,* 32 N.J. 358, 161 A.2d 69, 75 A.L.R. 2d 1, White is not seeking to enforce an industry-wide disclaimer of liability for personal injuries. Here, plaintiff, whose business is trucking, could have shopped around until he found the truck that would fulfill his business needs. He could be fairly charged with the risk that the product would not match his economic expectations, unless the manufacturer agreed that it would. Indeed, the Uniform Commercial Code expressly recognizes this distinction by providing that limitation of damages is prima facie unconscionable in personal injury cases, but not in cases of commercial loss (Citation).

Plaintiff contends that, even though the law of warranty governs the economic relations between the parties, the doctrine of strict liability in tort should be extended to govern physical injury to plaintiff's property, as well as personal injury. We agree with this contention. Physical injury to property is so akin to personal injury that there is no reason for distinguishing them (Citations). In this case, however, the trial court found that there was no proof that the defect caused the physical damage of the truck. The finding of no causation, although ambiguous, was sufficient absent a request by plaintiff for a specific finding (Citation). Since the testimony on causation was in conflict, the trial court's resolution of the conflict is controlling.

The judgment is affirmed, each side to bear its own costs on these appeals. . . .

PETERS, Justice (concurring and dissenting).

I concur in the affirmance of the judgment, but on grounds different from the majority. The majority permit recovery on the theory that there was a breach of an express warranty. Then the majority say, unnecessarily and gratuitously, that plaintiff cannot recover on the theory of strict liability. Both the holding and the dicta are, in my opinion, incorrect.

There was no breach of express warranty. It is fundamental that no one is liable for the breach of an express warranty unless the buyer *relies* upon that warranty (Citation) or unless the warranty constitutes "part of the basis of the bargain" (Citation). Here, the undisputed facts show that plaintiff did *not* rely on White being responsible under the warranty, and it is clear that White's responsibility was not "part of the basis of the bargain." The uncontradicted evidence demonstrates that plaintiff had no idea that White was a party to the warranty and that he relied solely on Southern's responsibility. The majority say that the statute requires only that plaintiff rely on "the warranty," and not that he be aware of who made it. But one does not rely upon a mere scrap of paper which calls itself a warranty. He relies on the fact that a certain responsible party (which he may know as "the manufacturer" rather than by name) will "stand behind" the product and perform in accordance with the terms of the warranty. Here plaintiff admits that he relied on Southern's responsibility under the warranty, but not on White's.

The majority, having found in favor of the plaintiff on the theory of an express warranty, completely decided the case. There was no need to discuss the strict liability doctrine. Everything said by the majority on that subject is obviously dicta. The problem of what damages may be recovered in an action based on strict liability is a most important question of first impression in this state. It is too important to be decided in a mere "advisory opinion." But because the majority have elected to discuss it, and have done so, I submit, erroneously, I cannot allow the erroneous dicta to go unchallenged.

Given the rationale of *Greenman v. Yuba Power Products, Inc.,* 59 Cal. 2d 57, 63, 27 Cal. Rptr. 697, 377 P.2d 897, it cannot properly be held that plaintiff may not recover the value of his truck and his lost profits on the basis of strict liability. The nature of the damage sustained by the plaintiff is immaterial, so long as it proximately flowed from the defect. What *is* important is not the nature of the damage but the relative roles played by the parties to the purchase contract and the nature of their transaction.

[I]n *Santor v. A & M Karagheusian, Inc.,* . . . the plaintiff bought carpeting from a local retailer. When the carpeting became useless because of certain defects, plaintiff sued the manufacturer. In allowing plaintiff to recover the difference between the price he paid and the actual market value of the carpeting, the court expressly disapproved the concept that the strict liability doctrine should be restricted to personal injury claims. "[A]lthough the doctrine has been applied principally in connection with personal injuries sustained by expected users from products which are dangerous when defective, . . . the responsibility of the maker should be no different where damage to the article sold or to other property of the consumer is involved" (Citation). It should be noted that there, as here, the court was faced with a statutory scheme covering implied warranties. Unlike the majority here, however, the New Jersey court expressly refused to draw an arbitrary distinction between different types of damages in order to give effect to those statutes in a greater number of situations.

Of course, the application of the strict liability theory to property damage (including "economic loss") will limit the applicability of several sections of the recently enacted Commercial Code dealing with implied warranties (Citations). But this result, even if unfortunate, follows from the rationale of *Greenman,* which limited the effect of a statute requiring the purchaser to give defendant notice of a breach of warranty within a reasonable time (Citation). In the present case, it is not necessary to "extend" *Greenman* in order to reach the proper result. All that is required is that we apply its reasoning to a factual situation which cannot be distinguished analytically from that case.

In *Greenman* we allowed recovery for "personal injury" damages. It is well established that such an award may include compensation for past loss of time and earnings due to the injury (Citation), for loss of future earning capacity (Citation), and for increased living expenses caused by the injury (Citation). There is no logical distinction between these losses and the losses suffered by plaintiff here. All involve economic loss, and all proximately arise out of the purchase of a defective product. I find it hard to understand how one might, for example, award a traveling salesman lost earnings if a defect in his car causes his *leg* to break in an accident but deny that salesman his lost earnings if the defect instead disables only his *car* before any accident occurs. The losses are exactly the same; the chains of causation are slightly different, but both are "proximate." Yet the majority would allow recovery under strict liability in the first situation but not in the second. This, I submit, is arbitrary.

The "history" of products liability law does not compel a dichotomy between "economic loss" and other types of damage. Although the various products liability doctrines developed in the field of personal injury claims, the overwhelming majority of courts *today* make no distinction between personal injury damages and property damages (including "economic loss") in products liability cases. If no such distinction was made under the products liability doctrines in use *before Greenman,* then such a distinction *under Greenman's* strict-liability doctrine may be reasonably (though not necessarily) made only on the basis that protection of life and limb is of greater social value than protection against financial loss. But, as money damages do not replace the life or limb lost, this basis is sound only to the extent that allowing recovery for personal injuries on a strict liability theory operates as a *deterrent* (vis-à-vis the theories formerly used) which induces manufacturers to be *more* careful in their production methods. But it is highly doubtful that *Greenman's* imposition of strict liability does furnish such a deterrent, in view of the fact that, at the time *Greenman* was rendered, the doctrine of res ipsa loquitur and the weakening of the "privity" requirement in implied warranty actions would have often subjected the manufacturer to liability, or at least to litigation, in any event, whenever a defect in his product caused an injury. (Citations.). . . . The purpose of the strict liability rule as expressed in *Greenman* is not to deter, but "to insure that the costs of injuries resulting from defective products are borne by the manufacturers that put such products on the market rather than by the injured persons who are powerless to protect themselves" (Citation). The initial breakthroughs in products liability law may well have operated as deterrents when measured against the former status of the law, which gave the consumer little protection against the manufacturer's carelessness. At that time, a distinction between personal injuries and other types of damage might have been justified. But given the equal treatment of all types of damage under the law as it existed just before *Greenman,* it makes no sense to adopt a new doctrine (strict liability in tort) for reasons *other* than deterrence and then hold that this doctrine is limited by a distinction which can be justified only if the doctrine were a deterrent. The New Jersey Supreme Court responded to this historical argument in *Santor,* "True, the rule of implied warranty had its gestative stirrings because of the greater appeal of the personal injury claim. But, once in existence, the field of operation of the remedy should not be fenced in by such a factor" (Citation).

The majority suggest that the manufacturer should bear (and spread) the risk of personal injury damages because "the cost of an injury and the loss of time or health may be an overwhelming misfortune to the person injured. . . ." This is no reason to distinguish between personal injury damages and other types of damage. Such "overwhelming misfortune" may not be present in a given personal injury case, but the majority do not indicate that they would deny recovery in a personal injury case if this element were lacking. Conversely, an economic loss might be an "overwhelming misfortune" in a given case, but I doubt that any court would allow recovery in such a case and deny it in other economic loss cases. "Overwhelming misfortunes" *might* occur more often in personal injury cases than in property damage or economic loss cases (although the majority cite no evidence to this effect), but this is no reason to draw the line between these types of injury when a more sensible line is available. Suppose, for example, defective house paint is sold to two home owners. One suffers temporary illness from noxious fumes, while the other's house is destroyed by rot because the paint proved ineffective (a loss generally uninsured). Although the latter buyer may clearly suffer the greater misfortune, the majority would not let him recover under the strict liability doctrine because *his* loss is solely "economic," while letting the first buyer recover the minimal costs and lost earnings caused by his illness.

The majority unduly fear that, if the strict liability rule is applied to economic loss, "the manufacturer would be liable for damages of unknown and unlimited scope." This would not be so if the notion of "defective" in the strict liability doctrine is viewed as coextensive with the concept of "unmerchantable" in the implied warranty field. This term has been well defined by case law and has been deemed to be certain enough for use in our recently enacted Commercial Code (Citation). Equating "defective" with "unmerchantable" comports with the purpose of *Greenman*, which was not to expand the notion of when the manufacturer has breached his initially implied duty to the purchaser, but only to eliminate the sales law's restrictions on *recovery* for that breach of duty (the privity and notice requirements and the operation of disclaimers) where the buyer is an ordinary consumer.

The majority also point to Mr. Barefield's alleged success with the truck and state that "If under these circumstances defendant is strictly liable in tort for the commercial loss suffered by plaintiff, then it would be liable for business losses of other truckers caused by the failure of its trucks to meet the specific needs of their businesses, even though those needs were communicated only to the dealer." Here the majority seem to equate strict liability and the implied warranty of fitness for a particular purpose (Citation). No authority is cited for this proposition, and I have found none. So far as I know, no proponent of the concept of manufacturers' strict liability has ever seriously argued that the manufacturer should be liable for the product's inability to serve specific needs which the buyer communicates only to the retailer, except insofar as those needs conform to what the product is ordinarily expected (by the manufacturer and the consuming public) to do. Mr. Barefield's testimony went only to show that the truck *could do* "the jobs for which it was built" (Citations), i.e., that it was merchantable. Apparently, he did not convince the trial court. I fail to see how this testimony tends to support the majority's "horrible consequences" argument, for there is no indication that the trial court relied on plaintiff's or Barefield's *communications* of their needs to the dealer in finding the truck to be "defective."

The majority recognize that the rules governing warranties were developed to meet the needs of "commercial transactions." If this is so, then why not look to the *transaction* between the buyer and the seller and see if it was a "commercial" transaction rather than a sale to an ordinary consumer at the end of the marketing chain? How can the nature of the damages which occur *later*, long after the transaction has been completed, control the characterization of the transaction? Any line which determines whether damages should be covered by warranty law or the strict liability doctrine should be drawn at the time the sale is made.

In *Greenman*, we relied to some degree upon *Henningsen v. Bloomfield Motors, Inc.* (1960) 32 N.J. 358, 161 A.2d 69, 75 A.L.R. 2d 1. *Henningsen* held a manufacturer liable by holding privity to be unnecessary in an implied warranty action and held that the manufacturer's disclaimer of all warranties was contrary to public policy and therefore void. This was based upon a realistic appraisal of the "freedom of contract" commonly vested in the consumer in today's economy. where gross inequality of bargaining power is pervasive. "The traditional contract is the result of free bargaining of parties who are brought together by the play of the market, and who meet each other on a footing of approximate economic equality. In such a society there is no danger that freedom of contract will be a threat to the social order as a whole. But in present-day commercial life the standardized mass contract has appeared. It is used primarily by enterprises with strong bargaining power and position. 'The weaker party, in need of the goods or services, is frequently not in a position to shop around for better terms, either because the author of the standard contract has a monopoly (natural or artificial) or because all competitors use the same clauses. His contractual intention is but a subjection more or less voluntary to terms dictated by the stronger party, terms whose consequences are often understood in a vague way, if at all' " (Citation).

I am not concerned over the fact that if damages on the strict liability theory are allowed here, this may limit the application of some of the restrictive statutory provisions relating to warranty. In my opinion those restrictive provisions should not apply to the ordinary consumer, who is usually unable to protect himself from insidious contractual provisions such as disclaimers, foisted upon him by commercial enterprises whose bargaining power he is seldom able to match, and who "is seldom 'steeped in the business practice which justifies' " the notice requirement (Citation), and who should not be barred by the privity requirement (Citation). The purpose of the strict liability rule adopted in Greenman was to protect people who are "powerless to protect themselves" (Citation). This does not mean, however, that the implied warranty sections of the code should not apply within the world of commerce, where parties generally bargain on a somewhat equal plane and may be presumed to be familiar with the legal problems involved when defective goods are purchased.

Although this is a close case, I would find that plaintiff was an ordinary consumer insofar as the purchase involved here was concerned, even though he bought the truck for use in his business. Plaintiff was an owner-driver of a single truck he used for hauling and not a fleet-owner who bought trucks regularly in the course of his business. He was the final link in the marketing chain, having no more bargaining power than does the usual individual who purchases a motor vehicle on the retail level.

I recognize that this "ordinary consumer" test needs judicial definition. This should be done on a case-by-case basis as is customarily done with any new doctrine. It is, however, the best resolution of the dilemma facing this court. I assume that the majority do not wish to overrule Greenman. On the other hand, neither the majority nor I wish to extend Greenman so as to completely deny any effect to the disclaimer and notice provisions of the Commercial Code. Thus, a line must be drawn somewhere. The line drawn by the majority is arbitrary and artificial, there being no sound basis for distinguishing between the types of damage assigned to opposite sides of the majority's line. The line I suggest would seem to fit squarely within the reasons for the strict liability rule.

The majority object to applying the strict liability doctrine to economic loss because they feel that the manufacturer should be able to sell its product "as is." But this objection overlooks the fact that the strict liability rule would allow the manufacturer to do this in certain cases. The strict liability rule, for example, permits the defense of assumption of risk. "Here, as elsewhere, the plaintiff will not be heard to complain of a risk which he has encountered voluntarily, or brought upon himself with full knowledge and appreciation of the danger" (Citation).

To sum up, all the strict liability rule does to implied warranty law is abolish the notice requirement, restrict the effectiveness of disclaimers to situations where it can be reasonably said that the consumer has freely assumed the risk, and abolish privity requirement, where ordinary consumers are involved. It does not introduce a notion of "defective" which is different from that of "unmerchantable" in implied warranty law. These changes properly adapt traditional sales law to the marketing position of today's ordinary consumer. Under the majority dicta, which would deny plaintiff the price of his truck as well as his lost profits on a strict liability theory, the housewife who buys a new refrigerator with such a serious defect as to make it useless cannot recover for the loss of her purchase price from the manufacturer (unless there is an express warranty), because of the privity doctrine (Citation). Should the privity doctrine be abolished, the manufacturer's disclaimer of implied warranties would bar her, even if she could not buy a new refrigerator without a similar disclaimer. Further, if there were no disclaimer, her failure to give the manufacturer reasonable notice of the defect would bar her effort to recover. These results cannot be reconciled with the holding and rationale of *Greenman*.

Thus, although I would affirm, I would do so on the basis of the strict liability doctrine. . . .

□   □   □

1. The majority opinion argues that strict liability is not a suitable theory if the plaintiff suffers only economic loss, that warranty is the only suitable theory. The dissent argues a contrary view. On what bases would you support either of these positions?

2. The dissent equates the "unreasonably dangerous defect" of strict liability with the "unmerchantable" concept of warranty to reach the result. Are these equivalent concepts? In what situations would recovery be denied under the concept of strict liability?

3. Assume, in this case, plaintiff established that the brakes malfunctioned owing to a production or design flaw, caused the damage to his truck, and caused him very minor injuries. Would you agree with the majority's view that this should be treated as a breach of warranty, since the only significant loss claimed was economic? Presumably at some point, as plaintiff's injuries increased, the majority would permit strict liability to operate. How would this be established? What considerations would govern?

Selected Statutes and Legal Principles from the Restatement of Torts (2d)

RESTATEMENT OF TORTS (2d)

§ 291. Unreasonableness; How Determined; Magnitude of Risk and Utility of Conduct

Where an act is one which a reasonable man would recognize as involving a risk of harm to another, the risk is unreasonable and the act is negligent if the risk is of such magnitude as to outweigh what the law regards as the utility of the act or of the particular manner in which it is done.

§ 292. Factors Considered in Determining Utility of Actor's Conduct

In determining what the law regards as the utility of the actor's conduct for the purpose of determining whether the actor is negligent, the following factors are important:

(a) the social value which the law attaches to the interest which is to be advanced or protected by the conduct;
(b) the extent of the chance that this interest will be advanced or protected by the particular course of conduct;
(c) the extent of the chance that such interest can be adequately advanced or protected by another and less dangerous course of conduct.

§ 293. Factors Considered in Determining Magnitude of Risk

In determining the magnitude of the risk for the purpose of determining whether the actor is negligent, the following factors are important:

(a) the social value which the law attaches to the interests which are imperiled;
(b) the extent of the chance that the actor's conduct will cause an invasion of any interest of the other or of one of a class of which the other is a member;
(c) the extent of the harm likely to be caused to the interests imperiled;
(d) the number of persons whose interests are likely to be invaded if the risk takes effect in harm.

§ 402A. Special Liability of Seller of Product for Physical Harm to User or Consumer

(1) Who sells any product in a defective condition unreasonably dangerous to the user or consumer or to his property is subject to liability for physical harm thereby caused to the ultimate user or consumer, or to his property, if
    (a) the seller is engaged in the business of selling such a product, and
    (b) it is expected to and does reach the user or consumer without substantial change in the condition in which it is sold.
(2) The rule stated in Subsection (1) applies although
    (a) the seller has exercised all possible care in the preparation and sale of his product, and
    (b) the user or consumer has not bought the product from or entered into any contractual relation with the seller.

Caveat*:

The Institute expresses no opinion as to whether the rules stated in this Section may not apply

(1) to harm to persons other than users or consumers;
(2) to the seller of a product expected to be processed or otherwise substantially changed before it reaches the user or consumer; or
(3) to the seller of a component part of a product to be assembled.

Comment:

a. This Section states a special rule applicable to sellers of products. The rule is one of strict liability, making the seller subject to liability to the user or consumer even

---

*Authors' Note: Since publication of the Restatement, the courts have extended protection under Section 402A to include bystanders. Lessors and component part manufacturers have been held as defendants.

though he has exercised all possible care in the preparation and sale of the product. The Section is inserted in the Chapter dealing with the negligence liability of suppliers of chattels, for convenience of reference and comparison with other Sections dealing with negligence. The rule stated here is not exclusive, and does not preclude liability based upon the alternative ground of negligence of the seller, where such negligence can be proved.

b. *History.* Since the early days of the common law those engaged in the business of selling food intended for human consumption have been held to a high degree of responsibility for their products. As long ago as 1266 there were enacted special criminal statutes imposing penalties upon victualers, vintners, brewers, butchers, cooks, and other persons who supplied "corrupt" food and drink. In the earlier part of this century this ancient attitude was reflected in a series of decisions in which the courts of a number of states sought to find some method of holding the seller of food liable to the ultimate consumer even though there was no showing of negligence on the part of the seller. These decisions represented a departure from, and an exception to, the general rule that a supplier of chattels was not liable to third persons in the absence of negligence or privity of contract. In the beginning, these decisions displayed considerable ingenuity in evolving more or less fictitious theories of liability to fit the case. The various devices included an agency of the intermediate dealer or another to purchase for the consumer, or to sell for the seller; a theoretical assignment of the seller's warranty to the intermediate dealer; a third party beneficiary contract; and an implied representation that the food was fit for consumption because it was placed on the market, as well as numerous others. In later years the courts have become more or less agreed upon the theory of a "warranty" from the seller to the consumer, either "running with the goods" by analogy to a covenant running with the land, or made directly to the consumer. Other decisions have indicated that the basis is merely one of strict liability in tort, which is not dependent upon either contract or negligence.

Recent decisions, since 1950, have extended this special rule of strict liability beyond the seller of food for human consumption. The first extension was into the closely analogous cases of other products intended for intimate bodily use, where, for example, as in the case of cosmetics, the application to the body of the consumer is external rather than internal. Beginning in 1958 with a Michigan case involving cinder building blocks, a number of recent decisions have discarded any limitation to intimate association with the body, and have extended the rule of strict liability to cover the sale of any product which, if it should prove to be defective, may be expected to cause physical harm to the consumer or his property.

c. On whatever theory, the justification for the strict liability has been said to be that the seller, by marketing his product for use and consumption, has undertaken and assumed a special responsibility toward any member of the consuming public who may be injured by it; that the public has the right to and does expect, in the case of products which it needs and for which it is forced to rely upon the seller, that reputable sellers will stand behind their goods; that public policy demands that the burden of accidental injuries caused by products intended for consumption be placed upon those who market them, and be treated as a cost of production against which liability insurance can be obtained; and that the consumer of such products is entitled to the maximum of protection at the hands of someone, and the proper persons to afford it are those who market the products.

d. The rule stated in this Section is not limited to the sale of food for human consumption, or other products for intimate bodily use, although it will obviously include them. It extends to any product sold in the condition, or substantially the same condition, in which it is expected to reach the ultimate user or consumer. Thus the rule stated applies to an automobile, a tire, an airplane, a grinding wheel, a water heater, a gas stove, a power tool, a riveting machine, a chair, and an insecticide. It applies also to products which, if they are defective, may be expected to and do cause only "physical harm" in the form of damage to the user's land or chattels, as in the case of animal food or a herbicide.

e. Normally the rule stated in this Section will be applied to articles which already have undergone some processing before sale, since there is today little in the way of consumer products which will reach the consumer without such processing. The rule is not, however, so limited, and the supplier of poisonous mushrooms which are neither cooked, canned, packaged, nor otherwise treated is subject to the liability here stated.

f. *Business of selling.* The rule stated in this Section applies to any person engaged in the business of selling products for use or consumption. It therefore applies to any manufacturer of such a product, to any wholesale or retail dealer or distributor, and to the operator of a restaurant. It is not necessary that the seller be engaged solely in the business of selling such products. Thus the rule applies to the owner of a motion picture theatre who sells popcorn or ice cream, either for consumption on the premises or in packages to be taken home.

The rule does not, however, apply to the occasional seller of food or other such products who is not engaged in that activity as a part of his business. Thus it does not apply to the housewife who, on one occasion, sells to her neighbor a jar of jam or a pound of sugar. Nor does it apply to the owner of an automobile who, on one occasion, sells it to his neighbor, or even sells it to a dealer in used cars, and this even though he is fully aware that the dealer plans to resell it. The basis for the rule is the ancient one of the special responsibility for the safety of the public undertaken by one who enters into the business of supplying human beings with products which may endanger the safety of their persons and property, and the forced reliance upon that undertaking on the part of those who purchase such goods. This basis is lacking in the case of the ordinary individual who makes the isolated sale, and he is not liable to a third person, or even to his buyer, in the absence of his negligence. An analogy may be found in the provision of the Uniform Sales Act, § 15, which limits the implied warranty of merchantable quality to sellers who deal in such goods; and in the similar limitation of the Uniform Commercial Code, § 2-314, to a seller who is a merchant. This Section is also not intended to apply to sales of the stock of merchants out of the usual course of business, such as execution sales, bankruptcy sales, bulk sales, and the like.

g. *Defective condition.* The rule stated in this Section applies only where the product is, at the time it leaves the seller's hands, in a condition not contemplated by the ultimate consumer, which will be unreasonably dangerous to him. The seller is not liable when he delivers the product in a safe condition, and subsequent mishandling or other causes make it harmful by the time it is consumed. The burden of proof that the product was in a defective condition at the time that it left the hands of the particular seller is upon the injured plaintiff; and unless evidence can be produced which will support the conclusion that it was then defective, the burden is not sustained.

Safe condition at the time of delivery by the seller will, however, include proper packaging, necessary sterilization, and other precautions required to permit the product to remain safe for a normal length of time when handled in a normal manner.

h. A product is not in a defective condition when it is safe for normal handling and consumption. If the injury results from abnormal handling, as where a bottled beverage is knocked against a radiator to remove the cap, or from abnormal preparation for use, as where too much salt is added to food, or from abnormal consumption, as where a child eats too much candy and is made ill, the seller is not liable. Where, however, he has reason to anticipate that danger may result from a particular use, as where a drug is sold which is safe only in limited doses, he may be required to give adequate warning of the danger (see Comment j), and a product sold without such warning is in a defective condition.

The defective condition may arise not only from harmful ingredients, not characteristic of the product itself either as to presence or quantity, but also from foreign objects contained in the product, from decay or deterioration before sale, or from the way in which the product is prepared or packed. No reason is apparent for distinguishing between the product itself and the container in which it is supplied; and the two are purchased by the user or consumer as an integrated whole. Where the container is itself dangerous, the product is sold in a defective condition. Thus a carbonated beverage in a bottle which is so weak, or cracked, or jagged at the edges, or bottled under such excessive pressure that it may explode or otherwise cause harm to the person who handles it, is in a defective and dangerous condition. The container cannot logically be separated from the contents when the two are sold as a unit, and the liability stated in this Section arises not only when the consumer drinks the beverage and is poisoned by it, but also when he is injured by the bottle while he is handling it preparatory to consumption.

i. *Unreasonably dangerous.* The rule stated in this Section applies only where the defective condition of the product makes it unreasonably dangerous to the user or consumer. Many products cannot possibly be made entirely safe for all consumption, and any food or drug necessarily involves some risk of harm, if only from over-consumption. Ordinary sugar is a deadly poison to diabetics, and castor oil found use under Mussolini as an instrument of torture. That is not what is meant by "unreasonably dangerous" in this Section. The article sold must be dangerous to an extent beyond that which would be contemplated by the ordinary consumer who purchases it, with the ordinary knowledge common to the community as to its characteristics. Good whiskey is not unreasonably dangerous merely because it will make some people drunk, and is especially dangerous to alcoholics; but bad whiskey, containing a dangerous amount of fusel oil, is unreasonably dangerous. Good tobacco is not unreasonably dangerous merely because the effects of smoking may be harmful; but tobacco containing something like marijuana may be unreasonably dangerous.

Good butter is not unreasonably dangerous merely because, if such be the case, it deposits cholesterol in the arteries and leads to heart attacks; but bad butter, contaminated with poisonous fish oil, is unreasonably dangerous.

j. *Directions or warning.* In order to prevent the product from being unreasonably dangerous, the seller may be required to give directions or warning, on the container, as to its use. The seller may reasonably assume that those with common allergies, as for example to eggs or strawberries, will be aware of them, and he is not required to warn against them. Where, however, the product contains an ingredient to which a substantial number of the population are allergic, and the ingredient is one whose danger is not generally known, or if known is one which the consumer would reasonably not expect to find in the product, the seller is required to give warning against it, if he has knowledge, or by the application of reasonable, developed human skill and foresight should have knowledge, of the presence of the ingredient and the danger. Likewise in the case of poisonous drugs, or those unduly dangerous for other reasons, warning as to use may be required.

But a seller is not required to warn with respect to products, or ingredients in them, which are only dangerous, or potentially so, when consumed in excessive quantity, or over a long period of time, when the danger, or potentiality of danger, is generally known and recognized. Again the dangers of alcoholic beverages are an example, as are also those of foods containing such substances as saturated fats, which may over a period of time have a deleterious effect upon the human heart.

Where warning is given, the seller may reasonably assume that it will be read and heeded; and a product bearing such a warning, which is safe for use if it is followed, is not in defective condition, nor is it unreasonably dangerous.

k. *Unavoidably unsafe products.* There are some products which, in the present state of human knowledge, are quite incapable of being made safe for their intended and ordinary use. These are especially common in the field of drugs. An outstanding example is the vaccine for the Pasteur treatment of rabies, which not uncommonly leads to very serious and damaging consequences when it is injected. Since the disease itself invariably leads to a dreadful death, both the marketing and the use of the vaccine are fully justified, notwithstanding the unavoidable high degree of risk which they involve. Such a product, properly prepared, and accompanied by proper directions and warning, is not defective, nor is it *unreasonably* dangerous. The same is true of many other drugs, vaccines, and the like, many of which for this very reason cannot legally be sold except to physicians, or under the prescription of a physician. It is also true in particular of many new or experimental drugs as to which, because of lack of time and opportunity for sufficient medical experience, there can be no assurance of safety, or perhaps even of purity of ingredients, but such experience as there is justifies the marketing and use of the drug notwithstanding a medically recognizable risk. The seller of such products, again with the qualification that they are properly prepared and marketed, and proper warning is given, where the situation calls for it, is not to be held to strict liability for unfortunate consequences attending their use, merely because he has undertaken to supply the public with an apparently useful and desirable product, attended with a known but apparently reasonable risk.

l. *User or consumer.* In order for the rule stated in this Section to apply, it is not necessary that the ultimate user or consumer have acquired the product directly from the seller, although the rule applies equally if he does so. He may have acquired it through one or more intermediate dealers. It is not even necessary that the consumer have purchased the product at all. He may be a member of the family of the final purchaser, or his employee, or a guest at his table, or a mere donee from the purchaser. The liability stated is one in tort, and does not require any contractual relation, or privity of contract, between the plaintiff and the defendant.

"Consumers" include not only those who in fact consume the product, but also those who prepare it for consumption; and the housewife who contracts tularemia while cooking rabbits for her husband is included within the rule stated in this Section, as is also the husband who is opening a bottle of beer for his wife to drink. Consumption includes all ultimate uses for which the product is intended, and the customer in a beauty shop to whose hair a permanent wave solution is applied by the shop is a consumer. "User" includes those who are passively enjoying the benefit of the product, as in the case of passengers in automobiles or airplanes, as well as those who are utilizing it for the purpose of doing work upon it, as in the case of an employee of the ultimate buyer who is making repairs upon the automobile which he has purchased.

Illustration:

1. A manufactures and packs a can of beans, which he sells to B, a wholesaler. B sells the beans to C, a jobber, who resells it to D, a retail grocer. E buys the can of beans from D, and gives it to F. F serves the beans at lunch to G, his guest. While eating the beans, G breaks a tooth, on a pebble of the size, shape, and color of a bean, which no reasonable inspection could possibly have discovered. There is satisfactory evidence that the pebble was in the can of beans when it was opened. Although there is no negligence on the part of A, B, C, or D, each of them is subject to liability to G. On the other hand E and F, who have not sold the beans, are not liable to G in the absence of some negligence on their part.

m. *"Warranty."* The liability stated in this Section does not rest upon negligence. It is strict liability, similar in its nature to that covered by Chapters 20 and 21. The basis of liability is purely one of tort.

A number of courts, seeking a theoretical basis for the liability, have resorted to a "warranty," either running with the goods sold, by analogy to covenants running with the land, or made directly to the consumer without contract. In some instances this theory has proved to be an unfortunate one. Although warranty was in its origin a matter of tort liability, and it is generally agreed that a tort action will still lie for its breach, it has become so identified in practice with a contract of sale between the plaintiff and the defendant that the warranty theory has become something of an obstacle to the recognition of the strict liability where there is no such contract. There is nothing in this Section which would prevent any court from treating the rule stated as a matter of "warranty" to the user or consumer. But if this is done, it should be recognized and understood that the "warranty" is a very different kind of warranty from those usually found in the sale of goods, and that it is not subject to the various contract rules which have grown up to surround such sales.

The rule stated in this Section does not require any reliance on the part of the consumer upon the reputation, skill, or judgment of the seller who is to be held liable, nor any representation or undertaking on the part of that seller. The seller is strictly liable although, as is frequently the case, the consumer does not even know who he is at the time of consumption. The rule stated in this Section is not governed by the provisions of the Uniform Sales Act, or those of the Uniform Commercial Code, as to warranties; and it is not affected by limitations on the scope and content of warranties, or by limitation to "buyer" and "seller" in those statutes. Nor is the consumer required to give notice to the seller of his injury within a reasonable time after it occurs, as is provided by the Uniform Act. The consumer's cause of action does not depend upon the validity of his contract with the person from whom he acquires the product, and it is not affected by any disclaimer or other agreement, whether it be between the seller and his immediate buyer, or attached to and accompanying the product into the consumer's hands. In short, "warranty" must be given a new and different meaning if it is used in connection with this Section. It is much simpler to regard the liability here stated as merely one of strict liability in tort.

n. *Contributory negligence.* Since the liability with which this Section deals is not based upon negligence of the seller, but is strict liability, the rule applied to strict liability cases (see § 524) applies. Contributory negligence of the plaintiff is not a defense when such negligence consists merely in a failure to discover the defect in the product, or to guard against the possibility of its existence. On the other hand the form of contributory negligence which consists in voluntarily and unreasonably proceeding to encounter a known danger, and commonly passes under the name of assumption of risk, is a defense under this Section as in other cases of strict liability. If the user or consumer discovers the defect and is aware of the danger, and nevertheless proceeds unreasonably to make use of the product and is injured by it, he is barred from recovery.

Comment on Caveat:

o. *Injuries to non-users and non-consumers.* Thus far the courts, in applying the rule stated in this Section, have not gone beyond allowing recovery to users and consumers, as those terms are defined in Comment l. Casual bystanders, and others who may come in contact with the product, as in the case of employees of the retailer, or a passer-by injured by an exploding bottle, or a pedestrian hit by an automobile, have been denied recovery. There may be no essential reason why such plaintiffs should not be brought within the scope of the protection afforded, other than that they do not have the same reasons for expecting such protection as the consumer who buys a marketed product; but the social pressure which has been largely responsible for the development of the rule stated has been a consumers' pressure, and there is not the same demand for the protection of casual strangers. The Institute expresses neither approval nor disapproval of expansion of the rule to permit recovery by such persons.

p. *Further processing or substantial change.* Thus far the decisions applying the rule stated have not gone beyond products which are sold in the condition, or in substantially the same condition, in which they are expected to reach the hands of the ultimate user or consumer. In the absence of decisions providing a clue to the rules which are likely to develop, the Institute has refrained from taking any position as to the possible liability of the seller where the product is expected to, and does, undergo further processing or other substantial change after it leaves his hands and before it reaches those of the ultimate user or consumer.

It seems reasonably clear that the mere fact that the product is to undergo processing, or other substantial change, will not in all cases relieve the seller of liability under the rule stated in this Section. If, for example, raw coffee beans are sold to a buyer who roasts and packs them for sale to the ultimate consumer, it cannot be supposed that the seller will be relieved of all liability when the raw beans are contaminated with arsenic, or some other poison. Likewise the seller of an automobile with a defective steering gear which breaks and injures the driver, can scarcely expect to be relieved of the responsibility by reason of the fact that the car is sold to a dealer who is expected to "service" it, adjust the brakes, mount and inflate the tires, and the like, before it is ready for use. On the other hand, the manufacturer of pigiron, which is capable of a wide variety of uses; is not so likely to be held to strict liability when it turns out to be unsuitable for the child's tricycle into which it is finally made by a remote buyer. The question is essentially one of whether the responsibility for discovery and prevention of the dangerous defect is shifted to the intermediate party who is to make the changes. No doubt there will be some situations, and some defects, as to which the responsibility will be shifted, and others in which it will not. The existing decisions as yet throw no light upon the questions, and the Institute therefore expresses neither approval nor disapproval of the seller's strict liability in such a case.

q. *Component parts.* The same problem arises in cases of the sale of a component part of a product to be assembled by another, as for example a tire to be placed on a new automobile, a brake cylinder for the same purpose, or an instrument for the panel of an airplane. Again the question arises, whether the responsibility is not shifted to the assembler. It is no doubt to be expected that where there is no change in the component part itself, but it is merely incorporated into something larger, the strict liability will be found to carry through to the ultimate user or consumer. But in the absence of a sufficient number of decisions on the matter to justify a conclusion, the Institute expresses no opinion on the matter.

§ 402B. Misrepresentation by Seller of Chattels to Consumer

One engaged in the business of selling chattels who, by advertising, labels, or otherwise, makes to the public a misrepresentation of a material fact concerning the character or quality of a chattel sold by him is subject to liability for physical harm to a consumer of the chattel caused by justifiable reliance upon the misrepresentation, even though

(a) it is not made fraudulently or negligently, and

(b) the consumer has not bought the chattel from or entered into any contractual relation with the seller.

Caveat:

The Institute expresses no opinion as to whether the rule stated in this Section may apply

(1) where the representation is not made to the public, but to an individual, or
(2) where physical harm is caused to one who is not a consumer of the chattel.

Comment:

a. The rule stated in this Section is one of strict liability for physical harm to the consumer, resulting from a misrepresentation of the character or quality of the chattel sold, even though the misrepresentation is an innocent one, and not made fraudulently or negligently. Although the Section deals with misrepresentation, it is inserted here in order to complete the physical harm caused by the chattel. A parallel rule, as to strict liability for pecuniary loss resulting from such a misrepresentation, is stated in § 552D.

b. The rule stated in this Section differs from the rule of strict liability stated in § 402A, which is a special rule applicable only to sellers of products for consumption and does not depend upon misrepresentation. The rule here stated applies to one engaged in the business of selling any type of chattel, and is limited to misrepresentations of their character or quality.

c. *History.* The early rule was that a seller of chattels incurred no liability for physical harm resulting from the use of the chattel to anyone other than his immediate buyer, unless there was privity of contract between them. (See § 395, Comment a.) Beginning with Langridge v. Levy, 2 M. & W. 519, 150 Eng. Rep. 863 (1837), an exception was developed in cases where the seller made fraudulent misrepresentations to the immediate buyer, concerning the character or quality of the chattel sold, and because of the fact misrepresented harm resulted to a third person who was using the chattel. The remedy lay in an action for deceit, and the rule which resulted is now stated in § 557A.

Shortly after 1930, a number of the American courts began, more or less independently, to work out a further extension of liability for physical harm to the consumer of the chattel, in cases where the seller made misrepresentations to the public concerning its character or quality, and the consumer, as a member of the public, purchased the chattel in reliance upon the misrepresentation and suffered physical harm because of the fact misrepresented. In such cases the seller was held to strict liability for the misrepresentation, even though it was not made fraudulently or negligently. The leading case is Baxter v. Ford Motor Co., 168 Wash. 456, 12 P.2d 409, 88 A.L.R. 521 (1932), adhered to on rehearing, 168 Wash. 465, 15 P.2d 1118, 88 A.L.R. 527, second appeal, 179 Wash. 123, 35 P.2d 1090 (1934), in which the manufacturer of an automobile advertised to the public that the windshield glass was "shatterproof," and the purchaser was injured when a stone struck the glass and it shattered. In the beginning various theories of liability were suggested, including strict liability in deceit, and a contract resulting from an offer made to the consumer to be bound by the representation, accepted by his purchase.

d. *"Warranty."* The theory finally adopted by most of the decisions, however, has been that of a non-contractual "express warranty" made to the consumer in the form of the representation to the public upon which he relies. The difficulties attending the use of the word "warranty" are the same as those involved under § 402A, and Comment m under that Section is equally applicable here so far as it is pertinent. The liability stated in this Section is liability in tort, and not in contract; and if it is to be called one of "warranty," it is at least a different kind of warranty from that involved in the ordinary sale of goods from the immediate seller to the immediate buyer, and is subject to different rules.

e. *Sellers included.* The rule stated in this Section applies to any person engaged in the business of selling any type of chattel. It is not limited to sellers of food or products for intimate bodily use, as was until lately the rule stated in § 402A. It is not limited to manufacturers of the chattel, and it includes wholesalers, retailers, and other distributors who sell it.

The rule stated applies, however, only to those who are engaged in the business of selling such chattels. It has no application to anyone who is not so engaged in business. It does not apply, for example, to a newspaper advertisement published by a private owner of a single automobile who offers it for sale.

f. *Misrepresentation of character or quality.* The rule stated applies to any misrepresentation of a material fact concerning the character or quality of the chattel sold which is made to the public by one so engaged in the business of selling such chattels. The fact misrepresented must be a material one, upon which the consumer may be expected to rely in making his purchase, and he must justifiably rely upon it. (See Comment j.) If he does so, and suffers physical harm by reason of the fact misrepresented, there is strict liability to him.

Illustration:

1. A manufactures automobiles. He advertises in newspapers and magazines that the glass in his cars is "shatterproof." B reads this advertising, and in reliance upon it purchases from a retail dealer an automobile manufactured by A. While B is driving the car, a stone thrown up by a passing truck strikes the windshield and shatters it, injuring B. A is subject to strict liability to B.

g. *Material fact.* The rule stated in this Section applies only to misrepresentations of material facts concerning the character or quality of the chattel in question. It does not apply to statements of opinion, and in particular it does not apply to the kind of loose general praise of wares sold which, on the part of the seller, is considered to be "sales talk," and is commonly called "puffing"—as, for example, a statement that an automobile is the best on the market for the price. As to such general language of opinion, see § 542, and Comment d under that Section, which is applicable here so far as it is pertinent. In addition, the fact misrepresented must be a material one, of importance to the normal purchaser, by which the ultimate buyer may justifiably be expected to be influenced in buying the chattel.

h. *"To the public."* The rule stated in this Section is limited to misrepresentations which are made by the seller to the public at large, in order to induce purchase of the chattels sold, or are intended by the seller to, and do, reach the public. The form of the representation is not important. It may be made by public advertising in newspapers or television, by literature distributed to the public through dealers, by labels on the product sold, or leaflets accompanying it, or in any other manner, whether it be oral or written.

Illustrations:

2. A manufactures wire rope. He issues a manual containing statements concerning its strength, which he distributes through dealers to buyers, and to members of the public who may be expected to buy. In reliance upon the statements made in the manual, B buys a quantity of the wire rope from a dealer, and makes use of it to hoist a weight of 1,000 pounds. The strength of the rope is not as great as is represented in the manual, and as a result the rope breaks and the weight falls on B and injures him. A is subject to strict liability to B.

3. A manufactures a product for use by women at home in giving "permanent waves" to their hair. He places on the bottles labels which state that the product may safely be used in a particular manner, and will not be injurious to the hair. B reads such a label, and in reliance upon it purchases a bottle of the product from a retail dealer. She uses it as directed, and as a result her hair is destroyed. A is subject to strict liability to B.

i. *Consumers.* The rule stated in this Section is limited to strict liability for physical harm to consumers of the chattel. The Caveat leaves open the question whether the rule may not also apply to one who is not a consumer, but who suffers physical harm through his justifiable reliance upon the misrepresentation.

"Consumer" is to be understood in the broad sense of one who makes use of the chattel in the manner which a purchaser may be expected to use it. Thus an employee of the ultimate purchaser to whom the chattel is turned over, and who is directed to make use of it in his work, is a consumer, and so is the wife of the purchaser of an automobile who is permitted by him to drive it.

j. *Justifiable reliance.* The rule here stated applies only where there is justifiable reliance upon the misrepresentation of the seller, and physical harm results because of such reliance, and because of the fact which is misrepresented. It does not apply where the misrepresentation is not known, or there is indifference to it, and does not influence the purchase or subsequent conduct. At the same time, however, the misrepresentation need not be the sole inducement to purchase, or to use the chattel, and it is sufficient that it has been a substantial factor in that inducement. (Compare § 546 and Comments.) Since the liability here is for misrepresentation, the rule as to what will constitute justifiable reliance stated in §§ 537–545A are applicable to this Section, so far as they are pertinent.

The reliance need not necessarily be that of the consumer who is injured. It may be that of the ultimate purchaser of the chattel, who because of such reliance passes it on to the consumer who is in fact injured, but is ignorant of the misrepresentation. Thus a husband who buys an automobile in justifiable reliance upon statements concerning its brakes, and permits his wife to drive the car, supplies the element of reliance, even though the wife in fact never learns of the statements.

Illustration:

4. The same facts as in Illustration 2, except that the harm is suffered by C, an employee of B, to whom B turns over the wire rope without informing him of the representations made by A. The same result.

UNIFORM COMMERCIAL CODE

§ 2-313. Express Warranties by Affirmation, Promise, Description, Sample

(1) Express warranties by the seller are created as follows:
  (a) Any affirmation of fact or promise made by the seller to the buyer which relates to the goods and becomes part of the basis of the bargain creates an express warranty that the goods shall conform to the affirmation or promise.
  (b) Any description of the goods which is made part of the basis of the bargain creates an express warranty that the goods shall conform to the description.
  (c) Any sample or model which is made part of the basis of the bargain creates an express warranty that the whole of the goods shall conform to the sample or model.

(2) It is not necessary to the creation of an express warranty that the seller use formal words such as "warrant" or "guarantee" or that he have a specific intention to make a warranty, but an affirmation merely of the value of the goods or a statement purporting to be merely the seller's opinion or commendation of the goods does not create a warranty.

§ 2-314. Implied Warranty: Merchantability; Usage of Trade

(1) Unless excluded or modified (Section 2-316), a warranty that the goods shall be merchantable is implied in a contract for their sale if the seller is a merchant with respect to goods of that kind. Under this section the serving for value of food or drink to be consumed either on the premises or elsewhere is a sale.

(2) Goods to be merchantable must be at least such as
  (a) pass without objection in the trade under the contract description; and
  (b) in the case of fungible goods, are of fair average quality within the description; and
  (c) are fit for the ordinary purposes for which such goods are used; and
  (d) run, within the variations permitted by the agreement, of even kind, quality and quantity within each unit and among all units involved; and
  (e) are adequately contained, packaged, and labeled as the agreement may require; and
  (f) conform to the promises or affirmations of fact made on the container or label if any.

(3) Unless excluded or modified (Section 2-316) other implied warranties may arise from course of dealing or usage of trade.

§ 2-315. Implied Warranty: Fitness for Particular Purpose

Where the seller at the time of contracting has reason to know any particular purpose for which the goods are required and that the buyer is relying on the seller's skill or judgment to select or furnish suitable goods, there is unless excluded or modified under the next section an implied warranty that the goods shall be fit for such purpose.

§ 2-316. Exclusion or Modification of Warranties

(1) Words or conduct relevant to the creation of an express warranty and words or conduct tending to negate or limit warranty shall be construed wherever reasonable as consistent with each other; but subject to the provisions of this Article on parol or extrinsic evidence (Section 2-202) negation or limitation is inoperative to the extent that such construction is unreasonable.

(2) Subject to subsection (3), to exclude or modify the implied warranty of merchantability or any part of it the language must mention merchantability and in case of a writing must be conspicuous, and to exclude or modify any implied warranty of fitness the exclusion must be a writing and conspicuous. Language to exclude all implied warranties of fitness is sufficient if it states, for example, that "There are no warranties which extend beyond the description on the face hereof."

(3) Notwithstanding subsection (2)

    (a) unless the circumstances indicate otherwise, all implied warranties are excluded by expressions like "as is," "with all faults" or other language which in common understanding calls the buyer's attention to the exclusion of warranties and makes plain that there is no implied warranty; and

    (b) when the buyer before entering into the contract has examined the goods or the sample or model as fully as he desired or has refused to examine the goods there is no implied warranty with regard to defects which an examination ought in the circumstances to have revealed to him; and

    (c) an implied warranty can also be excluded or modified by course of dealing or course of performance or usage of trade.

(4) Remedies for breach of warranty can be limited in accordance with the provisions of this Article on liquidation or limitation of damages and on contractual modification of remedy (Sections 2-718 and 2-719).

§ 2-317. Cumulation and Conflict of Warranties Express or Implied

Warranties whether express or implied shall be construed as consistent with each other and as cumulative, but if such construction is unreasonable the intention of the parties shall determine which warranty is dominant. In ascertaining that intention the following rules apply:

(a) Exact or technical specifications displace an inconsistent sample or model or general language of description.

(b) A sample from an existing bulk displaces inconsistent general language of description.

(c) Express warranties displace inconsistent implied warranties other than an implied warranty of fitness for a particular purpose.

§ 2-318.   Third Party Beneficiaries of Warranties Express or Implied

A seller's warranty whether express or implied extends to any natural person who is in the family or household of his buyer or who is a guest in his home if it is reasonable to expect that such person may use, consume or be affected by the goods and who is injured in person by breach of the warranty. A seller may not exclude or limit the operation of this section.

§ 2-607.   Effect of Acceptance; Notice of Breach; Burden of Establishing Breach after Acceptance; Notice of Claim or Litigation to Person Answerable Over

(1) The buyer must pay at the contract rate for any goods accepted.

(2) Acceptance of goods by the buyer precludes rejection of the goods accepted and if made with knowledge of a non-conformity cannot be revoked because of it unless the acceptance was on the reasonable assumption that the non-conformity would be seasonably cured but acceptance does not of itself impair any other remedy provided by this Article for non-conformity.

(3) Where a tender has been accepted

   (a) the buyer must within a reasonable time after he discovers or should have discovered any breach notify the seller of breach or be barred from any remedy; and

   (b) if the claim is one for infringement or the like (subsection (3) of Section 2-312) and the buyer is sued as a result of such a breach he must so notify the seller within a reasonable time after he receives notice of the litigation or be barred from any remedy over for liability established by the litigation.

(4) The burden is on the buyer to establish any breach with respect to the goods accepted.

(5) Where the buyer is sued for breach of a warranty or other obligation for which his seller is answerable over

   (a) he may give his seller written notice of the litigation. If the notice states that the seller may come in and defend and that if the seller does not do so he will be bound in any action against him by his buyer by any determination of fact common to the two litigations, then unless the seller after seasonable receipt of the notice does come in and defend he is so bound.

(b) if the claim is one for infringement or the like (subsection (3) of Section 2-312) the original seller may demand in writing that his buyer turn over to him control of the litigation including settlement or else be barred from any remedy over and if he also agrees to bear all expense and to satisfy any adverse judgment, then unless the buyer after seasonable receipt of the demand does turn over control the buyer is so barred.

(6) The provisions of subsections (3), (4) and (5) apply to any obligation of a buyer to hold the seller harmless against infringement or the like (subsection (3) of Section 2-312).

§ 2-719. Contractual Modification or Limitation of Remedy

(1) Subject to the provisions of subsections (2) and (3) of this section and of the preceding section on liquidation and limitation of damages,

(a) the agreement may provide for remedies in addition to or in substitution for those provided in this Article and may limit or alter the measure of damages recoverable under this Article, as by limiting the buyer's remedies to return of the goods and repayment of the price or to repair and replacement of non-conforming goods or parts; and

(b) resort to a remedy as provided is optional unless the remedy is expressly agreed to be exclusive, in which case it is the sole remedy.

(2) Where circumstances cause an exclusive or limited remedy to fail of its essential purpose, remedy may be had as provided in this Act.

(3) Consequential damages may be limited or excluded unless the limitation or exclusion is unconscionable. Limitation of consequential damages for injury to the person in the case of consumer goods is prima facie unconscionable but limitation of damages where the loss is commercial is not.

CONSUMER PRODUCT SAFETY ACT*

§ 2056. Consumer Product Safety Standards

(a) (1) Standards authorized; types of requirements. The Commission may by rule, in accordance with this section and section 9 [15 USCS § 2058], promulgate consumer product safety standards. A consumer product safety standard shall consist of one or more of any of the following types of requirements:

(A) Requirements as to performance, composition, contents, design, construction, finish, or packaging of a consumer product.

(B) Requirements that a consumer product be marked with or accompanied by clear and adequate warnings or instructions, or requirements respecting the form of warnings or instructions.

*All sections as amended in 1976.

Any requirement of such a standard shall be reasonably necessary to prevent or reduce an unreasonable risk of injury associated with such product. The requirements of such a standard (other than requirements relating to labeling, warnings, or instructions) shall, whenever feasible, be expressed in terms of performance requirements.

(2) No consumer product safety standard promulgated under this section shall require, incorporate, or reference any sampling plan. The preceding sentence shall not apply with respect to any consumer product safety standard or other agency action of the Commission under this Act (A) applicable to a fabric, related material, or product which is subject to a flammability standard or for which a flammability standard or other regulation may be promulgated under the Flammable Fabrics Act [15 USCS §§ 1191 *et seq.,* or (B) which is or may be applicable to glass containers.

(b) Publications, in Federal Register, of notice of proceedings for development of consumer product safety standard; contents of notice; time period during which standard is to be developed. A proceeding for the development of a consumer product safety standard under this Act shall be commenced by the publication in the Federal Register of a notice which shall—

(1) identify the product and the nature of the risk of injury associated with the product;

(2) state the Commission's determination that a consumer product safety standard is necessary to eliminate or reduce the risk of injury;

(3) include information with respect to any existing standard known to the Commission which may be relevant to the proceeding; and

(4) include an invitation for any person, including any State or Federal agency (other than the Commission), within 30 days after the date of publication of the notice (A) to submit to the Commission an existing standard as the proposed consumer product safety standard or (B) to offer to develop the proposed consumer product safety standard.

An invitation under paragraph (4)(B) shall specify the period of time in which the offeror of an accepted offer is to develop the proposed standard. The period specified shall be a period ending 150 days after the date the offer is accepted unless the Commission for good cause finds (and includes such finding in the notice) that a different period is appropriate.

(c) Publication of existing standard as proposed consumer product safety standard. If the Commission determines that (1) there exists a standard which has been issued or adopted by any Federal agency or by any other qualified agency, organization, or institution, and (2) such standard if promulgated under this Act, would eliminate or reduce the unreasonable risk of injury associated with the product, then it may, in lieu of accepting an offer pursuant to subsection (d) of this section, publish such standard as a proposed consumer product safety rule.

(d) Offers to develop proposed consumer product safety standard.

(1) Except as provided by subsection (c), the Commission shall accept one, and may accept more than one, offer to develop a proposed consumer product safety standard pursuant to the invitation prescribed by subsection (b)(4)(B), if it determines that the offeror is technically competent, is likely to develop an

appropriate standard within the period specified in the invitation under subsection (b), and will comply with regulations of the Commission under paragraph (3) of this subsection. The Commission shall publish in the Federal Register the name and address of each person whose offer it accepts, and a summary of the terms of such offer as accepted.

(2) If an offer is accepted under this subsection, the Commission may agree to contribute to the offeror's cost in developing a proposed consumer product safety standard, in any case in which the Commission determines that such contribution is likely to result in a more satisfactory standard than would be developed without such contribution, and that the offer is financially responsible. Regulations of the Commission shall set forth the items of cost in which it may participate, and shall exclude any contribution to the acquisition of land or buildings. Payments under agreements entered into under this paragraph may be made without regard to section 3648 of the Revised Statutes of the United States (31 U.S.C. 529) [31 USCS § 529].

(3) The Commission shall prescribe regulations governing the development of proposed consumer product safety standards by persons whose offers are accepted under paragraph (1). Such regulations shall include requirements—

    (A) that standards recommended for promulgation be suitable for promulgation under this Act, be supported by test data or such other documents or materials as the Commission may reasonably require to be developed, and (where appropriate) contain suitable test methods for measurement of compliance with such standards;

(e) (1) If the Commission publishes a notice pursuant to subsection (b) to commence a proceeding for the development of a consumer product safety standard for a consumer product and if—

    (A) the Commission does not, within 30 days after the date of publication of such notice, accept an offer to develop such a standard, or

    (B) the development period (specified in paragraph (3)) for such standard ends,

the Commission may develop a proposed consumer product safety rule respecting such product and publish such proposed rule.

(2) If the Commission accepts an offer to develop a proposed consumer product safety standard, the Commission may not, during the development period (specified in paragraph (3)) for such standard—

    (A) publish a proposed rule applicable to the same risk of injury associated with such product, or

    (B) develop proposals for such standard or contract with third parties for such development, unless the Commission determines that no offeror whose offer was accepted is making satisfactory progress in the development of such standard.

In any case in which the sole offeror whose offer is accepted under subsection (d)(1) of this section is the manufacturer, distributor, or retailer of a consumer product proposed to be regulated by the consumer product safety standard, the Commission may independently proceed to develop proposals for such standard during the development period.

(3) For purposes of paragraph (2), the development period for any standard is a period (A) beginning on the date on which the Commission first accepts an offer under subsection (d)(1) for the development of a proposed standard, and (B) ending on the earlier of—

  (i) the end of the period specified in the notice of proceeding (except that the period specified in the notice may be extended if good cause is shown and the reasons for such extension are published in the Federal Register), or

  (ii) the date on which it determines (in accordance with such procedures as it may by rule prescribe) that no offeror whose offer was accepted is able and willing to continue satisfactorily the development of the proposed standard which was the subject of the offer, or

  (iii) the date on which an offeror whose offer was accepted submits such a recommended standard to the Commission.

(f) If the Commission publishes a notice pursuant to subsection (b) to commence a proceeding for the development of a consumer product safety standard and if—

(1) no offer to develop such a standard is submitted to, or, if such an offer is submitted to the Commission, no such offer is accepted by, the Commission within a period of 60 days from the publication of such notice (or within such longer period as the Commission may prescribe by a notice published in the Federal Register stating good cause therefor), the Commission shall—

  (A) by notice published in the Federal Register terminate the proceeding begun by the subsection (b) notice, or

  (B) develop proposals for a consumer product safety rule for a consumer product identified in the subsection (b) notice and within a period of 150 days (or within such longer period as the Commission may prescribe by a notice published in the Federal Register stating good cause therefor) from the expiration of the 60-day (or longer) period—

    (i) by notice published in the Federal Register terminate the proceedings begun by the subsection (b) notice, or

    (ii) publish a proposed consumer product safety rule; or

(2) an offer to develop such a standard is submitted to and accepted by the Commission within the 60-day (or longer) period, then not later than 210 days (or such later time as the Commission may prescribe by notice published in the Federal Register stating good cause therefor) after the date of the acceptance of such offer the Commission shall take the action described in clause (i) or (ii) of paragraph (1)(B).

§ 2057. Banned Hazardous Products

Whenever the Commission finds that—

(1) a consumer product is being, or will be, distributed in commerce and such consumer product presents an unreasonable risk of injury; and

(2) no feasible consumer product safety standard under this Act would adequately

protect the public from the unreasonable risk of injury associated with such product,

the Commission may propose and, in accordance with section 9 [15 USCS § 2058], promulgate a rule declaring such product a banned hazardous product.

§ 2058. Administrative Procedure Applicable to Promulgation of Consumer Product Safety Rules

(a) Promulgation of consumer product safety rule; withdrawal of notice of proceeding regarding proposed rule that is not reasonably necessary or not in the public interest; applicability of administrative procedure law; opportunity for oral argument or written submission.

   (1) Within 60 days after the publication under section 7(c), (e)(1), or (f) or section 8 [15 USCS § 2056(c), (e)(1), (f), or 2057] of a proposed consumer product safety rule respecting a risk of injury associated with a consumer product, the Commission shall—

      (A) promulgate a consumer product safety rule respecting the risk of injury associated with such product if it makes the findings required under subsection (c), or
      (B) withdraw by rule the applicable notice of proceeding if it determines that such rule is not (i) reasonably necessary to eliminate or reduce an unreasonable risk of injury associated with the product, or (ii) in the public interest;

      except that the Commission may extend such 60-day period for good cause shown (if it publishes its reasons therefor in the Federal Register).

   (2) Consumer product safety rules which have been proposed under section 7(c), (e)(1), or (f) or section 8 [15 USCS § 2056(c), (e)(1), (f), or 2057] shall be promulgated pursuant to section 553 of title 5, United States Code [5 USCS § 553], except that the Commission shall give interested persons an opportunity for the oral presentation of data, views, or arguments, in addition to an opportunity to make written submissions. A transcript shall be kept of any oral presentation.

(b) Statement of risk of injury; consideration of product data. A consumer product safety rule shall express in the rule itself the risk of injury when the standard is designed to eliminate or reduce. In promulgating such a rule the Commission shall consider relevant available product data including the results of research, development, testing, and investigation activities conducted generally and pursuant to this Act. In the promulgation of such a rule the Commission shall also consider and take into account the special needs of elderly and handicapped persons to determine the extent to which such persons may be adversely affected by such rule.

(c) Required considerations and findings.

   (1) Prior to promulgating a consumer product safety rule, the Commission shall

consider, and shall make appropriate findings for inclusion in such rule with respect to—

(A) the degree and nature of the risk of injury the rule is designed to eliminate or reduce;

(B) the approximate number of consumer products, or types or classes thereof, subject to such rule;

(C) the need of the public for the consumer products subject to such rule, and the probable effect of such rule upon the utility, cost, or availability of such products to meet such need; and

(D) any means of achieving the objective of the order while minimizing adverse effects on competition or disruption or dislocation of manufacturing and other commercial practices consistent with the public health and safety.

(2) The Commission shall not promulgate a consumer product safety rule unless it finds (and includes such finding in the rule)—

(A) that the rule (including its effective date) is reasonably necessary to eliminate or reduce an unreasonable risk of injury associated with such product.

(B) that the promulgation of the rule is in the public interest; and

(C) in the case of a rule declaring the product a banned hazardous product, that no feasible consumer product safety standard under this Act would adequately protect the public from the unreasonable risk of injury associated with such product.

(d) Effective date of rules; stockpiling.

(1) Each consumer product safety rule shall specify the date such rule is to take effect not exceeding 180 days from the date promulgated, unless the Commission finds, for good cause shown, that a later effective date is in the public interest and publishes its reasons for such finding. The effective date of a consumer product safety standard under this Act shall be set at a date at least 30 days after the date of promulgation unless the Commission for good cause shown determines that an earlier effective date is in the public interest. In no case may the effective date be set at a date which is earlier than the date of promulgation. A consumer product safety standard shall be applicable only to consumer products manufactured after the effective date.

(2) The Commission may by rule prohibit a manufacturer of a consumer product from stockpiling any product to which a consumer product safety rule applies, so as to prevent such manufacturer from circumventing the purpose of such consumer product safety rule. For purposes of this paragraph, the term "stockpiling" means manufacturing or importing a product between the date of promulgation of such consumer product safety rule and its effective date at a rate which is significantly greater (as determined under the rule under this paragraph) than the rate at which such product was produced or imported during a base period (prescribed in the rule under this paragraph) ending before the date of promulgation of the consumer product safety rule.

(e) Amendments and revocations. The Commission may by rule amend or revoke any consumer product safety rule. Such amendment or revocation shall specify the date on which it is to take effect which shall not exceed 180 days from the date the amendment or revocation is published unless the Commission finds for good cause shown that a later effective date is in the public interest and publishes its reasons for such finding. Where an amendment involves a material change in a consumer product safety rule, sections 7 and 8 [15 USCS §§ 2056, 2057], and subsections (a) through (d) of this section shall apply. In order to revoke a consumer product safety rule, the Commission shall publish a proposal to revoke such rule in the Federal Register, and allow oral and written presentations in accordance with subsection (a)(2) of this section. It may revoke such rule only if it determines that the rule is not reasonably necessary to eliminate or reduce an unreasonable risk of injury associated with the product. Section 11 [15 USCS § 2060] shall apply to any amendment of a consumer product safety rule which involves a material change and to any revocation of a consumer product safety rule, in the same manner and to the same extent as such section applies to the Commission's action in promulgating such a rule.

§ 2059. Commission Responsibility; Petition for Consumer Product Safety Rule

(a) Petition by interested person for commencement of proceeding for issuance, amendment, or revocation of consumer product safety rule. Any interested person, including a consumer or consumer organization, may petition the Commission to commence a proceeding for the issuance, amendment, or revocation of a consumer product safety rule.

(b) Place of filing and contents of petition. Such petition shall be filed in the principal office of the Commission and shall set forth (1) facts which it is claimed establish that a consumer product safety rule or an amendment or revocation thereof is necessary, and (2) a brief description of the substance of the consumer product safety rule or amendment thereof which it is claimed should be issued by the Commission.

(c) Public hearing or investigation as to whether petition should be granted. The Commission may hold a public hearing or may conduct such investigation or proceedings as it deems appropriate in order to determine whether or not such petition should be granted.

(d) Grant or denial of petition. Within 120 days after filing of a petition described in subsection (b), the Commission shall either grant or deny the petition. If the Commission grants such petition, it shall promptly commence an appropriate proceeding under section 7 or 8 [15 USCS §§ 2056, 2057]. If the Commission denies such petition it shall publish in the Federal Register its reasons for such denial.

(e) Civil action to compel action requested in petition.

  (1) If the Commission denies a petition made under this section (or if it fails to grant or deny such petition within the 120-day period) the petitioner may commence a civil action in a United States district court to compel the

Commission to initiate a proceeding to take the action requested. Any such action shall be filed within 60 days after the Commission's denial of the petition, or (if the Commission fails to grant or deny the petition within 120 days after filing the petition) within 60 days after the expiration of the 120-day period.

(2) If the petitioner can demonstrate to the satisfaction of the court, by a preponderance of evidence in a *de novo* proceeding before such court, that the consumer product presents an unreasonable risk of injury, and that the failure of the Commission to initiate a rule-making proceeding under section 7 or 8 [15 USCS §§ 2056, 2057] unreasonably exposes the petitioner or other consumers to a risk of injury presented by the consumer product, the court shall order the Commission to initiate the action requested by the petitioner.

(3) In any action under this subsection, the district court shall have no authority to compel the Commission to take any action other than the initiation of a rule-making proceeding in accordance with section 7 or 8 [15 USCS §§ 2056, 2057].

(4) In any action under this subsection the court may in the interest of justice award the costs of suit, including reasonable attorneys' fees and reasonable expert witnesses' fees. Attorneys' fees may be awarded against the United States (or any agency or official of the United States) without regard to section 2412 or title 28, United States Code [28 USCS § 2412], or any other provision of law. For purposes of this paragraph and sections 11(c), 23(a), and 24 [15 USCS §§ 2060(c), 2072(a), 2073], a reasonable attorney's fee is a fee (A) which is based upon (i) the actual time expended by an attorney in providing advice and other legal services in connection with representing a person in an action brought under this subsection, and (ii) such reasonable expenses as may be incurred by the attorney in the provision of such services, and (B) which is computed at the rate prevailing for the provision of similar services with respect to actions brought in the court which is awarding such fee.

(f) Availability of other remedies. The remedies under this section shall be in addition to, and not in lieu of, other remedies provided by law.

(g) Availability of provisions of subsec. (e). Subsection (e) of this section shall apply only with respect to petitions filed more than 3 years after the date of enactment of this Act [enacted Oct. 27, 1972].

§ 2061. Imminent Hazards

(a) Filing of action. The Commission may file in a United States district court an action (1) against an imminently hazardous consumer product for seizure of such product under subsection (b)(2), or (2) against any person who is a manufacturer, distributor, or retailer of such product, or (3) against both. Such an action may be filed notwithstanding the existence of a consumer product safety rule applicable to such product, or the pendency of any administrative or judicial proceedings under any other provisions of this Act. As used in this section, and hereinafter in this Act, the term "imminently hazardous consumer product" means a consumer product which presents imminent and unreasonable risk of death, serious illness, or severe personal injury.

(b) Scope of jurisdiction.

   (1) The district court in which such action is filed shall have jurisdiction to declare such product an imminently hazardous consumer product, and (in the case of an action under subsection (a)(2)) to grant (as ancillary to such declaration or in lieu thereof) such temporary or permanent relief as may be necessary to protect the public from such risk. Such relief may include a mandatory order requiring the notification of such risk to purchasers of such product known to the defendant, public notice, the recall, the repair or the replacement of, or refund for, such product.

   (2) In the case of an action under subsection (a)(1), the consumer product may be proceeded against by process of libel for the seizure and condemnation of such product in any United States district court within the jurisdiction of which such consumer products is found. Proceedings and cases instituted under the authority of the preceding sentence shall conform as nearly as possible to proceedings *in rem* in admiralty.

(c) Concurrent initiation of proceeding to promulgate consumer product safety rule. Where appropriate, concurrently with the filing of such action or as soon thereafter as may be practicable, the Commission shall initiate a proceeding to promulgate a consumer product safety rule applicable to the consumer product with respect to which such action is filed.

(d) Consultation with Product Safety Advisory Council.

   (1) Prior to commencing an action under subsection (a), the Commission may consult the Product Safety Advisory Council (established under section 28) [15 USCS § 2077] with respect to its determination to commence such action, and request the Council's recommendation as to the type of temporary or permanent relief which may be necessary to protect the public.

   (2) The Council shall submit its recommendations to the Commission within one week of such request.

   (3) Subject to paragraph (2), the Council may conduct such hearing or offer such opportunity for the presentation of views as it may consider necessary or appropriate.

(e) Venue of certain actions; service of process; subpoenas.

   (1) An action under subsection (a)(2) of this section may be brought in the United States district court for the District of Columbia or in any judicial district in which any of the defendants is found, is an inhabitant or transacts business; and process in such an action may be served on a defendant in any other district in which such defendant resides or may be found. Subpoenas requiring attendance of witnesses in such an action may run into any other district. In determining the judicial district in which an action may be brought under this section in instances in which such action may be brought in more than one judicial district, the Commission shall take into account the convenience of the parties.

(2) Whenever proceedings under this section involving substantially similar consumer products are pending in courts in two or more judicial districts, they shall be consolidated for trial by order of any such court upon application reasonably made by any party in interest, upon notice to all other parties in interest.

(f) Appearance of Commission by attorneys. Notwithstanding any other provision of law, in any action under this section, the Commission may direct attorneys employed by it to appear and represent it.

§ 2064.   Notification and Repair, Replacement, or Refund

(a)   "Substantial product hazard." For purposes of this section, the term "substantial product hazard" means—

(1) a failure to comply with an applicable consumer product safety rule which creates a substantial risk of injury to the public, or

(2) a product defect which (because of the pattern of defect, the number of defective products distributed in commerce, the severity of the risk, or otherwise) creates a substantial risk of injury to the public.

(b) Manufacturers, distributors, and retailers of non-compliant or defective product to inform Commission. Every manufacturer of a consumer product distributed in commerce, and every distributor and retailer of such product, who obtains information which reasonably supports the conclusion that such product—

(1) fails to comply with an applicable consumer product safety rule; or

(2) contains a defect which could create a substantial product hazard described in subsection (a)(2),

shall immediately inform the Commission of such failure to comply or of such defect, unless such manufacturer, distributor, or retailer has actual knowledge that the Commission has been adequately informed of such defect or failure to comply.

(c) Manufacturers, distributors, and retailers to give notice to one another, to public, or to purchasers. If the Commission determines (after affording interested persons, including consumers and consumer organizations, an opportunity for a hearing in accordance with subsection (f) of this section) that a product distributed in commerce presents a substantial product hazard and that notification is required in order to adequately protect the public from such substantial product hazard, the Commission may order the manufacturer or any distributor or retailer of the product to take any one or more of the following actions:

(1) To give public notice of the defect or failure to comply.

(2) To mail notice to each person who is a manufacturer, distributor, or retailer of such product.

(3) To mail notice to every person to whom the person required to give notice knows such product was delivered or sold.

Any such order shall specify the form and content of any notice required to be given under such order.

(d) Repair, replacement, or refund. If the Commission determines (after affording interested parties, including consumers and consumer organizations, an opportunity for a hearing in accordance with subsection (f)) that a product distributed in commerce presents a substantial product hazard and that action under this subsection is in the public interest, it may order the manufacturer or any distributor or retailer of such product to take whichever of the following actions the person to whom the order is directed elects:

(1) To bring such product into conformity with the requirements of the applicable consumer product safety rule or to repair the defect in such product.

(2) To replace such product with a like or equivalent product which complies with the applicable consumer product safety rule or which does not contain the defect.

(3) To refund the purchase price of such product (less a reasonable allowance for use, if such product has been in the possession of a consumer for one year or more (A) at the time of public notice under subsection (c), or (B) at the time the consumer receives actual notice of the defect or noncompliance, whichever first occurs).

An order under this subsection may also require the person to whom it applies to submit a plan, satisfactory to the Commission, for taking action under whichever of the preceding paragraphs of this subsection under which such person has elected to act. The Commission shall specify in the order the persons to whom refunds must be made if the person to whom the order is directed elects to take the action described in paragraph (3). If an order under this subsection is directed to more than one person, the Commission shall specify which person has the election under this subsection. An order under this subsection may prohibit the person to whom it applies from manufacturing for sale, offering for sale, distributing in commerce, or importing into the customs territory of the United States (as defined in general headnote 2 to the Tariff Schedules of the United States [19 USCS § 1202]), or from doing any combination of such actions, the product with respect to which the order was issued.

(e) Expenses.

(1) No charge shall be made to any person (other than a manufacturer, distributor, or retailer) who avails himself of any remedy provided under an order issued under subsection (d), and the person subject to the order shall reimburse each person (other than a manufacturer, distributor, or retailer) who is entitled to such a remedy for any reasonable and foreseeable expenses incurred by such person in availing himself of such remedy.

(2) An order issued under subsection (c) or (d) with respect to a product may require any person who is a manufacturer, distributor, or retailer of the product to reimburse any other person who is a manufacturer, distributor, or retailer of such product for such other person's expenses in connection with carrying out the order, if the Commission determines the reimbursement to be in the public interest.

(f) Hearings. An order under subsection (c) or (d) may be issued only after an opportunity for a hearing in accordance with section 554 of title 5, United States

Code [5 USCS § 554], except that, if the Commission determines that any person who wishes to participate in such hearing is a part of a class of participants who share an identity of interest, the Commission may limit such person's participation in such hearing to participation through a single representative designated by such class (or by the Commission if such class fails to designate such a representative).

(g) (1) If the Commission has initiated a proceeding under this section for the issuance of an order under subsection (d) with respect to a product which the Commission has reason to believe presents a substantial product hazard, the Commission (without regard to section 27(b)(7) [15 USCS § 2076(B)(7)]) or the Attorney General may, in accordance with section 12(e)(1)]15 USCS § 2061(e)(1)], apply to a district court of the United States for the issuance of a preliminary injunction to restrain the distribution in commerce of such product pending the completion of such proceeding. If such a preliminary injunction has been issued, the Commission (or the Attorney General if the preliminary injunction was issued upon an application of the Attorney General) may apply to the issuing court for extensions of such preliminary injunction.

(2) Any preliminary injunction, and any extension of a preliminary injunction, issued under this subsection with respect to a product shall be in effect for such period as the issuing court prescribes not to exceed a period which extends beyond the thirtieth day from the date of the issuance of the preliminary injunction (or, in the case of a preliminary injunction which has been extended, the date of its extension) or the date of the completion or termination of the proceeding under this section respecting such product, whichever date occurs first.

(3) The amount in controversy requirement of section 1331 of title 28, United States Code [28 USCS § 1331], does not apply with respect to the jurisdiction of a district court of the United States to issue or exend [extend] a preliminary injunction under this subsection.

§ 2068. Prohibited Acts

(a) It shall be unlawful for any person to—

(1) manufacture for sale, offer for sale, distribute in commerce, or import into the United States any consumer product which is not in conformity with an applicable consumer product safety standard under this Act;

(2) manufacture for sale, offer for sale, distribute in commerce, or import into the United States any consumer product which has been declared a banned hazardous product by a rule under this Act;

(3) fail or refuse to permit access to or copying of records, or fail or refuse to establish or maintain records, or fail or refuse to make reports or provide information, or fail or refuse to permit entry or inspection, as required under this Act or rule thereunder;

(4) fail to furnish information required by section 15(b) [15 USCS § 2064(b)];

(5) fail to comply with an order issued under section 15(c) or (d) [15 USCS § 2064(c), (d)] (relating to notification, to repair, replacement, and refund, and to prohibited acts);

(6) fail to furnish a certificate required by section 14 [15 USCS § 2063] or issue a false certificate if such person in the exercise of due care has reason to know that such certificate is false or misleading in any material respect; or to fail to comply with any rule under section 14(c) [15 USCS § 2063(c)] (relating to labeling);

(7) fail to comply with any rule under section 9(d)(2) [15 USCS § 2058(d)(2)] (relating to stockpiling); or

(8) fail to comply with any rule under section 13 [15 USCS § 2062] (relating to prior notice and description of new consumer products); or

(9) fail to comply with any rule under section 27(e) [15 USCS § 2076(e)] (relating to provision of performance and technical data).

(b) Paragraphs (1) and (2) of subsection (a) of this section shall not apply to any person (1) who holds a certificate issued in accordance with section 14(a) [15 USCS § 2063(a)] to the effect that such consumer product conforms to all applicable consumer product safety rules, unless such person knows that such consumer product does not conform, or (2) who relies in good faith on the representation of the manufacturer or a distributor of such product that the product is not subject to an applicable product safety rule.

MAGNUSON-MOSS WARRANTY ACT

§ 2302. Warranty Provisions

(a) Rules requiring full and conspicuous disclosure; contents of written warranty. In order to improve the adequacy of information available to consumers, prevent deception, and improve competition in the marketing of consumer products, any warrantor warranting a consumer product to a consumer by means of a written warranty shall, to the extent required by rules of the Commission, fully and conspicuously disclose in simple and readily understood language the terms and conditions of such warranty. Such rules may require inclusion in the written warranty of any of the following items among others:

(1) The clear identification of the names and addresses of the warrantors.

(2) The identity of the party or parties to whom the warranty is extended.

(3) The products or parts covered.

(4) A statement of what the warrantor will do in the event of a defect, malfunction, or failure to conform with such written warranty—at whose expense—and for what period of time.

(5) A statement of what the consumer must do and expenses he must bear.

(6) Exceptions and exclusions from the terms of the warranty.

(7) The step-by-step procedure which the consumer should take in order to obtain performance of any obligation under the warranty, including the identification of any person or class of persons authorized to perform the obligations set forth in the warranty.

(8) Information respecting the availability of any informal dispute settlement procedure offered by the warrantor and a recital, where the warranty so provides, that the purchaser may be required to resort to such procedure before pursuing any legal remedies in the courts.

(9) A brief, general description of the legal remedies available to the consumer.

(10) The time at which the warrantor will perform any obligations under the warranty.

(11) The period of time within which, after notice of a defect, malfunction, or failure to conform with the warranty, the warrantor will perform any obligations under the warranty.

(12) The characteristics or properties of the products, or parts thereof, that are not covered by the warranty.

(13) The elements of the warranty in words or phrases which would not mislead a reasonable, average consumer as to the nature or scope of the warranty.

(b) Availability of warranty terms prior to sale; advertising, labeling, point-of-sale material, etc.; duration of warranties.

(1) (A) The Commission shall prescribe rules requiring that the terms of any written warranty on a consumer product be made available to the consumer (or prospective consumer) prior to the sale of the product to him.

(B) The Commission may prescribe rules for determining the manner and form in which information with respect to any written warranty of a consumer product shall be clearly and conspicuously presented or displayed so as not to mislead the reasonable, average consumer, when such information is contained in advertising, labeling, point-of-sale material, or other representations in writing.

(2) Nothing in this title [15 USCS §§ 2301 et seq.] (other than paragraph (3) of this subsection) shall be deemed to authorize the Commission to prescribe the duration of written warranties given or to require that a consumer product or any of its components be warranted.

(3) The Commission may prescribe rules for extending the period of time a written warranty or service contract is in effect to correspond with any period of time in excess of a reasonable period (not less than 10 days) during which the consumer is deprived of the use of such consumer product by reason of failure of the product to conform with the written warranty or by reason of the failure of the warrantor (or service contractor) to carry out such warranty (or service contract) within the period specified in the warranty (or service contract).

(c) Warranty conditioned on using other designated article or service. No warrantor of a consumer product may condition his written or implied warranty of such product on the consumer's using, in connection with such product, any article or service (other than article or service provided without charge under the terms of the warranty) which is identified by brand trade, or corporate name; except that the prohibition of this subsection may be waived by the Commission if

(1) the warrantor satisfies the Commission that the warranted product will function properly only if the article or service so identified is used in connection with the warranted product, and

(2) The Commission finds that such a waiver is in the public interest.

The Commission shall identify in the Federal Register, and permit public comment on, all applications for waiver of the prohibition of this subsection, and shall publish in the Federal Register its disposition of any such application, including the reasons therefor.

(d) Standard warranty provisions for incorporation by reference into warranties. The Commission may by rule devise detailed substantive warranty provisions which warrantors may incorporate by reference in their warranties.

(e) Section applicable only to products costing more than $5. The provisions of this section apply only to warranties which pertain to consumer products actually costing the consumer more than $5.

§ 2303.   Designation of Warranties

(a) "Full (statement of duration)" and "Limited" warranties. Any warrantor warranting a consumer product by means of a written warranty shall clearly and conspicuously designate such warranty in the following manner, unless exempted from doing so by the Commission pursuant to subsection (c) of this section:

(1) If the written warranty meets the Federal minimum standards for warranty set forth in section 104 of this Act [15 USCS § 2304], then it shall be conspicuously designated a "full (statement of duration) warranty."

(2) If the written warranty does not meet the Federal minimum standards for warranty set forth in section 104 of this Act [15 USCS § 2304], then it shall be conspicuously designated a "limited warranty."

(b) Exemption for expressions of general policy regarding customer satisfaction. Sections 102, 103 and 104 [15 USCS §§ 2302, 2303, and 2304] shall not apply to statements or representations which are similar to expressions of general policy concerning customer satisfaction and which are not subject to any specific limitations.

(c) Written warranties that do not have to be designated "Full (statement of duration)" or "Limited." In addition to exercising the authority pertaining to disclosure granted in section 102 of this Act [15 USCS § 2302], the Commission may by rule determine when a written warranty does not have to be designated either "full (statement of duration)" or "limited" in accordance with this section.

(d) Applicability of subsecs. (a) and (c). The provisions of subsections (a) and (c) of this section apply only to warranties which pertain to consumer products actually costing the consumer more than $10 and which are not designated "full (statement of duration) warranties."

§ 2304. Federal Minimum Standards for Warranty

(a) Requirements, generally. In order for a warrantor warranting a consumer product by means of a written warranty to meet the Federal minimum standards for warranty—

   (1) such warrantor must as a minimum remedy such consumer product within a reasonable time and without charge, in the case of a defect, malfunction, or failure to conform with such written warranty;

   (2) notwithstanding section 108(b) [15 USCS § 2308(b)], such warrantor may not impose any limitation on the duration of any implied warranty on the product;

   (3) such warrantor may not exclude or limit consequential damages for breach of any written or implied warranty on such product, unless such exclusion or limitation conspicuously appears on the face of the warranty; and

   (4) if the product (or component part thereof) contains a defect or malfunction after a reasonable number of attempts by the warrantor to remedy defects or malfunctions in such product, such warrantor must permit the consumer to elect either a refund for, or replacement without charge of, such product or part (as the case may be). The Commission may by rule specify for purposes of this paragraph, what constitutes a reasonable number of attempts to remedy particular kinds of defects or malfunctions under different circumstances. If the warrantor replaces a component part of a consumer product, such replacement shall include installing the part in the product without charge.

(b) Imposition of duties upon consumer as condition of securing remedy; applicability and extent of warrantor's duties under subsec. (a).

   (1) In fulfilling the duties under subsection (a) respecting a written warranty, the warrantor shall not impose any duty other than notification upon any consumer as a condition of securing remedy of any consumer product which malfunctions, is defective, or does not conform to the written warranty, unless the warrantor has demonstrated in a rulemaking proceeding, or can demonstrate in an administrative or judicial enforcement proceeding (including private enforcement), or in an informal dispute settlement proceeding, that such a duty is reasonable.

   (2) Notwithstanding paragraph (1), a warrantor may require, as a condition to replacement of, or refund for, any consumer product under subsection (a), that such consumer product shall be made available to the warrantor free and clear of liens and other encumbrances, except as otherwise provided by rule or order of the Commission in cases in which such a requirement would not be practicable.

   (3) The Commission may, by rule define in detail the duties set forth in section 104(a) of this Act [subsec. (a) of this section] and the applicability of such duties to warrantors of different categories of consumer products with "full (statement of duration)" warranties.

   (4) The duties under subsection (a) extend from the warrantor to each person who is a consumer with respect to the consumer product.

(c) Damage, or unreasonable use, while in possession of consumer. The performance of the duties under subsection (a) of this section shall not be required of the warrantor if he can show that the defect, malfunction, or failure of any warranted consumer product to conform with a written warranty, was caused by damage (not resulting from defect or malfunction) while in the possession of the. consumer, or unreasonable use (including failure to provide reasonable and necessary maintenance).

(d) Definition and construction of "without charge." For purposes of this section and of section 102(c) [15 USCS § 2302(c)], the term "without charge" means that the warrantor may not assess the consumer for any costs the warrantor or his representatives incur in connection with the required remedy of a warranted consumer product. An obligation under subsection (a)(1)(A) to remedy without charge does not necessarily require the warrantor to compensate the consumer for incidental expenses; however, if any incidental expenses are incurred because the remedy is not made within a reasonable time or because the warrantor imposed an unreasonable duty upon the consumer as a condition of securing remedy, then the consumer shall be entitled to recover reasonable incidental expenses which are so incurred in any action against the warrantor.

(e) Effect of designation of warranty as "Full (statement of duration)" warranty on suits by consumer. If a supplier designates a warranty applicable to a consumer product as a "full (statement of duration)" warranty, then the warranty on such product shall, for purposes of any action under section 110(d) [15 USCS § 2310(d)] or under any State law, be deemed to incorporate at least the minimum requirements of this section and rules prescribed under this section.

§ 2308.   Limitation on Disclaimer of Implied Warranties

(a) Where written warranty is made or service contracts is entered into. No supplier may disclaim or modify (except as provided in subsection (b)) any implied warranty to a consumer with respect to such consumer product if (1) such supplier makes any written warranty to the consumer with respect to such consumer product, or (2) at the time of sale, or within 90 days thereafter, such supplier enters into a service contract with the consumer which applies to such consumer product.

(b) Where implied warranties are limited in duration to duration of written warranty. For purposes of this title [15 USCS §§ 2301 et seq.] (other than section 104(a)(2)) [15 USCS § 2304(a)(2)] implied warranties may be limited in duration to the duration of a written warranty of reasonable duration, if such limitation is conscionable and is set forth in clear and unmistakable language and prominently displayed on the face of the warranty.

(c) Violative disclaimer, modification, or limitation ineffective. A disclaimer, modification, or limitation made in violation of this section shall be ineffective for purposes of this title [15 USCS § 2304(a)] and State law.

§ 2310. Remedies

(a) Informal dispute settlement procedures.

(1) Congress hereby declares it to be its policy to encourage warrantors to establish procedures whereby consumer disputes are fairly and expeditiously settled through informal dispute settlement mechanisms.

(2) The Commission shall prescribe rules setting forth minimum requirements for any informal dispute settlement procedure which is incorporated into the terms of a written warranty to which any provision of this title [15 USCS §§ 2301 *et seq.*] applies. Such rules shall provide for participation in such procedure by independent or governmental entities.

(3) One or more warrantors may establish an informal dispute settlement procedure which meets the requirements of the Commission's rules under paragraph (2). If—

(A) a warrantor establishes such a procedure,

(B) such procedure, and its implementation, meets the requirements of such rules, and

(C) he incorporates in a written warranty a requirement that the consumer resort to such procedure before pursuing any legal remedy under this section respecting such warranty.

then (i) the consumer may not commence a civil action (other than a class action) under subsection (d) of this section unless he initially resorts to such procedure; and (ii) a class of consumers may not proceed in a class action under subsection (d) except to the extent the court determines necessary to establish the representative capacity of the named plaintiffs, unless the named plaintiffs (upon notifying the defendant that they are named plaintiffs in a class action with respect to a warranty obligation) initially resort to such procedure. In the case of such a class action which is brought in a district court of the United States, the representative capacity of the named plaintiffs shall be established in the application of rule 23 of the Federal Rules of Civil Procedure [USCS Federal Rules of Civil Procedure, Rule 23]. In any civil action arising out of a warranty obligation and relating to a matter considered in such a procedure, any decision in such procedure shall be admissible in evidence.

(4) The Commission on its own initiative may, or upon written complaint filed by any interested person shall, review the bona fide operation of any dispute settlement procedure resort to which is stated in a written warranty to be a prerequisite to pursuing a legal remedy under this section. If the Commission finds that such procedure or its implementation fails to comply with the requirements of the rules under paragraph (2), the Commission may take appropriate remedial action under any authority it may have under this title [15 USCS §§ 2301 *et seq.*] or any other provision of law.

(5) Until rules under paragraph (2) take effect, this subsection shall not affect the validity of any informal dispute settlement procedure respecting consumer

warranties, but in any action under subsection (d), the court may invalidate any such procedure if it finds that such procedure is unfair.

(b) Violation of or non-conformity with 15 USCS §§ 2301 *et seq.* as unfair trade practice. It shall be a violation of section 5(a)(1) of the Federal Trade Commission Act (15 U.S.C. 45(a)(1)) for any person to fail to comply with any requirement imposed on such person by this title [15 USCS §§ 2301 *et seq.*] (or a rule thereunder) or to violate any prohibition contained in this title [15 USCS §§ 2301 *et seq.*] (or a rule thereunder).

(c) Jurisdiction of District Courts; actions·by Attorney General or by Commission; "deceptive warranty."

    (1) The district courts of the United States shall have jurisdiction of any action brought by the Attorney General (in his capacity as such), or by the Commission by any of its attorneys designated by it for such purpose, to restrain (A) any warrantor from making a deceptive warranty with respect to a consumer product, or (B) any person from failing to comply with any requirement imposed on such person by or pursuant to this title [15 USCS §§ 2301 *et seq.*] or from violating any prohibition contained in this title [15 USCS §§ 2301 *et seq.*]. Upon proper showing that, weighing the equities and considering the Commission's or Attorney General's likelihood of ultimate success, such action would be in the public interest and after notice to the defendant, a temporary restraining order or preliminary injunction may be granted without bond. In the case of an action brought by the Commission, if a complaint under section 5 of the Federal Trade Commission Act [15 USCS § 45] is not filed within such period (not exceeding 10 days) as may be specified by the court after the issuance of the temporary restraining order or preliminary injunction, the order or injunction shall be dissolved by the court and be of no further force and effect. Any suit shall be brought in the district in which such person resides or transacts business. Whenever it appears to the court that the ends of justice require that other persons should be parties in the action, the court may cause them to be summoned whether or not they reside in the district in which the court is held, and to that end process may be served in any district.

    (2) For the purposes of this subsection, the term "deceptive warranty" means (A) a written warranty which (i) contains an affirmation, promise, description, or representation which is either false or fraudulent, or which, in light of all of the circumstances, would mislead a reasonable individual exercising due care, or (ii) fails to contain information which is necessary in light of all of the circumstances, to make the warranty not misleading to a reasonable individual exercising due care; or (B) a written warranty created by the use of such terms as "guaranty" or "warranty," if the terms and conditions of such warranty so limit its scope and application as to deceive a reasonable individual.

(d) Suits by consumers; class actions.

    (1) Subject to subsections (a)(3) and (e), a consumer who is damaged by the failure of a supplier, warrantor, or service contractor to comply with any obligation under this title [15 USCS §§ 2301 *et seq.*], or under a written

warranty, implied warranty, or service contract, may bring suit for damages and other legal and equitable relief—

    (A) in any court of competent jurisdiction in any State or the District of Columbia; or

    (B) in an appropriate district court of the United States, subject to paragraph (3) of this subsection.

  (2) If a consumer finally prevails in any action brought under paragraph (1) of this subsection, he may be allowed by the·court to recover as part of the judgment a sum equal to the aggregate amount of cost and expenses (including attorneys' fees based on actual time expended) determined by the court to have been reasonably incurred by the plaintiff for or in connection with the commencement and prosecution of such action, unless the court in its discretion shall determine that such an award of attorneys' fees would be inappropriate.

  (3) No claim shall be cognizable in a suit brought under paragraph (1)(B) of this subsection—

    (A) if the amount in controversy of any individual claim is less than the sum or value of $25;

    (B) if the amount in controversy is less than the sum or value of $50,000 (exclusive of interests and costs) computed on the basis of all claims to be determined in this suit; or

    (C) if the action is brought as a class action, and the number of named plaintiffs is less than one hundred.

(e) Opportunity to cure. No action (other than a class action or an action respecting a warranty to which subsection (a)(3) applies) may be brought under subsection (d) for failure to comply with any obligation under any written or implied warranty or service contract, and a class of consumers may not proceed in a class action under such subsection with respect to such a failure except to the extent the court determines necessary to establish the representative capacity of the named plaintiffs, unless the person obligated under the warranty or service contract is afforded a reasonable opportunity to cure such failure to comply. In the case of such a class action (other than a class action respecting a warranty to which subsection (a)(3) applies) brought under subsection (d) for breach of any written or implied warranty or service contract, such reasonable opportunity will be afforded by the named plaintiffs and they shall at that time notify the defendant that they are acting on behalf of the class. In the case of such a class action which is brought in a district court of the United States, the representative capacity of the named plaintiffs shall be established in the application of rule 23 of the Federal Rules of Civil Procedure [USCS Federal Rules of Civil Procedure, Rule 23].

(f) Persons against whom remedies may be enforced. For purposes of this section, only the warrantor actually making a written affirmation of fact, promise, or undertaking shall be deemed to have created a written warranty, and any rights arising thereunder may be enforced under this section only against such warrantor and no other person.

Federal Regulation—The Highlights of Some Important Acts

C.1 THE CONSUMER PRODUCT SAFETY ACT

C.1.1 Overview

In response to increasing public concern about the hazards connected with using certain consumer products, the Congress and President created the National Commission on Product Safety in 1967 to "conduct a comprehensive study and investigation of the scope and adequacy of measures now employed to protect consumers against unreasonable risk of injuries which may be caused by hazardous household products" [C-1]. Concluding that the current methods were inadequate, the Commission recommended the establishment of a permanent Consumer Product Safety Commission (CPSC). In response Congress enacted the Consumer Product Safety Act (CPSA) in 1972 [C-2].

The Act established an independent regulatory commission to be headed by five commissioners, selected by the President. The Commission was to carry out the Act's enumerated purposes:

1. To protect the public against unreasonable risks of injury associated with consumer products.

2. To assist consumers in evaluating the comparative safety of consumer products.

3. To develop uniform safety standards for consumer products and to minimize conflicting state and local regulations.

4. To promote research and investigation into the causes and prevention of product-related deaths, illnesses, and injuries [C-3].

It is clear from the Act's legislative history that the words "associated with" were intentionally employed to indicate that the CPSA would also cover reasonably foreseeable misuse [C-4].

The term "consumer product" is broadly defined as any article produced or distributed for sale to, or the personal use of, a consumer in or around a household, a school, in recreation, or otherwise. But the definition explicitly excludes tobacco and tobacco products, motor vehicles and motor vehicle equipment, firearms, aircraft, boats, drugs and cosmetics, food, and pesticides, among others [C-5]. Generally the items excluded are regulated by other statutes. Moreover, whereas all the provisions of the Act apply to imported products, they do not apply to exports unless the product is in fact distributed in the United States or eventually is to be sold or used in a United States installation outside of the United States [C-6].

The CPSC was given a number of mechanisms to implement the Act's purposes. The following sections outline the meaning and some implications of these mechanisms.

C.1.1 Information Gathering, Research, and Public Disclosure

The CPSC is directed to maintain an Injury Information Clearinghouse to collect and analyze injury data and to disseminate this information to the public [C-7]. Among the methods used to collect such information is the National Electronic Injury Surveillance System (NEISS). NEISS is a computerized data collection system connected to 119 representative hospital emergency rooms across the United States. Information about any product-related injury treated in one of these emergency rooms is transmitted by computer to the CPSC in Washington, D.C. If the Commission staff decides that more detailed information is necessary, an in-depth field investigation is conducted. Admittedly, this system provides the Commission with information about only those injuries for which patients received emergency room treatment, which is estimated to be only 38 percent of all product-related injuries. It is estimated that another 41 percent of injuries are treated in doctor's offices, 18 percent at home, and 3 percent by direct hospital admissions [C-8].

In an attempt to increase public participation in the data collection process the Commission has established a toll-free "Hotline" to answer inquiries and accept product hazard notifications [C-9].

Note that the NEISS data provide only the frequency of *product-related* injuries. They do not indicate whether the product caused the injury. Whereas adequate, in-depth field investigations of the injury-producing event could focus on this critical question, the Commission has thus far not gathered sufficient information to give much assistance in this regard.

In addition to this data-gathering function the Commission may:

1. Require any manufacturer to keep records, make reports and submit any information the CPSC may require.
2. Inspect any factory or warehouse, or any records and papers, related to the manufacture of consumer products.

3. Require any manufacturer to furnish notice and a description of any new consumer product to the Commission before the product's distribution in commerce.
4. Conduct any other hearings or inquiries that it may deem necessary [C-10].

Beyond its data collection functions the Commission is authorized to conduct research into the causation and prevention of product-related injuries, to develop product safety methods and testing devices, and to offer training in product safety investigation and test methods.

Generally, any information gathered by the Commission is to be made available to the public [C-11]. Information not required to be disclosed by the Freedom of Information Act [C-12], or otherwise protected by law from disclosure, need not be revealed. Trade secrets are considered confidential. Otherwise, information can be made public.

The Commission publishes information about its proceedings and the rules it promulgates in the *Federal Register* [C-13] but has adopted a number of other practices to make information more generally available to the public. For instance, NEISS published a monthly newsletter of its findings and the toll-free "Hotline" is available for a broad range of consumer inquiries [C-14].

C.1.3 Consumer Product Safety Rules and Product Bans

The fundamental purpose of the CPSA is to protect consumers from *unreasonable risks of injury*. One of the prime methods the Commission uses for the direct regulation of the products themselves is the issuance of consumer product safety rules. These rules may make requirements "as to performance, composition, contents, design, construction, finish, or packaging of a consumer product," or requirements "that a consumer product be marked with or accompanied by adequate warnings or instructions" [C-15]. The Commission may also impose a complete ban on a product when it poses an unreasonable risk of injury that cannot be protected against by the promulgation of any feasible consumer product safety standard [C-16]. But the initial inquiry in all cases is always whether an unreasonable risk of injury exists.

The Act does not define an "unreasonable risk," but the legislative history of the Act reveals that Congress intended very much the same type of risk-utility balancing as is incorporated in Restatement (Second) of Torts, § 402A [C-17]. See Section 4.4. Indeed, the Act itself requires that, before a consumer product safety rule be promulgated, the Commission must make findings with respect to:

1. The degree and nature of the risk of injury the rule is designed to eliminate or reduce.
2. The approximate number of consumer products, or types or classes thereof, subject to such rule.
3. The need of the public for the consumer products subject to such rule, and the probable effect of such rule upon the utility, cost, or availability of such products to meet such need.

4. Any means of achieving the objective of the order while minimizing adverse effects on competition or disruption or dislocation of manufacturing and other commercial practices consistent with the public health and safety [C-18].

The process of developing, amending, or revoking a standard may be initiated by either the Commission or any other interested person, including a consumer or consumer organization, by petition to the Commission. See Figure C-1 for the procedural steps in the petition process.

Such a petition must set forth the facts suggesting that a rule, revocation, or amendment is necessary and must briefly describe the substance of a proposed rule or amendment. The Commission is required to act on such a petition. If the petition is denied or the Commission fails to respond to it, the petitioner may bring an action in a United States District Court to compel the Commission to take action.

Once the Commission has determined that a consumer product safety standard is necessary, it will publish notice of its determination in the Federal Register and will invite any person, other than the Commission, to submit an existing standard as the proposed standard. The Commission may accept a previously existing standard, in lieu of an offer to develop one, but only if it determines that the standard has already been issued or adopted by a Federal agency or other qualified institution and that such standard would eliminate or reduce the unreasonable risk of injury. It is unclear exactly what a "qualified institution" might be, but unless the Commission accepts an existing standard as its proposal, it must accept at least one qualified offer to develop the proposal. To qualify, the Commission must find that the offeror is technically competent, is likely to develop an appropriate standard within the period specified, and will provide supporting test data, suitable testing methods, notice to interested persons and opportunities for them to participate, and Commission access to all records.

The emphasis is clearly on standards development outside of the Commission, but in certain circumstances the CPSC may engage in standards development itself. If the Commission does not accept an offer within 30 days, or the development period for the standard ends without a standard's having been produced, or the sole accepted offer is made by a manufacturer, retailer, or distributor of the product proposed to be regulated, the Commission may proceed to develop a standard itself.

Once a standard is promulgated, the rule is applicable only to products manufactured after its effective date, although the Commission is empowered to prohibit a manufacturer from stockpiling goods before the effective date [C-19].

The Commission may also promulgate a rule completely banning a consumer product from the market if it finds that it presents an unreasonable risk of injury that cannot be protected against by any feasible consumer product safety standard [C-20]. As with a consumer product safety standard, amendment, or revocation, any interested person may petition for a product ban [C-21]. The procedures applicable to promulgating a safety standard are also applicable to promulgating a product ban.

Whatever the rule, any person adversely affected by it may petition for its review in a United States Court of Appeals. The court will not uphold the rule unless it finds that the Commission's findings in regard to need for such a rule are supported by "substantial evidence on the record taken as a whole." The Act makes clear that the

Procedures under the Consumer Product Safety Act*

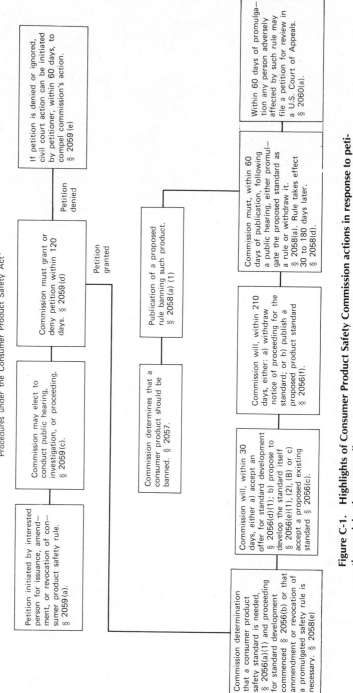

Figure C-1. Highlights of Consumer Product Safety Commission actions in response to petitions originating externally.

"record" for these purposes includes more than merely the record from the rule-making proceedings and that the Commission may include any other information that it considers relevant [C-22].

The Commission may also prescribe reasonable testing programs to be conducted by third parties to discover whether products conform to safety rules and may require the use of labels identifying the date and place of manufacture and the manufacturer's identity [C-23].

At this writing, while there are many proposed safety standards pending promulgation, the Commission has actually promulgated only three safety standards, for bicycles, architectural glass, and matchbooks. The Commission has also promulgated only one product ban, that directed at certain refuse bins. Thus, it is difficult, as yet, to judge the effectiveness of the rules promulgation process.

C.1.4 Imminent Hazards

When the Commission determines that a consumer product presents an "imminent and unreasonable risk of death, serious illness, or severe personal injury," it may file in a United States District Court: (a) an action for seizure of the product; (b) an action against the manufacturer; or (c) both of these [C-24]. In an action against the manufacturer the court may grant such temporary or permanent relief as may be necessary to protect the public from the risk. Such relief orders may require notice of the risk to the public or to purchasers of the product; recall, repair, or replacement of the product; or refund for the product.

The Commission has employed this section to seize firecrackers, which contained a charge in excess of a regulation limit, and carpeting, which did not comply with federal standards for flammability. When necessary, then, the CPSC will take the drastic action mandated by this section of the Act.

C.1.5 Substantial Product Hazards

Among the most important provisions of the CPSA is the section dealing with "substantial product hazards" [C-25]. Unlike the sections dealing with the promulgation of consumer product safety rules, this provision enables the Commission to regulate products that are already in the hands of consumers, and its sanctions can be applied to products manufactured before the enactment of the CPSA.

While the Act nowhere distinguishes between an "unreasonable risk" [C-26], a "substantial product hazard," and an "imminent hazard" [C-27], the distinction seems to be one of degree. The Commission considers the severity of the risk and the necessity for quick action in assigning a risk to any particular category.

An "unreasonable risk" is identified through the risk-utility balancing process. However, an "imminent hazard" is one that presents an imminent risk of "death, serious illness, or severe personal injury" [C-28]. The possible consequences of the risk are more grave than those associated with a "substantial product hazard."

The Act defines a "substantial product hazard" as:

1. A failure to comply with an applicable consumer product safety rule which creates a substantial risk of injury to the public.
2. A product defect which (because of the pattern of defect, the number of defective products distributed in commerce, the severity of the risk, or otherwise) creates a substantial risk of injury to the public [C-29].

The first part of the definition suggests that only those violations of a consumer product safety rule that rise to the level of a "substantial risk" will be treated under this section. "Substantial risk" is left undefined but probably incorporates the factors enumerated parenthetically in the second part of the definition. In any event most of the Commission's actions under this section will be taken under the second part of the definition, since few consumer product safety rules have thus far been promulgated.

    The Act mandates that any manufacturer, distributor, or retailer of a product who obtains information that reasonably supports the conclusion that the product contains a "substantial product hazard" must immediately inform the Commission of the hazard unless such person knows that the CPSC has already been adequately informed by other sources. If the Commission concludes that a substantial product hazard exists, it may order the manufacturer, distributor, or retailer to do one or more of the following:

1. Give public notice of the defect or failure to comply.
2. Mail notice to each person who is a manufacturer, distributor, or retailer of such product.
3. Mail notice to every person to whom the person required to give notice knows such product was delivered or sold.
4. Elect to bring the product into conformity with the applicable standard, to repair the defect in the product, to replace the product with a like product that does not contain the defect, or to refund the purchase price of the product [C-30].

Where notice is ordered, the Commission will specify the form and content of the notice. Where the order directs the manufacturer, distributor, or retailer to elect some other action, the Commission may require such person to submit a plan for taking such action and may also order such person to cease manufacturing, selling, distributing, or importing the product.

    When the Commission initiates a proceeding to order election to repair, replace, or refund, the Commission or Attorney General may apply to a United States District Court for a preliminary injunction to restrain the distribution of the product pending the completion of the proceeding.

    This part of the CPSA has probably been used most frequently thus far because of both the flexibility of remedy and the possibility of quick action it provides. These advantages will probably encourage the Commission to continue to use this provision.

C.1.6   Compliance and Enforcement

While both the "imminent hazard" provision and the "substantial product hazard" provision contain compliance and enforcement aspects, the CPSA includes separate provisions directed *solely* at enforcement.

One such provision lists activities prohibited under the Act. This section makes it unlawful for any person to:

1. Manufacture, sell, distribute, or import any product that is not in conformity with an applicable consumer product safety standard.
2. Manufacture, sell, distribute, or import any product that has been declared a banned, hazardous product.
3. Fail or refuse to permit access to or copying of records, to establish or maintain records, to make reports or provide information, or to permit entry or inspection, as required under the Act.
4. Fail to furnish information as required under the substantial product hazard provision.
5. Fail to comply with an order relating to notification, repair, replacement, refund, or other prohibited acts under the substantial product hazard provision.
6. Fail to furnish a certificate as required by the Act or issue a false certificate that the person could have discovered contained false information by the exercise of due care; or fail to comply with any rule relating to labeling.
7. Fail to comply with any rule relating to stockpiling.
8. Fail to comply with any rule relating to prior notice and description of new consumer products.
9. Fail to comply with any rule requiring the submission of performance and technical data to the Commission [C-31].

The Act provides that any person who *knowingly* violates any of these prohibited acts may be subject to a fine not to exceed $2000 for each separate violation and not to exceed $500,000 for any related series of violations [C-32]. A person may be presumed to have the knowledge deemed to be possessed by a reasonable man in the circumstances for the purposes of this provision.

Any person who *knowingly and willfully* violates a prohibited act, after receiving notice of noncompliance from the Commission, may be subject to criminal liability [C-33]. A director, officer, or agent of a corporation who authorizes, orders, or performs a prohibited act and who has knowledge of the notice of noncompliance may be subject to penalties in addition to any penalties the corporation may suffer.

The United States District Courts may restrain any violation of the prohibited acts; any manufacturing, selling, distributing, or importing of a product subject to an order to repair, replace, or refund; or any distribution of a product that does not comply with a consumer product safety rule, when such action is sought by either the Commission or the Attorney General [C-34]. The District Courts may also seize and actually remove from the marketplace any consumer product that fails to conform to a consumer product safety rule or that has been manufactured, sold, distributed, or imported in violation of an order issued under the "substantial product hazard" provision.

Finally, compliance with any rules or orders issued under the CPSA does not relieve a manufacturer from liability to any party under the common law or state statutory law [C-35].

C.2   THE MAGNUSON-MOSS WARRANTY—FEDERAL TRADE COMMISSION IMPROVEMENT ACT

C.2.1   Overview

Consumer sales transactions are generally governed under state law by the Uniform Commercial Code [C-36]. See Section 1.3.2. The Code provides for an implied warranty of merchantability from the seller to the buyer of a product. Moreover, when the seller knows the buyer intends to use the product for a particular purpose, an implied warranty for that purpose arises upon the sale. These provisions would seem to supply the consumer with adequate guarantees of protection. The Code also provides, however, for the liberal modification and disclaimer of implied warranties [C-37]. See Section 5.5.

Commonly, warrantors give a limited express warranty followed by a general disclaimer of any implied warranties. For example, a typical new car warranty reads as follows:

The manufacturer warrants each new motor vehicle (including original equipment placed thereon by the manufacturer except tires), chassis or parts manufactured by it to be free from defects in material or workmanship under normal use and service. Its obligations under this warranty being limited to making good at its factory any part or parts thereof which shall, within the time and mileage limitations as specified . . . be returned to it with transportation charges prepaid and which its examination shall disclose to its satisfaction to have been thus defective; *this warranty being expressly in lieu of all other warranties expressed or implied, and all other obligations or liabilities on its part,* and it neither assumes nor authorizes any other person to assume for it any other liability in connection with the sale of its vehicles. [Emphasis added.]

Consumers may well believe that they are actually being given some added protection with this type of express warranty, rather than that they are being denied the general protection of an implied warranty. Moreover, even where a consumer can claim the benefit of an implied warranty, the Code allows for the limitation or modification of the damages and remedies available under it [C-38].

One of the basic premises of the Code is that the buyer and seller are able to bargain freely on the terms of their agreement. While this may be true in a commercial context, it is rare indeed that a consumer can bargain with the company warranting the product he considers buying. This inability to bargain from positions of equal power lies at the heart of the Code's inadequacy in protecting consumers.

In 1968 the president created the Task Force on Appliance Warranties and Service. The Task Force studied the servicing, repair, and durability of consumer products and concluded that some warrantors did not live up to their commitments, that often no real means of enforcement were available to the consumer, that many warranties were inadequately understood by consumers, and that some warranties were plainly deceptive. It also concluded that competitive pressures probably dissuaded companies from offering better warranties.

The Magnuson-Moss Warranty—Federal Trade Commission Improvement Act [C-39] was a federal response to these problems and to the inadequacy of state law to deal with them. The Act's purpose is to "improve the adequacy of information available to consumers, prevent deception, and improve competition in the marketing of consumer products" [C-40]. It was anticipated that, by the regulating of what a warranty can say and how it can be said, consumers would be able to compare warranties and to make them a real part of their deliberations in deciding which product to purchase. The warranty would then become an essential part of the product and there would be greater incentive for warrantors to offer better warranties.

The scope of the Magnuson-Moss Warranty Act is to establish nationally uniform minimum disclosure standards for written warranties, restrict disclaimers of implied warranties, and provide more effective means for consumers to enforce their warranty rights [C-41].

C.2.2 Disclosure, Designation, and Disclaimers

The Magnuson-Moss Warranty Act applies only to *written* warranties on consumer products. A "consumer product" is defined as "any tangible personal property which is distributed in commerce and which is normally used for personal, family, or household purposes" [C-42]. Because Congress foresaw that suppliers might attempt to get around the provisions of the Act by supplying service contracts in lieu of warranties, the Federal Trade Commission (FTC) has the power to prescribe rules concerning the form and content of service contracts [C-43] as well as the form and content of warranties.

The Act requires that all warranties must "fully and conspicuously disclose in simple and readily understood language" their terms and conditions. The FTC may promulgate rules more specifically governing warranty content to help achieve this goal. Some of the items the rules may require be included in a written warranty are enumerated in the Act:

1. The clear identification of the names and addresses of the warrantors.
2. The identity of the party or parties to whom the warranty is extended.
3. The products or parts covered.
4. A statement of what the warrantor will do in the event of a defect, malfunction, or failure to conform with such written warranty—at whose expense—and for what period of time.
5. A statement of what the consumer must do and expenses he must bear.
6. Exceptions and exclusions from the terms of the warranty.

7. The step-by-step procedure which the consumer should take in order to obtain performance of any obligation under the warranty, including the identification of any person or class of persons authorized to perform the obligations set forth in the warranty.

8. Information respecting the availability of any informal dispute settlement procedure offered by the warrantor and a recital, where the warranty so provides, that the purchaser may be required to resort to such procedure before pursuing any legal remedies in the courts.

9. A brief, general description of the legal remedies available to the consumer.

10. The time at which the warrantor will perform any obligations under the warranty.

11. The period of time within which, after notice of a defect, malfunction, or failure to conform with the warranty, the warrantor will perform any obligations under the warranty.

12. The characteristics or properties of the products, or parts thereof, that are not covered by the warranty.

13. The elements of the warranty in words or phrases which would not mislead a reasonable, average consumer as to the nature or scope of the warranty [C-44].

The Commission has promulgated a rule incorporating many of these provisions and additionally requiring that, if a warrantor includes a warranty registration card with his product, he must disclose whether or not the return of the card is an absolute requirement to warranty coverage and performance [C-45]. Though the Act allows the Commission to promulgate such rules for all products costing more than $5, the Commission has thus far opted to afford such protection only to consumers purchasing products costing at least $15.

The FTC must also promulgate rules governing the presale availability of warranty terms and their incorporation in advertising, labeling, and other sales materials. It has promulgated a rule that requires retailers to provide the full text of the warranty prior to sale. The rule makes similar requirements of catalog and door-to-door sellers.

Finally, the Commission may promulgate a rule waiving the Act's prohibition against a warrantor requiring that the product may be used only in conjunction with another product identified by brand, trade, or corporate name. The warrantor must, however, be able to satisfy the Commission that the warranted product will not function properly if not used in conjunction with the specified product and the Commission must find that its waiver would be in the public interest.

Beyond these disclosure requirements and rules the Act requires that any warranty on a consumer product costing more than $10 be designated as either a "full" or "limited" warranty [C-46]. To be labeled a "full" warranty, the warranty must meet Federal minimum standards, which require that a warrantor:

1. Must remedy the consumer product within a reasonable time and without charge, in case of a defect, malfunction, or failure to conform with the warranty.

2. May not impose any limitation on the duration of any implied warranty on the product.

3. May not exclude or limit consequential damages for breach of any written or implied warranty, unless the exclusion or limitation conspicuously appears on the face of the warranty.

4. After a reasonable number of attempts by the warrantor to remedy the defects in the product, must permit the consumer to elect either a refund for or replacement of the product without charge [C-47].

The warrantor generally may not impose any duty on the consumer as a condition of securing a remedy except those of notifying the warrantor of the defect and making the product available to him. It is, however, a defense to the necessity of warrantors' performing the duties enumerated above that the malfunction of the product was caused by damage or unreasonable use while in the possession of the consumer. In any case any warranty that does not meet all of these standards must be designated a "limited" warranty.

There are several narrow exceptions to these requirements. Expressions of general policy regarding customer satisfaction, for example, "Satisfaction guaranteed," need not be designated as either "full" or "limited"; need not meet the enumerated standards; and are not subject to FTC rules concerning warranty disclosure [C-48]. Moreover, a consumer product may have *both* "full" and "limited" warranties if such warranties are clearly and conspicuously differentiated [C-49].

The Act also contains a separate provision directed at the limitation and disclaimer of implied warranties [C-50]. No implied warranty may be disclaimed or modified if a supplier makes a written warranty or enters into a service contract within 90 days of the time of sale. Note however that no supplier is required to issue *any* warranty. This leaves disclaimers valid if no express warranty is set forth. Furthermore, an implied warranty may be limited in duration, but only in a "limited warranty," and if it is limited to the duration of the written warranty and such limitation is conscionable and is set forth prominently in clear and unmistakable language.

While the FTC can enforce the provisions of this Act under its powers as a commission to prohibit deceptive trade practices [C-51], the Act also provides remedies for the individual consumer.

C.2.3 Remedies

To encourage warrantors to provide informal dispute settlement procedures, the Act provides that, if such a procedure is established and conforms to FTC rules concerning such procedures, the warrantor can require that a consumer resort to the procedure before seeking any judicial remedy under the Act [C-52]. The Commission has promulgated a rule concerning dispute settlement [C-53]. Perhaps its most interesting aspects are that, if a dispute procedure complies with the rule's requirements, its decisions are not binding but are admissible evidence in any related civil action. However, even though a warrantor provides such a procedure, consumers are still free to pursue any remedies they may have under state or other federal law [C-54]. This latitude afforded the consumer may serve to dissuade warrantors from providing any procedures at all.

Subject to these limitations, a consumer or consumer class may bring a suit for damages or other equitable relief for a failure to comply with any obligation under the Act or under a written or implied warranty or service contract. The warrantor must, however, be given an opportunity to cure the failure to comply before any action may be brought [C-55].

C.3 OCCUPATIONAL SAFETY AND HEALTH ACT

In 1970 Congress passed the Occupational Safety and Health Act (OSHA) [C-56]. Its purpose is "to assure so far as possible every working man and woman in the nation safe and healthful working conditions" [C-57]. To implement this goal, employers are required to furnish their employees a place of employment "free from recognized hazards that are causing or are likely to cause death or serious physical harm to his employees" [C-58]. The Act also provides that employers may be required to maintain records relating to their activities under the Act and that records and places of employment may be subject to federal inspection.

Federal authorities are directed to conduct employee safety training and education programs. They are also authorized to conduct research directly, or by grant or contract, into injury-related matters, to collect and analyze occupational safety and health statistics, and to disseminate information concerning these activities to interested persons. Finally, the Secretary of Labor has the power to promulgate and enforce occupational safety and health standards.

While the Act itself is directed solely at employers, once a safety standard has been promulgated, it may be used as evidence of the standard of care to which manufacturers of industrial machinery should conform. Indeed, violation of an occupational health and safety standard may be found to establish a *prima facie* case of liability or negligence *per se*. For example, the Fifth Circuit Court of Appeals held, in *Arthur v. Elota Mercante Gran Centro Americana S.A.* [C-59], that violations of OSHA regulations constitute negligence *per se*. In that case there was an employer-employee relationship, but there is no reason to believe that such rules will not be used to establish the standard of care against manufacturers, where they are relevant.

C.4 A FINAL NOTE

While the Consumer Product Safety Act, the Federal Warranty Act, and the Occupational Safety and Health Act are the most pervasive federal legislation likely to affect the products liability field, the manufacturer must ascertain whether there exist any other federal or state laws that could affect his liability. For instance, there are separate federal acts dealing with certain product categories, for example, the Flammable Fabrics Act [C-60], the Refrigerator Safety Act [C-61], the Federal Hazardous Substances Act [C-62], the Poison Prevention Packaging Act [C-63], and the Food, Drug, and Cosmetics Act [C-64]. It is evident that manufacturers must remain current with new as well as updated legislation, regulations, and rules promulgated by federal and state governments.

BIBLIOGRAPHY

[C-1]   Act of November 20, 1967, Public Law No. 90-146, 81 Stat. 466.

[C-2]   Consumer Product Safety Act, Public Law No. 92-573 (October 27, 1972), 15 U.S.C. §§ 2051-2081 [hereinafter cited only as 15 U.S.C.].

[C-3]   15 U.S.C. § 2051 (1972).

[C-4]   118 Cong. Rec. 36198 (1972) (remarks of Senator Moss).

[C-5]   15 U.S.C. § 2052(a)(1) (1972) and 1976 amendment.

[C-6]   15 U.S.C. § 2066 (1972); 15 U.S.C. § 2067 (1972).

[C-7]   15 U.S.C. § 2054(a) (1972).

[C-8]   2 *NEISS News,* September 1973, No. 1 at 8.

[C-9]   The "Hotline" number is (800) 638-2666, or, in Maryland (800) 492-2937. It is attended from 8:00 A.M. to 8:00 P.M., Monday through Friday and is provided with a taping system at other times.

[C-10] 15 U.S.C. §§ 2062, 2065, 2076 (1972).

[C-11] 15 U.S.C. § 2054(a)(1) (1972).

[C-12] 5 U.S.C. § 552 *et seq.* (1970).

[C-13] The *Federal Register* is the official source for publication of the rules and regulations of the federal agencies.

[C-14] *Supra* note 11.

[C-15] Consumer Product Safety Improvements Act of 1976, Public Law 94-284 (May 11, 1976) 15 U.S.C. § 2056(a)(1) (1976) (amending 15 U.S.C. §§ 2051-2081 [1972]) [hereinafter cited only as 15 U.S.C.].

[C-16] 15 U.S.C. § 2057 (1972).

[C-17] S. Rep. No. 92-749, 92d Cong., 2d Sess. 6 (1972). Also see Chapter 4 regarding § 402A.

[C-18] 15 U.S.C. § 2058(c)(1) (1972).

[C-19] 15 U.S.C. § 2058 (1972).

[C-20] 15 U.S.C. § 2057 (1972).

[C-21] 15 U.S.C. § 2059(a) (1972).

[C-22] 15 U.S.C. § 2060 (1972) and 1976 amendment.

[C-23] 15 U.S.C. § 2063 (1972).

[C-24] 15 U.S.C. § 2061 (1972).

[C-25] 15 U.S.C. § 2064 (1972) and 1976 amendment.

[C-26] 15 U.S.C. § 2058 (1972).

[C-27] 15 U.S.C. § 2061 (1972).

[C-28] 15 U.S.C. § 2061 (1972).

[C-29] 15 U.S.C. § 2064(a) (1972).

[C-30] 15 U.S.C. § 2064 (1972).

[C-31] 15 U.S.C. § 2068 (1972) and 1976 amendment.

[C-32]   15 U.S.C. § 2069 (1972) and 1976 amendment.

[C-33]   15 U.S.C. § 2070 (1972).

[C-34]   15 U.S.C. § 2071 (1976).

[C-35]   15 U.S.C. § 2074 (1972).

[C-36]   The Uniform Commercial Code [hereinafter the U.C.C.] has been adopted by every state except Louisiana. California and Massachusetts have passed state warranty laws, but their effectiveness is limited solely to those states.

[C-37]   U.C.C. §§ 2-314, 2-315, 2-316 (1972).

[C-38]   *Id.* § 2-719.

[C-39]   Magnuson-Moss Warranty—Federal Trade Commission Improvement Act, Public Law No. 93-637 (January 4, 1975), 15 U.S.C. §§ 2301–2312 and amendments to 15 U.S.C. §§ 45, 46, 49, 50, 52, 56, 57 [hereinafter cited as 15 U.S.C.].

[C-40]   15 U.S.C. § 2302 (1975).

[C-41]   15 U.S.C. §§ 2301–2312 (1975).

[C-42]   *Id.* § 2301.

[C-43]   *Id.* § 2306.

[C-44]   *Id.* § 2302.

[C-45]   40 Fed. Reg. 60188 (1975).

[C-46]   15 U.S.C. § 2303 (1975).

[C-47]   *Id.* § 2304.

[C-48]   *Id.* § 2303.

[C-49]   *Id.* § 2305.

[C-50]   *Id.* § 2308.

[C-51]   15 U.S.C. § 45 (1975).

[C-52]   15 U.S.C. § 2310 (1975).

[C-53]   40 Fed. Reg. 60218 (1975).

[C-54]   15 U.S.C. § 2311 (1975).

[C-55]   *Id.* § 2310.

[C-56]   Occupational Safety and Health Act of 1970, Public Law 91-596 (December 29, 1970), 29 U.S.C. § 651–678 [hereinafter cited as 29 U.S.C.].

[C-57]   29 U.S.C. § 651 (1970).

[C-58]   *Id.* § 654.

[C-59]   487 F.2d 561 (5th Cir. 1973).

[C-60]   15 U.S.C. §§ 1191 *et seq.* (1967).

[C-61]   15 U.S.C. §§ 1211 *et seq.* (1956).

[C-62]   15 U.S.C. §§ 1261 *et seq.* (1960).

[C-63]   15 U.S.C. §§ 1471 *et seq.* (1970).

[C-64]   21 U.S.C. §§ 301 *et seq.* (1938).

Index of Cases

Subject Index

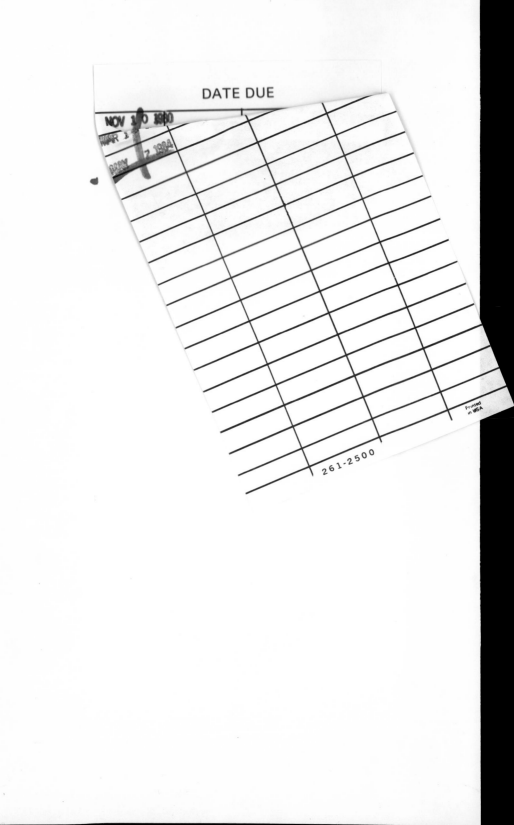

DATE DUE

NOV 10 1980

MAR 1

7 1984

261-2500

Printed
in USA